HIGHER GROUND

Also by Craig Werner

A Change Is Gonna Come: Music, Race & the Soul of America
Playing the Changes: From Afro-Modernism to the Jazz Impulse
Up Around the Bend: The Oral History of Creedence Clearwater Revival

Stevie

HIGHER

Curtis

Stevie Wonder, Aretha Franklin, Curtis Mayfield,
and the Rise and Fall of American Soul

GROUND

Aretha

CRAIG WERNER

 CROWN PUBLISHERS · NEW YORK

Published by Crown Publishers, New York, New York.
Member of the Crown Publishing Group, a division of Random House, Inc.
www.crownpublishing.com

CROWN is a trademark and the Crown colophon is a registered trademark of
Random House, Inc.

Printed in the United States of America

DESIGN BY LEONARD HENDERSON

Library of Congress Cataloging-in-Publication Data
Werner, Craig Hansen, 1952–
Higher ground : Stevie Wonder, Aretha Franklin, Curtis Mayfield, and the
Rise and Fall of American Soul / Craig Werner.—1st ed.
1. Franklin, Aretha. 2. Wonder, Stevie. 3. Mayfield, Curtis. 4. Soul
musicians—United States—Biography. 5. Rock musicians—United States—
Biography. I. Title.
ML400.W36 2004
781.644'092'2—dc21   2003009187

ISBN 0-609-60993-9

First Edition

For
the Dadooronron-ers
and
the Freedom Riders
(then and now)

ACKNOWLEDGMENTS

Higher Ground echoes with the voices of dozens of people who have blessed me with their insights into life and music since I first heard Stevie Wonder on radio station KYSN in Colorado Springs back in 1963. A few of those who nurtured the sense of musical community that led to this book were Brian Berry, Mike DeLong, Jim Allen, Kent Lawyer, Rob Wilson (co-host of the countdown on the first virtual radio station, WWCS), my brothers Blake (on the country side) and Brian (who caught on to *Music of My Mind* before I did), and Geoff King. Barbara Talmadge, Missy Kubitschek, and soul man Steve Schultz helped get me through some rough transitions. During my years in Mississippi, Kevin Stewart, Jon and Martha Scott, Karah Stokes, and Mike Reese helped me understand the sound of the South. In Madison, Wisconsin, where I've been fortunate to teach Afro-American Studies for two decades, my musical communities have been rich and various. When I name Robert Philipson, Eric Schumacher-Rasmussen, Alexander Shashko, Keisha Bowman, Juan Gonzalez, Rhea Lathan, Leah Mirakhor, Lisa Photos, David Ikard, Wendy Schneider, Rhonda Lee, Trudi Witonsky, Dan Schultz, Scott Sherman, Kassia Conway, Yoseph Tekla-marian, Duer Sharp, Howard Moore, Charles Hughes, Shanna Benjamin, Michelle Gordon, Genella Taylor, Steve Kantrowitz, Natalia Santa Maria, Roberto Rivera, Glenn Berry, Brian Bischel, and Ed Pavlic, they'll be aware that they're standing in for a larger conversation. A major shout out to Keith and Allison at the Harmony Bar, Steve at Borders East, and Jeremiah, Michael, and Soren at Canterbury Books for negotiating the special orders and allowing their stores to be used as reference libraries. Many thanks to Irwin Soonachan and Bill Van Deburg for their roles in introducing me to Curtis Mayfield; and to Mavis Staples, Bobby Womack, Jerry Butler, Eddie Thomas, and Johnny Meadows for their willingness to help me tell the Chicago story right. My agent, Dan Greenberg, and my editor, Chris Jackson, have rendered the publication process painless. Chris pointed the way from a promising first draft to what the book has become. Thanks also to the production and design staff at Crown Publishers, notably Camille Smith and Lenny Henderson. Profound thanks to Dave Marsh for his role in convincing me that I had a story to tell and that someone outside my immediate community might care. The virtual community Dave holds together played a major role in my thinking as this book came together. Again, when I name Marsha Cusic, Sue Martinez, Stewart Francke, David Cantwell, John Floyd, Daniel Wolff, Lee Ballinger, and Danny Alexander, they'll know we're all part of a larger chorus. From the proposal through the final draft, Tim Tyson functioned more as coauthor than as editor. And always, my deepest love to Leslee, Riah, and Kaylee, who put up with Dad when he goes into that weird writing space.

CONTENTS

Introduction 1

"Moving On Up"

Soul Music and the Gospel Vision

Chapter One 13

"There Is a Fountain Filled with Blood"

The Roots of the Gospel Vision

Chapter Two 63

"Keep On Pushing"

The Soul of the Freedom Movement

Chapter Three 126

"Spirit in the Dark"

Music and the Powers of Blackness

Chapter Four 188

Songs in the Key of Life

The Gospel Vision in Changing Times

Chapter Five 236

"Who's Zoomin' Who?"

Megastars, Monuments, Elders

A Note on Sources   291

Notes   295

Discography   313

Recommended Compilations   325

Index   327

HIGHER GROUND

"Moving On Up"

Soul Music and the Gospel Vision

T HE BITTER END WASN'T EXACTLY A CHURCH, but Curtis Mayfield was feeling the spirit. Contemplating the salt-and-pepper crowd that had braved a cold snap to pack the New York City club in the first week of 1971, Mayfield peered over the steel-rimmed glasses that gave him the look of a street-corner philosopher. "Y'all got some strength tonight," he said with a gentle chuckle. "You lit a fire up under us." With the audience shouting out its approval, Mayfield rapped over the groove of "We're a Winner," the controversial anthem he'd written and sung with the Impressions a few years earlier. "A whole lotta stations didn't want to play that particular recording. Can you imagine such a thing?" Mayfield asked the Bitter End crowd, shaking his head. "Well, I would say what most of you would say—we don't give a damn, we're a winner anyway." From the back of a club best known as the launching pad for Bob Dylan, Joan Baez, and Peter, Paul and Mary, a voice boomed out, "They don't want to play Aretha either," eliciting a flurry of "Right on" and "Tell it." "We're believing very strongly in equality and freedom for all, but especially we people who are darker than blue," Mayfield said. This was the heart of the gospel vision he'd been preaching alongside the Queen of Soul, Stevie Wonder, and a host of other artists who reshaped American popular music while battling in the streets for the soul of America. "I'm not trying to offend anyone," Mayfield explained in the quiet tones that had earned him the nickname "the Gentle Genius," "but just basically telling it like it is."

From there Mayfield conducted the Greenwich Village crowd on a musical tour of the storefront churches he'd known as a child growing up in Chicago's Cabrini-Green ghetto. The band was still playing "We're a Winner," but by the time Mayfield finished, everyone in the club understood that what mattered wasn't the hit song but the spirit that brought them together. Ignoring the boundaries between the sacred and the secular, Mayfield mixed lines from the classics he'd penned for the Impressions with images from the gospel standards that had steeled the souls of the everyday people he called the "invisible heroes" of the civil rights movement: "People get ready, I got good news for you. How we got over and you know it's true." Like a church mother calling on Jesus, he summoned the spirit of his people's martyred leader: "We gotta keep on pushing like Martin Luther told you to." Circling back to the text of the soul sermon, he concluded, "Let us all say amen and together we'll clap our hands, 'cause we're movin' on up." By then no one was worrying about the boundaries that, back on the streets of Nixon's America, separated personal salvation and political redemption, or the musical worlds of gospel, pop, and soul.

Decades later, it's hard to imagine why dozens of radio stations banned "We're a Winner" when it was released in the final weeks of 1967. In a musical world defined by hip-hop and MTV, the song's celebration of the "blessed day" when black people wipe away the tears and move on up to a better world seems as innocently reassuring as *The Jeffersons*. But for those who saw the freedom movement as a threat to the American way—and they were many—the marriage of soul music and the movement represented a real threat. The movement's leaders and their opponents were in perfect agreement on the central point. Soul music wasn't just entertainment. Comedian-turned-activist Dick Gregory was dead serious when he compared Aretha's political impact with King's: "You heard her three or four times an hour. You heard Reverend King only on the news." Poet Nikki Giovanni, a leading voice in the generation that turned from civil rights to Black Power, was even more assertive. "Aretha was the riot was the leader," Giovanni wrote in "Poem for Aretha," "if she had said, 'come, let's do it,' it would have been done." Insisting that people take the Bible and the Declaration of Independence seriously, the gospel vision was intent on changing the world. That was the good news the singers sang on high and the movement brought down to earth.

Higher Ground tells the story of how Aretha Franklin, Stevie Wonder, and Curtis Mayfield set about realizing that vision with some of the most powerful music ever to grace the nation. It's a story about black suffering, sorrow, and survival; but it's also a story about the most promising interracial dialogue America has ever seen. For anyone who believes in democratic art, Aretha, Stevie, and Curtis should be taken as seriously as the visionaries who have insisted the nation remember what it has been and helped it imagine what it can be: Walt Whitman and Emily Dickinson; Woody Guthrie and Bruce Springsteen; Duke Ellington and Mahalia Jackson; William Faulkner and James Baldwin.

As I worked on *Higher Ground,* I was often asked why I chose Aretha, Stevie, and Curtis rather than, for example, Marvin Gaye, Otis Redding, and James Brown. My first inclination was simply to fill the CD changer with *Spirit in the Dark, Innervisions,* and *The Very Best of the Impressions* and hit "random." But, of course, you can do the same thing with *What's Going On, Otis Blue,* and *James Brown Live at the Apollo.* The deeper answer to this question reflects the complicated relationships between African Americans and the larger culture; the past and the future; the South and the North. On one level, it's perfectly accurate to hear Stevie, Aretha, and Curtis as part of the long black song that has sustained African Americans since the first of the slave poets responded to the hard truth of "Nobody knows the trouble I've seen" with the paradoxical hope of "Glory Hallelujah!" But time and place combined to position Aretha, Stevie, and Curtis where they could add a new and uniquely meaningful voice to the communal chorus. It's crucial that all three grew up in the North in families and communities that had migrated from the Jim Crow South. Most southern-bred singers came of age in a world where segregation seemed intractable. Stevie, Curtis, and Aretha belonged to the first generation of African Americans who could reasonably hope to participate in the mainstream culture on something like an equal basis. Their music plowed a soul-deep memory of a history steeped in blood into an even deeper determination to create a new world where that hope could be realized. Grounded in the specifics of African American life but open to anyone willing to answer its call for change, their music offered— and still offers—an unsurpassed vision of shared possibility.

It's impossible to understand the power of this music apart from the political energy of the African American freedom movement. Like the movement, soul music emerged at a unique moment in American history. For a brief moment, a substantial majority of blacks managed to balance a deep sense of connection to traditional communities with a real desire to move closer to an American mainstream where blacks and whites could find common ground. Martin Luther King's dream was, as he told the world, "very deeply rooted in the American dream." Survival in America didn't necessarily imply bleaching your soul. For that same brief moment a significant number of whites seemed willing to expand their own dream. Many seemed poised to dive into what James Baldwin called the "deep waters" of America's interracial reality. It didn't happen. But that doesn't diminish the importance of the moment when it seemed like it might. That healing vision of shared struggle defined both soul music and the civil rights movement, and it remains the best vision that America has had for itself and the world.

The daughter of the renowned Detroit preacher C.L. Franklin, Aretha took that vision as an article of faith. Growing up in a household where the stars of the gospel world ate soul food and talked politics with Martin Luther King and Ralph Abernathy, Aretha soaked in the sound and spirit of the southern freedom movement. Before she reached her teens, she was singing on the "gospel highway," an informal network of churches and concert halls that took her into every corner of black America as the movement gathered momentum during the fifties. While her decision to pursue a career as a jazz/pop singer might seem a betrayal of her gospel roots, both Aretha and her father understood the move as part of a broader political commitment to desegregation. That she found her voice, and financial success, only when she returned to her gospel roots with "I Never Loved a Man (The Way I Love You)" and "Respect" speaks both to the problems with the crossover strategy and to the enduring power of the community that nurtured her. Once she returned to her foundation, however, her music provided an emotional center that transcended ideology. While Aretha never wavered from her personal commitment to King's interracialist dream, "Think," "Rock Steady," and "Spirit in the Dark" spoke equally clearly to the aspirations of the Black Power movement. Through the late sixties and early seventies, responses to her call echoed in the voices of Vietnam veterans, feminists of all races, and countless white Americans who first heard her voice sandwiched between the Young Rascals and the Strawberry Alarm Clark on the Top Twenty countdown. It truly was, as one contemporary called it, the "Age of Aretha."

If Aretha sang the spirit of the political preachers who took the movement into America's living rooms on the six o'clock news, Curtis Mayfield harmonized with the souls of the thousands of ordinary people who provided the leaders with their foot soldiers. Like Aretha, Curtis grew up in the church and started out singing straight gospel. Like the poor Chicagoans who formed the congregation of the storefront church where his grandmother preached, he supported the movement as it battled against Jim Crow in Montgomery, Little Rock, and the Mississippi Delta. But the distance between the Traveling Souls Spiritualist Church and Reverend Franklin's New Bethel Baptist wasn't just geographical. Mayfield grew up in a community where the southern movement's gains contrasted all too clearly with the harsh reality of life at the bottom of a beleaguered industrial economy. No one in Chicago's Cabrini-Green projects was likely to confuse the North with the promised land. Blessed with an extraordinarily warm and winning personality, Mayfield matured into an urban Griot, a new-world version of the West African singer/historian/genealogists who passed their people's stories down through the generations. The songs Mayfield wrote for the Impressions—"People Get Ready," "Keep On Pushing," "This Is My Country"—told his people's story in a way that radiated the healing energy of the gospel vision. But as "(Don't Worry) If There's a Hell Below We're All Gonna Go" made clear, he never forgot or minimized the burdens that made the healing necessary. Where Aretha kept a certain distance from Black Power, Mayfield had an intuitive sympathy with the militants' insistence on self-acceptance and self-determination. While he never achieved superstardom, he developed a realistic resistance strategy for those determined not to succumb to bitterness and despair. The economic and psychological self-sufficiency he sought, and to an impressive degree achieved, earned him near-legendary status in a music business that had destroyed dozens of his elders.

Where Aretha and Curtis kept their best music firmly grounded in the African American church, Stevie Wonder lit out joyously for territories usually associated with "white" music. That's not to say he wasn't "black enough." His early hits "Fingertips, Part 2" and "I Was Made to Love Her" infused Motown with pure gospel fervor at a time when the label was aggressively pursuing a pop crossover strategy. It's just that Wonder's idea of blackness was as comfortable with the Beatles and New Age mysticism as it was with Duke Ellington and Detroit's Whitestone Baptist Church, where he sang in the choir. By the time he embarked on his beautifully baffling *Journey Through the Secret Life of Plants* at the end of the seventies, he'd made it clear that he was a true American original. Stevie took America at its word and, like Walt Whitman, set about remaking it in his own quirky and charismatic image. In the series of albums he created during the seventies—*Music of My Mind, Talking Book, Innervisions, Fulfillingness' First Finale,* and his supreme statement, *Songs in the Key of Life*—he almost pulled it off.

During the eighties and nineties Stevie and Aretha would struggle, not always successfully, with the complicated and confusing demands of superstardom and celebrity. Both would find it increasingly difficult to remain in contact with the communities that had supported them as they made their way from black America to the world. In part because of the extreme demands he'd taken on as singer, songwriter, producer, and business owner, Mayfield fell into near-anonymity before a catastrophic 1990 accident that left him paralyzed for the last decade of his life. The problems all three faced weren't really susceptible to individual solution. With the ascendancy of Ronald Reagan and the emergence of hip-hop as one center of an increasingly fragmented African American cultural landscape, the values embedded in the gospel vision came under increasing pressure. While all three continued to make moving music—including the biggest-selling album of Aretha's career, *Who's Zoomin' Who?,* and Mayfield's near-miraculous *New World Order*—their later music was no longer changing many people's lives. That simply highlights the importance of understanding and appreciating the reasons why it did, when it did.

Embedding the movement's call in the texture of everyday life, Stevie, Curtis, and Aretha each played a key role in the ongoing call and response between the gospel vision and what novelist Ralph Ellison called the "blues impulse." Describing a way of life rather than a musical form, Ellison defined the blues as "an impulse to keep the painful details and episodes of a brutal experience alive in one's aching consciousness, to finger its jagged grain, and to transcend it, not by the consolation of philosophy but by squeezing from it a near-tragic, near-comic lyricism. As a form," he concluded, "the blues is an autobiographical chronicle of personal catastrophe expressed lyrically." Ellison's fellow writer and friend Albert Murray agreed, describing the blues as black America's version of "the most fundamental of existential imperatives: affirmation, which is to say, reaffirmation and continuity in the face of adversity." The blues speak frankly of isolation and despair, the sense that black people have been cast adrift in a world where the devil has taken control. Rather than giving in to those feelings, blues artists tell their stories in voices that walk the line between despair and laughter, asserting black humanity in a world predicated, as Martin Luther King Jr. observed, on the "thingification" of human beings. Bluesmaster Willie Dixon summed up the blues response when he sang, "I'm here, everybody knows *I'm* here."

Like the blues, the gospel vision refuses to submit passively to the burdens of history. Seizing control of their own stories, gospel artists testify to the value of their lives and to the power that offers more than mere survival. Inside the church most call that power the Lord God, Jehovah, or more frequently and personally, Jesus. But the gospel vision is elastic enough to accept those who called the power Jah, Allah, Yemaya, or—like funkmaster George Clinton—"the Mothership." At its best, the gospel vision helps people experience themselves *in relation to others* rather than *on their own*. Where the blues offers reaffirmation, gospel offers redemption. If the blues gives you the strength to face another day, gospel holds out the possibility that tomorrow may be different, better. With the help of the spirit and your people—in church, at a political rally, or on the dance floor—you can get over, walk in Jerusalem, dance to the music. But it takes an energy bigger than yourself: Jesus, Jah, the Spirit. Whatever its specific incarnation, gospel redemption breaks down the difference between personal salvation and communal liberation. No one makes it alone. Where the blues men and women focus on the immediate problem of finding the strength to face another blues-torn day, the gospel vision holds out the hope that, if we stick together and keep faith with the spirit, a change is gonna come.

It would be a mistake to draw too sharp a line between gospel and the blues. The relationship between the blues impulse and the gospel vision presents a clear example of the fundamental principle of African American culture called "call and response." The basic structure of call and response is straightforward. An individual voice, frequently a preacher or singer, calls out in a way that asks for a reply. As Wilson Pickett and Marvin Gaye liked to say, "Can I get a witness?" The response can be verbal, musical, physical—anything that puts it across. It can affirm, argue, redirect the dialogue, raise a new question. Any response that elicits a response becomes a new call. Usually the individual who issued the first call responds to the response and remains the focal point of an ongoing dialogue. But, both in its political contexts and in its more strictly musical settings, call and response moves the emphasis from the individual to the community, from the present predicament to the ongoing tradition.

For African American performance to work, the performer *must* receive a response, be it the rallying of the community around the political leader calling them to action, the punctuated cries of "Yes, Lord" and "Tell it" greeting Mahalia Jackson and James Brown, or the classic soul samples in twenty-first-century hip-hop. Drawing on the experience and insights of the entire community, call and response forms the living, breathing core of African American politics. The individual maintains a crucial role; a carefully crafted call will yield the most fruitful insight. But the individual does not necessarily, or ideally, maintain *control.* Aretha's brother Cecil described her use of call and response perfectly: "It's just like being in church. She does with her voice exactly what a preacher does with his when he moans to a congregation. That moan strikes a responsive chord in the congregation, and somebody answers you back with their own moan, which means, 'I know what you're moaning about, because I feel the same way.' So you have something sort of like a thread spinning out and touching and tying everybody together in a shared experience."

While Aretha, Stevie, and Curtis created music that felt *like* church, most of their records weren't gospel music per se. If they'd been content to stay *in* church, they certainly wouldn't have had the impact they had, because most white listeners would never have heard their names. Setting out to attract an audience that was certain to shy away from openly religious lyrics, Curtis, Aretha, and Stevie benefited from the pioneering efforts of Ray Charles and Sam Cooke. Aware of the financial and political benefits of crossing over to the pop charts, the pioneering R&B artists had introduced gospel singing styles to white audiences by the simple expedient of reworking a few lyrics. Crystallizing the strategy that allowed the soul singers to take the gospel vision to the center of an aggressively secular music industry, Charles laughingly observed, "Gospel and the blues are really, if you break it down, almost the same thing. It's just a question of whether you're talkin' about a woman or God." While some black churchgoers shook their heads over the move from choir loft to nightclub, few resisted Cooke's or Charles's love songs. Most understood the crossover strategy as part of the larger political movement intent on opening every area of American society to black participation. Jerry Wexler, who'd produced Ray Charles and Aretha, spoke for many when he claimed that "the green dollar and the black song did more to eliminate segregation than all the polemics and preaching in the world." By the end of the century, the green dollar would, ironically enough, become the defining element of a new form of segregation that mocked the vision the singers and Wexler shared.

That irony underscores the value of focusing on Aretha, Stevie, and Curtis, whose voices reverberate through the mostly untold, and distinctly sobering, story of the freedom movement in the North. Most civil rights histories concentrate on the campaigns in the South and the legal skirmishes in Washington, D.C. If the North enters the story at all, it is usually only in the later stages and then in connection with the shift from civil rights to Black Power. That story is less wrong than it is deceptive. Its incomplete narrative seriously underestimates the depth of white supremacy in the North and renders the specific history of black northerners invisible. *Higher Ground* seeks to recover part of that history and to reflect on the political lessons to be gained from a broader picture of American life in the last half of the twentieth century. While the story begins amid the hopes of the movement, it continues through and beyond the Reagan years. What emerges is a sobering account of broken hopes and betrayed trust. In the South the enemy was clearly identified; in the North it was hard to tell your friends from your foes. Northern liberals who supported civil rights legislation aimed at the Jim Crow South frequently resisted efforts to desegregate their own neighborhoods and their own children's schools. Similarly, a handful of northern blacks held a degree of political and economic power unthinkable in Birmingham or Memphis. But that power depended on the continued existence of its base in the ghetto. As the story played out over the decades, it became increasingly clear that poor blacks in Chicago and Detroit weren't much better off than their grandparents had been in Alabama and Mississippi, and that problem could not be read only in black and white.

Charting the cross-currents of American racial politics since World War II, *Higher Ground* follows Aretha Franklin, Curtis Mayfield, and Stevie Wonder as they grappled with the enduring dilemmas of race and democracy. Like the movement itself, their personal stories mingle trouble and triumph. Each overcame obstacles that would have broken the spirits of most ordinary people: Stevie's blindness and near-fatal injury in an automobile accident, Curtis's childhood poverty and grown-up paralysis, Aretha's troubled private life. Each survived to create art of transcendent beauty. But despite their success in changing America's musical landscape, they failed to realize the dream at the center of the gospel vision. Far too many people remained stranded on the platform when the freedom train pulled out of the station. The movement won the cultural battle but lost the political war. That's the irony at the center of this book. You can see it in the juxtaposition of the White House ceremonies honoring Stevie and Aretha with the nightmare moonscapes of Chicago's West Side and Detroit's Eight Mile Road.

However bleak the picture, the struggle hasn't ended. The black southerners who forged the gospel vision in the fiery furnace of slavery and the fleeting hopes of Reconstruction wouldn't have been surprised by the return of the hard times. From the beginning they'd understood that trouble was simply a part of life. And that it didn't always last. That wisdom echoed in the songs their children and grandchildren carried out of the southern wilderness into an ambiguous promised land that, for many, turned out to be a mirage. Over the generations the rhythm and the words of the songs changed, but the vision persisted. In 2004, as in 1804 and 1904 and 1954, the challenge was to respond in ways that made it real. As James Baldwin wrote in "Sonny's Blues," "For, while the tale of how we suffer, and how we are delighted, and how we may triumph, is never new, it always must be heard. There isn't any other tale to tell, it's the only light we've got in all this darkness." It was the song that Aretha, Curtis, and Stevie had been singing all along as they summoned countless thousands aboard the gospel train to the higher ground. For those with the ears to hear and the will to respond, the invitation remains open. As Curtis Mayfield once sang to the weary and the wary as well as to the warriors: "You don't need no ticket, you just get on board."

CHAPTER ONE

"There Is a Fountain Filled with Blood"

The Roots of the Gospel Vision

Listen at her. Amen." Reverend C.L. Franklin's words rose up above the swell of voices that greeted his fourteen-year-old daughter as she surrendered to the moan at the timeless heart of "Precious Lord (Take My Hand)," the most tormented and triumphant of gospel classics. The quickening rhythm of the church mothers' fans beat an expectant murmur from the crowd, which gave way to joyous cries of "Amen" and "Tell it," and the hum of Detroit record store owner Joe Von Battle's portable recording equipment. Her fingers flowing over the keys of the battered piano, young Aretha immersed herself in a healing river of spirit and song. Closing her eyes as the spotlight glinted off the crown of her perfectly coifed hair, Aretha sank into the depths of the song she'd sung so many times beneath the bright blue cross above the pulpit of her father's New Bethel Baptist Church, nestled in the heart of Detroit's dirt-poor Paradise Valley ghetto. Crying out "Ain't no harm to moan," she flooded out a cascade of tones that lifted her five thousand listeners above the killing streets of the cities that had promised much and delivered little, and carried them back to the southern crossroads churches where many had first felt the power of the Lord.

Those who weren't caught up entirely in their own trials might have paused to reflect on the song Aretha used as her gospel chariot. It was no secret that Thomas Dorsey, the reformed whorehouse piano player whose songs defined modern gospel music, had written "Precious Lord" the night he heard that his wife and son had died in childbirth. Those who attended New Bethel would have understood that Aretha's moan bore witness to her still-fresh pain over her mother's death. Raising her face to heaven and pounding out a shattering series of chords, Aretha struggled to twist the moan back into language. "At," she began, shouting with an intensity that testified to the loving attention she'd received from the great gospel singers—Mahalia Jackson, Clara Ward, Marion Williams—who'd helped raise her in a house where the regular visitors included Adam Clayton Powell Jr. and Martin Luther King. The word stretched almost ten seconds until Aretha brought the line home. "At the river," she continued, her words resonating with a chorus of African American voices, among them Paul Robeson's "Deep River" and Langston Hughes's vision of a deep deep river flowing from West Africa and the slave markets of New Orleans into the souls of black folk as they spread across a land in which they remained pilgrims of sorrow.

Praying that his ancient reel-to-reel equipment would hold out, Joe Von Battle recognized Aretha as something special. His keen grasp of the connection between the spiritual, aesthetic, and commercial dimensions of black music led him to believe she had the potential to reach music lovers far beyond the walls of the drafty old arena or the stained glass at New Bethel Baptist. A central figure in Detroit's African American music scene who had recorded down-and-dirty R&B singers Washboard Willie, Tye Tongue Hanley, and the Detroit Count as well as C.L. Franklin's sermons, Von Battle had navigated the cross-currents between gospel, jazz, and rhythm and blues. He'd stood in Reverend Franklin's living room trading stories with Mahalia, Sam Cooke, jazz pianist Art Tatum, "Queen of the Blues" Dinah Washington, and New Bethel's talented young music director, James Cleveland. Reverend Franklin was reluctant to rush his daughter into a music business that had chewed up more than a few young black singers, but Von Battle had little difficulty convincing him to approve a series of recordings. The songs he committed to acetate on a series of Sundays in 1956 document the first steps on a path that would make Aretha one of the most deeply loved singers of her time and establish her as an American artist of the stature of Walt Whitman, Woody Guthrie, William Faulkner, and Duke Ellington.

Twelve years later Aretha would again turn to "Precious Lord" as she and her gospel people—a few of them white—staggered beneath a burden that seemed too heavy to bear. As a mule-drawn cart carried Martin Luther King's body through the streets of Atlanta, Aretha offered up a quieter version of "Precious Lord" as a meditation on the most basic human question: how to keep hope alive in a world where the devil holds sway. Her face a twisted mask of grief, Aretha's voice illuminated the gospel vision that sustained the foot soldiers of the movement, the ordinary people whose tears, sweat, and—far too often—blood had changed America in ways that seemed impossible to all but the most audacious dreamers a generation before.

As it has done since the first cries rose up from the festering holds of the slave ships, the gospel vision sounds the central predicaments of African American history: to flee or fight white power, to affirm black identity or assimilate into the larger society, to transcend the material world or try to conquer it, to pursue innovation or preserve tradition. Giving voice to the ongoing drive for freedom that remains the beating heart of African American history, gospel-based music bears witness to the burdens of life, the same experiences that gave rise to the blues. But where the blues celebrates survival, gospel seeks redemption. Whatever its specific form— traditional gospel, reggae, soul, the celebratory moments of disco and house music—the gospel impulse reconnects individuals with powers and communities larger than themselves: God and a community determined, as Mahalia Jackson sang, to "move on up." Small wonder that gospel provided the guiding spirit of the civil rights movement that reshaped American life in the years following World War II.

For Aretha, the gospel vision and gospel music were inseparable. She'd grown up surrounded by the stars of the gospel firmament, and her earliest memories clustered around the legendary musicians who filled her father's social circle. When Mahalia Jackson sang in Detroit, she stayed with the

Franklin family and "taught me things a girl should know," as Aretha recalled. "Mahalia would come in and she'd head right for the kitchen. She'd put up a pot of greens," she reminisced, savoring her memories of the down-home smells that filled her world in those days. "We'd sit around and talk. I was shy, but I guess I did have a lot of questions. Then maybe we'd sing. They were so strong, those ladies. And always there for me. She'd sing in my father's church, and I would be thrilled listening to her. And feeling so lucky she would come home, to our house." When Mahalia finished whipping up her feasts of fried chicken, gumbo, cornbread, and sweet potato pie, she never lacked for good company. Easing back into the living room with its fine woodwork, plush green carpet, and purple satin drapes, she could relax with Franklin family friends like Clara Ward, Francis Steadman, Sam Cooke, Marion Williams, and James Cleveland. Attracted by the charismatic presence of Aretha's father, Reverend C.L. Franklin, the "High Priest of Soul Preaching," the gospel luminaries mingled with jazz musicians, R&B stars, and political leaders like Powell and King. For Reverend Franklin's talented daughter, the best times were when "somebody would start toying with the piano and something would start up. There was always music in our house. The radio was going in one room, the record player in another, the piano banging away in the living room."

Like the sounds and smells that surrounded her, Aretha came to Detroit from the South. She was born on March 25, 1942, in Memphis, Tennessee, the musical crossroads of the mid-South. Best known for the freewheeling night life of the Beale Street blues clubs, the sprawling cotton market at the bend of the Mississippi River was equally well known among African Americans as the headquarters of the Church of God in Christ and the home of renowned gospel composers W. Herbert Brewster and Lucy Campbell. Migrants fleeing the backbreaking labor of the Delta filled their Saturday nights with blues consolations and their Sunday mornings with gospel exultations, both of which testified to their hard times and their enduring hopes. The Franklins would soon join the thousands for whom Memphis served as a halfway house on the journey to the killing floors of Chicago or the assembly lines of Detroit. In Memphis they occupied a modest single-story home in a neighborhood that would nurture an impressive roster of musicians including Maurice White, the guiding spirit of Earth, Wind & Fire.

Named after her father's sisters, Aretha Louise Franklin was the fourth of five children. While her brothers Vaughn and Cecil would pursue careers in the military and the ministry respectively, Aretha's older sister Erma and younger sister Carolyn would add to the family's musical legacy. Erma would enter soul music history for her superior version of Janis Joplin's signature song, "Piece of My Heart," while Carolyn would make her mark as the composer of Aretha's mid-seventies soul ballad "Angel." Together Erma and Carolyn would provide memorable backup vocals on classics from "Do Right Woman—Do Right Man" and "Respect" to "Chain of Fools."

Aretha's family had carried their songs to Memphis from the Mississippi Delta, where the young Clarence LaVaughn Franklin had pastored a series of churches in and around Greenville and Clarksdale, the mythic cradle of the blues. Born January 22, 1915, in Sunflower County, Mississippi, C.L. lived the harsh reality that echoed through the music of Robert Johnson and Muddy Waters. Unwilling to accept his place in the Jim Crow South after returning from World War I, C.L.'s father had abandoned the family. His mother remarried a caring and hardworking but illiterate sharecropper, Henry Franklin. The family moved from plantation to plantation before settling in the parched cotton fields of Bolivar County outside Doddsville. As he grew up, C.L. witnessed white supremacy's relentless assault on his stepfather's sense of self-worth. The intensely intelligent youngster perceived the obvious injustices of Jim Crow: the inadequate schools and the way the white farmers cheated his stepfather each year when the price of the cotton never quite balanced the accrued cost of food and supplies. He raged at the everyday indignities that constantly reminded blacks of their place on the fringes of humanity. Decades later Franklin rankled at the memory of being intentionally sprayed by bus drivers taking white children to school while C.L. and his friends trudged along the muddy spring roads.

Chopping cotton alongside his father in the fields next to Highway 61 and the Illinois Central Railroad line, Aretha's father dreamed of a better life as he waved back to blacks driving cars with northern plates. Walking the tracks, he hailed migrants aboard the "Chicken Bone Special" headed for the promised lands of Chicago, Cleveland, and Detroit. Returning to the sharecroppers' quarters at the end of the day, he would relax listening to the blues moans of Blind Lemon Jefferson and Roosevelt Sykes as well as his favorite recorded sermon, Reverend J.M. Gates's "Dead Cat on the Line."

Although he always insisted that he never felt a conflict between gospel and the blues, C.L. Franklin's path out of the Delta led not to Beale Street but to the pulpit of Memphis's respectable New Salem Baptist Church. From his early childhood in Mississippi, he had been steeped in the spirit of the church, walking two miles to choir practice and traveling in a horse-drawn wagon to the churches where he heard the backwoods preaching style that would shape his own. When he was thirteen, he experienced a fiery vision on the wall of his bedroom. "A voice spoke to me from behind the plank and said something like, 'Go and preach the gospel to all nations,'" he later told an interviewer. "I went and told my mother what I had seen and heard." A few years later he formally accepted the call to preach after hearing an inspirational sermon by the Memphis-based Reverend Benjamin Perkins. C.L. established himself by rotating through a series of small rural churches, often serving as many as four congregations at a time. Like their blues-playing brothers and cousins, Delta preachers grappled in a highly competitive culture that required both insight and showmanship. The charisma that would propel C.L. to stardom first emerged, he fondly recalled, at Delta "preaching rallies," where four or five young ministers would deliver short sermons, "trying to outdo the others" and capture the hearts and financial support of the crowd. Rivalries grew fierce, but from the beginning C.L.'s voice and flair for showmanship set him apart.

His growing reputation enabled C.L. to establish a home base in Clarksdale, although he continued to visit churches throughout the area. One day in Shelby, Mississippi, he met a young pianist and singer named Barbara Siggers. Attracted by her quiet beauty and resonant voice, he began courting her. A few months later, as a persistent rain drenched the cotton fields, they were married at the house of one of C.L.'s Clarksdale parishioners. The young couple stayed in Clarksdale for a year before moving on to Greenville and then, at the invitation of Reverend Perkins, whose sermon had set C.L. on his spiritual path, to Memphis and New Salem Baptist Church. C.L. busied himself serving New Salem and was soon pastoring a second church in the new Hollywood subdivision while pursuing studies at LeMoyne College. His young wife sang in the choir.

At home Barbara Franklin exercised an influence that was not only personal but musical. "I was young but I remember how warm and beautiful she was," Aretha wrote in her autobiography. "I was very close to her and I can't say which, if either of my parents was the greater influence on me." The legendary producer John Hammond, who would sign Aretha to her first pop music contract, remembered hearing that "Aretha's mother was one of the really great gospel singers. Aretha said she had more talent than C.L." Still, without question, Aretha's father provided the family's center of gravity. And her mother suffered in the fishbowl of life in a preacher's household. C.L.'s respectful and admiring assessment of her glossed over the difficulties faced by a talented woman in a church culture dominated by charismatic men: "People loved her. We weren't too involved with them socially; we were involved with them in terms of the church program. She got along beautifully, beautifully. She had no problem. To me, people who respect the minister's wife and encourage her, admire her for what she is doing, like to hear her sing—I don't see why she has any difficulty, although I have often heard it said that it is difficult to be a minister's wife."

Whatever his wife's hardships, Franklin had embarked on a journey that would carry him to the forefront of the National Baptist Convention. In those days "for a black boy," the illustrious African American photographer Ernest Withers explained, "growing up to be President of the Convention was like a white boy becoming President of the United States." C.L.'s first step to that end took place when he delivered the eulogy for a friend who had pastored Friendship Baptist Church in Buffalo, New York. His sermon so impressed the mourners that they asked him to fill the vacancy, an invitation Franklin eagerly accepted. That same year his sermon at the annual meeting of the National Baptist Convention mesmerized a Detroit audience that included members of that city's New Bethel Baptist, which was embroiled in conflicts that would soon lead half the congregation to walk out and form a new church. The members who stayed behind agreed that the charismatic young Franklin was an ideal figure to rebuild the congregation. Much to the dismay of his Buffalo flock, he agreed to move once more. C.L. Franklin served the Lord *and* C.L. Franklin.

When C.L. Franklin climbed into the pulpit of New Bethel on the first Sunday in June of 1946, the church huddled in a dilapidated former bowling alley on Hastings Street in the heart of Detroit's Paradise Valley ghetto. Located on the city's Lower East Side, Paradise Valley was the point of arrival for most of the black migrants who streamed to Michigan in search of the economic opportunities promised by Detroit's wartime emergence as the "Arsenal of Democracy." When they arrived, however, they found themselves in what the *Pittsburgh Courier,* a black newspaper with a national audience, called "the largest Southern city in the United States." As early as 1942 a *Life* magazine headline noted, "Detroit Is Dynamite," warning that the uneasy racial situation could "either blow up Hitler or blow up the United States."

A migrant's first problem was simply finding a place to live. The black population of Detroit doubled between 1940 and 1950, putting enormous pressure on an already overtaxed and rigidly segregated housing market. As the ghetto expanded north from Paradise Valley on the east side of Woodward Avenue, conditions in the "rat belt"—residents reported more than two hundred bites in a two-year period—deteriorated. Over a quarter of Lower East Side apartments lacked plumbing and full kitchens. Migrants who prospered fled to middle-class black neighborhoods like Oakland Avenue and Conant Gardens; the growing divisions along class lines mocked the dreams that had drawn the migrants to Detroit in the first place.

Tensions between new migrants and old settlers in the black community, however, paled beside the seething fear and anger that the black migration provoked among whites in Detroit. In 1943 the tensions exploded into one of the worst riots in American history. The riot began on the bridge over the Detroit River that linked the city with the Belle Isle recreation area, which local whites sometimes called "Nigger Island." Historian Timothy Tyson describes what happened when word of white attacks on black motorists reached Paradise Valley: "A young black man mounted the stage at the Forest Club, a popular black hangout in Paradise Valley, seized the microphone from the band leader, and told the crowd, 'There's a riot at Belle Isle. The whites have killed a colored lady and her baby. Thrown them over the bridge. Everybody come on.' The rumor about the woman and her baby was not true, but thousands of African Americans raged through the streets, stoning white motorists and looting white businesses. White agitators spread similar rumors of outrage, many of which were sexual in nature, as white mobs rampaged on streetcars and set fire to blacks' automobiles. Many white rioters traveled substantial distances from all-white communities, as one put it, 'to kill us a nigger.' White police ignored and sometimes encouraged white rioters; some became active participants in the violence." The riot left 38 dead, including 17—all of them black—killed by police. Officials reported 676 serious injuries and $2 million in property damage.

In 1946, when Reverend Franklin and his young family arrived in Detroit, memories of the Belle Isle riot remained fresh, but those nightmare images could not overshadow the vitality and energy of their new home. On any Friday or Saturday night the clubs clustered along John R Street between Forest and Canfield overflowed with the music that accompanied the migrants on their journey north. They talked, drank, and danced to "Boogie Chillen" by John Lee Hooker, the Clarksdale-born bluesman who held down a janitor's job at Dodge Main. They rocked to "Fever" by Little Willie John, who'd moved from Arkansas to the Motor City when he was four. R&B belter LaVern Baker, billed as "Little Miss Sharecropper," fronted Todd Rhodes's jump blues band while trumpeter Howard McGhee, saxophonist Bill Evans (who would soon change his name to Yusef Lateef), and singer Betty Carter helped establish Detroit as a center of the burgeoning bebop movement. Hank Ballard, first with the Royals and then with the Midnighters, delighted crowds with his salacious smash "Work with Me Annie." The three Jones brothers from Pontiac—drummer Elvin, who would form part of John Coltrane's great band of the sixties, soulful pianist Hank, and trumpeter Thad, whom Charles Mingus once called "Bartok with valves for a pencil that's directed by God"—joined a jazz world that included vibe virtuoso Milt Jackson and trumpeter Donald Byrd. A parade of Detroit-born or -based musicians sparkled at night spots like the Flame Show Bar, famous for its hundred-foot-long bar and the mirrors covering three walls. Thomas "Beans" Bowles, who would play a key role in the Motown story as a member of the Funk Brothers house band, described the scene outside the Flame at its peak in the late thirties: "On weekends the traffic would line up; you could not drive down Canfield or John R. That was hustle night, girls were on the streets, pimps were out, everybody was makin' money. Lights and glitter, valet parking. Nobody bother you or nothin'."

By the time the young preacher took the pulpit at New Bethel, Paradise Valley was surrendering its preeminence in black nightlife to Oakland Avenue, a north-end district that prided itself on comparisons with Los Angeles's "Miracle Mile." The name "Paradise Valley" grew increasingly ironic. A writer for Detroit's leading black newspaper, the *Michigan*

Chronicle, described the changes in the area around the young Reverend Franklin's church: "No longer is the Valley the gay, charming, and alluring young lady she once was, instead she is a withered, ugly old hag whom no one loves and whom everyone is beginning to forsake for a younger more beautiful companion." Thousands of returning veterans and new migrants came hoping the Paradise Valley boom would resume but finding little sign of it. Aretha's brother Cecil fleshed out the picture: "The people you saw who had any measure of success were the pimp and the hustler, the numbers man and the dope man. Aretha knew what they were all about, without having to meet them personally."

Rather than lamenting his bad timing, C.L. Franklin embraced the challenge. "Hastings is a fine place for a church because the church is for everyone," he announced. The exuberant preacher set about marshaling the resources for that mission. If, as Franklin observed, "raising money in church is an art," music historian Daniel Wolff was certainly correct in anointing Franklin "one of the premier artists." By March 1949 New Bethel had been transformed from a crumbling bowling alley into a palace. Entering through an outer lobby with new picture windows on three sides, the growing congregation worshiped amid towering stained-glass depictions of Jesus and the disciples.

Aretha always retained her affection for the church where her father preached beneath the glowing blue neon crucifix above the altar. In her autobiography she admitted to feeling "the pull of those days in the old neighborhood down on Hastings with the Willis Theater across the street, small shops and storefront churches as far as the eye could see." Aretha remembered the musical allure of the clubs where black musicians from Duke Ellington to Dinah Washington bedazzled appreciative audiences. She also relished memories of the storefront Holiness Church across the street from New Bethel where "they were shouting and praising His name so strong that I was drawn inside."

Reverend Franklin called upon the Holy Spirit in a somewhat more cerebral style. From his days studying sociology and English literature at LeMoyne, C.L. enjoyed being called "Rabbi," a nickname that suggested the intellectual content of his sermons. Developing a "more historically minded and less evangelical" style than most of his Baptist peers, Franklin argued that his thoughtful approach would have "a more lasting effect because you're reaching their minds as well as their emotions." Still, he shared his flock's appreciation for the intermingling of music and spirit. Every Sunday, New Bethel raised its own chorus of voices bearing witness to the burdens of life in the promised land and testifying to the spirit that bestowed the strength to face another week on the loading docks or in the white folks' kitchens. From the start music played a central role at New Bethel, reflecting Franklin's belief that "gospel music mends the broken heart, raises the bowed down head, and gives hope to the weary traveler."

At New Bethel C.L. perfected the inimitable style that would soon allow him to command fees of up to four thousand dollars per sermon. Future Supreme Mary Wilson, whose family attended New Bethel, described the weekly scene of women "rocking back and forth in the pews, saying, 'Yes, Jesus. Yes, Lord.' There were several women in starched white nurse's uniforms and they would go over to the most hysterical churchgoers and fan them.... We would sit back and bet which of these middle-aged women was going to 'get happy' first." Blues great B.B. King expressed his admiration for the man he called "my main minister. Whenever I was in Detroit, I'd make it a point to get myself up to New Bethel on Sunday mornings.... He spoke simply and beautifully, telling stories in hypnotic cadences that called forth the power of Scripture. He gave examples I could understand. His sermons were musical, moving with the rhythms of his emotions, building to a climax, and leaving you renewed. He also injected strong messages about racial pride. Listening to Reverend Franklin's messages was like listening to a good song. You felt hope." By the time the Chrysler Freeway Project forced New Bethel to relocate to the old Oriole Theater, the splintered congregation C.L. Franklin had encountered in 1946 had grown to between three and four thousand.

Even as "the Man with the Million Dollar Voice" advanced toward the preeminent place he would maintain for the next thirty years, the Franklin family was facing difficulties that would shape Aretha's personality. In 1948, when Aretha was six, Barbara Franklin left the family and took Vaughn, her oldest son, to Buffalo. While C.L. Franklin rarely mentioned his wife's departure, the split shook the children. Aretha has always rejected suggestions that her mother betrayed the family's trust. "In no way, shape, form or fashion did our mother desert us," she wrote. "She simply moved with Vaughn back to Buffalo, where she lived with her parents." Remembering summer visits to her mother, who supported herself working as a nurse's aide at Buffalo General Hospital, Aretha painted a warm picture of carefree childhood games and ice cream treats. The visits came to a tragic end in 1952 when Barbara Franklin died suddenly of a heart attack. Even a half century later Aretha would say only, "I cannot describe the pain, nor will I try."

Many of those who knew Aretha well believe that Barbara's departure and death affected Aretha even more deeply than she acknowledged. Mavis Staples, who first met Aretha when they were both teenagers on the gospel circuit, remembered that Aretha "had a brush and a case. And I asked, 'That's your mother's brush?' And she said, 'Yeah, that's my mother's brush. It's still got a little bit of hair in it.' I think that was the worst thing that could've happened for her, not to know her mother." Mahalia Jackson concluded simply, "After her mama died, the whole family wanted for love."

As she would throughout her life, Aretha turned to the church and song for solace. The same year her mother died, she accepted Jesus as her Lord and personal savior, a formal commitment that Aretha took with the utmost seriousness. By the time she was ten, she'd already found her way to the piano, "just bangin', not playin', but findin' a little something here and there," she later told an *Ebony* magazine interviewer. When C.L. overheard his daughter imitating popular hits like Eddie Heywood's "Canadian Sunset," he arranged for professional lessons. Frustrated by "too much 'Chopsticks,' " Aretha asserted her musical independence. When the teacher arrived, Aretha recounted, "I'd hide. I tried for maybe a week, but I just couldn't take it. She had all these little baby books, and I wanted to go directly to the tunes." Listening carefully to visitors like jazz master Art Tatum and future gospel legend James Cleveland provided Aretha with all the schooling she needed. As Smokey Robinson, a close friend of Aretha's brother Cecil, remembered, "We poke our heads into the music room and I'm amazed. Seated behind the baby grand is a baby herself, singing like an angel."

In later life Aretha would minimize the burdens she experienced during her childhood; at times, her memories evoke a sepia *Father Knows Best*, complete with comic interludes. Family friend Dorothy Swan remembered entering the kitchen to find C.L. Franklin, who had not yet hired a permanent cook or housekeeper, cooking beans. Exasperated, the reverend complained, "I keep cooking them and they just get harder and harder." To which Dorothy responded succinctly, "Put some water in!" Fortunately, the arrival of Aretha's grandmother Rachel and a new housekeeper saved the family from starvation. With the help of visits from Mahalia, they gave Aretha a schooling in the kitchen arts that made her proud. "I'm good and mean with the pots," she would later say. "These were the serious soul sisters with those big black cast-iron skillets."

Living in a comfortable brick house in a shaded half-acre lot near Oakland Avenue, Aretha was shielded from the increasing problems of Paradise Valley. Although she had heard about the Detroit riot and felt the community's outrage over President Truman's 1952 seizure of the steel mills, she remembered the early fifties as "a time of high optimism in Detroit," accompanied by "music [that] reflected that optimism, the belief that things were getting better for black folks." From as far back as she could remember, music was part of the world that included parties at Belle Isle, movies at the Echo Theater, treats from Mr. Wiggins's Sweetshop, car rides with the family in C.L.'s Cadillac convertible, and the excitement of listening to broadcasts of fights featuring Sugar Ray Robinson and Detroit's own Joe Louis. "My childhood was a happy one," Aretha wrote. "We roller-skated, sat on the back porch—some people would call it a stoop—and told a lot of jokes late into the midnight hour. I had a piano right off the back porch, and sometimes I'd sing."

The children benefited from the attentions of C.L.'s companion, Lola Moore, whom Aretha remembered as "fashionable, fun and a dynamite cook." Although some members of the congregation raised their eyebrows at the presence of an unmarried woman in the minister's home, no one publicly challenged the story that she was just helping out with the children. For a while Lola lived with the Franklins, and the children hoped their father would marry her. But the relationship came to an end, and although Aretha cried when Lola caught a cab to the train station, she concluded simply, "Daddy's personal affairs were not our business, and we knew not to question him."

Ensconced behind the mahogany desk in his study or charming the visitors at his many parties, C.L. Franklin was the social and emotional fulcrum of the household. But his impact on his talented daughter was not simply psychological. When he lifted his expressive hands in benediction and filled New Bethel with his soaring words and rhythms, he provided his daughter a graduate education in giving voice to the spirit. Aretha frequently paid tribute to her father's influence on her style: "Most of what I learned vocally came from him. He gave me a sense of timing in music and timing is important in everything." In her autobiography she described what happened when C.L. felt the spirit: "When he would get into what I call high or third gear, it was called whooping. Later Harry Belafonte called Daddy a super-whooper, a description that made me smile.... Whooping is a powerful and highly rhythmic way of preaching in which words take the form of song—half speech, half melody. Reverend Jesse Jackson, whose ordination sermon was delivered by Daddy, said, 'C.L. Franklin was the most imitated soul preacher in history, a combination of soul and science and sweetness and substance.' " When Reverend Franklin reached the climax of a classic sermon like "Dry Bones in the Valley," "The Man at the Pool," or "A Bigot Meets Jesus," the line dividing speech from song existed mostly in theory. When the choir joined their minister in a favorite hymn such as "Father I Stretch My Hand to Thee" or "The Old Ship of Zion," the emotional unity of individual performer and responsive congregation set a standard that Aretha would carry with her into the world of secular entertainment.

While C.L. Franklin never crossed over into that world, his performances earned him an audience beyond the walls of his church. In 1951 he began broadcasting his sermons on Detroit radio, first on a small station out of suburban Dearborn and a year later on powerhouse WJLB. Reaching out to a national audience, Reverend Franklin bought time on a Memphis station where rates were cheap. Broadcasting giant WLAC out of Nashville quickly picked him up. At WLAC, ostensibly a black station targeting a black audience, DJs Gene Nobles, William "Hoss" Allen, and John R, whose full name was John Richbourg, were fully aware that the airwaves paid little heed to segregation. At any given moment upward of half their listeners, like the DJs, were white.

The broadcasts also caught the attention of Detroit record store owner and producer Joe Von Battle, who convinced Reverend Franklin to record his sermons on the JVB label. Neither Franklin nor Von Battle saw anything unusual about mixing commerce and politics with sincere expressions of faith. Since slavery times African Americans had used biblical images to comment on political issues, and the gospel circuit had been one of the few spheres in which blacks could express themselves and earn a decent living.

Seeking a larger audience and a bigger payday, Von Battle licensed the recordings to Chicago-based Chess Records, where Franklin rapidly ascended to stardom. He eventually headlined his own show on the gospel circuit and attained legendary status for his classic sermon "The Eagle Stirreth Her Nest." B.B. King summed up the message. "God stirs the nest of our personal history," the bluesman reflected. "He challenges us, like He challenged Daniel in the lions' den. Reverend Franklin would remind me that God's angels made the lions lie down like lambs. Like an eagle, God is swift and strong in healing our hearts."

The sermon is widely recognized as one of the classics of American preaching. Taking a passage in Deuteronomy as his text, Franklin offers a stirring exhortation that echoes the gospel vision of the movement leaders. He opens the sermon by saying he is using the eagle "to symbolize God's care and God's concern for his people." Then he lays out the take-home message in straightforward terms: "History has been one big nest that God has been eternally stirring to make man better—and to help us achieve world brotherhood." As the sermon unfolds, Franklin abandons the abstractions and spins out a fable about a farmer who builds a cage for an eagle he discovers living among his chickens. "The man went out and built a cage," Franklin chants, sweeping his listeners up in a wave of sound and rhythm:

> *And*
> > *every day he'd go in*
> > > *and feed the eagle.*
> *But*
> > *he grew*
> > > *a little older*
> > > > *and a little older.*
> *Yes he did.*
> > *His wings*
> > > *began*
> > *to scrape on the sides*
> > > *of the cage.*
> *And*
> > *he had to build*
> > > *another cage*

Finally, the farmer's heart melts at the sight of the eagle's distress, and he opens the door, freeing the eagle to fly, first to the branches of a nearby tree, and then into the heavens toward the mountain where the other eagles soar. "My soul is an eagle in the cage that the Lord has made for me," Franklin half-says, half-sings:

> *My soul,*
> > *My soul,*
> *my soul*
> > *is caged in,*
> > *in this old body,*
> > *yes it is,*
> *and one of these days*
> *the man who made the cage*
> *will open the door*
> *and let my soul*
> *Go.*
> *Yes he will.*

The sermon climaxes in a frenzy of moans wrapped around the most basic promise of the gospel vision: "One of these days, my soul will take wings... A few more days. O Lord."

Aretha understood that her father's sermons echoed the messages of the freedom movement. "Daddy preached self-pride," she observed, paraphrasing his social philosophy. "We are black not because we are cursed, for blackness is not a curse; it is a curse only if you think so, and it's not really a curse then; it's just the way you think. All colors are beautiful in the sight of God. The only reason why you entertain a thought like that is because you have been culturally conditioned by white people to think that way, and they conditioned you that way because they used this as a means to an end, to give you a feeling of inferiority, and to then take advantage of you, socially, economically, and politically."

The luminaries who gathered in the Franklin living room and kitchen represented the mainstream civil rights movement at its best. The traditional leadership class, they were well dressed, articulate, and confident that their cause was righteous. Cloaking their legal and moral appeals in the fiery words of the Old Testament, they supplemented their idealism with a hard-headed use of black economic power. During the Montgomery bus boycott, Martin Luther King claimed the moral high ground, but the power of black dollars did as much to carry the day. Organized around the presence of charismatic leaders including Franklin family friends Powell, Abernathy, and of course King, that movement embraced a "best foot forward" strategy designed to win white liberal allies and establish blacks as worthy of full participation in American society. They celebrated the individual breakthroughs of Jackie Robinson, General Benjamin Davis, and Nat King Cole, the first African American to host a network television show. They cheered Thurgood Marshall's victories in the courts and King's successful campaign to end segregation on the Montgomery buses. As the conversation around the Franklin dinner table gave way to the music that filled the house when the guests adjourned to the living room, Reverend Franklin's young daughter was learning that, in black America, music and the movement could share a voice.

GROWING UP IN the Cabrini-Green housing projects, a black island on Chicago's overwhelmingly white Near North Side, Curtis Mayfield never met the black political leaders or entertainers who frequented the Franklin household. Nevertheless, he and most other Cabrini residents joined their brothers and sisters throughout the nation in rejoicing over the Supreme Court's 1954 *Brown vs. Board of Education* decision and thrilling to Dr. King's stirring speeches. Few of them were aware that they were already playing central roles in an unpublicized drama that would shape the fate of the freedom movement not only in Chicago but throughout the United States. Even as the southern movement brought the walls of Jim Crow tumbling down, poor African Americans in Chicago found themselves losing battles that would leave them more isolated in the final years of the century than they had been prior to *Brown*. If freedom was really just another word for nothing left to lose, many of the people of Cabrini-Green were free.

In Cabrini-Green as in the Georgia woods and the Mississippi Delta, hard-pressed residents turned to music and religion for strength and inspiration. Born June 3, 1942, Curtis was the first child of Curtis Lee Mayfield (who had been born Curtis Lee Cooper) and Marion Washington. Raised by his mother and his maternal grandmother, Sadie Riley, he couldn't remember a time when he wasn't listening to gospel music, especially the music that resounded out of the church presided over by his grandmother, Anna Belle Mayfield. "My grandmother was working to become a minister back in the early fifties. So I saw a lot of church. We had a little storefront place. It was known as the Traveling Souls Spiritualist Church. And so it was just automatic for us young kids. We had Sunday school every Sunday, so after we'd come up in age of course we'd heard a lot of gospel music." Like many storefront churches, Traveling Souls relocated several times before finding a resting place in the Lawndale District at the heart of the city's mushrooming West Side ghetto. Curtis and the small congregation pitched in to touch up the peeling blue paint on the building and inscribe the church's name in big white letters on the front window.

Reverend Mayfield presided over services in a room heated by a black potbellied stove. Rising from a chair behind the rostrum, she would share her experience of the spirit with a congregation that numbered forty or fifty. Jerry Butler, who had been born in Mississippi and raised in the Pentecostal Church of God in Christ, remembers that when the spirit descended, services that began in the afternoon might last until midnight. He never forgot the emotional fire unleashed by the men and women as they spoke in tongues, "got the Holy Ghost," and testified to the power of the spirit in their lives.

For Butler and his young friend Curtis, the spiritual message came through more strongly in the music than in the words. "Whereas the preaching would kind of tire you out and put you to sleep," Mayfield admitted, "the music was an outburst just full of love that would build your heart up." Reflecting on the energy unleashed in spiritualist services, Butler saw African Americans recovering dimly apprehended aspects of their cultural heritage: "They had gone spiritually back to their African roots. Yes, the songs they were singing were about Christ—and in English—but the rhythms and the dances, the shouts and calls and responses between that woman and the congregation, were African."

It's unlikely that many of his Cabrini neighbors in the forties would have endorsed Butler's Afrocentric interpretation of their spiritual life. In the heady days after the project first opened in 1942, many saw Cabrini-Green as the harbinger of a future in which blacks and whites would live together in harmony. The Chicago Housing Authority had created the Cabrini project in 1937, choosing a site in a Sicilian neighborhood nicknamed "Little Hell," tearing down the run-down tenements at the intersection of Oak and Cleveland Streets, better known as "death corner," and replacing them with 581 two- and three-story row houses with flat roofs, private entrances, and small yards. For those who relocated to the interracial neighborhood from the overcrowded South Side slums, where rats outnumbered people, Cabrini-Green promised a taste of the American dream.

Almost from the start the project found itself caught up in the battle over public housing that would define the movement in the North. Like Detroit, black Chicago suffered from a severe housing shortage. In 1948 the Urban League reported that 375,000 South Side residents were crammed into an area that could legally accommodate 110,000. The saturation of the South Side created enormous pressure for redefining Chicago's racial boundaries. In neighborhood after neighborhood events followed a familiar script. A relatively well-off black family seeking to escape the ghetto would agree to pay higher-than-market value for a house on a previously all-white block; panicked whites would flee the area, allowing landlords to scoop up their property at bargain prices; the landlords would then neglect maintenance and subdivide apartments, re-creating the conditions the black pioneers had fled at the start of the cutthroat cycle. In Chicago's "bungalow belt," where a large number of European ethnic working-class families owned their own homes, the first signs of the depressing pattern understandably generated fierce resistance.

The result was a state of what one historian called "chronic urban guerrilla warfare." Whenever a black family moved into a white neighborhood, white residents mobilized to defend their turf. When black World War II veteran Roscoe Johnson and his wife, Ethel, moved into the Park Manor neighborhood, residents clustered on porches and in backyards, drinking, shouting "Bring out Bushman!" and "String him up!" and singing "Old Black Joe" and "Carry Me Back to Ole Virginny." As the night wore on, the verbal attacks escalated into physical violence. "We barricaded the door and put a mattress behind it," Mrs. Johnson reported. "We crawled on our hands and knees when the missiles started coming through the windows. Then they started to throw gasoline-soaked rags in pop bottles. They also threw flares and torches. The crowds didn't leave until daybreak."

Similar scenes played out with distressing regularity throughout the city. Through the late forties and early fifties Chicago authorities reported scores of racially motivated bombings. When Curtis Mayfield was growing up, the primary difference between Chicago and Birmingham was the absence of news coverage up North. Fearing that the racial tinder littering the city could blaze up in a major conflagration, the city had convinced newspaper editors, including the editors of black America's flagship paper, the *Chicago Defender,* to limit coverage of racial disturbances to brief factual accounts and to avoid editorials, inflammatory pictures, or emotionally charged language. Even though the city's "tension map" blossomed with colored pins mapping incidents of racial violence, Chicagoans in unaffected areas, to say nothing of the rest of the nation, rarely even knew the clashes had occurred. Although the headlines of the *Defender* screamed out news of racial atrocities in the South, the black press minimized and sometimes altogether ignored the violence in their own backyards.

The complicity of the black press in hushing up the hostilities was part of a larger pattern of race in Chicago politics. Unlike most of their relatives down South, blacks in Chicago could vote. Black ballots were a crucial cog in the most effective political machine ever assembled in an American city. In exchange for control of a substantial number of patronage jobs for blacks and protection for South Side numbers rackets and jitney cabs, a black sub-machine run by one-legged black boss William Dawson delivered votes for Richard Daley's machine on request, including some of the questionable ones that swung the 1960 presidential election to John Kennedy. Dawson and his allies also tacitly agreed not to challenge the racial status quo. Black politicians might speak out against racial injustice in Mississippi and Alabama. But their power base and economic self-interest were tied to the continuing existence of the Chicago ghetto.

Nonetheless, for the young Curtis Mayfield and his family, the Cabrini row houses *did* offer a glimpse of a better future, albeit one that vanished almost as soon as it came into sight. Under the leadership of Elizabeth Woods, the Chicago Housing Authority envisioned a solution to Chicago's intense postwar housing shortage based on building small integrated projects scattered throughout the city. The CHA believed that small projects offered the best chance of providing real educational and employment opportunities for all Chicagoans. But the approach never got an honest chance. Before long a set of deals redirected resources from small projects to the endless miles of all-black high-rise projects lining the State Street Corridor on the South Side. Woods herself would be driven from office by a segregationist coup.

But before that happened, the Cabrini-Green of the early 1950s provided one of the rare test cases for Woods's vision. Most of the first blacks to move to Cabrini, including the Mayfields, were fleeing the South Side slums. When black families began moving into Cabrini-Green on August 1, 1942, their new homes seemed promising. Retreating from Chicago's steaming summer streets to the shade beneath the trees outside the row houses, dancing to the music at the frequent block parties or partaking of the feasts provided by the neighborhood's established St. Philip Benizi Church, most of the neophyte North Siders shared the feelings of Margaret Wilson, who said: "In the early days, I didn't feel a boundary to the community. I didn't feel like Cabrini was separated from the rest of the area at all." For future jazz pianist Ramsey Lewis, his interracial group of friends seemed like a natural part of a comfortable childhood: "It wasn't until I was in college that I realized I was from what others might consider a 'poor' family as far as money was concerned. But growing up in Cabrini, I never wanted for anything. We had clothes to go to church in, clothes to go to school in, and clothes to play in." Ramsey ran with a mixed group—two or three whites, two or three blacks: "I didn't realize there was anything unusual about the fact that our neighborhood was mixed."

All too soon, however, events would justify Chicago activist Saul Alinsky's sardonic definition of *integration* as "the period of time between the arrival of the first black and the departure of the last white." At Cabrini the 1958 opening of the "Reds"—fifteen buildings of between seven and nineteen stories housing seven thousand new residents—marked the point of no return. Initially, as Jerry Butler remembered, the Reds seemed to expand the opportunity offered by the low-rise "Greens." "When the red high-rises were built, the initial reaction was, wow, this is gonna be great," he recalled. "And I think in its embryonic stages, it was great. It was a mixed community with all types of blue-collar workers. We had bus drivers and plumbers and sanitation workers." Fellow Red resident Viola Holmes concurred: "I thought I was livin' in heaven.... We had a big playground for the kids to play in during the day and all the grown folk would take over in the night time and set out there in back." Rochelle Satchell underlined the communal spirit that permeated the projects: "Everybody took care of everybody. You never had to lock your doors. You never had fear of anybody just coming out. You never felt like they were going to do any harm."

For the young Curtis Mayfield, life in the projects was simply life. Without romanticizing the era, Mayfield remembered the forties and fifties as a time of communal sharing. "Mostly everybody that had a little something or that had a little home or even an apartment, they had grandfathers, they had uncles and aunties, and many times those people lived right within the same household. And of course the women had their men and everybody had the support and took what little you might have to make it work for everybody." Mayfield traced the values of his community to its roots in the rural South, where most of the older generation had grown up. "I was fortunate enough to be amongst a lot of folks who helped to strengthen my mental abilities as a youngster," he said appreciatively. "I learned through the streets and through the wise old people. I used to love to listen to old folks. Though you have to sort things out and make certain amends because a lot of what they say's BS. But there's a lot of truth to it, too. You know, everything in its place. I got my learning talking to elderly people who'd had to do the same because of the times. Even prior to my time that was the only way to get a learning."

The economic realities of life in the projects, however, placed those values under extreme pressure. The prospects for residents of Cabrini-Green during the early fifties couldn't be divorced from a metropolitan economy teetering on the brink of collapse. The periodic recessions that plagued the postwar economy justified the old saying that "when white America sneezes, black America gets pneumonia." Soaring unemployment rates squeezed black families hard. Carl Sandburg had celebrated Chicago as the "city of the big shoulders," "the nation's freight handler," and the "hog butcher for the world," but by the time Mayfield reached his teens, the slaughterhouses and railroad yards had lost much of their business to regional centers developed with federal subsidies. Casting uneasy glances at the run-down slums encroaching on the Loop business district, Chicago merchants began relocating to the mushrooming northwestern suburbs.

For young African Americans seeking blue-collar jobs that would allow them to support a family, it was an unmitigated disaster. Cut out of the job market before they'd entered it, some turned to hustling. Many struggling to scrape by on seasonal employment and service-sector jobs succumbed to despair. Mayfield lamented the changes that would ultimately transform Cabrini into a symbol of social collapse and cut the younger generation off from the community that had nurtured him: "As you got older, you began to see a different way of life, and the men and the women, they became divided. The men went their way and you could see families just sort of deteriorating simply because they didn't have that background. A lot of kids can't look back one generation. Everybody wanted to become individuals, independent individuals. Which has its place. But to have a foundation you need a very strong beginning, and you have to know where you come from."

Mayfield's foundation lay in his family and the music that suffused his life. Although his father left the family when Curtis was an infant, his mother helped develop his deep love for language. He fondly recalled that she "was very much into poetry. She wrote poems herself and had a lot of books of poetry which I used to read all the time. She read me Paul Laurence Dunbar, Dr. Seuss, limericks. These became the foundations for my hook lines and rhythmic patterns."

Although Cabrini was located far from the glittering theaters and funky blues clubs that stretched along State Street between Thirty-first and Thirty-fifth Streets on the South Side, music filled Mayfield's childhood. "I never really had to acquire an interest in music," he reminisced. "I just grew up around people who were a constant inspiration." Jerry Butler agreed: "I shrink away from saying music was part of the black community because it makes it sound like it wasn't part of any other community, but music was always there for us. It was part of the neighborhood. We grew up singing." Ramsey Lewis echoed Butler and emphasized the different styles of music available in the Cabrini mix: "There was always talk about different kinds of music. I was exposed to all kinds of music—jazz, pop, R&B, blues.... My dad never said, 'Don't listen to Frank Sinatra because he's white,' or anything like that. He brought Art Tatum's music into the house and all sorts of stuff, but at the time I was so into gospel and classical music that I didn't appreciate it until later." Mayfield relished the variety, drawing deeply from Chicago's blues scene and finding particular inspiration in legends Muddy Waters and Little Walter.

Mayfield's first contacts with blues, R&B, and jazz came primarily via radio. Curiously, despite the area's large and rapidly growing black population, when Curtis was young there was no radio station devoted entirely to black music. Until 1963, when Phil Chess purchased WVON, black radio had been one part of an "ethnic" mix on stations that also programmed, among others, Greek, Lithuanian, German, and Bohemian music. As a result, the young Mayfield was forced to scan the dial in search of black DJs like Holmes Daylie, aka "Daddy-O" Daylie, whose *Jazz from Dad's Pad* aired on WAIT; Herb Kent, who always closed his show with the Gospel Clefs' "Open Our Eyes"; and Al Benson, a whiskey-drinking Democratic precinct captain whose ten hours a day on the air were split between WGES, WJJD, and WAAF.

The pioneer DJs combined music, ads, and announcements targeted toward the black community, with an outrageous showmanship that made them stars on and off the air. "Daddy-O" Daylie, for instance, developed his rhyming rapping style while working as a bartender. Chicago DJ Sid McCoy remembered that celebrities loved to hang out and watch him perform: "He would get up there with a glass and pour that drink, and he'd be rhyming all the time that he was making that drink. He would wrap the glass in a napkin, and at the end of a couplet he would set the glass down. Then he'd take the ice and throw it up in the air and catch it behind his back. He was fantastic. Everybody loved him." The first Chicago DJ to speak in a southern accent on the air, Benson was so popular that in 1949 he was elected to the honorary position of "Mayor of Bronzeville," the affectionate term used by residents to describe the black South Side. A firm supporter of R&B and the civil rights movement, Benson chartered an airplane the day before the 1956 presidential election and blanketed his hometown of Jackson, Mississippi, with five thousand copies of the U.S. Constitution.

The DJs provided the young Mayfield with an inexhaustible supply of fresh musical ideas: "I had so much to go back on for ideas and sounds and rhythms and feels." The deepest of those ideas and rhythms came from gospel music. Chicago's gospel heritage ran deep. Thomas Dorsey wrote most of his songs there, and once Mahalia Jackson followed the Illinois Central rail line north from New Orleans, Chicago was the undisputed capital of the gospel world. Sallie Martin nurtured a generation of great gospel vocalists, and despite their name, the Five Blind Boys of Mississippi called the South Side home. "Most of my life it was almost automatic," Mayfield recalled. "Most black folks connected one way or another with the quartets and the little chorus groups and what have you." While his grandmother provided the religious center of the family, Mayfield picked up his earliest musical inspiration from the male relatives who introduced him to the gospel quartet tradition that exerted a profound influence on the Impressions. "My grandfather and my uncle, they were affiliated with my grandmother, but they were into the music. They listened to a lot of old-timers like the Original Five Blind Boys and the Dixie Hummingbirds. The Soul Stirrers when Sam Cooke was there as a young kid. That was my foundation, connecting music with the church." Mayfield remembered standing on tiptoe, peering over the top of the old Victrola, and watching the black-and-white labels on the Specialty gospel records spin around and around while he basked in the voices of some of the greatest singers the nation has ever known.

Chicago permitted Mayfield to see his idols in person. His good friend and future band mate Jerry Butler attended Mt. Sinai Baptist, a prominent church that attracted leading gospel stars including frequent guest vocalist Mahalia Jackson, while James Cleveland served as choir director after leaving Detroit. On occasion Mayfield would join Butler on expeditions to the South Side. At Union Hall near Forty-eighth and State, he heard the Five Blind Boys of Mississippi, the Soul Stirrers, the Pilgrim Travelers, the Bells of Joy, the Staple Singers, and a powerful group that never got out of Chicago, the Morning Glory Singers. "We heard plenty of church music, plenty of harmonizing," Butler recalled. "To hear these people sing the way I always wished I could sing, to go so deep and then so high, just so strong. Those guys could belt out a tune. That was just good singing and good music. I was a quartet man, the four- and five-man groups. When it comes to quartets, it could even be barbershop. I just loved harmony. The church is where the foundation was laid down for us."

The intense competition in the gospel quartet scene inspired singers like Ira Tucker of the Dixie Hummingbirds, Claude Jeter of the Swan Silvertones, and the greatest of them all, Archie Brownlee of the Five Blind Boys of Mississippi. The quartets faced off in front of the most demanding audiences imaginable, developing their stage shows and musical licks in response to the most recent round of battles. The Dixie Hummingbirds immortalized the battle style in "Let's Go Out to the Programs," which incorporates affectionate parodies of their main rivals. What ultimately determined the winner of a showdown, however, was the spiritual fire of the audience's response.

Mayfield remembered seeing Brownlee running up and down the aisles of the Union Hall, drenched with sweat as he unleashed the soul-shattering screams that brought the audience to tears of ecstatic joy.

Mayfield and Butler began to build on that foundation as members of their own family-based gospel group, the Northern Jubilee Gospel Singers. Composed of Butler, Mayfield, and Curtis's cousins Sam, Tommy, and Charles Hawkins, the group performed in the highly competitive Chicago quartet scene of the early fifties. Though the group never reached the level of the adult quartets, the local showdowns honed the skills of the two future Impressions—and fed their spirits. "The church had plenty of little affairs with other churches," Mayfield recalled. "We'd go visit other churches and they'd visit us, and every church would have a group, a young kid singer vocalist or someone who was singing music. A lot of a cappella and group singing and that was good for the youngsters. That would build your heart up." As the youngest member of the Northern Jubilees, Mayfield began to develop the distinctive near-falsetto tenor that made his mature singing so distinctive. "I was maybe seven when they got started, and I guess within a few months I found that I could carry a tune. I had just an automatic high-pitched voice being that young. I fit right in as a tenor singer."

By the time he was eleven Curtis had begun to display his multifaceted musical talent. When he visited his paternal relatives in Ducoine, Illinois, he started picking out tunes on the piano. Never having taken music lessons, Mayfield experimented and decided that he liked the sound of the black keys. The attraction carried over when he picked up a guitar that one of the Hawkins brothers had brought home after a stint in the army. "The guitar used to sit in my grandmother's home in a corner, but no one would ever touch it," Mayfield said. "It would just draw me closer. It wasn't mine, but finally I had to go pick this instrument up, and when I strummed across it, it probably tuned in the key of Spanish, which is natural tuning—when you strum across it, it sounds out of tune. So subconsciously I tuned it to the key of F sharp, which I found later was all the black keys on the piano. Being self-taught, I never changed it. It used to make me proud because no matter how good a guitarist was, when he grabbed my axe, he couldn't play it." By the time Curtis reached fourteen, it was obvious to Butler that "he was an exceptional talent, but no one was quite sure how exceptional or how talented. All we knew was that one day while cleaning out a closet, he found this old beat-up guitar, and in a few weeks' time he was playing 'Jingle Bells' and other songs by ear. Inside of three or four months he could play every song we knew, plus he had this great tenor voice. When he hooked up with us, the Northern Jubilee Singers took on a new dimension."

Despite their youth the Northern Jubilees set out on the gospel highway, performing throughout the city. Once they had honed their skills in the neighborhood churches, they were able to book shows throughout the Midwest and, occasionally, in the South. "Uncle Charles kept us running," Mayfield recalled. "Whether we were in the city or on the road, we were moving quite a bit. We were running, playing the cities, trying to keep our little group up." Butler recalled traveling to Tampa on a church bus in the summer of 1953 where the young people sang at the National Spiritualist Convention. During that journey, Butler became aware of the thin line dividing the sacred and the profane: "A guy doing any kind of singing," he reminisced, "in any kind of limelight, could attract pretty girls who would do anything, even have sex with you, just to say they were in your company."

The lure of feminine appreciation no doubt played a part in Mayfield's decision to form the Alphatones, a doo-wop-style group whose members included his West Side Grammar School friends Al Boyce, James Weems, and Dallas Dixon. Short and dark-skinned, Curtis had a round face and a gap-toothed smile that in later years would become part of his charm and appeal. But as a teenager, his shy demeanor provided no competition for the taller, more self-assured Butler. They rehearsed in the practice rooms at the neighborhood center in Seward Park and sometimes in the apartments of neighbors like Lillian Davis Swope, who cherished her memories of Cabrini's musical ferment: "We had a lot of things goin' on over here. We had Ramsey Lewis and we had Curtis Mayfield. I used to let Curtis practice his music in my house when I lived down on Hudson. I knowed all of them, Jerry Butler too. I had to finally take Curtis over to Seward Park and got the park to give him a room because my house wasn't a conducive place for him to practice in." Zora Washington remembered the Alphatones' performances at dances in the basement of the Cabrini Reds. If the Alphatones were seeking to establish themselves with the young ladies, Washington laughed, they fell short of their dreams: "As far as dealing with Curtis, he was not my speed. As a kid, he just wasn't it. As I got older, yes, I grew to appreciate his music, but as a girl, nooooo." Mayfield would soon enter a larger world, musically and socially, but he never moved away from the laughter and the spirit of Cabrini-Green.

❧

WHERE CURTIS AND ARETHA both grew up in worlds defined by the gospel vision, Stevie Wonder seemed destined to live the blues. Born six weeks prematurely on May 13, 1950, in Saginaw, Michigan, the young Steveland Morris, as the last name on his birth certificate read, was blinded, probably by an excess of oxygen during the fifty-two days he spent in an incubator while doctors worked to save his life. Stevie's infancy was a difficult time for his mother, Lula Hardaway, and his two older brothers. His biological father, Calvin Judkins, was a handsome hard-living hustler who did little to support his family. Wonder's friend Lee Garrett, who was also blind, recalled telling Lula about his unhappy childhood as a despised "blind brat": "When I was telling Lula that story," Garrett said, "she shrugged her shoulders, saying that she knew the expression 'the blind brat' only too well herself. If it were up to Judkins, Steve would have ended up in a corner like myself."

Although she had been abandoned by her parents, Lula grew up in a hardworking, close-knit family ruled by her uncle, Henry Wright, near the small town of Hurtsboro in the heart of the Alabama black belt. As a child, Lula soaked in the gospel vision through the songs she sang in the church choir. She cherished her uncle's inspirational stories about the family's proud history and a distant past when black men had been kings. When her uncle died suddenly, however, the good times came to an end. Lula was exiled to East Chicago, where for a brief time she lived with her birth father in a neighborhood nicknamed "Alabama North." Shuttled from relative to relative, she dropped out of school and gave birth to her first son before she moved in with Stevie's father in Saginaw, which Stevie's father would tell him was only twelve miles from the North Pole. Calvin Judkins turned out to be Lula's worst mistake. When money was short, he beat her and sent her out onto the street, where she earned the money she needed to feed her sons by selling sexual favors.

Desperate to escape her nightmarish life with Judkins as well as

Saginaw's depressed economy and the frigid winds that blew in off Lake Huron, Lula moved the family to Detroit. Rising at 4:30 A.M. to work in the city's fish markets, she scrimped and saved enough money to buy a small brick house on Breckenridge Avenue in the heart of the East Side ghetto. Her life continued to improve when she met and married Paul Lynch, who supported Stevie, Milton, Calvin, and the younger siblings born over the next few years—Larry, Timothy, and Renee—by working in a bakery. On the rare occasions when Stevie saw his biological father, the results could be traumatic. After one excursion his father brought Stevie back to his apartment. "He stayed away for a long time and left me alone. I got upset, and I started to cry about that," Stevie told an interviewer. "But after a while I just said, hey, forget it, and I just went on to sleep. I was just afraid because the surroundings weren't familiar to me."

Even if his eyesight had been perfect, the prospects greeting Wonder would have been bleak. The primary difference between his world in the mid-fifties and Mayfield's Chicago was that Detroit promised more and delivered even less. Although the myth of Detroit as a land of economic opportunity would linger through the sixties, the process that would later be called "deindustrialization" began almost immediately after V-J Day. By the time Lula Hardaway moved her family to Detroit, the large automakers had begun their exodus to the suburbs and were busily relocating plants to small towns in the South and Midwest where the labor force would be less militant. Lacking seniority and pull within the union hierarchies, the fortunate black workers who had made inroads during the war sought mostly to protect their own hard-won gains. Even so, they were concentrated in jobs that white workers considered demeaning or dangerous. As one auto industry executive told a white reporter in a moment of stunning forthrightness, "Some jobs white folks will not do, so they have to take niggers in, particularly in dice work, spraying paint on car bodies. This seems to kill a white man." While he acknowledged that the work also "shortens [Negro] lives, cuts them down," he shrugged, "They're just niggers."

No one familiar with Detroit's history as a stronghold of the Black Legion and Ku Klux Klan was surprised by the intensity of white resistance that began in 1941 when the city announced that the Sojourner Truth housing project on the city's Northeast Side would be open to blacks. Local whites immediately formed the Seven Mile–Fenelon Improvement Association and geared up to resist the plan. Posting signs that announced succinctly, "Negroes who move in here will be burned. Signed, Neighbors," the association invoked the language of war, calling the plans an "invasion" and their neighborhood a "battleground." When the first blacks moved in on February 28, 1942, the battle led to 220 arrests and left 40 injured. The clash established a pattern in Detroit that resembled Chicago's. Like their cousin vultures in Chicago, realtors sought to capitalize on black desperation and white fear by "blockbusting," reaping predatory profits and feeding the cycle of flight and violence.

These brutal dynamics created a painful dilemma for economically secure black communities like Conant Gardens, which formed an unholy alliance with the Seven Mile–Fenelon Improvement Association during the Sojourner Truth conflict. Like the whites who saw the projects as an assault on the good life they felt they had earned for their children, the black homeowners of Conant Gardens feared that the projects would drive out respectable citizens and lower property values. Aware of Conant Gardens' position, many Sojourner Truth residents found the class divide as painful as the racial hostility, which was at least expected. Kenneth G. Booker was aware that "the people in Conant Gardens didn't want us out here as well as the whites didn't want us to be a project either." Acknowledging that "it wasn't everybody in Conant Gardens," Sojourner resident Gerald Blakely understood their position, even if he didn't sympathize with it. "What happened was that during that particular period that was the only area that blacks could get FHA loans. They were more concerned about the property values going down. It was the idea that it was a project and would take the property values down." But the bottom line for "project boys," as Robert Bynum, who was one of them, put it, was simply that "they didn't want us."

Never as secure or affluent as its white counterpart, the black middle class faced a no-win situation. On the one hand, no one should begrudge the residents of Conant Gardens, or of C.L. Franklin's Oakland Avenue enclave, the fruits of their arduous labors. On the other hand, protecting those advances sometimes set the interests of those who had made it against the desire of others to escape the worsening conditions in Paradise Valley. In the long run the resolution of the Sojourner Truth conflict would mirror the economic fate of the nation as a whole: a fortunate few would attain unimaginable riches; a substantial number of African Americans, though many fewer, proportionately, than whites, would rise to middle- and upper-middle-class comfort. But all too many would find themselves abandoned, with neither a realistic chance for escape nor the long-term hope offered by a growing freedom movement in the South.

Against that backdrop, Stevie Wonder was probably fortunate to grow up in what he called "upper lower circumstances." "I would love to do a TV special that would tell many things people don't know about me," he once told a *Newsweek* interviewer, "like how when I was younger my mother, my brothers and I had to go on the dry dock where there was coal and steal some to keep warm. To a poor person that is not stealing, that is not crime, it's a necessity." When Stevie's mother denied the story was true, Stevie, who unlike George Washington may have occasionally told mutually incompatible versions of a story, clarified his underlying point: "My mother wasn't very happy with the reference to the fact that I stole coal when I was young. I'm not ashamed to talk about it, but my mother felt very bad. I tried to explain to her that I told the story only because it's *sad* that in a country that is as wealthy as the United States stealing for survival is a *necessity* as well as a *crime*." To which Lula responded, "Politics or not, we never were *that* badly off."

Lula's refusal to fixate on the family's problems carried over to Stevie's attitude toward his blindness. Initially, Lula worried over her son's condition and spent precious dollars on a series of doctors and faith healers, but Stevie did his best to convince her he didn't feel deprived of a sense he'd never known: "I never really wondered much about my blindness or asked questions about it, because to me, really, being blind was normal. But I knew it used to worry my mother, and I know she prayed for me to have sight someday, so I finally just told her that I was happy being blind, and I thought it was a gift from God, and I think she felt better after that." Noting that a girl born the same day in Saginaw had died in the incubator, he added sincerely, "I personally think I'm lucky to be alive." Once Lula accepted Stevie's condition as permanent, she did her best to assure him a normal childhood. She allowed him to explore the neighborhood with his brothers and encouraged him to swim, skate, and go bowling. "I always loved her for giving me that independence," Stevie reminisced. "She let me feel the breeze of riding a bicycle."

At times Wonder would credit his blindness with providing a buffer against discontent: "We were poor all right but I wasn't aware of it as much as other kids would be. Being blind I didn't see the things I didn't have, like on television. I was sort of lucky." As he matured, Wonder would often observe that, in a society obsessed with superficial appearances, his blindness conferred certain advantages. "I'm glad that I'm blind," he told *Rolling Stone* interviewer Ben Fong-Torres. "Being blind, you don't judge books by their covers. You go through things that are relatively insignificant, and you pick out the things that are more important." Wonder insists that he has a clear understanding of sight. "I'm almost sure that the forms I see look exactly like yours. I mean even with textures of skin, or the different colors of skin, you can touch someone and you can get a pretty good picture in your mind, your mind's eye. It's no longer coming from your eyes, it's coming from inside you. Well the same thing happens to me."

One of Stevie's earliest memories, which like many of his stories rings like a cross between an exaggerated family story and an urban tall tale, concerned his brothers' attempt to alleviate his blindness. "When I was just a little baby I remember my brothers Milton and Calvin were messing around with a lot of stuff in the house, they had stuff all over everywhere, jam and bubble gum and stuff," Wonder said. "They had a garbage can and some matches in the house, and they were saying, 'God, you know Stevie needs some more light. Wonder what we can do to get him some light? Maybe we can set this thing... like start a fire in here and he'll have some more light.' So they went and started a fire and almost blew the house down."

A relaxed blues humor recurs in many of the childhood stories Stevie has told over the years, many of which portray him as a mischievous adventurer predisposed to pushing boundaries. The salacious comedy routines of ghetto raconteur Redd Foxx inspired his first experiments with the opposite sex. "It was the playhouse trip," Wonder recalled with a smile. "And I really was like taking the girl's clothes off and everything. I don't understand how I did that stuff, but I was into it. I had her in my room with my clothes off. And she gave it away 'cause she started laughin' and gigglin'." Although once again the details stretch credibility, Stevie told several versions of an incident that earned him his mother's more serious displeasure. "You know those small sheds they used to have in back of houses?" he asked. "In the ghetto where I lived, we'd hop them from one to the other. I remember one time my aunt came in and said, 'Okay Steve, Mama said don't be doin' that,' and I said 'Aw, fuck you.' " Stevie continued his roof-jumping exploits until his mother caught up with him and rewarded his language with an electrical-cord whipping.

When no one was available to watch over him, Stevie gravitated to the family radio, which he called "one of my best friends." His favorite DJs, especially Larry Dixon, who hosted the *Sundown* show on WCHB, introduced him to the rapidly changing black music scene of the fifties. The radio equivalent of Motown, WCHB was a black-owned station that redefined the Detroit soundscape. When Stevie's and Aretha's families moved to Detroit, the color barrier remained very much in effect on Detroit radio. As late as the end of the forties, even a popular white DJ like Bill Randle, the host of the *Interracial Goodwill Hour* on WJLB, could be fired for playing "obviously black music" during daylight hours; Randle's hanging offense was to expose unwitting whites to Nat King Cole. Still, in comparison to Chicago, Detroit radio opened up much more rapidly to the R&B explosion of the fifties. Detroit DJ LeRoy G. White, the jive-talking host of *Rockin' with LeRoy,* and six-foot-four, three-hundred-pound white R&B lover Mickey Shorr assaulted musical segregation by appealing to teenagers of all races with a barrage of Johnny Otis, the Dominoes, Ruth Brown, Ray Charles, Muddy Waters, LaVern Baker, the Drifters, and Howlin' Wolf. The most popular DJ of all, Frantic Ernie Durham, frequently broadcast his WJLB show from the Twenty Grand Club on the edge of the expanding black enclave on the city's West Side. Serving up an aural gumbo that was part black music, part advertising hustle, and part street poetry, Durham was famous for the surreal song introductions that shaped the verbal approach of descendants like P-Funk's George Clinton. "Great googa mooga, shooga wooga!" Durham might begin. "Welcome to another inning of spinning with Ernie Durham, your ace from inner space, on the swinging-est show on the ra-di-o! Let's cut the chatter with another platter! It's 'Treasure of Love' from Mr. Clyde McPhatter!"

However silly it might sound to outside ears, Durham's "nonsense" carried serious undertones. Martha Jean "The Queen" Steinberg, who took her regal presence from WDIA in Memphis to WCHB in 1963, outlined the implications. Emphasizing black radio's role in the spread of the movement, she claimed, "If it hadn't been for black radio, Martin Luther King would not have gotten off the ground, because we were the first to talk about it. It was new, it was exciting. Everybody became curious. We talked like the

African drummers used to talk years ago. We talked in a code—'Yes Mammy o Daddy, get on down!' We talked about what to do, but some people didn't know what we were talking about. After the movement started moving about the nation, we let everybody know what was going on, because no one would interview Martin Luther King. No one knew Jesse Jackson. Nobody interviewed these preachers, so we did that ourselves, on a low-key basis, but we did."

Sitting in his room listening to Steinberg, Durham, and Larry Dixon, who incorporated quiet social commentary into the mix of jazz and R&B on the *Sundown* show, young Steveland Morris heard hints of the gospel vision in African American politics. But his first love was the music. Stevie's early favorites included Johnny Ace's "Pledging My Love," Bill Doggett's funky "Honky Tonk," and the Drifters' "On Broadway," as well as songs by Mary Wells, the Coasters, Clyde McPhatter, and the Five Royales. As he listened to the R&B hits that prepared the way for Motown's crossover success, Wonder also was being exposed to the music's southern sources. He listened to the electrified down-home blues of John Lee Hooker and Howlin' Wolf and became a fan of gospel groups like the Staple Singers and the Dixie Hummingbirds featuring Ira Tucker, whose daughters, Linda and Sundray, would sing backup for Wonder during the seventies, and whose son Ira Jr. would become a staff member and confidant.

As long as he lived in the ghetto, Wonder had relatively little direct contact with racial prejudice. But when he entered Detroit's Fitzgerald School, he encountered teachers who saw neither blindness nor blackness as a blessing: "They made me feel like because I was black I could never be or would never be successful." One of his first realizations of racial difference came when he tuned in to a black radio station on the school bus. "I was the only black kid on the bus, and I would always turn the radio down, because I felt ashamed to let them hear me listening to B.B. King. But I *loved* B.B. King. Yet I felt ashamed because—because I was *different* enough to want to hear him and because I had never heard him anywhere else." The incident made a deep impression on Wonder, and in later years it would serve as a touchstone for his political sensibility. "Freedom begins in the simplest things, even in such things as feeling free enough to turn on a radio to a particular station," he said. "You have to seize that for yourself and then demand that kind of freedom for others."

Although Wonder's first ambition was to become a DJ on the imaginary radio station WBMB—"Blind Man's Bluff" radio—it soon became clear that he would not be satisfied playing music made by others. "The first time I really felt the power of music was on a family picnic at Belle Isle," he recalled. "Someone had hired a band, and I sat on the drummer's lap. He let me play the drums. It was a thrill I'll never forget. People applauded and one man gave me three quarters. Man, I felt like I had a fortune in my pocket. Later, when I'd sing or play for fun at functions, people would give me dollars, but I'd never take them. I just wanted quarters. Paper money doesn't jingle."

By the time he was seven, Wonder had begun fooling around with the piano, harmonica, and drums. "I was always beating things, like beating tables with a spoon, or beating on those little cardboard drums they used to give kids. I'd beat 'em to death," he reported with pride. At a Lion's Club Christmas party for blind children, he received a small drum kit. "I started playing the drums on the wrong side. So they came over to me and said, 'Hey, you don't do it like this, try it over on the other side' and I'd say, 'Oh no, I wanna hear the side with the snares,' " he laughed. At about the same time a neighbor moved out, bequeathing her piano to the Hardaways. Even though he could barely reach the pedals, Stevie liked picking out tunes on the keys and claimed to have written his first songs when he was eight.

But the instrument that truly fascinated him was the harmonica. He first encountered it in the form of a tiny harmonica dangling off a family friend's key ring. Noticing Stevie's love for the toy instrument, an uncle gave him a Hohner chromatic harmonica. Before long his nephew was playing day and night. "I started playing the blues," he said, naming Jimmy Reed, Bobby "Blue" Bland, and Chicago harmonica wizard Little Walter as his inspirations. "I took a little bit of everybody's style and made it my own. I guess I practiced, but I never considered it practice because I loved it too much. It was like searching in a new place you've never been before. I kept finding new things, new chords, new tunes."

Before long Wonder joined forces with neighborhood friend John Glover to form a street-corner group. Establishing themselves in the area around Twenty-fifth and Twenty-sixth Streets, the young duo harmonized on a repertoire of popular hits including Frankie Lymon's "Why Do Fools Fall in Love?" and two early Smokey Robinson songs, "She's Not a Bad Girl" and "My Momma Told Me to Leave Those Girls Alone." John played the guitar while Stevie beat out rhythms on his newly acquired bongos. Already Wonder was developing the flair that would make him a favorite at Harlem's Apollo Theater. "I used to love to do the imitations of Jackie Wilson," Wonder said. "I heard he was a very exciting performer, so I used to do all kinds of flips and stuff."

While Motown circulated the youngster's wry comment that his first ambition was to be "a minister, or maybe a sinner," his close friend and mentor Clarence Paul laughingly dismissed his protégé's claims that he had been a junior deacon and church soloist as a concoction of the label's publicity machine. Still, there's no reason to doubt that his street-corner performances earned the disapproval of some respectable churchgoers. "We used to get pretty big crowds of people playing on those porches. I remember this one time, this lady who was a member of our church—she was Sanctified Holiness, but she was still a member of our church, the Whitestone Baptist Church—came along, and she said, 'Oh, Steve, I'm ashamed of you for playing this worldly music out here. I'm so ashamed of you.' I really blew it. I'd been a junior deacon in the church, and I used to sing solo at the services. But she went and told them what I was doing, and they told me to leave. And that's how I became a sinner." Sooner than anyone would have imagined, the sinner-in-training would embark on a career that would provide the strongest imaginable proof that rock 'n' roll, the devil's music, could be drafted into the service of the gospel vision.

GLIDING ACROSS THE gleaming hardwood surface of the Arcadia skating rink, feeling herself a part of "young black America at its best," Aretha Franklin surrendered to the spell of the same music that enchanted Stevie Wonder. For Aretha, who used the first fifteen dollars she earned singing in church to buy a pair of white roller skates, the sounds of Johnny Ace, Ruth Brown, LaVern Baker, Frankie Lymon, and the Flamingos—the "Four Tops of yesteryear," as she'd later call them—melted into her warm memories of her early teenage years. Announcing proudly that "Detroiters were serious skaters," she described the Arcadia on Woodward Avenue as "a sepia scene of budding innocence, all-American teenage stuff, sipping on cherry Cokes or hugged up as we skated to couples-only, listening to Dinah asking the musical question, 'Did you say I got a lot to learn?' " A few years younger than Aretha, future Supreme Mary Wilson admired Aretha's style and self-assurance: "I remember skating, timidly keeping to the rail, and watching Aretha Franklin whiz by. She didn't just skate: she bopped."

Wilson belonged to a sizable group of Motown stars-to-be who grew up near the Franklins. Aretha knew but never became friends with Wilson, Diana Ross, and Otis Williams of the Temptations. But her brother Cecil's best friend, Smokey Robinson, spent a great deal of time helping Cecil and future Miracle Pete Moore operate a hair-processing business out of the Franklins' first-floor bathroom. Charging two dollars rather than the seven that their youthful patrons would have paid at the local barbershop, Cecil mastered the fine art of making waves with a comb and using his finger to set the 'do. When he went away to college at Morehouse in Atlanta, Smokey inherited the clientele. For Robinson, the sounds of the Franklin household only added to the attraction of the job. He remembered gospel star Clara Ward singing in the kitchen while she cooked. Quickly Robinson fell under the spell of his friend's talented sister. "I fell in love with her when she was seven," Smokey smiled, but a few years later when he asked Cecil to set him up, he found that his friend was "too much of a protective big brother." The romantic regrets didn't stop Smokey from appreciating Aretha's budding musical talent. "Me and my friends fooled with music," Smokey wrote in his autobiography, "but none of us, like little Aretha, could sit down and play two-fisted full-blooded stomp-down piano. As a child, she played nearly as good as she does now."

Barely into her teens, Aretha had already begun playing piano for the choir at New Bethel. Shortly thereafter she moved up to become one of three featured soloists, earning fifteen dollars a week. Her first performance remained a blur in Aretha's memory. Facing a congregation of fifteen hundred, she sang "Jesus Be a Fence Around Me," which she'd first heard performed by Sam Cooke and the Soul Stirrers. "Next thing I know, I'm just out there," she reported. "Out there singing. But right then I knew that was for me." So did the members of the congregation, who shared Mary Wilson's assessment that from the start "Aretha had a way of singing gospel that transcended all musical boundaries. Sometimes in gospel music you can only enjoy it in the framework of religion. Gospel was part of my religion, but I was into pop and R&B music. Aretha had a way of making me enjoy my gospel roots in a pop context. In church, she would make you feel you were listening to good music and not being preached to from the Bible. That was the beauty of her style." Aretha's reputation spread rapidly, but the contrast between her spirit-filled performances and her shy personality surprised many who knew her. Otis Williams of the Temptations, who had first encountered Aretha and her sisters at the Arcadia, was one of them: "I got friendly with her sister and I used to walk her home from school. I remember one day doing that and finally getting to meet Aretha. There she was, real quiet and shy—the same little girl who was layin' folks out in church. I guess I was surprised, she was *so* quiet."

Like Stevie Wonder, Aretha followed the exploits of charismatic Detroit DJs like Frantic Ernie Durham and LeRoy White as they popularized a new style of black music. A few years earlier the lines between gospel and secular music had seemed set in stone. But many mid-1950s stars heeded the example of Ray Charles, who had scandalized many churchgoing black citizens by incorporating sanctified singing styles into down-and-dirty hits like "I've Got a Woman" and "What'd I Say." Charles responded to the criticism with his matter-of-fact observation, "All you needed to do to change gospel to blues was substitute a woman's name for the Lord's." Then Charles went about the serious business of redrawing America's cultural map. Musical terrain that was previously marked "white" and "black," "smooth" and "raw," and above all "sacred" and "secular" turned out to share some territory. Before long the man Julian Bond called "the Bishop of Atlanta" for his role in inspiring the freedom movement had won over all but his most rigid detractors while clearing the path for a host of church-tinged R&B singers interested in selling records on the "other side" of the color line.

Aretha's favorite examples of the emerging sound ranged from Little Willie John's bluesy "Talk to Me, Talk to Me" and the Clovers' novelty goof "Love Potion Number Nine" through the ethereal harmonies of the Moonglows' "Ten Commandments of Love" and Ruth Brown's exuberant "Mama, He Treats Your Daughter Mean" to near-gospel hits like Clyde McPhatter's "A Lover's Question" and LaVern Baker's "Soul on Fire." At the same time she loved tuning in to "Senator" Bristol Bryant's gospel hour to hear the Caravans, the Sensational Nightingales, the Dixie Hummingbirds, and the Swan Silvertones.

First at Alger Elementary School and then at Hutchins Junior High and Northern High School, Aretha usually fulfilled the role of good student, earning "A's, B's, some C's, maybe a D here and there." In most respects, she lived the life of a regular pupil, but her classmates and teachers knew that her musical talents went way beyond playing tuba and flute in the school band. When unruly students threatened to reduce study hall sessions to chaos, teachers would sometimes summon Aretha to help restore order. "They'd be throwing spitballs or fighting, and I'd have to play the piano to entertain," Aretha said. "That was my first experience with a tough audience."

Even if Aretha hadn't been such a performer, Reverend Franklin's prominence made it difficult for his children to blend into the crowd. "In Detroit, the Franklin girls were celebrities," Mary Wilson observed. Erma Franklin responded by developing a dignified bearing that earned her the nickname "Madam Queen." To Aretha, she "could be loving and caring or cool and aloof." Honing her intellectual talents at Clark University in Atlanta, Erma developed the ability, as Aretha phrased it, to "spar intellectually" with her father. Many shared Wilson's view of Carolyn Franklin as "a big wheel in school" and the most powerful personality among the sisters: "She was the baby in the family, but she always had street gangs and she was the leader." Carolyn's tough veneer developed in part as defense against her ostensibly tamer big sister. "I could have killed Aretha sometimes," Carolyn told an interviewer. "When I was a child, she'd take me to the rabbit field across the street from our house, place me in the hole, and hide. I'd scream my head off in fright, damn near had a stroke screaming and crying, while I'd hear Aretha laugh her head off behind some bushes." But Carolyn never doubted her sister's love or support: "She was like the mama lion with me. If anyone messed with me at school, they had Aretha to deal with."

In later years Aretha, Carolyn, and Erma would at times clash; twice C.L. was forced to restore peace when an argument threatened to escalate into physical violence. But they also shared profound emotional and musical bonds. It seemed natural that they would form their own singing group, the Cleopatrettes. For a while they filled the house with their versions of songs by the Drifters, Ruth Brown, and LaVern Baker. Soon, however, Carolyn and Erma began to resent Aretha's intensity, ambition, and desire for musical control. "She always wanted to sing in a key that didn't blend with the harmonies of the group," Erma laughed. "So we decided to let her go do her own thing." "I suppose I might have been sort of a bully," Aretha admitted. "I wanted to go on through the night. And they'd be tired. And I would *yell* at them. 'Sing, sing, I want you to sing.' " Giving up the girl group idea, the sisters shifted their attention to gospel. Hoping that spiritual messages would generate sisterly harmony, they formed a group that appeared at local churches for about eight months. Again the group collapsed because, as Aretha sighed, "we were too busy fussin' and fightin'."

A serious threat to Aretha's future came when she found out she was pregnant shortly before she turned fourteen. Up to that time Aretha had enthusiastically joined her girlfriends' pursuit of harmless romantic fantasies. She fell in puppy love with a boy she called "Romeo" when she was twelve and loved holding hands while skating to the romantic strains of the Penguins' "Earth Angel" or "I Only Have Eyes for You" during "couples only" at the Arcadia. Things grew more serious when she fell for an older boy who wore open-collared shirts and tight jeans and, best of all, drove a Ford Fairlane convertible. What Aretha thought was true love collapsed into something more mundane when she told her beau about her condition. "When I was pregnant, he would drive past the house with the top dropped, blow the horn and keep going," Aretha wrote in her autobiography. "I couldn't believe he was going to be this cold. He never stopped to spend any time or to check on my condition. Finally, though, I saw him for what he was—a big dog."

In her sixth month Aretha dropped out of school and lived at home until the birth of her first son, whom she named Clarence in honor of her father. Although she feared that the news of her pregnancy would anger him, C.L. proved supportive. "He was not judgmental, or scolding," she said. "He simply talked about the responsibilities of motherhood. He was a realist and he expected me to face the reality of having a child." Aretha realized that "the days of spiced ham and Popsicles were over." Mary Wilson emphasized that even in the upscale Oakland Avenue neighborhood, out-of-wedlock births were not unusual. "Many of the neighborhood girls had babies when they were thirteen, fourteen, and fifteen years old," she wrote, emphasizing that middle-class children like the Franklin sisters belonged to the same world as the residents of the nearby Brewster Housing Projects. "That was the bad part about being in the projects, because that kind of thing was happening all around us. So many people living in such close proximity has a lot to do with it." With the help of her grandmother and Erma, Aretha cared for her new baby and returned to school. When she found out she was pregnant once more, with her second son, Eddie, she dropped out again, this time for good at age sixteen.

Aretha appreciated her father's support and never questioned his decisions. But his reputation as a man who loved the high life as well as the holy life created tensions for his children. Jerry Wexler, who would later spend many late-night hours on the phone listening to Aretha talk about her burdens, painted a clear picture of C.L. Franklin's complex relationship with his favorite daughter. Reverend Franklin was "a national leader," Wexler wrote in his autobiography, but he was also "a charismatic character who reputedly took an occasional walk on the wild side. He'd been busted for pot possession and liked to party. Some say the preacher used his children, especially the precocious Aretha, as props and pawns; others called him a devoted father."

Reverend Franklin made no secret of his love of good music, fashionable attire, and the night spots where the African American elite released its burdens and celebrated its successes. Bass player Herman Wright recalled C.L.'s visits to the Southland Lounge on Chicago's South Side: "He liked music. He frequented clubs. He had an active life. Reverend Franklin was a real nice man, a smooth guy." Franklin's tailored suits, complete with diamond stick pins and alligator shoes, justified his nicknames "Black Beauty" and "the Jitterbug Preacher." Mary Wilson testified that even in the pulpit, he exerted a hypnotizing influence over his female parishioners. "Women absolutely loved him. He was a ladies' man. My mother adored him." Some speculated that Reverend Franklin's appeal played a substantial part in his wife's decision to leave Detroit. New Bethel deacon Willie Todd observed that problems in the marriage arose because "Reverend was gone so much. He was a playboy. I mean, truth is the light. That wasn't their first separation." Observing caustically that once her mother departed, "some women pursued him aggressively," Aretha described what happened when one pursuer showed up at the family house with a suitcase, ready to set up housekeeping: "Carolyn snapped into action. She grabbed a kitchen knife, ran up the steps, jumped in front of the woman, and backed her down the stairs and out of the house." Sounding a theme that many have echoed,

Wilson speculated on C.L.'s long-term effect on his daughter: "That charisma he had . . . I can see why his children would be as enamored of him as everyone else. It's as if none of the men in Aretha's life could ever match her father, because he was so dynamic." For a while it appeared that C.L. might marry the mother of poet and music critic Al Young, who grew up in the Franklins' neighborhood, but Mary Young put an end to the relationship. Years later she explained the reason to her son: "He would spend Saturday night with me. Then, at the crack of dawn, he would hop out of bed, shove his little bottle of whiskey in his coat pocket and say, 'Oh, Mary, I have to go preach.' I just couldn't marry anybody like that."

Reverend Franklin's daughters did not hate all of his girlfriends. C.L.'s relationship with gospel singer Clara Ward presented his daughter with a particularly complicated emotional situation. Aretha traced her desire to become a singer to hearing Clara sing "Peace in the Valley" at a relative's funeral when she was ten years old. Although the Ward Singers' flashy style caused some heads to shake and tongues to cluck, Aretha loved their flair. Their sequined gowns and bouffant hairdos contributed to Aretha's conviction that there was "nothing inconsistent between a flashy presentation and passionate love of God." A striking woman whose piercing eyes flashed out from her thin face, Ward was in her late twenties when she fell under C.L. Franklin's spell. When she began visiting the Franklin home, she fell under the spell of the young Aretha. Clara's sister Willa Ward-Royster observed that her sister was "so amazed by Aretha's singing voice and delivery that she offered all the guidance she could to advance that huge talent. Aretha had an inherent gift from Mother Africa or Mother Earth. . . . No one could have taught her how to reach back up to where the heart joins soul, gather the treasures trembling there, and then, song by song, present her glory to the listening world. Here was this shy, unaffected child who could without plan yank the covers off folks' emotions." Meditating on the good fortune that brought her together with an ideal vocal mentor, Aretha counted her blessings: "You can't explain it yourself. But you can sense it in other people, I guess. Clara knew. She knew I *had* to sing."

Clara Ward's entanglement with Aretha's father began shortly after he moved to Detroit, and they frequently shared the bill on gospel shows in the late forties and early fifties. The relationship between Clara and C.L. took on new depth one night at Philadelphia's Metropolitan Opera House, where they were appearing on a program with Mahalia Jackson, Brother Joe May, and midget evangelist Sammy Bryant. In Willa's words, "The Reverend and Clara seemed to share the Holy Spirit intermingled with the human spirit. It was the start of my sister's only heart, soul, and flesh real romance."

As Ward's visits to Detroit grew more frequent, her bond with Aretha deepened. The recently widowed reverend's need for help with the children allowed Clara to justify those visits. As Willa wrote, "Although Mom was jealous of Clara's closeness to C.L., she liked his children well enough, which made her receptive to the idea of Clara's traveling to Detroit to sit with them occasionally. If she knew that the good Reverend was doing most of the sitting—and more—with my sister Clara, she did not let on." What did upset Mrs. Ward was her suspicion that her daughter was being exploited. "Franklin just wants you to build his congregation up," she lectured her daughter. "You've come too far and worked too hard to be singing there for free."

As murmurings about C.L. and Clara spread, the stylish couple attracted the attention of the African American press. When they traveled together to the World Baptist Alliance Convention in Europe, photographers were there to greet them on their arrival in Paris and again when they returned to the United States. Eventually the fires would cool, but the two remained close. C.L. joined the Ward Singers for their twenty-first-anniversary program in 1954 and paid an emotional visit to Clara in the hospital after she suffered a stroke onstage in 1967. Always sensitive to the lingering rumors that assigned Clara partial blame for her parents' separation, Aretha avoided the topic. "Daddy and Clara were great friends," she said flatly. "They were broad-minded in their attitudes and absolutely subscribed to the biblical mandate that the gospel be spread all over the world."

Whatever the complexities of her relationship with C.L. Franklin, Clara Ward helped provide his daughter with an unmatchable musical education. When Aretha was small, she would sit at the top of the stairs and peer down through the banister at a shifting parade of visitors including Art Tatum, B.B. King, Arthur Prysock, Lionel Hampton, Oscar Peterson, Dorothy Donegan, Lou Rawls, Erroll Garner, and of course gospel stars like Mahalia Jackson, James Cleveland, and Sam Cooke. Aretha took special delight in meeting Cooke and Dinah Washington, another of her singing idols. A hardworking, savagely stylish singer, Washington was equally at ease with the no-nonsense R&B of "Baby, Get Lost," a blues standard like "Trouble in Mind," a torch song like "What a Diff'rence a Day Makes," or a jazzy pop ballad like "Unforgettable." Widely recognized as "Queen of the Blues," Washington set the standard to which Aretha aspired in her first secular records.

Sometimes C.L. would summon his daughter from her watching point or even rouse her from sleep so she could entertain his guests with renditions of "Canadian Sunset" or "Don't Get Around Much Anymore." In return, Aretha received personal attention from some of the most influential keyboard players of the era. She imitated Erroll Garner's "raining tremolos and easy swing" and marveled at the unsurpassed inventiveness of houseguest Art Tatum, although she never tried to re-create his dense modernist style: "I just cancelled [his playing style] out for me and knew I could never do that, but he left a strong impression on me as a pianist and a person."

On the other hand, Aretha said, James Cleveland "helped shape my basic musical personality in profound ways. James was a gospel genius. He was one of those people modernizing gospel while honoring its traditional soul and message." Barely out of his teens when he accepted the position of minister of music at New Bethel, Cleveland had already established himself as an accompanist for the Caravans and Mahalia Jackson. Along with his close friend gospel singer Melvin Rencher, Cleveland lived with the Franklins until, family legend had it, he was banished for the unpardonable sin of eating a bowl of banana pudding Reverend Franklin had reserved for himself. Fortunately, before his exile he had already helped Aretha take her first steps toward the piano style that would ground her great love songs in the sound and feel of the gospel vision. Paying tribute to Cleveland, who would remain one of her closest musical friends until his death, Aretha wrote, "He showed me some real nice chords and I liked his deep, deep sound. There's a whole lot of earthiness in the way he sings and what he was feelin', I was feelin', but I just didn't know how to put it across. The more I watched him, the more I got out of it."

Aretha got as much inspiration and even more pleasure out of her friendship with Sam Cooke, who rose to stardom after he replaced the legendary R.H. Harris in the Soul Stirrers. Aretha had grown up listening to gospel quartets and considered the Swan Silvertones, the Dixie Hummingbirds, and the Sensational Nightingales "monuments of pure gospel power." She appreciated their style almost as much as their spirit. "Rather than robes, the men might wear matching green or blue or even gold suits. They were servants of God to be sure, but they were also showmen." Like many young girls, she fell in love with Cooke's boyish charm and the spiritual sensuality of his voice on Soul Stirrer hits "Nearer to Thee," "Wonderful," and "Touch the Hem of His Garment." Aretha kept a Sam Cooke scrapbook, switched from Kools to Kents because that was the brand Sam smoked, and treasured a crumpled cigarette package he had thrown away.

Although Cooke's fellow Soul Stirrer S.R. Crain may have exaggerated when he claimed that Sam and Aretha had been lovers "when they were still little children," Aretha was only seven years old when Cooke first met C.L. Franklin in 1949. Making his Detroit debut as a member of the Highway QCs on a bill with the Harmony Kings of St. Louis and Detroit's Flying Clouds, Cooke impressed the minister, who asked the group to stay in town. Almost immediately, however, the QCs accepted a spot on powerhouse Memphis radio station WDIA, widely known as the "Mothership of the Negroes." When Cooke returned to Detroit, he did so as a member of the Soul Stirrers and later as a crossover solo sensation headlining the Flame Show Bar. Still not old enough for admission to the night spot, Aretha eagerly awaited her heartthrob's visits to the family home. "I'd have died to go to the Flame. But I was too young. It drove me crazy," she lamented. "I would hear Sam Cooke was coming, and I would be beside myself. I truly loved that man. He would come to the house, so polite and gentle. And so handsome." Although the age difference and Cooke's constant travels discouraged a full-blown romance in later years, Cooke clearly enjoyed his young fan and fed her dreams when he invited her and her father to his house and gave her a fringed suede jacket.

Cooke's importance to Aretha went beyond romantic fantasies. As one of the first gospel singers to successfully navigate both the musical and the financial transitions from gospel to secular music, Cooke pursued the crossover strategy as part of an explicitly political agenda. Following the path opened by Ray Charles, Cooke believed that as white audiences grew accustomed to the gospel touches in his crossover hits, they would gradually open up to the real thing. The dollars they funneled into the black music world would help fuel the community's economic development. A constant reader who would later befriend both Malcolm X and Muhammad

Ali, Cooke believed in African American solidarity. He guarded against losing contact with the fans who had lifted him to stardom by playing gospel versions of his hits when he performed in black clubs. "When the whites are through with Sammy Davis, Jr., he won't have anywhere to play," commented Cooke even as he was preparing to play the Copacabana Club. "I'll always be able to go back to my people 'cause I'm never gonna stop singing to them.... I'm not gonna leave my base."

He was certain Aretha had what it took to follow in his footsteps. "As much as anybody, Sam Cooke made me want to sing," she said. "He would just say, 'Sing, girl.' And believe me, that was enough." Aretha paid close attention to Cooke's vocal technique as well as his winning smile: "He did so many things with his voice—so gentle one minute, so swinging the next, then electrifying, always doing something else." While he was still a member of the Soul Stirrers, Cooke played the Franklins a rough recording of "You Send Me" and encouraged C.L. Franklin to consider a pop career for his daughter. Although C.L. responded that he "didn't want her to start out *too* young," Aretha took the message to heart: "I guess I figured if Sam could do it, I could too."

Aretha's initiation into show business began in her early teens when she spent her summer vacations traveling with her father's gospel revue. As a small child she had occasionally joined her father onstage, sometimes with comic results. Atlanta DJ Zenas Sears remembered being asked to introduce Aretha at a show when she was five or six: "All the acts were around in a circle—there was no running in from the wings in those days, they were all there—and so I introduced [C.L.] and finished with it, and I forgot Aretha. She kicked me in the shins. So I did it—and she kicked me again and sat down." Sears no doubt nodded in amusement years later when he heard the tiny spitfire issue her grown-up demand for respect. On tour with her father, Aretha earned fifty dollars a night for singing one or two songs before the climactic sermon. But she put an equal value on the opportunity to perform on bills with the Dixie Hummingbirds, the Roberta Martin Singers, and the Ward Singers. "They were real gospel giants," she remarked. "It was great training."

At times the gospel highway seemed more like a backwoods road. While C.L. flew from city to city with frequent trips back to Detroit to attend to his congregation, Aretha and her siblings put in countless miles in rickety buses and overcrowded cars. "We'd drive thousands and thousands of miles," Aretha recalled with a shudder. "I've been to California from Detroit about four times through the desert. Negotiating those narrow Rocky Mountain curves left me with big eyes." When the highway led them to the Deep South, the Franklins encountered the Jim Crow world they had heard their father discussing with Dr. King. Cecil Franklin underscored the hardships attendant on a schedule that might take them to Richmond on Sunday, Wilmington on Monday, Raleigh on Wednesday, Durham on Friday, and Atlanta over the weekend. He described "driving 8 or 10 hours to make a gig, and being hungry and passing restaurants all along the road, and having to go off the highway into some little city to find a place to eat because you're black—that had its effect."

For gospel performers, as for their colleagues in jazz, R&B, and the blues, financial exploitation was a matter of course. Erma provided a sardonic description of the standard operating procedures: "When you were singing gospel, it was very hard to get your money after the program was over. The promoter would run off with all the money, so it was almost a knock-down-drag-out fight to get on the show with Reverend Franklin, because then you didn't have to worry about your money." Not even personal friendship guaranteed fair treatment, as Aretha discovered when she went to Chicago at the invitation of the notoriously penurious Mahalia Jackson. Aretha was thrilled when Mahalia praised her singing, but she hadn't been paid and "was just too shy to ask her for money." When she finally summoned the courage to ask, Mahalia said she'd "talk to your dad about it," and Aretha "left Chicago with my heart broken."

Before she was eighteen, Aretha would amass a life's worth of experiences that blurred the line between gospel and the blues. Smokey Robinson described her world-weary report on a trip that had taken her to Chicago, Memphis, and St. Louis: " 'I meet all kinds of people, Smoke. There's a lot of stuff happening out there on the road. Sometimes it's even more than I want to see.' She turned her eyes from me and gazed out the window, looking like a wise woman in the body of a child."

The road provided some compensations for the hardships. Erma seconded Cecil's descriptions of travel in the South, noting, "Blacks had to stay with blacks in the South. You had to stay in black motels, so you had your gospel groups and your rhythm-and-blues groups at the same motel." But, she continued, because the R&B groups were familiar with C.L.'s sermons, "they'd introduce themselves and they'd become fast friends with everyone else who were stars on the road. So when they'd come to Detroit they would call my dad and come over to the house. Invariably, they'd start to singing and then it'd be one big party." The moments of camaraderie could materialize without warning. Aretha remembered a "rainy night on a dark Mississippi road" when the Franklins stopped for gas at a station "in the middle of nowhere." A second car pulled up, and out spilled the Staple Singers—Mavis, Pervis, Yvonne, Cleotha, and Pops. After a brief reunion, Aretha headed back into the night with the Staples' "Uncloudy Day" and "The Downward Road Is Crowded" ringing in her head.

Whatever the hardships and contradictions of the gospel highway, the singers and preachers who traveled along it transmitted their redemptive vision to black audiences in every corner of the country. Few expressed the role of music in that vision more strongly than C.L. Franklin in his sermon "Without a Song," based on the 137th Psalm, verses 1–4: "By the rivers of Babylon, there we set down, yea, we wept when we remembered Zion. We hanged our harps upon the willows in the midst thereof, for they that carried us away captive required of us a song; and they that wasted us required of us mirth, saying, Sing us one of the songs of Zion. How shall we sing the Lord's song in a strange land?"

The question had echoed down through the generations, transmitting the anguish of Middle Passage and slavery to the parishioners of New Bethel and the thousands who heard Franklin's recorded sermons in their living rooms. Even as he expressed the lure of withdrawal, he cried out against silence. The Hebrews should have sung, he intoned: "Yes, they were in a strange land; yes, they were among so-called heathens; yes, the situation in which they found themselves was an unfamiliar situation.... But even under adverse circumstances, you ought to sing sometimes." Sounding a keynote of the gospel vision, Franklin affirmed a power in music that reached deeper than words. "Sometimes you don't have to know what the words of the singer may be, but you appreciate the melody and the music of the song," he assured the congregation, calling out for their assent. "Some things you can't say, you can sing. Isn't it so?"

As the congregation called out its "Amen"s and "Yes, sir"s and the tempo of the church women's fans quickened, Reverend Franklin shifted gears, offering a story that illuminated the connection between personal and political tribulations and that reminded the beloved community of the power of its voice. Long years before, back when black people lived in bondage, Franklin began, an old black woman, answering the call of a sermon delivered by John Wesley's brother, sought to join a white church. When the minister turned her away, Franklin thundered, the black folks who had witnessed her repudiation raised their voices in song. "As the old lady's name was Mary," Franklin chanted, his voice taking on the sadness and joy of his people's history, "they sang, 'Oh Mary, don't weep, don't mourn; Pharaoh's army got drownded; Mary, don't weep, and then don't mourn.' Think of the message that is wrapped up in that song."

Fully aware that Pharaoh continued to shape the lives of black people from Clarksdale to Cabrini-Green, Reverend Franklin reminded his listeners of how their ancestors had used "Steal Away to Jesus" to "create unity and give rise to thoughts of liberation," and he challenged them to bring the singing spirit of song into the struggles they would face once the sermon ended. No matter how bleak the prospect, he assured them, "the Negro sang. Through his darkness, through his trials, and through his tribulations, he sang." Surrendering entirely to the rhythmic chants and whoops, Reverend Franklin ended by bearing witness to a power beyond words:

> *great God,*
> > *I want to keep on singing,*
> > > *until somebody knows,*
>
> *yes,*
>
> > *that my rock in a wearied land*
> > *is salvation*
> > *to every lost soul.*

When Aretha recorded "Precious Lord" and the other songs on her 1956 debut album, *Songs of Faith*, she was echoing her father's exhortations. Throughout the album Aretha sings with a raw power and spiritual depth that stakes her claim to the legacy of her gospel mothers. Accompanied by her father's affirming words and the responsive claps and murmurs welling up from the congregations at New Bethel and the Oakland Auditorium, where the cuts were recorded, Aretha plumbs the history locked up in the gospel classics: Thomas Dorsey's "Precious Lord (Take My Hand)" and two Clara Ward standards, "Never Grow Old" and "There Is a Fountain Filled with Blood," a tour de force that transforms the blood at the root of black life into the sacred source of redemption. Mapping the roots of the gospel vision as clearly as Mahalia's "How I Got Over" or Marion Williams's piercing gospel blues "The Moan," Aretha stretches the words until they break, opening herself to something that can only be said in song. Testifying to the self-shattering power flowing from the spirit into the answering moans of her beloved community, she celebrates the possibility of redemption in a world ravaged, now as then, by war and rumors of war. Aretha would go on to make more polished and popular music. She would even become world famous. But she would never bear witness to the power of the gospel vision with greater anguish or greater depth than she did in her father's church at fourteen.

CHAPTER TWO

"Keep On Pushing"

The Soul of the Freedom Movement

ARTIN LUTHER KING JR. wiped his brow and gazed out over the salt-and-pepper crowd sweating in front of Buckingham Fountain in Chicago's Grant Park on a blistering day in late July 1965. "Let us pray," King intoned, urging the Lord and tens of thousands of demonstrators to turn their thoughts to the "nonwhite citizens of this city, who have walked for years through the darkness of racial segregation, a nagging sense of nothingness." As his lieutenants and bodyguards cleared a path through the jostling crowd, King descended from the fountain and assumed his place at the front of the march. As the marchers set off west down Balbo Drive, they raised their voices in song: "Ain't gonna let nobody turn me round." Bringing the point home in the stirring chorus that had rung out in Montgomery, Birmingham, and Selma, they promised to "keep on walking, keep on talking, marching up to freedom land."

Carrying signs that read "Segregation Hurts Children," "Keep Your Eye on the Prize," and "This Could Be the Start of Something New," marchers adjusted the lyrics to local conditions, vowing "Ain't gonna let Mayor Daley turn me round." As the front ranks rounded the corner from State Street and turned onto Madison Avenue, traffic in the downtown Chicago Loop came to a halt. Passing through the shadows of the skyscrapers, a pocket of marchers sang, "People are you ready," the opening line of the Impressions' recent hit "Meeting Over Yonder." "Don't forget to be there," they went on, using the lyrics that had been circulated on mimeographed sheets in the week before the march. "Dr. King's gonna be there at the meeting over yonder." By the time it reached City Hall, where King hoped to present Richard Daley with a list of demands centered on housing and education, the march had swelled to almost a hundred thousand. Disappointed to find that Daley had ducked the planned photo opportunity by leaving town to attend a convention in Detroit, King invited the throng to join him in another prayer. When he raised his head, his voice rang out with phrases he had used repeatedly in the days before the march: "Chicago is a great city. We want it to be a greater city. We must learn to live together as brothers, or we will all perish together as fools."

King had come to Chicago to fulfill a promise that Southern Christian Leadership Conference staffer James Bevel had made that March in the wake of the movement's stirring victory in Selma, Alabama. "Chicago is not that different from the South," Bevel had observed. "Black Chicago is Mississippi moved a few hundred miles north. We are going to have a movement in Chicago." As he prepared to do battle for the future of the city ruled by the machine politician whose biographers would call him "American Pharaoh," King prayed for a new exodus. He hoped that the nation would see the Chicago movement as a continuation of the drama that had been unfolding in the South, a drama in which the disciplined interracial group of marchers raising their voices in song represented the fundamental values of Christian brotherhood and American democracy.

~☙~

FEW OF THE MILLIONS WHO WATCHED images of the carefully orchestrated march that evening on the network news broadcasts were aware that a second march had taken place simultaneously along the same streets. The "shadow march" did not compete with King's march, and the people who shuffled down the sidewalk carried the same vision of freedom as King's marchers on the pavement. Nor did the shadow marchers reject King's political goals altogether. But nonviolence was a hard sell in Chicago—maybe even harder than it had been in Birmingham. Onlookers who supported the march but had not accepted the disciplines of nonviolence followed at a short distance, cheering King and jeering the police. The second march was angrier and blacker than its official counterpart—and it was heavily armed. Winding their way down the sidewalks outside the police lines and beyond the awareness of the reporters covering the march, the shadow marchers responded to white supremacist hecklers in kind, refusing to turn the other cheek when pushed or taunted. No major incidents erupted that day in Chicago. But the bitter fellow travelers of nonviolence served as a stark reminder of the violence simmering just beneath the surface of racial relations, even when the public story was being defined by apostles of Gandhian nonviolence. By the time the throng arrived at City Hall, the two marches effectively merged into a single body representing the actual complexity of the movement rather than its official public image.

Many shadow marchers dismissed as dangerously naïve King's belief that moral persuasion would change Richard Daley's Chicago. Few were surprised by the reception that comedian-turned-activist Dick Gregory received less than a week later when he led a march into Mayor Daley's home neighborhood of Bridgeport, an Irish enclave on the front lines of the city's battles over public housing. Ordered by police to remain silent and walk two by two, the marchers encountered a mob of Bridgeport residents shouting, "Go back to the zoo," and throwing rocks. Hand-lettered signs extolled the Ku Klux Klan and Alabama's segregationist governor, George Wallace. Recalling the still-fresh images of the violence that had greeted marchers on the Edmund Pettis Bridge in Selma, a group of teenage girls adapted an Oscar Mayer advertising jingle, singing, "I wish I was an Alabama trooper. That is what I'd truly like to be. I wish I was an Alabama trooper, 'cause then I could kill niggers legally."

The contrast between that song and "Ain't Gonna Let Nobody Turn Me Round" reflects the shifting contours of the struggle as it moved from the South to the cities of the North and West in the mid-sixties. But what united the two theaters of the movement, as well as the official marchers and their shadow counterparts, was the soul music that provided the movement's day-by-day soundtrack. And during the first half of the decade, no music garnered a deeper response than the redemptive anthems of Curtis Mayfield and the Impressions. Both King's interracialist followers and the street nationalists heard "Meeting Over Yonder" as a call to battle. When the struggle seemed too much to bear, followers of both Martin and Malcolm took heart from Mayfield's gentle exhortation to "Keep On Pushing." As they savored the bonds of love and friendship that bound their families and the movement itself together, they sank into the soothing harmonies of "I'm So Proud" and "Woman's Got Soul." "People Get Ready" tapped the deepest wellsprings of the gospel vision and gave many a weary soul a place to rest.

"It was warrior music," affirmed Gordon Sellers, a Florida-born activist who had begun as an angry participant in the shadow marches before converting to a nonviolent philosophy in the mid-sixties. "It was music you listened to while you were preparing to go into battle. Curtis inspired us, but he also took us to task. He was writing at a time we were struggling. But he knew we were struggling for the right things." Joanne Bland, who had been on the Edmund Pettis Bridge and now directs the National Voting Rights Museum in Selma, reversed Sellers's trajectory. "I started out with civil rights and moved to Black Power," she reflected. "But wherever I was, Curtis's music was there. 'Keep On Pushing,' 'People Get Ready,' 'This Is My Country.' " As SNCC organizer Stanley Wise told music historian Brian Ward, "Curtis always seemed to be right on time. You could see his records on every movement turntable." Wise's SNCC colleague Jimmy Collier concurred, rattling off a list that included the less-known Impressions cuts "I've Been Trying," "Never Too Much Love," and "It's Been a Long, Long Winter," as well as "Keep On Pushing," "Meeting Over Yonder," and "People Get Ready."

Like most soul singers, Mayfield inspired the movement with his music rather than by marching in its front lines. He performed benefits such as the "Freedom Show" that Philly DJ George Woods organized in support of the Selma crusade, but "the music is really what connected us," Mayfield's business partner Eddie Thomas observed. "Everything we were feeling and talking about was tied in with Martin Luther King and the movement and black rights." Mayfield was aware that his music flowed from the wellsprings of black political aspiration. "As a young man I was writing songs like 'Keep on Pushing' and 'This Is My Country' and feeling all the love and all the things I observed politically. Of course with everything I saw on the streets as a young black kid, it wasn't hard during the later fifties and early sixties for me to write [in] my own heartfelt way of how I visualized things, how I thought things ought to be."

Stevie Wonder's and Aretha Franklin's contributions to the movement followed similar patterns. Because of her father's friendship with King and Detroit's black political establishment, Aretha had more direct contact with the movement. She idolized King and took pride in Detroit's "Great March to Freedom," a midwestern counterpart of the more famous 1963 March on Washington that her father had helped organize. Joining Mahalia Jackson and Dinah Washington at a Chicago benefit for the Birmingham movement, Aretha mesmerized the overflow audience at McCormack Place with a rendition of "Precious Lord (Take My Hand)." Hesitant to risk offending potential record buyers, Motown discouraged its stars from making political statements. But in 1963 the company broke from its common practice and allowed Stevie to perform at a benefit in support of the March on Washington. As Brian Ward speculates, the label's primary motivation may well have been to expose him to the affluent audience that had come to see Carmen McRae, Paul Newman and Joanne Woodward, and Tony Bennett. Unconcerned with show business maneuvering, movement warriors went right on mixing "I Was Made to Love Her" and the exuberant rhythms of "Fingertips" with politically resonant soul songs like "Keep On Pushing" or Sam Cooke's "A Change Is Gonna Come."

Black DJs played a central role in encouraging listeners to hear soul music politically. Chicago DJ Herb Kent described the approach that his home station, WVON, had taken while supporting the Freedom Summer of 1964. "WVON played a big part in the civil rights era, both with the music being played—like homeboy Curtis Mayfield—and because we talked about it on the air. We did a sit-in in this trailer. People would come and look at us in there fasting. We were certainly right there in the middle of the civil rights movement and the music delivered the messages. We let people know and talked about what was going on." Chuck Scruggs, of KSOL in San Francisco, specified the Impressions' "sermon songs" as part of a political mix: "As a jock during that time I would take those message songs and add a line or two of editorial…something that would fit the title or the theme of the song…. I didn't play a message song in isolation, and then go from that to something else that had no connection. I'd go from a message song like 'Keep On Pushing' to, say, 'Stand by Me.' You see what I mean? I'd make the transition with words of hope for my listeners. You know—'Stand by me people 'cause we gotta keep on pushing for our freedom.' "

Mayfield's ability to spark his people's imagination grew directly out of his gospel roots, but his grounding in doo-wop helped him reach listeners who never entered a church. Throughout the fifties Chicago was home to a thriving doo-wop scene that developed groups such as the Flamingos, the Spaniels, and the Dells, whose sweet harmonies and gospel intensities paralleled those in Mayfield's gospel soul. Like most big-city doo-wop scenes, Chicago's South Side featured highly competitive street-corner singing. Paralleling the competition between gospel quartets and anticipating later forms such as hip-hop freestyling, doo-wop groups would battle for control of street corners, where they could attract an audience and establish a reputation. Reggie Smith, a member of the Five Chances, remembered Mayfield's incursion on the group's turf at Forty-fourth and Prairie: "Curtis Mayfield was living around there before his mother and him moved to Cabrini-Green. His mother had bought him a banjo, something of the sort. He used to come around beating on the banjo and we'd tell him to get away from us with all that noise, cause we're trying to sing [but] he went on to beat us to death."

Both the gospel and doo-wop scenes centered on the South Side black belt, but the Near North Side, where Mayfield moved when he was still a toddler, was by no means a musical wasteland. The Cabrini-Green doo-wop scene centered on the recreation center in Seward Park. Billy Butler, one of several North Siders who later recorded Mayfield compositions, described the scene: "We were all into trying to sing. That was the only thing to do really. The area didn't have street gangs at the time. Everyone would form a group and go into Seward Park." Jerry Butler added that Seward Park provided a place where young musicians could learn from elders, such as a somewhat disreputable wino named Doug. "He had this old beat-up guitar, but man could he play it," Butler reminisced. "Me and Curtis would just sit and listen to him play all day, and I think it was from him that Curtis picked up a lot of his stuff."

Herb Butler, a member of the Players, loved the competitive energy: "At that time everybody sang. You know that Major Lance lived right down the street. Everybody who was anybody would rehearse there. They had like seven rooms, and you could come in and tell which room which group was gonna be in, because people would be hanging around the doors, or rooms would be full and they would not be letting anybody in." Undeterred, fans clustered around the practice rooms hoping to overhear the Serenades, the Capris, the Players, the Medallionaires, and the Van Gayles, who had a local hit with "The Twirl." "Joe [Breckenridge] and the guys would never do their song until everybody in the other rooms had stopped singing," Herb Butler recalled. "When there was a moment of silence, you could hear them start that song 'ah hoo,' and everybody would leave whatever they were doing and go up to the door and hear them guys do that song."

Even when he was singing with the Northern Jubilee Gospel Singers, Mayfield began toying with secular music as part of the short-lived Alphatones, which included schoolmates Al Boyce, James Weems, and Dallas Dixon. But the real move toward popular music came when Jerry Butler, who had sung with the Northern Jubilees, invited his friend to join the Roosters, who specialized in a funky southern style of R&B. The original members of the Roosters—Sam Gooden, Emmanuel Thomas, Fred Cash, and brothers Richard and Arthur Brooks—had moved from Chattanooga to Chicago, where they recruited Butler. Aware of Mayfield's ability to harmonize and play guitar, Butler convinced the other Roosters to give him a chance.

"Curtis was not easily convinced," Butler recalled. "He had a group of his own, the Alphatones, and didn't want to drop everything and come with us. I suggested a compromise. 'Dig Curt,' I said. 'Let's do it like this: You rehearse three nights a week with us and three with your group. Whoever improves first will be the group you go with.'" From Mayfield's perspective, Butler's persistence determined the decision. "We had a long debate for about two or three weeks, but Jerry would never give up. Eventually, he won me over, and I joined with these older guys. We woodshedded for a good year, and finally we came along with a few songs."

Practicing at the Seward Center and in the apartments of family and friends, the Roosters tried out their songs at street carnivals, neighborhood centers, and the parties thrown by Cabrini residents in the basement of the high-rise Reds. They played, Butler recalled, "anywhere we were allowed to play." As the group began to attract a following, Butler's cousin, a drug addict and would-be music promoter, convinced them to rent the Washburne Auditorium to put on a kind of coming-out show. "He convinced me to take three hundred dollars—my entire savings—and invest it in a show at the Washburne Auditorium," Butler groaned. "Come the day of the show, we couldn't get in the building because he hadn't paid the deposit and the insurance. People were lined up around the block to see us." When the same cousin failed to pay the Roosters for their performance at a South Side show featuring jazzmen Gene Ammons and Sonny Stitt, the would-be impresario's career crashed to a halt.

Still looking for their breakthrough, the Roosters entered a talent show at Washburne. As they entered the auditorium, another aspiring manager, Eddie Thomas, pulled up in his canary-yellow-and-white Cadillac. When Thomas heard the Roosters, he was impressed. "I thought they were fabulous," Thomas recalled. "They'd heard of me because I was managing the Medallionaires, and they said, 'Why don't you come work with us too? You can handle two groups.'" Thomas accepted but insisted that the group change its name. "The Roosters just don't ring a bell," he announced, "they do not ring a bell at all." Mayfield was already dubious about the down-home name. "Down South they had been the Roosters and a Chick because they had a lady singer with them. So they come to the big North with that Roosters name. We couldn't get through a song after we told the audience the name. They'd be crowing and making all kinds of barnyard sounds." After first proposing the "Victorians," Thomas came up with the name that stuck. "I said to them, 'I was so impressed when I met you guys, how about the Impressions?' And they said, 'Yeah, yeah.'" At first the original members resisted, worrying that the change would hurt their popularity back home, but when Thomas promised heavy Chattanooga publicity, they went along with the switch.

When Thomas assumed control of the Impressions' business fortunes in 1957, both black music and the freedom movement had arrived at a dangerous crossroads. Following the Supreme Court's 1954 *Brown* decision and the success of the Montgomery bus boycott in 1955, the movement had fallen into disarray. Recovering from its initial shock and disorientation, the white South mounted a campaign of "massive resistance" to desegregation.

Relying on sympathetic judges, economic reprisals, and state "sovereignty commissions" that operated like a homegrown KGB, as well as fists, guns, and homemade bombs, white supremacists tried hard to hold a lid on black protest from the Montgomery bus boycott until the sit-in movement blew it off in 1960.

The situation "up south," as the migrants called their new homes north of the Mason-Dixon Line, wasn't much better. The economic bleeding in Detroit had become a hemorrhage. Novelist Nelson Algren described the Chicago of the mid-fifties as "a jukebox running down in a deserted bar." Integration had been a complete flop. When Richard J. Daley ascended to Chicago's mayoral throne in 1956, one of his first acts was to approve the building of a series of major housing projects: the Henry Horner Homes, the Clarence Darrow Homes, Stateway Gardens, the Robert Brooks Homes, and the Robert Taylor Homes. The projects did alleviate the housing shortage in black Chicago, but they did so in the worst conceivable manner for the African American children destined to live in them. By the time the last of the high-density high-rise buildings opened its doors, over forty thousand blacks, almost all of them desperately poor, were packed into the State Street Corridor, an area a quarter of a mile wide and four miles long between Cermak (Twenty-second Street) and Fifty-first Street. The only alternative for most blacks was the growing West Side ghetto, which lacked even the South Side's established black institutions.

It was easy to blame the decisions that created the ghetto nightmare on the white working-class homeowners who had been on the front lines of previous housing battles. Belligerent, openly racist, and sometimes violent, lower-class whites made excellent scapegoats. But in fact those discriminatory decisions had been made with the tacit, and sometimes active, complicity of both the black power structure and white liberals. William Dawson's black submachine understood clearly that its prosperity depended on de facto segregation. Whatever their public statements on racial injustice, black elected officials never pressured the city to create integrated projects. "Dawson didn't want black voters dispersed," the chair of the Chicago Housing Authority concluded. "Many of the black aldermen didn't want them dispersed."

As Mayfield set out on his career in music, the prospects facing black musicians in the north mirrored those of the community as a whole. At the end of the fifties avenues that a few years earlier had seemed to be opening up suddenly were filled with roadblocks. Hypersensitive to the threat of international Communism, mainstream politicians painted any challenge to the American racial status quo as part of an all-encompassing Communist plot. Rock 'n' roll, which ardent segregationists condemned as "mongrel music," provided an inviting target. Pictures of Little Richard, eyes rolled back underneath a distinctly bizarre mountain of hair, confronted Cold War America with one of its worst nightmares. The hysterical tone of the attacks on rock 'n' roll comes through clearly in a pamphlet distributed to white parents by an Alabama branch of the White Citizens Council: "Help save the youth of America! Don't let your children buy or listen to these Negro records. The screaming idiotic words and savage music are undermining the morals of our white American youth!"

The authorities cracked down on the threatening interracial music scene. In city after city panicky promoters summoned police to restore order while horrified white parents condemned rock 'n' roll as a Communist conspiracy to reduce America to an outpost of the rhythm-crazed African jungle. Chuck Berry went to jail on trumped-up charges of corrupting the morals of a minor; Little Richard was hounded into retirement. Pioneering DJ Alan Freed, who made no distinction between rock 'n' roll and R&B, was exiled in a trumped-up "payola" scandal that somehow let clean-cut pop impresario Dick Clark escape unscathed. And in a series of events that would shape the future of rock 'n' roll, Elvis Presley was drafted into the army, cleaned up, and transformed from the missionary of musical miscegenation into a safely sanitized matinee idol.

ALTHOUGH THE IMPRESSIONS were aware of rock 'n' roll, they felt more closely connected to the gospel soul of Ray Charles, Clyde McPhatter, and Sam Cooke. Despite the similarity of their origins and sound, R&B and rock 'n' roll had already begun moving apart. On many radio stations the new Elvis presided over Top Forty lists that excluded all but the least threatening black singers. While Cooke and Berry Gordy struggled gallantly to control that battle, many black listeners, among them Mayfield, preferred R&B's grittier gospel stylings. Mayfield praised Charles for pioneering the approach he would later perfect in "Keep On Pushing" and "People Get Ready." "At first it was strange listening to Ray Charles," Mayfield confessed. "He's been singing gospel all his life even though his music's considered rhythm and blues. He changed the lyrics but never changed his way of singing, which you could hear was out of the church." Mayfield felt an even deeper affinity with fellow Chicagoan Cooke, who had left gospel's Soul Stirrers after his 1957 classic "You Send Me" reached the top of the charts. "When that came out, man, we thought it was a fantastic piece of music. I just loved it," Mayfield enthused. At the beginning, however, Mayfield and Eddie Thomas hesitated to commit themselves to Cooke's crossover strategy. "We knew the pop stations were very prejudiced, and it would take a certain kind of sound to get over," Thomas reflected, referring to the bright harmonies and catchy melodies of Cooke's pop records. "But if we would produce that, we would lose our support from our own people. So at least we know we'll survive." Thomas cited Jerry Butler's 1961 rendition of "Moon River," the theme song from *Breakfast at Tiffany's,* as the worst-case scenario: "Vee-Jay spent a ton, that was a $35,000 recording session, they went gung ho. The blacks didn't support it, they weren't interested in 'Moon River.' The whites played at it, but they didn't support Jerry Butler because he was black, so it went down the drain, all of that money."

In the fifties such dilemmas must have seemed distant to Butler and Mayfield. First the Impressions needed a recording contract. Eddie Thomas arranged for a series of auditions and herded his charges to the offices of Chicago's leading R&B labels. In Mayfield's version of the story, it was virtually a fluke that the Impressions wound up signing with Vee-Jay. The day they were scheduled to audition for Chess, he recalled, a major snowstorm hammered the city: "The snow was about five feet to walk through when we went to Chess Records and knocked on the door. I guess there was a secretary in there, but no one would let us in. So we turned around, and what's across the street: Vee-Jay Records. We just went right across through the snow, dragging our amplifier and guitar. Ewart Abner was upstairs with the A&R [Artists and Repertoire] man, Calvin Carter—they let us in. It must have been a weekend—no one was really working—and we sang 'For Your Precious Love' for Calvin right on the steps. He loved it. About a week later I was in the studio for the first time. And that's really how we got off."

Carter provided a slightly different version of the story. "They sang about five or six numbers and sounded pretty good," he recalls, "but I was not hearing that thing that sounds like money in the bank. On a hunch, I told them, 'Sing something you're ashamed to sing! Sing something you don't usually feel like singing in public.' So one of them told the rest, 'Hey, how about that spiritual thing we worked out?' The rest of them argued about it, but they finally sang it." Written by Jerry Butler with the help of the Brooks brothers, "For Your Precious Love" sold nearly a million copies when released as a single.

Less given to myth-making, Eddie Thomas attributed the way things played out to nuts-and-bolts commercial concerns. "We went down to King Records at Seventeenth and Wabash, where Ralph Bass was the A&R guy. He listened to us and said, 'Well, no.' They had the big boy, James Brown, so they had the whole world by the handle. We went to Chess Records next. They had the Dells, Billy Stewart, the Moonglows, they were doing okay, they didn't feel like they needed another act." Thomas confirmed that Calvin Carter made the decision to sign the Impressions after hearing "For Your Precious Love," but he offered a different explanation of why they hadn't planned to include it in the audition. "We were very hesitant about doing 'For Your Precious Love' because we'd heard about how much thievery was going on in the business," Thomas observed. "They take your songs and somebody else would do 'em. We sang 'Sweet Was the Wine' and a couple of other tunes. He liked the group a little, said, 'You've got a sound, but something…' So I said we gotta go for broke now, we already struck out twice. So we sang 'For Your Precious Love,' and when we did that, pop! goes the weasel, bing!" Butler remembered Carter's eyes lighting up as he called out to his sister and business partner Vi and Vee-Jay executive Ewart Abner, who would go on to become president of Motown: "That's it! That's it! That's the one! Abner, get me some contracts. Vi, you, Eddie, and Abner better talk."

The group crashed back to earth when the Spaniels, one of Chicago's hottest doo-wop groups, showed up at the studio. Butler and Mayfield realized immediately that "For Your Precious Love" would be an ideal vehicle for the Spaniels' Pookie Hudson, whose soulful lead vocals had lifted "Goodnight Sweetheart" and "Since I Fell for You" into the Top Ten. The situation deteriorated further when Carter asked the Impressions to sing the song again. "There was a long pause as paranoia set in," Butler remembered. "Here comes the rip-off. He likes our song, and he wants them to record it. That's why they called them and told them to come over right away. This ain't no accident. I'll bet that bastard's got a tape recorder in his desk. Oh shit, what do we do now? Well, we'll sing it fast, and then they can't remember it. But what about the tape recorder in his desk? Well, we'll think of something before we leave." Not until they entered the studio two weeks later did the Impressions' fears fully subside. When the group released "For Your Precious Love" in the summer of 1958, it introduced several elements of the gospel soul style Mayfield later brought to perfection. A powerful bass line and softly strumming guitar provide a deceptively peaceful setting for Butler's solemn testifying. The call and response between the lead vocalist, whose baritone contrasts with Mayfield's sweet tenor, and the background chorus emphasizes the cut's gospel roots and points like a compass needle straight to the production techniques that would define Chicago soul.

Unlike Chess, which concentrated on marketing distinctly black music to black audiences, mostly tunes recorded by southern-born musicians, Vee-Jay actively pursued the crossover market. In the early sixties it would establish itself as an industry powerhouse with hits like Gene Chandler's "Duke of Earl," the Four Seasons' "Sherry," "Big Girls Don't Cry," and "Walk Like a Man," and, for a brief time, the Beatles' first American LP. The label's leadership team consisted of Abner, Vivian Carter Bracken, who remains one of the few black women to exert real power in the record industry, and her brother Calvin, the center of Vee-Jay's talent department. Irritated when the McGuire Sisters' cover of "Goodnight Sweetheart" outsold the Spaniels' original, he set about remedying the situation. Butler remembers hearing Carter explain, "Why did that happen? Because mine sounded black and theirs didn't. So now I've got to try to figure out how to make mine sound not so black." Although Carter was not himself a musician, Butler emphasizes that "he had a great ear, a great feel for songs, a great feel for artists, and a great feel for people. He's got a track record that Phil Spector would be envious of, but his recognition is nonexistent."

Ironically, or perhaps typically, the success of "For Your Precious Love" contributed to the breakup of the original Impressions. The problems began when the group got its first look at the record label. "They pressed up the records with the name Jerry Butler written across the sky, and they put the Impressions in magnifying glass," Eddie Thomas recalled, grimacing. "I didn't know whether to laugh or cry," Butler admitted. "Laugh because I had just made the featured name in the group, or cry because I knew that Curtis, Sam, Arthur, and Richard didn't like it one bit. Each of their faces was twisted up into a half-smile that did nothing to hide their hurt and envy." Butler tried to rectify the situation by telling Eddie Thomas and Abner they'd have to reprint the label. Abner resisted, pointing out the cost of reprinting fifty thousand labels and arguing that a featured vocalist would increase airplay, promotion, and publicity. "By the time he got through talking, we were feeling sorry for feeling sorry," Butler said. "He was one of those guys who could sell you the Brooklyn Bridge and then buy it back five minutes later for half the price." Still, Butler acknowledged, the damage was irreparable. "When the record came out that way, all the attention went to Jerry," Mayfield observed. "And of course you can understand all these fellows having worked and sacrificed evenly in trying to become somebody, for anyone's name to be put out front was a sort of a blow. When disc jockeys played the record, it was 'Now here's Jerry Butler and "For Your Precious Love." ' And of course the fan mail would come, which we got gobs of, to Jerry Butler."

Butler's soulful delivery and the gospel undertones of "For Your Precious Love" quickly caught the attention of influential black DJs, including George Woods of WHAT in Philadelphia and Stevie Wonder's idol Larry Dixon, who introduced the Impressions to the economic realities of life on the road. Thomas booked a two-day trip to Detroit, which was to be followed by a quick return home for an appearance on Jim Lounsbury's *Bandstand Matinee,* Chicago's equivalent of *American Bandstand.* When they arrived in Detroit, Dixon informed them that he had talked to Vee-Jay and arranged for them to stay an extra day and appear on a free show he was promoting. The Detroit audience loved "For Your Precious Love." "The place went up in screams," Butler recalls with satisfaction. "It was strange, but I got the same feeling that night that I had experienced with the Northern Jubilee Singers when the church was with us. It's a feeling of pushing up to your limit and then over, and your spirit lifts your body. It all becomes so real that it's unreal." Once church ended, however, reality set in. Dixon made three thousand dollars on the show but "didn't even buy us a hamburger." Nor, it turned out, had he mentioned the change of plans to the group's management, who sat by in despair as the Impressions missed

Bandstand Matinee. "Detroit was Larry's town," Butler observed, "and if we wanted to sell records there, we needed him. In other words, Larry could pee on us and tell us it was raining, and we had better believe it."

A few weeks later—resplendent in uniforms consisting of gray silk jackets, black pants, white shirts, black ties, and pocket scarves they had purchased in the open-air market on Maxwell Street—the Impressions embarked on a promotional tour that would take them to Philadelphia, Miami, and Harlem's Apollo Theater. At the Apollo they appeared on a bill with Huey Smith and the Clowns, the Coasters, and Frankie Lymon. Before they left, however, Curtis's grandmother dispatched them to visit a spiritualist healer who would administer a blessing. When they arrived, the old woman blessed the water and sprinkled a few drops on Arthur, Richard, and Sam. But "when she got to Curtis and me," Butler recalled, "she took the cup and flung the water in our faces, capping the whole thing off by letting the cup slip out of her hand and hitting me in the face with it." Once they'd made their escape, Curtis looked at his partner, shook his head, and said, "She sure did bless the hell out of us, didn't she, man?"

By the end of the tour, Butler was "wondering if the little old lady who had blessed us when we were leaving Chicago had instead put a curse on us." The marquees blazoning Butler's name in giant letters and relegating the Impressions to an afterthought, if that, aggravated the underlying tensions. "The guys knew I didn't have anything to do with what was happening," Butler observed, "but it was still a bit much for them to swallow. They became quiet and distant. I felt like a stranger among guys who were my friends." To make matters worse, the group's repertoire, with the exception of its big hit, failed to impress the hardened audiences out east. When they opened their set at the Apollo with versions of recent hits by Elvis Presley and Tony Bennett, Butler remembers a leather-lunged member of the audience shouting out, "Y'all take that white shit someplace else and sing what I came here to hear." Sometimes simply singing the song wasn't enough. "I used to get down on one knee and sing 'For Your Precious Love,' " Butler said. "This guy came all the way from Baltimore and brought a whole bunch of his friends to see me get down on my knees. But that night I didn't get down on my knees; I just finished the song and walked off the stage. The guy hollered out, 'Naw, motherfucker, come back here. I brought all these people up here to see you get down on your knees. Get down on your knees!' The audience rolled. He wouldn't let the show go on until I got down on my knees."

When the Impressions returned to Cabrini at the end of July, they had become, in Butler's words, "lightweight celebrities." "All of a sudden the smells we used to ignore—the pee in the elevators and on the stairs, wine bottles and junkies—suddenly became too much to bear," he added. Setting out on a tour on a bill with the Coasters and Clyde McPhatter, the Impressions discovered the grinding tedium of life on the road. Long rides, run-down hotels, and a relentless schedule of thirty-one one-nighters stoked tensions to the boiling point. The end came before a performance at the Sam Houston Auditorium in San Antonio, when the group realized it would be stranded without enough money to fly to Philadelphia for a scheduled promotional appearance. Butler described the end of the original Impressions, beginning with the moment when Arthur Brooks turned to him and announced, "We ain't going on, and you can do all the singing." When Richard and Sam Gooden agreed, all eyes turned to Curtis. " 'I'm going on, man,' said Curtis, 'because I want to get paid.' 'Okay, Curtis,' I said, 'I guess it's just me and you.' " Sam changed his mind, but Arthur and Richard made good on their promise to walk. "It occurred to me, as we went along that night, that Arthur and Richard weren't missed at all," Butler recalled. "No one in San Antonio knew they existed. It was then that I made my decision to leave the group."

Eddie Thomas believed that Vee-Jay had consciously orchestrated the split. "After record sales took off, they took off like a rocket ship. It started in Gary and Chicago and spread. Vee-Jay realized they had a great voice in Jerry Butler, and to them he was the next Roy Hamilton. They gave him a new car, a 1957 white Mercury, and two thousand dollars. Here's Jerry Butler living deep in the heart of Cabrini-Green. That was a big move to have that much in hand at one time in his life, 'cause he didn't have anything. They decided to move him out into the forefront." Calvin Carter, who believed he'd made a mistake by not advertising Pookie Hudson as a solo star when he was with the Spaniels, was unapologetic about Vee-Jay's strategy. Mayfield acknowledged that it was common practice: "Back during those times most record companies, if they had a five-man group that was beginning to do well, they immediately wanted to pull the lead artist away, sensing they could sell more records and get into the crossover market, over into the white market. They did it with Dee Clark and the Kool Gents, they did it with Frankie Lymon and the Teenagers, Clyde McPhatter and the Drifters—I mean you name it, they did it with all of them."

Going solo made perfectly good commercial sense. But from a broader perspective, it also tipped the call-and-response dynamic toward the individual *I* and away from the communal *we*. The African American tradition certainly didn't suppress individuality or discourage strong voices. Archie Brownlee, Robert Johnson, and Billie Holiday remained unmistakably themselves. But as Albert Murray emphasizes in *Stomping the Blues,* even the most alienated "blues I" drew its power from the listeners' recognition that they shared the brutal experiences behind the alienation. Like Muddy Waters or Bessie Smith, solo soul stars could tap into that power. But there was a real advantage to the group format, which drew directly from the collective energy of the "gospel we." The Original Gospel Harmonettes and the Swan Silvertones didn't really sing "backup" for Dorothy Love Coates or Reverend Claude Jeter; their hopes and burdens thicken the texture and deepen the meaning of the lead vocalists' tales of how they got over. Groups like the Drifters, the Temptations, and the Impressions domesticated the energies of live gospel performance, providing a commercially viable version of call and response. But they still modeled communities where the individual needed the group. When industry pressures separated leader from community, it was part of the larger process that would shift the balance toward individual commercial success. It was, to be sure, part of the journey toward the American mainstream. But the ticket came at a price.

For the Impressions, the immediate cost of the split with Butler was high. The remaining Impressions released several unsuccessful follow-ups, including "Come Back My Love" and "Hey Senorita." "We scuffled some," Mayfield noted. "For a time we would do gigs as the Impressions, but nobody was really aware of the Impressions. So it was quite hard for us to get gigs." Even after Butler left the group, the Impressions sometimes benefited from his name. "Sometimes we did gigs in little towns as Jerry Butler and the Impressions, and Sam would do 'For Your Precious Love.' This was in some of the lowlands, like down in Mississippi, just in little night spots like that." At the end of 1959 Vee-Jay released the group from its contract because, as Calvin Carter admitted, "I was not excited about Curtis's falsetto voice. A falsetto voice has never gotten over to me. At that time we also had the Dells, the Magnificents, the Spaniels, the Orioles—we had acts coming out of our ears. We just couldn't launch the Impressions."

Butler's departure would prove to be a blessing in disguise. "When Jerry left, it allowed us to regroup and start getting into our own selves," Mayfield said. "It allowed me to generate and pull out my own talents as a writer and a vocalist." Still living in Cabrini-Green, Mayfield considered going on the road with Butler as a guitarist at a salary of three hundred dollars a week. Instead, he took a job selling cigars for Alfred Dunhill Co., where his route ran up and down the North Shore "Gold Coast." But he always knew that his real passion lay in music. Soon he was writing songs and playing guitar on sessions for several labels. Billy Butler, himself an accomplished guitarist, described Mayfield's playing as "not rigid. Very liquidy. Soft sound. Almost fluid." Soon, as Gerald Simms, a staff member at the Chicago-based blues label Okeh, observed, "everyone in Chicago was imitating his guitar style."

Mayfield developed that style backing up powerful blues singers including Jimmy Reed, whose unstructured approach to recording forced the young sideman to hone his skills. "Everybody had to circle him like he was the fire and we was circling around him to get warm," Mayfield said. "We all watched his mouth and watched his guitar because he was one of those guys that bars meant nothing to. He may change right in the middle, he may get back to the one and then back to the bass. But you had to watch him and keep tempo and change when he changed." Mayfield chuckled when he remembered Reed's notorious inability to remember the words to his songs. "Of course he could never remember his lyrics, so his wife was always feeding him the words. If you listen to the old Jimmy Reed stuff, you can hear his wife singing right behind him."

As good a guitarist as Mayfield was, he was a better songwriter. Eddie Thomas summed up the consensus within the Chicago soul community when he said, "Curtis is a genius. That says it all. The man was like a factory all by himself. He could wake up and write a song in the middle of the night." As Mayfield entered adulthood, he turned to music to help him sift through his troubles. "Songwriting was an escape if I was hurt too bad or if something wasn't going right," he meditated. "I could always retire to writing my sentiments and my personal feelings. Anger, love, everything in my life would come out on paper. I wrote my songs for myself first. I was the one trying to learn the first lesson because I didn't have actual arguments. My fights and arguments, even with God, went down on paper."

Mayfield began devoting himself seriously to writing when he accepted Jerry Butler's renewed invitation to return to the road as a backup guitarist. Eddie Thomas, who was working as Butler's driver and valet, recalled that the opportunity arose when the previous guitarist, Phil Upchurch, accepted a better-paying job with Chicago soulman Dee Clark. Butler realized that he missed Curtis's "sense of humor, his pragmatism, his instincts, his great musical sense." The timing couldn't have been better. "When Jerry called, I had nothing to do," Mayfield admitted. "As a matter of fact the Internal Revenue Service was looking for me for four hundred bucks. They found me in Cabrini-Green and wanted payment. I had a Webcor tape recorder, and they wanted me to sell it to get them money. Anyway I got away from them by playing for Jerry. I did nothing but play for Jerry and sleep with my guitar and write songs." The payoff of the renewed collaboration, Thomas reports, was instantaneous. "I told Jerry, 'Let's call Curtis,' and the rest was 'He Will Break Your Heart,' 'He Don't Love You Like I Love You,' 'Find Yourself Another Girl,' and 'I'm A-Telling You,'" Thomas concluded, reeling off the list of hits Mayfield would pen for Butler over the next few years.

Along with early Impressions cuts like "Grow Closer Together," "Never Let Me Go," and "I'm the One Who Loves You," those songs established the sound and sensibility that would define Chicago soul. Combining seductive hooks and angelic harmonies with a call-and-response style straight out of the Traveling Souls Spiritualist Church, Mayfield aspired to write songs that were, in his words, "hard and soft but never harsh." Sometimes he dealt directly with the problems he'd seen growing up in Cabrini-Green; music historian Brian Ward rightly labels "I'm A-Telling You" "a compelling account of working-class life on the breadline." Like many soul anthems, "Grow Closer Together" works equally well as a love song or as a paean to the southern movement Curtis read about in the *Chicago Defender* and watched on the evening news.

More frequently, however, Mayfield's lyrics simply gave voice to the realities of African American life without dwelling on the underlying social sources. "He Will Break Your Heart," for example, sympathetically portrays what happens when different worlds intersect. Written during a late-night drive from Philadelphia to Atlantic City after a gig, the song began as a melody in Butler's head and developed into a vignette of life on the road told from the perspective of the brokenhearted boyfriend of a woman hypnotized by the chance for a brief escape from her everyday problems. "It was something I'd lived," Butler admitted. "You go into a town; you're only gonna be there for one night; you want some company; you find a girl; you blow her mind. Now you know this girl hasn't been sittin' in that town waitin' for you to come in. She probably has another fellow, and the other fellow's probably in love with her; they're probably planning to go through a whole thing, right? But you never take that into consideration on that particular night. You're lonesome, you want company; she's available or she's there—you know. But looking at it from the standpoint of the guy that's in town all the time and that's been lovin' this girl for years and years—that was basically the reason for that lyric. The lyric was an experience rather than a revelation."

Imagining a distinctive variation of the sound pioneered by Ray Charles and Sam Cooke, Mayfield and Eddie Thomas laid the foundation for the Impressions' success while both were working for Butler. "Being with Jerry Butler, we did two things," Thomas recounted. "Number one, we saved our money, piled it away. We lived together, stayed together, roomed together. In the morning I'd get up early, before the rest of the group. I was at radio stations, introducing myself to the DJs, promoting Jerry but at the same time promoting Eddie Thomas. I did that everywhere we went, all throughout the South, Baltimore, Washington, Detroit, Cleveland."

By 1961 Mayfield and Thomas had saved enough touring to stake the post-Butler Impressions to a second chance. Recently married to Helen Williams and awaiting the birth of his first son, Mayfield was determined to establish financial independence. "I had saved a thousand dollars and we went to New York to record," said Mayfield, now clearly established as the front man of the group. "All the fellows came together again, and we checked into this hotel in Manhattan, and I guess we were there about a week when we recorded 'Gypsy Woman.' " Meanwhile Thomas scrambled to get the group a record deal. "While Jerry's playing the Apollo, I'm getting up early in the morning going to the record companies trying to find a deal. I went to RCA—Ray Ellis threw me out. He didn't like Curtis's picture, said he looked like a rabbit with that front tooth stickin' out." Thomas's friend and Chicago soul historian Johnny Meadows agreed: "Ray Ellis passed on Curtis because of his appearance. I'm serious. They had Sam Cooke, they had Harry Belafonte, and this was the clean-cut image they were looking for." Thomas finally succeeded in convincing Clarence Avent of ABC-Paramount, which had begun making inroads into the R&B market with the signing of Ray Charles, to take a chance. "Clarence said, 'Give it a shot, what have we got to lose,'" Thomas recalled. "And I agreed, 'Yeah, give us a shot,' and I said, 'I'll tell you what. Being with Jerry Butler I know a lot of DJs across the country. I got their home phone numbers and everything. I think I can support this record. If you guys will distribute it, I can get the airplay to get it started.'"

Mayfield recognized Thomas's dedication and business acumen as the key to the group's success—Thomas would later receive the prestigious James Foster Peabody Award for lifetime contributions to the recording industry. "Eddie was such a hustler man," Mayfield said with a smile. "Everywhere we went, anything even looked like an antenna, maybe five or ten miles away, we'd come on and Eddie would hustle 'Gypsy Woman' to whoever was there." Thomas capitalized on a radio world that had not yet locked itself in to rigid formats and prefabricated playlists. "Country and western, gospel, any kind of station, didn't matter what the format was," Mayfield noted. "Eddie would pull over and take us into the station. People just appreciated you coming in and making the stop, so they'd give you a play. So that's how we began to build up 'Gypsy Woman.' Finally it broke out and began to do very well in Philadelphia."

For Thomas, this would prove to be the breakthrough moment for the Impressions and for his own career. "We had a gig at the Uptown Theater in Philadelphia. The black jocks I knew got the record started, Philadelphia just took off, Baltimore and Washington picked up. Naturally, Chicago's gonna be last. ABC called me in and asked me would I like to work for them, and they offered me a job as national promotions, they'd never had a black national promotions man. That was great, I've got a group on one hand and a national promotions job on the other hand. I can promote the Impressions to no end. So I quit my job with Jerry Butler and launched my whole career."

A vignette inspired by Mayfield's affection for Western movies, "Gypsy Woman" reestablished the reconstituted Impressions and allowed Mayfield to give up his position as Butler's sideman. While he continued to spend much of his time on the road, he set up a home base in Chicago, moving from Cabrini-Green to the South Side, where his neighbors included the Staple Singers. Noting that their families had crossed paths briefly before Mayfield moved to Cabrini, Mavis Staples described their mutual affection: "We all lived in what we called the 'dirty thirties' in Chicago, us and Sam Cooke and Lou Rawls, all of us. But we didn't really meet him until we moved down to Eighty-ninth Street when Curtis and the fellows lived in three houses in a row on Eighty-seventh Street. Then we'd see them all the time. We were like family, still are. When we got together, we'd have a good time because all of us were down-home folks." Although Brian Hyland's 1970 bubblegum cover version got more airplay on white stations and outsold the Impressions' original, "Gypsy Woman" climbed into the Top Twenty. During 1961 and 1962 the group released a series of appealing but commercially marginal records including "Grow Closer Together," "Never Let Me Go," "Little Young Lover," and "Minstrel and Queen." "They were great records, but they didn't go pop," Meadows commented. "They were hits strictly in the black community."

Mayfield is a refreshing exception to a history littered with the tragic stories of gifted craftsmen falling victim to predatory record labels and failing to profit from their own genius. His control of the rights to his songs didn't happen by accident. He described his experience as a young songwriter in the highly competitive New York scene he'd dipped into during the Impressions' hiatus. "At one time all your big publishers were around the square at 1615 Broadway," he recalled. "When you come down in the streets around that building, you'd run into young people, black, Italian, Hispanic, it didn't matter. They were all peddling their songs. If they had a decent song, they could run up to the publisher and sell it for twenty dollars. Of course, the publisher would take it lock, stock, and barrel." Even success didn't guarantee security. "Maybe they'd go up to fifty or a hundred dollars if you got a little hot streak going for yourself, but nobody ever owned nothing except those big guys who had the money. Many of those songs became great, great hits."

Having witnessed the publishing companies' predatory treatment of songwriters up close, Mayfield investigated ways of establishing control over his economic fate. "It was important to me to own as much of myself as I could. So I found out where the Library of Congress was and how to register my own publishing company. Turned out it cost nothing." Thomas concurred: "At that time we had become very aware of what was going down in music. We knew that you'd better start learning about publishing because that can go on and on. A song can be done again and again, and those royalties will be yours later on in life. We looked way down the line and saw what time it was." Beginning with the Curtom publishing company, which was named after the partners, Mayfield would establish several publishing companies over the years, including Chi-Sound (established in 1965), Camad (1968), and Mayfield Music (1975).

Meanwhile the group was paying its dues on the road. "The country was our neighborhood," Mayfield said. "We were putting on 150,000 miles a year." "It was a grind," Thomas added. "You had very few theater places where you were gonna be there a week. You had the Royal Theater in Baltimore, the Howard in Washington, the Regal in Chicago, the Fox in Detroit, the Uptown, the Apollo. Those were the only long engagements, and they gave you time to take a coffee break. But on the road you had one-nighters. You're here one night, you had to pack up and get on the road and drive to the next gig and check into the hotel. One-nighters were tough." Thomas remembered that the most enthusiastic reception came in the South. "Virginia, North Carolina, Charlotte, all those places we went through twice or more. The gospel thing was strong down there. The South was definitely our territory."

The territory could be treacherous. In the civil rights era any car with Illinois plates and black occupants provided a potential target for lawmen on the lookout for "outside agitators." Thomas described the Impressions' reception in Jackson, Mississippi: "The speed limit there was 35 miles per hour. We were headed for the hotel, a black hotel, and we were cautious, doing about 25 or 30, below the speed limit. The police stopped us and said, 'You're driving too slow. Where are you going, where are you from, what are you doing here?' They gave us a ticket for driving too slow. We went downtown to pay the ticket. Guess how much the ticket was? A dollar! I can't forget that. Just things to interrupt you, all these little petty things they'd do."

That type of harassment constantly reminded black travelers that Jim Crow remained alive and well. Federal court rulings aside, the Impressions knew better than to seek accommodations outside the black community. "During that time the white hotels had not recognized the green dollar yet," Thomas said. "They got the message later on and went crazy, but at the time if you were black, you had to stay back. So if you were in Memphis, for example, they knew we were at the Lorraine Motel, that's where Martin Luther King was assassinated. In Atlanta there were black hotels on Peachtree. Hard times, that's just the way it was." Looking back with mixed feelings on a system that withheld equality but frequently compensated by enforcing a strong sense of community, Thomas meditated on the movement's ironic impact on the black economy. "All those motels died once the white folks realized that they were losing out on millions of those dollars. That mean green has changed the whole thing. They realized how dumb they were. We fought to make them give it to us, but then we destroyed the mamas and the papas in the course of it."

Mayfield took advantage of his time on the road to hone his songwriting skills. Distancing himself from the transitory pleasures and fleeting romances available to singers who brought a touch of glamour into their audiences' lives, he concentrated on the dramas playing out inside his head: "When the fellows would go out to have fun and maybe there'd be parties after the set, they would leave all their wallets with me, and I'd sit in my room and live through my own fantasies and write." His productivity amazed his friends and attracted the attention of Chicago producers like Carl Davis, who signed him on as a staff songwriter and associate producer with Chicago's Okeh label. "Curtis and I, we knew each other for a long time," Davis recalled. "I used to go out to his house a lot of times and sit down, and Curtis would have a shopping bag full of tapes, and a lot of them were songs that he would only have 6 or 8 bars to. Because when Curtis used to get an idea he would go to a tape recorder and put the idea down. Then he would go off into something else, and he would come back to it later on. A lot of times you'd pick up a tape and play it, and you'd get off into it, and then it would stop! You'd have to go back and ask him to finish this tune or finish that tune or finish this one. So he would do it; he was very obliging about it and would go write you a complete tune."

Gerald Sims, a member of the Okeh production team, offered the definitive statement on Mayfield's importance when he said, "The Chicago sound came from basically one source—Curtis Mayfield." Johnny Meadows elaborated: "Curtis had the real versatility. He had the ability to compose, the ability to write, the ability to arrange, the backward strings on the guitar giving the unique sound, the left-handed backward strings. There was a lot going there that was unique. In addition to the creative burst of the material, it was the way he presented it and put it together, the voicing on the records. You knew the Curtis Mayfield sound when you heard it." Eddie Thomas marveled at his friend's productivity: "There was no way we could record all the stuff he wrote, so he set up with Major Lance, Gene Chandler, so many artists in Chicago had his support and help, and Curtis was the kind of person who wanted to help other people, and of course he wanted to get his songs done and recorded." Mayfield's luminous and voluminous body of work fully justifies Thomas's assessment.

Aspiring singers clamored for a chance to record his songs. The sometimes-hard-to-find CDs *Curtis Mayfield's Chicago Soul, The Class of Mayfield High,* and *Impressed!* (released only in the U.K.) document Mayfield's creative contributions and far-reaching influence. In addition to Jerry Butler, Gene Chandler, Major Lance, and the family group the Five Stairsteps—all of whom built substantial careers singing Mayfield's compositions—the list of artists who rode his music to minor stardom includes Walter Jackson, Otis Leavill, Billy Butler and the Enchanters, the Opals, the Artistics, Holly Maxwell, Marlina Mars, and Jan Bradley, whose version of "Mama Didn't Lie" ranks with the best "girl group" records. Okeh's Carl Davis remembers that Major Lance would hang around the studio, bringing him coffee and stating his case. "I must have had ten cups of coffee a day," Davis laughed. "Major would just sit there and expound on the fact that if I gave him the chance, he would make us both some money. Curtis was going to write a tune for him." When Davis gave in, Lance made good on his promise by taking the exuberant dance floor classic "The Monkey Time" and the catchy ghetto fable "Um, Um, Um, Um, Um, Um, Um" into the Top Ten. Lance amassed a greatest-hits album full of Mayfield's songs including "Delilah," "Mama Didn't Know," "Hey Little Girl," "It Ain't No Use," "Ain't It a Shame," and the soaring meditation "Sometimes I Wonder."

Mayfield's most sensitive interpreter was Gene Chandler, best known for "Duke of Earl." Chandler's ability as a soul performer shines through more clearly on Mayfield compositions "What Now?" "Think Nothing About It," "Man's Temptation," "Just Be True," and the near-forgotten soul classic "Rainbow." "Gene seemed to sing my songs in his own way, and he had such an enthusiasm for them. He was a seller of them," Mayfield said. "Whatever it was, even if the song wasn't the best, Gene just had a way of putting himself totally into a tune. He always was capable of putting his own influences, his own feeling, into a tune, but also being true to the original intention of the writer."

Mayfield's chief problem was deciding which songs to reserve for the Impressions. Whenever possible, he farmed the dilemma out to his friends. "You would have to be careful with Curtis," Davis groaned. "Because if Curtis came up with six tunes and he'd play them, you'd say, 'That's the one I want!' He'd say, 'Oh, that's the one I'm cutting on the Impressions.' So what I would do is let him play all the tunes he had available, and then I'd ask him which songs were available to me. You had to learn to work around Curtis." It was a lesson well worth learning.

Mayfield's intimates sometimes wondered what would have happened if he'd had the creative and commercial support of a savvy company like Motown. "I loved Smokey Robinson, but Curtis was the greatest songwriter I've known," Thomas said. "If Curtis had been in Detroit, it would have been unbelievable, because they had so much power over the DJs. They'd just say, 'We're gonna play this Marvin Gaye, we're not gonna play the Curtis Mayfield.' Motown really had a stranglehold on it." Stressing that he didn't intend his comments as criticism of Motown, Davis contrasted Motown's methods with the Chicago-soul approach: "Motown used to put a picture frame together, paint in all the background, and then they would take the artist and put him in the picture. They would make a complete record, record it in a certain key that they thought would fit the song. Then the singer had to come in and sing the song. Our approach was to take each artist, paint the background in, and then put the frame around to fit the subject." For his part, Mayfield insisted that his relationship with Motown "wasn't really a rivalry. Those guys were just so much admired and they were so big there was no need. The best I could do was learn something from them. Berry Gordy, Smokey Robinson, they had fantastic writers over there, and all you could do was admire those folks for the contributions they made to America."

Like Berry Gordy, Mayfield "wanted to keep as much of the pie as possible." Thomas summed up their strategy, which resonated with the freedom movement's goals of economic equality and uplift: "You always hear, 'You gotta pay your dues.' It's true enough, but if you're not careful, you pay your whole life out in dues." Mayfield could see down the road in ways that many talented young artists could not. "Come the end or the middle of the road, you're only left a shell, and the publisher owns part of you, the record company owns all your masters, and you are the owner of a faded dream of fame," Mayfield reflected. "What does fame mean without a little fortune? I saw those things early in my life, and I have always advised people, whatever field, whatever business, the bottom line is to own as much of yourself as possible."

◈

ARETHA FRANKLIN'S QUEST FOR MUSICAL and economic independence bogged down almost as soon as it began. At first the outlook seemed promising. She arrived on the popular-music scene heralded as the spiritual and aesthetic daughter of Billie Holiday and Bessie Smith. Moving to New York City in early 1960 with the express purpose of taking the music world by storm, she quickly attracted the attention of John Hammond, who over the course of a half century in the music business discovered a list of stars ranging from Holiday and Count Basie to Bruce Springsteen and Bob Dylan. More important, as far as Aretha and her father were concerned, Hammond had played a central role in the history of black female vocalists. Over a four-day period in November 1933 he had supervised the final recording session of Bessie Smith and the first session of Billie Holiday. Before signing with Hammond, Aretha and her father had spurned overtures from Sam Cooke, who wanted Aretha to join him at RCA, and Motown, which they still thought of as an upstart local label. "Daddy and I had our sights set on something bigger," Aretha recalled, explaining their choice of Hammond, which they believed would stake Aretha's place in a great tradition that included Ella Fitzgerald and Dinah Washington as well as Bessie and Billie. It was a heavy burden for an eighteen-year-old to bear.

While Hammond clearly recognized Aretha's power and potential, his feel for the gospel world she had grown up in was limited. Overlooking the fact that Aretha's mentors included some of the most accomplished musicians from the worlds of R&B and jazz, not to mention the finest gospel singers imaginable, Hammond referred to her as an "untutored genius." It's tempting to speculate on the musical history of the alternate universes in which Aretha signed with Motown or Sam Cooke. With the possible exception of the Four Tops' Levi Stubbs, no Motown vocalist possessed Aretha's raw power. Backed by the driving rhythm of Motown's Funk Brothers rather than by the soft jazz combos Hammond preferred, Aretha might well have found her voice sooner than she did. In turn, she could have helped Motown bring its gospel roots a bit closer to the surface. And it's impossible to imagine a better mentor than Cooke, who knew exactly what it took to move back and forth between the upscale Copacabana Club and the chitlin circuit.

Speculation aside, the deal with Columbia was precisely what C.L. Franklin envisioned when he assented to his daughter's desire to move from gospel to pop. Believing that "one should make his own life and take care of his own business," Reverend Franklin helped Aretha weather the initial disapproval of the more staid members of the New Bethel congregation over her move away from traditional gospel. As he told African American journalist Phyl Garland after the release of "I Never Loved a Man (The Way I Love You)" and "Respect," "At first there was a quiet and subdued resentment, but now they acclaim her in loud terms." Aretha attributed her father's unstinting support to his certainty that, while she might record secular material, "I'd never *really* leave the church."

Aretha did leave Detroit, setting out for New York in search of secular stardom. Leaving baby Clarence in Detroit under the watchful eye of her grandmother, Big Mama, Aretha stayed first at the Thirty-eighth Street YWCA, followed by brief stints at the Bryant Hotel on Fifty-fourth and Broadway, the Chelsea Hotel, and a small hotel off Washington Square in Greenwich Village. In this haven for bohemians she took pleasure in the "artistic ambience" and savored the local diner's fried perch, which reminded her of Mahalia's down-home cooking. During the summer of 1960 she took dance lessons from Cholly Atkins, who also schooled Motown's budding stars, and enlisted New York pro Leora Carter as a voice coach for the auditions that would introduce her to the world of entertainment.

Arriving in New York from his travels on the gospel highway, Reverend Franklin took Aretha to meet Phil Moore, a choreographer and arranger with a reputation for packaging artists for major labels. After the audition Moore told C.L., "Reverend, your daughter doesn't need big choreography. She doesn't need to be fluffed up or polished over with New York sophistication. I wouldn't tamper with what she has naturally. Just let her do her thing, and she'll be fine." Jo King, a longtime record business insider who became Aretha's first manager, agreed. When Aretha auditioned at her apartment, King remembered, "she did everything wrong, but it came out right. She had something, a concept of her own about music that needed no gimmickry." Aretha's sense of herself came through clearly when King took her to study movement with a high-fashion model, who told her, "When you walk you should feel like you're floating." "Fine," Aretha responded, "but I'd rather walk than float."

To King, her quiet teenage client seemed "a desperately unhappy child." Gradually, however, she realized that Aretha's childlike bearing masked a complicated inner life that would express itself in her music. "For the first three months I thought I had an eighteen-year-old girl who had never left home before. And then it burst like a bubble. I realized I had a real woman here, one who knew more than I did when it came to men, alcohol, and everything. She had tremendous depth."

That depth began to express itself on the demo record Aretha made showcasing the songs of African American songwriter Curtis Lewis. King took Aretha's demos of four songs, including "Today I Sing the Blues," to Hammond in hopes of selling Lewis's compositions. Hammond's response has passed down into music-business lore: "I was distracted by the singer. Her name was Aretha Franklin, and even at first hearing, on a poorly made demo intended to sell songs rather than the singer, she was the most dynamic voice I'd encountered since Billie." Unaware that Aretha had already released a gospel album, *Songs of Faith,* Hammond approached her as a new talent. He immediately contacted King, who invited him to hear Aretha rehearse. "I went to the studio," Hammond recounted, "heard Aretha sing, and was convinced she would be a star. I knew exactly how I wanted to record her, keeping as much of the gospel feeling in her voice as possible, while using material which would attract jazz fans."

In retrospect, knowing how she would rise to R&B stardom, many have assumed that Columbia forced Aretha into a mold that didn't suit her talents. Reflecting on her repertoire of torch songs, jazz standards, show tunes, and soft blues, music historian Anthony Heilbut dismisses her work with Columbia as a misguided attempt "to wed Barbra Streisand with Clara Ward." Comparing Aretha's renditions of "Over the Rainbow" or "Bill Bailey Won't You Please Come Home" with "I Never Loved a Man" or

"Spirit in the Dark" makes it easy to regard her early work as a dilution of "black" music with "white" aesthetics, an upscale equivalent of Pat Boone's Boy Scout botching of Little Richard's "Tutti Frutti." The real story is a good deal more complicated.

In fact, Aretha's early records were oriented toward a crossover strategy that echoed the civil rights movement's commitment to desegregating American society. Aware that most American money flowed through white fingers and stayed in white hands, some black musicians of the fifties and early sixties tried to package themselves as sepia Sinatras or ebony Garlands. Setting out to garner their share of the riches waiting in Las Vegas and at upscale nightclubs like New York's Copacabana, entertainers like Sammy Davis Jr. and Nat King Cole envisioned a world where they could bask in the bright lights and cash the fat checks lining the Great White Way.

Aretha's repertory can be seen as a calculated attempt to win mainstream approval. But it also reflected her own taste. "I suppose you could say my early style was a combination of blues, gospel-based jazz, and rhythm and blues," she reflected. "I've always liked standards, so singing songs like 'Rock-a-bye Your Baby with a Dixie Melody' and 'How Deep Is the Ocean?' came naturally to me." When later asked to name her favorite secular singers, Aretha provided a list that ranged from Ella Fitzgerald, Sarah Vaughan, and Lena Horne through Nina Simone, Betty Carter, and Peggy Lee to pop crooners Rosemary Clooney and Doris Day. There's no reason to suspect her of irony. Among her African American contemporaries, she singled out Broadway sensation Leslie Uggams and Nancy Wilson as singers who had opened "major doors" and left "the buyers and promoters with the unmistakable impression that the African American chanteuse was responsible, qualified, and fabulous."

Given her eclectic embrace of American pop, it's not surprising that Aretha accepted Hammond's vision of her career without reservation. After signing Aretha to a five-year deal, Hammond's first move was to hire Ray Bryant, a jazz pianist with gospel roots, to serve as her musical director. Bryant, who had had a surprise R&B hit with "The Madison Time," recalled his first encounter with Aretha. "One night John called me," Bryant recalled. "It was pretty late at night, maybe nine or ten o'clock, and he said, 'Could you please come down to the Vanguard?' I said, 'Why?' and he said, 'Well, I signed this young girl singer from Detroit. We'd like for you to come down and meet her.' There were lots of people there, like a big party. Everybody just got up and did something. I played a little bit, she sang, and it was just sort of a welcome-to–New York party for Aretha. She was a very nice young lady—sort of shy. But when I heard her sing, I said, 'This girl can *sing!*' "

Entering Columbia's New York studios on August 1, 1960, with Aretha, Bryant, and a combo including bassist Bill Lee, the father of director Spike Lee, Hammond recorded what he'd later describe as one of his three or four favorite sessions. Supplemented by material recorded at two later sessions, those tracks provided the material for Aretha's first pop album, *The Great Aretha Franklin*, which was released in October. The record garnered critical praise and earned Aretha recognition from *Downbeat* magazine as the "New Female Star of the Year." The reception from the leading jazz magazine was welcome but intimated the difficulty Hammond and Aretha would have in realizing their plan to make a mark in what she called the "jukebox market." The first single, "Today I Sing the Blues," reached the R&B Top Ten. She edged onto the lower reaches of the pop charts with the follow-up, "Won't Be Long." A minor gem that hints at what might have resulted if Columbia had allowed Hammond more time to pursue his vision, "Won't Be Long" rings with the movement's forward-moving pulse and foreshadows gospel rockers like "Think" and "Rock Steady." Pushing the rhythm forward with a series of insistent piano runs, Aretha's voice transforms a pop ditty about a woman waiting for her man at the railroad station into a demand for change. "Hurry hurry hurry," she calls out, slipping out the back door of the studio and heading for the nearest church. She brings the song home with an urgent challenge that resonates with the energy of the sit-ins and the freedom rides. "I don't know about you, but I know, when the whistle blows, that it won't be long. It won't be long." Despite positive reviews and a strong response from the relatively small coterie of jazz aficionados, the album failed to crack the pop charts.

Hammond's second album with Aretha, *The Electrifying Aretha Franklin*, failed to substantially increase her audience, although it did yield her biggest Columbia hit, "Rock-a-bye Your Baby with a Dixie Melody." Only Aretha's unsweetened vocals keep the song from crossing the line into minstrelsy. While sentimental white listeners might have initially responded to the familiar melody and stereotypical lyrics, Aretha's bluesy tones under-

cut the nostalgia and, no doubt, limited its commercial appeal. Not surprisingly, black DJs and listeners preferred the flip side, "Operation
Heartbreak," a steamy cut worthy of Ruth Brown or LaVern Baker, which
gave Aretha her third R&B Top Ten hit. R&B hits did not, however, much
interest Columbia. In mid-1962 the label relieved Hammond of his production duties and assigned Aretha to Robert Mersey, who'd been working with
Andy Williams and would later produce Barbra Streisand's first number-
one album, *People*.

The change reflected the growing antipathy between Hammond and
Aretha's new husband, Ted White. A handsome man who'd entered into
Detroit's music scene as the owner of a chain of jukeboxes, White met Aretha
during one of her visits home during 1961. Sharing Aretha's March 25 birthday but eleven years older, White had been introduced to his future wife by
singer Della Reese at Detroit's Twenty Grand Club, a two-story extravaganza
subdivided into several plushly carpeted clubs and a twenty-two-lane bowling alley. Six months later the couple married in a ceremony conducted by
Aretha's father at New Bethel Baptist. Soon White took over as Aretha's manager, a source of constant irritation to everyone at Columbia. "I came in and
kind of upset the apple cart," White recalled, "by not wanting John Hammond
to produce another one of those Al Jolson–type albums." Declining this invitation to a mud fight, Hammond offered a different explanation: "I think I
made some very good records with Aretha at Columbia. I wanted to keep her
to a degree as a jazz singer, but Columbia wanted to make a big pop star out
of her, which I thought would ruin her integrity."

Despite his criticism of Hammond for pandering to white tastes, little
separated White's agenda from the one Columbia was already pursuing.
"Aretha was so multi-talented, we didn't want to get her bottlenecked into
one particular idiom at that time," White mused. "We thought she was
broad enough to attract people from all audiences. We wanted a little of the
jazz, a little of the pop, and a little of the so-called rock and roll. And we
just touched on all bases." The problems with the three Mersey-produced
albums—*The Tender, the Moving, the Swinging Aretha Franklin; Laughing on
the Outside;* and *Unforgettable—A Tribute to Dinah Washington*—is precisely
that they touch all the bases but never quite bring it home. The first features Aretha's tender but rarely swinging renditions of "Try a Little
Tenderness," a big hit in 1933 for bandleader Ted Lewis that had already

been covered by Bing Crosby and Frank Sinatra; Billie Holiday's signature song, "God Bless the Child"; and a deeply moving version of the meditative blues standard "Trouble in Mind." *Laughing on the Outside* consisted entirely of soft Streisand-esque ballads including Irving Berlin's "Say It Isn't So," Duke Ellington's "Solitude," and a version of "If Ever I Should Leave You" from the musical *Camelot,* which Jerry Wexler praised as "just superb, like the way Ella Fitzgerald would do Gershwin."

The material seemed perfectly suited to White's strategy of moving Aretha from the chitlin circuit to Caesar's Palace. That was the theory. The reality glittered less brightly. Even before White took control, Aretha's bookings reflected Columbia's uncertainty over her direction. Long engagements with jazz pianists like Horace Silver and Les McCann punctuated R&B tours headlined by Jackie Wilson and old friend Sam Cooke. During the first half of the sixties Aretha would share bills with everyone from Miles Davis and Patti LaBelle to Cannonball Adderley and James Brown, who appeared with her at the Shrine Auditorium in Los Angeles on a show that also included salsa legend Tito Puente. Despite Aretha's discomfort, "she could really sing from the first," Brown remembered. "At that time she had hit with 'Rock-a-bye Your Baby with a Dixie Melody.' We became close after that show. What I liked about her right away was how smart she was: you could tell just by talking to her once."

Musically, Aretha was happy to have a place in the jazz scene of the early sixties, which had moved away from bebop abstraction and was consciously reaching out to listeners more at home with gospel and the blues. "Jazz was going through a soul period, rediscovering its funky and churchy roots," Franklin recalled. "I was part of that mix. I'm talking about monster musicians like Freddie Hubbard and Blue Mitchell and Junior Mance. I was privileged to play dates at such a young age with the immortal John Coltrane. I observed Charles Mingus slap one of his pianists on stage.... Audiences accepted me on bills with Art Blakey and the Jazz Messengers." But she still wasn't really part of the new jazz movement, either in substance or in style.

Uprooted from audiences familiar with the intense vocal and emotional exchanges at the core of the gospel vision, Aretha "was afraid," she admitted. "I sang to the floor a lot. I did what I had to do." John Wilson, who played piano with the Ward Singers, described Aretha's 1962 appearance at the Showboat Club in Philadelphia. "After checking in at the hotel over the club," Wilson said, "she took a cab over to Mom Ward's house to get connected to familiar souls." When the Ward entourage arrived at the club to offer its support, "we heard that wonderful voice and saw that it was being wasted on an almost empty house. Aretha's face lit up with gratefulness when she saw Clara. On her intermission, Aretha's eyes welled up with tears as she said, 'These people don't want to hear me, I still sound like I'm in church.'" Clara replied encouragingly, "Well, Aretha, if you can't sing before these few, you'll never sing before thousands. You keep playing and singing like you're doing, and one day this place won't be able to hold the people. You just hang in there—you've got everything it takes to go to the top. You'll have them hanging on to every word, every note."

Sometimes Aretha must have felt like her blues would never end. Although she steadfastly refused to air her differences with her husband in public, Ted White found few defenders and no defense. Family friends reported repeated clashes between White and Aretha's father; one longtime intimate was quoted as saying, "They don't respect each other much." Teddy Harris, a member of Aretha's road band, told *Vanity Fair* that White was "kind of abusive," a charge Clyde Otis, who replaced Mersey as her producer in mid-1964, amplified angrily: "Ted beat her down unmercifully. This is a woman who is so insecure. She knows that she can sing well, but she's been so stepped upon and put upon by people who were close to her. She's never been able to stand up and say, 'This is what I will do, and this is why I want to do it.'"

Once Otis entered the picture, White's differences with Columbia escalated into open warfare. Frustrated with Aretha's lack of success on the charts, the label made the decision to release her when her contract expired. But it hedged its bets and charged Otis with the unenviable task of recording as much material as possible in the shortest possible time. "It was a catch-22 situation. Columbia didn't want her to go, but they could not reverse themselves and help her become a star. So they said to me, 'Well, look—cut as much stuff on her as you can,' because they felt that they might lose her—and in fact they did lose her. The way they talked about it was, 'Look, we've only got one more year left on her contract, and we'd like to have as much product on her in the can as possible.'" Otis cut five albums' worth of material in less than a year, complaining all the while that White's presence intimidated Aretha. "She refused to really blast," Otis grumbled. "He'd come in, and if she wanted to have a little bit of fun by cutting loose, he'd look at her, and that was it." Whatever his problems with White, Otis furnished no solutions for Aretha. Witness the inappropriately titled *Soul Sister* album, a hodgepodge of southern nostalgia ("Ol' Man River," "Swanee") and contemporary soul (Ashford and Simpson's "Cry Like a Baby," Van McCoy's "Sweet Bitter Love"). The disaster was topped off by Otis's own composition "Take a Look," a heavily orchestrated compendium of condescending clichés and sanctimonious moralizing. It was a long way from "There Is a Fountain Filled with Blood."

Predictably, none of the albums released during Aretha's final years with Columbia—*Runnin' Out of Fools, Yeah!!,* and *Soul Sister*—made much of a showing on the charts. "It seems like they won't really let me be me," a depressed Aretha told her old friend Smokey Robinson. "I've got so much music stored up inside me, Smoke, I can't hardly stand it." White blamed Aretha's failure to cross over on the label's penny-pinching approach. Columbia provided "very little money and very little outside support. In fact, I remember the first time we went to L.A. to work. I had to go down to Compton, in some very out-of-the-way record stores, to buy old Aretha albums and singles." The public relations people at Columbia, White believed, "weren't overly concerned. If you got a hit— great! If you didn't, then, 'We'll see you later.' " As a result, he contended, it was impossible to develop the type of show that would land his wife in Vegas: "Her earnings wouldn't have made it possible to take along the musicians who could back her up and show off her talents in the best way. Even in this country, you have to work for practically nothing if you don't have a hit."

Aretha's best chance for a breakthrough, a booking to sing her 1963 single "Skylark" on *The Ed Sullivan Show,* turned into a debacle. She prepared for her spot by having Cholly Atkins choreograph a new routine and purchasing a special gown. Things began to go wrong, Aretha recalled, during rehearsal. As she prepared to sing, "a voice from up in the booth said, 'We don't like the cut of the gown—change it.' " On the night of the show, a juggling act ran over its allotted time, and Aretha's slot was canceled. She was devastated.

Worse yet, in less than a year Aretha was confronted with the deaths of both Dinah Washington and Sam Cooke. Teddy Harris was playing piano with Aretha's band at Pasqual's Carousel in Atlanta when news broke of

Cooke's senseless shooting death at a tawdry motel in South Central Los Angeles. Cooke had gone to the motel with a woman who was later identified as a prostitute. When she absconded with his clothes, an angry Cooke, suspecting he'd been set up, stormed into the motel office. The motel clerk, who'd been told by the police after a string of robberies to shoot first and ask questions later, gunned Cooke down. "Aretha went berserk," Harris recounted. "After all the customers and employees had gone home from the club, she made all of the musicians in her group stay with her there, and she played Sam Cooke's music on the piano for hours. And she drank, too, with us."

While Aretha was less involved personally with Dinah Washington than she was with Sam Cooke, she responded deeply to her childhood idol's fatal overdose of pills and liquor. The heartfelt tribute album *Unforgettable* pays tribute to Washington's many-faceted talent. Aretha's performances of the tormented blues "Drinking Again" and "Nobody Knows the Way I Feel This Morning" support Clyde Otis's observation that "Aretha ached in the same way Dinah did." The ache reaches searing intensity on "This Bitter Earth." Tapping the emotional depths where memories of her mother and the stony roads of the gospel highway merged with her frustrations over her floundering marriage and career, Aretha walks the razor edge of despair before voicing the hard-won hope that maybe the earth she walks "isn't so bitter after all." *Unforgettable*, the only one of Aretha's Columbia albums since the debut to stand up as a whole, has attracted admirers including Bette Midler, who credits it with shaping her style: "It was like I had no idea what music was all about until I heard her sing. It opened up the whole world."

By the time *Unforgettable* was released in March 1964, Aretha was simply, in White's phrase, "waiting it out." Thinking back on the end of her time with Columbia, Aretha remembered a poignant moment that occurred when Columbia flew her to Puerto Rico to perform at an industry convention. "There was another young artist they'd signed," she recalled. "The guy had all these way-out lyrics, you know, like 'A hard rain's gonna fall' and all of that. We both had to be there. Anyhow, I was feeling pretty scared and down. And I remember looking out my hotel window at midnight. And there was this other artist out on the beach, just walking up and down, up and down alone. It was Bob Dylan. And I thought, 'My, he must be havin' a ball, and here I am miserable.' Believe me," she concluded, recognizing the irony of her misreading of Dylan's moment on the windy beach, "neither of us knew where we were headed then."

To no one's surprise or dismay, Columbia cut Aretha loose when her contract expired in 1966. Industry reports claimed that the label had lost $90,000 on her over six years. Songwriter Jerry Leiber articulated the general consensus when he sympathetically dismissed her Columbia work as a case of "upward mobility. We all do it." But Jerry Wexler, who would soon help guide her in a new and more profitable direction, provided a fairer assessment: "A lot of people missed the great licks she did at Columbia. It's become traditional to say, 'Well, Atlantic is where she really broke out.' But people are negating some of the beautiful things she did on Columbia—some of the ballads, some of the show tunes." Aretha agreed. "On Columbia I cut a lot of good stuff, and I feel that I gained an audience there," she said. "But I was having what is commonly known in the business, at Columbia, as 'turntable hits.' I was getting a lot of play, but not a lot of sales, and I think that was largely due to the kind of material I was doing. I was being classified as a jazz singer, and I never, ever felt I was a jazz singer. I can sing jazz, but that was not my format to begin with. I think the move from Columbia to Atlantic was about commercial success." Soul aficionado David Nathan, the editor of England's *Blues & Soul* magazine, defends Aretha's achievements at Columbia, calling *Aretha* a masterpiece and citing *Yeah!!* and *Runnin' Out of Fools* as "road maps for gospel-based vocalists singing secular material." John Hammond's judgment strikes nearer the truth: "I cherish the records we made together, but, finally, Columbia was a white company who misunderstood her genius."

IF ARETHA HAD LAUNCHED HER CAREER at black-owned Motown, the classic Atlantic recordings might never have happened—she might have had no reason to leave. For thirteen-year-old Stevie Wonder, at least, life at Motown couldn't have been much better. Since signing a contract in 1961 when he was eleven, he'd become the first artist to top the charts simultaneously with a single, "Fingertips, Part 2," and the album from which it came. He'd found a dedicated and sympathetic tutor and been adopted by the best soul band in the world, Motown's inimitable Funk

Brothers. Best of all, he'd become Motown's unofficial company mascot, the pampered darling of a bevy of solicitous big sisters, including most of Motown's leading female stars.

The chorus of adoring voices included Velvelette Bertha Barbee McNeal, who beamed, "He was like our little sweetheart, being younger. He would run around the studio. Being the baby of all of us, he was just pampered. I mean, we loved him to death. He knew everybody, and he'd come up to you and feel your whole face. That's how he knew, even before you said anything, who you were." Supreme Mary Wilson smiled over his antics. "Everyone loved him, and that was a good thing because he was full of mischief. Stevie seemed to always know who was standing near him, and one of his favorite pastimes was to run up and pinch young ladies on their bottoms. He would also tell one of us exactly what we were wearing—what color it was, and how it was styled. Some of us would act amazed, or at least feign amazement; of course, he was in cahoots with somebody. We all loved him."

Soul singer Mable John, the sister of ill-starred R&B great Little Willie John, observed that Stevie was not above taking advantage of his "disability": "When Stevie Wonder came there, being a little boy running up and down the stairs, bumping into folks—he was doing it on purpose, I think, 'cause he loved to play blind, and he could really find his way around. But he just loved getting your goat." By the time he'd been around Motown for a few years, Wonder's herd included dozens of goats, among them Motown songwriter Janie Bradford, who believed that Wonder "got around better than I did. I remember he came in my office one day, and I had a jar of pennies. I would take all my pennies and save them for my son. Stevie came in, and he took my pennies and ran! Ran out of the building—he was outside in the yard before I could catch him. And then when I took the pennies, he said, 'You gonna take a poor little blind boy's pennies?' He was always full of the devil." No wonder he cherished warm memories of his teenage years at Motown.

It's probably impossible to disentangle myth from reality concerning the chain of events that brought the talented ghetto boy under Motown's wing. If everyone who claims to have been present at the audition, which took place on the stoop in front of the Motown building, had actually been there, they would have had to move the event to Tiger Stadium. Ronnie

White of the Miracles credits his brother Gerald with setting things in motion. "I was just a victim of my family," he laughed, saying that his brother kept pestering him to come listen to one of his friends. "I kept putting it off. For some reason I never found the time to go over there. Until one day I had nothing much to do and remembered the favor I had promised my brother to do for a long time. When I went over to this house, Stevie was there with a guy who played guitar." Much to the amusement of Ronnie and fellow Miracle Pete Moore, who accompanied him to the impromptu audition, Stevie greeted them by announcing, "I can sing better than Smokey."

Amused and impressed with Stevie's rendition of "Lonely Boy," White set up a meeting with Brian Holland, a third of the Holland-Dozier-Holland team that wrote most of the hits that lifted the Supremes and the Four Tops to superstardom, including "Where Did Our Love Go?" and "(Sugar Pie Honey Bunch) I Can't Help Myself." Versions of what happened next differ slightly. Mary Wilson recalled that the Supremes were about to leave the studio when Gordy told them to stick around: "I think his mother was with him, and a couple of brothers. He's just a typical ten-year-old, comes running in." After hearing him play conga, drums, and organ, Wilson wrote, Gordy announced regally, "You are signed." Stevie's own report on the audition probably merges details from other early visits: "People were just walking around relatively casually. There were some people working on songs in different rooms, and I was taken into the main studio, Studio A, and I started playing the piano and singing. Somebody started playing drums, and I said, 'Oh, can I play those drums?' So I started playing drums."

Holland tells a more mundane version of what happened: "First of all let me tell you one thing: all the stuff that you hear about it is crazy. You know, like Stevie coming into Motown and everybody running for him and offering him milkshakes on golden trays. It was nothing like that. We sat on a curb on the sidewalk of Woodward Boulevard, and he was playing his harmonica and singing. And it was after that that Stevie met Berry Gordy, who then of course wanted to sign him at once." Gordy remembered that it was Motown producer Mickey Stevenson who burst in on him, crying out, "You got to come hear this little kid *now!*" "His voice didn't knock me out," Gordy said, "but his harmonica playing did. Something about him was infectious." While some credit Gordy himself with coming up with the "Little Stevie Wonder" nickname, others say that the suggestion came from Berry's sister Esther.

Whatever the details, Motown did offer the young musician a contract. At first Lula refused to sign. She was afraid that having a child in show business would disrupt a family life that, for the first time, was beginning to settle into a comfortable routine. And she didn't trust any record company to handle her son's finances. When she told Stevie of her decision, he embarked on a resistance campaign that consisted of beating on his drum every moment of the waking day. The incessant pounding finally broke his mother's resistance, and she agreed to sign. The result was a contract that provided an allowance for Stevie—it began at $2.50 a week—and payments to Lula for clothing and upkeep. The extra income was a blessing for the Hardaway family, who were struggling to make ends meet in the East Side ghetto. Other than stipulating that the underage performer could not appear in nightclubs, the contract was typical of the deals signed by other Motown performers.

In the early days, most of the singers who signed with Motown agree, the excitement and magic of what they were doing compensated for the fact that few of them were making much money. As the years have passed, several Motown veterans have grumbled that while they made Gordy rich, he didn't really return the favor. Wonder's first contract exemplifies the problem. When at age twenty-one he exercised his right to nullify the contracts signed for him when he was a minor, Wonder hired an auditing firm to examine Motown's books. While the audit uncovered no irregularities in the bookkeeping, the settlement amounted to just one million dollars, underlining how much of an upper hand standard industry practices gave to the company.

For the time being, though, Wonder was happy just to spend time at the magical building Gordy had dubbed "Hitsville, U.S.A." The young musician charmed Diana Ross and Martha Reeves, who was then working as a secretary. Describing Stevie as "hyper, bright, and brimming with talent," Smokey Robinson remembered him "leaping around the studio like a frog, beating the drums, blowing the harmonica, eating up sounds like they were candy." Although Clarence Paul laughingly referred to Wonder as a "pest" and Motown press kits reported that he had sometimes broken in on recording sessions because he couldn't see the red light above the door,

Brian Holland painted a more realistic picture. "His mother brought him into the studio. She always brought him. He'd never come by himself. She also was staying with him most of the time, and then someone else would come and pick them both up. When you saw Stevie, you saw his mother around. All the time. She would not take anything for granted and just leave him alone."

Motown's staff and stars gave Lula plenty of help. "I was very fortunate to meet a family like the Gordy family, like Motown," Wonder later beamed. "Everyone over eleven was a parent. Clarence Paul loved me like his own son. He was like a father, like a brother and a friend. Esther Edwards, Berry Gordy's sister, all the musicians and artists watched over me. Wanda Young of the Marvelettes would always tell me when she thought I was eating too much candy." Martha Reeves made it clear that "I was *not* Little Stevie Wonder's baby-sitter," but she lavished special attention on him, and he eagerly returned her affection. Clarence Paul traced Stevie's ability to move onstage to Reeves's attentions: "The way she taught that kid to dance was just a smash. Martha would stand behind the little one, take his arms, and while explaining the moves in words, she would simultaneously do them with him. It was just like his body had become hers or the other way around. He just adored Martha, and she felt more like a sister toward him than a teacher."

When Stevie needed a place to stay while waiting for a ride home, he'd frequently go to the house Reeves shared with her mother. "He knew and loved my family just like he's a member, because we took him in," Reeves said. "It's not like he was a little blind kid. Stevie was active! Stevie would beat everybody up; he was taller than most of them. They'd tear my mama's house up." One of his favorite pastimes was concocting musical skits and recording them on Reeves's tape recorder. She particularly enjoyed the monologues he delivered while doodling on the Hammond organ. "He'd play those silly chords and talk over them, make up dumb stories."

For the first time in his life, he had access to as many musical instruments as he wanted. "It was like a music store with all kinds of toys," he told an interviewer in the sixties, before adding another story to the legend of Stevie Wonder, mischief-maker. "Me and my friend, after a couple of days we kept going down there, and we went in the basement and stole some tapes. This is something Motown probably never knew I did, but it's cool now. I stole—

it must have been a two-track of 'Shop Around' by the Miracles. I kept it—I think we tore it up or something. But they were asking me, 'Steve, have you seen it? Somebody stole a tape. Where's the tape?' And I just never did say anything about it. 'Cause I thought I'd lose my contract."

Everyone who spent any time around Little Stevie testifies to his winning, if sometimes trying, sense of humor. One of his best-remembered stunts hinged on his finely honed ability as a mimic. He was particularly adept at imitating Gordy's voice. "He'd call my secretary and say, 'Send Stevie Wonder a check for half a million dollars right away. He needs the money right away,'" Gordy recounted. "So my secretary says, 'Wait a minute, boss. Just like that?' 'Yes, just like that, and do it right away.' She says, 'Have you lost your mind?' He says, 'No, Stevie's my friend, Stevie's a fine young man, just give him a check. He'll be in there shortly.' I don't think he got any checks, but who knows?" While he might not have gotten any six-figure checks, Stevie claimed that his mimicry resulted indirectly in his acquisition of a new tape recorder. "I'd call up and say, 'This is Berry, and I want you to get Stevie that tape recorder right away. He's a great new artist so it's okay to spend the money and buy it for him. I'm sure he'll get it back to us in a few days,'" Wonder reminisced. "After they fell for this stunt about three times and never got the tape recorder back, they gave me my first recorder as a belated birthday present."

Long before he engaged in a hilariously unforgettable tennis game on his 1983 appearance as host of *Saturday Night Live*, he had developed a set of comic routines that hinged on his blindness. Gordy recalled Wonder's delight in amazing attractive girls by praising their clothes or the color of their eyes (information that had been provided to him by his numerous partners in comedy). Aware of the routine, Gordy decided to strike back one day when Stevie greeted him by complimenting his attire: "I like that suit, Mr. Gordy. And that's a great tie, isn't it?" Deciding to take control, Gordy responded, "I'm not wearing a tie. I took it off just before I came into the studio." When Stevie came back with "Well, if you are wearing a tie, can I have it?" Gordy sighed in exasperation, "Okay, Stevie, who told you?" Taking mock offense, Stevie carried point, set, and match with the rejoinder, "What, am I blind?" Nor was Wonder above exploiting such gambits in the service of his growing interest in the opposite sex. On several occasions Wonder asked to feel a young woman's face, only to "accidentally" touch her breasts. After he apologized to the victim, Gordy remembered, Wonder would turn and smile "as if to say, 'Eat your heart out, fellas.'"

Like other eleven-year-olds, the young prankster spent part of each day attending to the more mundane demands of his schoolwork. Before Stevie came to Motown, his educational experiences had been less than encouraging. "I remember a teacher telling me that I should go on and make sure I studied very hard, because the only thing that I could probably do was tune pianos—no, I'm serious—or make baskets or potholders or rugs," he reported. "And this lady was being sincere. She didn't mean no harm by what she was saying. Being black and blind, that was all that was supposed to happen. They must have had visions of me being a hawker, peddling with shoelace and pencils or haunting some street corner with a Seeing-Eye dog begging for money or at the best sitting in some busy place playing the harmonica and holding a hat for alms."

Shortly after Wonder began appearing in public, the Detroit Board of Education raised a new set of concerns. Informing Lula and the company that the school system could not be expected to accommodate Stevie's travel schedule, the board announced that he would no longer be allowed to perform. The young musician was devastated. "I cried and cried and prayed for a long time," he admitted. Desperate, his mother placed a newspaper ad seeking suggestions on how Stevie could continue his education and still go on the road. The solution arrived via Helen Trauby, a teacher specializing in blind children, who introduced the family to Dr. Robert Thompson of the Michigan School for the Blind in Lansing. Together they worked out an acceptable response to the board's concerns.

The cornerstone of the plan was Ted Hull, who assumed the role of Stevie's tutor in September 1963. A kind, caring man devoted to nurturing his sole student's mind and character, Hull oversaw Stevie's day-to-day activities and managed his allowance. "The company, working through a booking agent, would consult with me and set up a tour," Hull recalled. "Then it was my job to provide Stevie's educational needs as coordinated through the School for the Blind. I established an allowance with Stevie, and I worked it out with his parents so he didn't develop champagne tastes at too early an age. He seems to appreciate it now, but he didn't appreciate it at the time." Being on the road placed heavy demands on Hull. "I was exhausted most of the time," he admitted. "Stevie held out extremely well, and I always recognized that he was holding down two full-time jobs, one as a student, one as an entertainer. I don't think he realized it. We wouldn't start school until about ten o'clock in the morning, but I would get up at six A.M. usually to prepare for school—to get a head start on the kid. Then we would have school for three and a half or four hours, and then it would be the entertainment business until maybe twelve or one o'clock in the evening. So I was absolutely exhausted." Stevie wasn't above taking advantage of the situation. Mary Wilson of the Supremes praised Hull as a "kind, studious young man" but added that "he could never bring himself to awaken the poor exhausted child. Stevie got away with murder."

In the long run Hull's efforts paid off. Stevie ultimately earned his diploma from the Michigan School for the Blind while developing the curiosity and knowledge he would later express in his songs. His favorite subject was history, and his favorite writers, Hull remembered, were Ernest Hemingway and James Baldwin, whose works he read in Braille. During the time he spent in residence in Lansing, Stevie participated in activities like choir and wrestling. Hull summed up his experience saying, "I think the nicest compliment I could pay Stevie, as a student, is that he was normal, a normal student."

While Wonder dutifully fulfilled Hull's requirements, he eagerly embraced the education he was receiving in the Motown studios. There he benefited from the attention of several members of Motown's Funk Brothers, the nonpareil house band that laid down the music tracks for almost every hit by the Four Tops, Supremes, Temptations, Smokey Robinson and the Miracles, Marvin Gaye, Martha and the Vandellas, and Mary Wells. Shortly after Wonder signed, Mickey Stevenson called pianist Earl Van Dyke, drummer Benny Benjamin, and James Jamerson—possibly the greatest electric-bass player who ever lived—into his office and told them management would appreciate it if they would work with Stevie. As Brian Holland remembered, Wonder's winning personality made their task an easy one: "Stevie made friends with every musician he met in the studio, and they would take the time actually to show him the elementary techniques he had to know about the various instruments. Sometimes they would even teach him more difficult things to do."

Stevie felt especially close to Benjamin, whom he called "Papa Zita." In an interview with *Rolling Stone* in the early seventies, Wonder celebrated

Benjamin as "one of the major forces in the Motown sound. He could play drums. You wouldn't even need a bass, that's how bad he was. Just listen to all the Motown hits, 'My World Is Empty' and 'This Old Heart of Mine' and 'Don't Mess with Bill.' On 'Girl's Alright with Me,' the drums would just pop!" At the same time Wonder acknowledged the personality quirks that sometimes drove the Motown staff to the verge of distraction. "Benny'd be late for sessions, Benny'd be drunk sometimes," Stevie said. "I mean, he was a beautiful cat, but Benny would come up with these stories like 'Man, you'd never believe it, but like a goddam *elephant*, man, in the middle of the road, stopped me from comin' to the session, so that's why I'm late, baby, so it's cool.' "

Even if they were sometimes erratic, playing with geniuses helped the boy wonder grow. Remembering that Motown recorded "hundreds and hundreds" of sides with Little Stevie, most of which remain unreleased, Brian Holland emphasizes that the publicity heralding him as a young genius wasn't entirely hype. "It was just amazing to watch him," Holland said. "That little one singing and doing such a great job. Every instrument that he found lying around in the studio, he would pick up and start playing it. He was so easy to work with, he could catch on so quickly—very, very quickly. His ear was fantastic. One day I came into the studio, and he sat at the drums. Just practicing, playing them over and over again. And it didn't take him long to get good at them either. The same with the piano. Whatever he did, Stevie always improved very fast."

It was equally clear to Gordy and Clarence Paul, the former gospel singer who supervised Wonder's career during its early stages, that their protégé possessed an unusual talent. As Smokey Robinson wrote in his autobiography, "It didn't take long for people to dub Stevie 'Baby Ray' 'cause he was like a little Ray Charles." By the early sixties Charles enjoyed universal acclaim as a musical wizard equally at ease with sanctified R&B, crossover pop, deep blues, and funky innovative jazz. Charles's surprise hit album *Modern Sounds in Country and Western* had even made him a star in a world where few African Americans felt at home. Backed up by a purely fictional Motown public relations campaign hinting that Charles was blood father to the "young genius," Wonder's first two albums—*Tribute to Uncle Ray* and *The Jazz Soul of Little Stevie Wonder*—present him as a miniature version of Charles. While no singer deserved to be asked to go toe to toe with Ray

Charles, *Tribute to Uncle Ray* includes creditable versions of "Hallelujah I Love Her So," "The Masquerade," and "Drown in My Own Tears."

Supported by Benjamin, Jamerson, Van Dyke, and Beans Bowles, Wonder showcased his formidable instrumental talents on *The Jazz Soul of Little Stevie Wonder.* He was already a skilled percussionist and pianist, but his first love was the harmonica. His approach to the instrument provided an early indication of the love of jazz he would later celebrate on "Sir Duke." "I think a harmonica for a long time was not really considered an instrument, but it's really like a small sax," he reflected later. "There's so much you can do with it. I try to play it with a sax or a certain feeling. It's another color of music. You can express the way you feel. You can get a vocal quality, it depends on how you play it." For days before the release of his debut albums, Stevie practiced signing his name. After presenting Gordy with an autographed copy, Wonder announced proudly, "This is the very best signature I have ever seen."

Wonder's first two albums failed to chart, as did his first three singles, "I Call It Pretty Music (But the Old People Call It the Blues)," "Waterboy," and "Contract on Love." But even as the label struggled to find the right studio sound, Wonder was beginning to blossom as a live performer. What he lacked in polish, he made up for in enthusiasm and intensity. "The first time I began to feel I was exciting to people, I threw my glasses out into the audience," Wonder recalled. "I used to have a bow tie on. I threw that out. It was so exciting that I wanted to get them to do it again, so the next night I tried it again, and it was still exciting."

Performing alongside the Miracles, the Supremes, and Motown's other top stars, Wonder participated in the landmark Motown Revue tours that began in 1962. The initial tour was a memorable marathon of ninety-four one-nighters at venues including the Howard Theater in Washington, D.C., the Franklin Theater in Boston, the Raleigh City Auditorium, and the Bamboo Club in Savannah, Georgia, capped by a week-long engagement at Harlem's Apollo, where the troupe performed six shows a day beginning at noon and ending at one A.M. To make things worse, Otis Williams of the Temptations groaned, "Motown's buses were in notoriously bad shape." Several tour participants have singled out Little Stevie's presence as a blessing of a particularly mixed variety. In his autobiography Williams wrote, "The one guy everybody loved was Stevie Wonder. Stevie liked to make people laugh and had an impish charm. Usually he sat at the back of the bus with the musicians and played his harmonica for hours. Everyone understood that he was wood-shedding, but only to a point. When it got to be about two or three in the morning, someone would yell, 'Stevie, man, put that damn harmonica down and go to sleep.' If that didn't work, we tried, 'Stevie, we're going to beat your ass if you don't take that harmonica...' and he'd laugh, because he knew we'd never do that. Not that the thought didn't cross our minds now and then."

As the Motown Revue set off for the South, it was entering a rapidly changing and potentially explosive political situation. Following the lull of the late fifties, the freedom movement had again taken the offensive, inspired by the sit-ins that spread rapidly from Greenville to Nashville and then to cities throughout the South. While the new Student Nonviolent Coordinating Committee took inspiration from the words of Martin Luther King, it based its campaigns more directly on a version of the gospel vision developed by Ella Baker, a brilliant organizer who had left the NAACP in despair over the "pulpit mentality" of the leaders. Declaring that "strong people don't need strong leaders," Baker set about organizing the young organizers.

Many on the front lines of the sit-in movement shared student organizer Diane Nash's deeply Christian belief in the transformative power of love. One of the most stirring moral triumphs of the movement occurred when, taking the lessons she had learned in her philosophy classes seriously, Nash challenged Nashville mayor Ben West to live up to his professed beliefs. A moderate on racial issues, West initially responded to the sit-ins that were paralyzing downtown Nashville by decrying violence against the protesters but claiming he was powerless to tell businessmen how to conduct their affairs. When West attempted to placate a group of students, asking them to pray together as good Christians, a Fisk student shouted, "What about eating together?" When West issued a general statement on the immorality of discrimination, Nash confronted him point-blank: "Do you mean that to include lunch counters?" When Nash refused to accept an equivocal answer, West paused and responded quietly, "Yes." Headlines trumpeted a victory for the movement, and within a month downtown shop owners agreed to the movement's central demands.

Even as they applauded the triumph of agapic love, however, few movement organizers or foot soldiers deluded themselves about the realities of violence. Even the leaders committed to nonviolence, whether out of principle or simply as a useful strategy, knew that their opposition was heavily armed and largely unhindered by moral compunctions. The cornerstone of the movement lay not only in Gandhian nonviolence but in traditions of armed self-defense that stretched back to Reconstruction. Most leaders, including King, kept guns in their houses. Colonel Stone Johnson, the black labor organizer who served as bodyguard for Birmingham movement leader Reverend Fred Shuttlesworth, provided the perfect summation of the grim blues humor embedded in the situation. When asked how, given his commitment to nonviolence, he managed to protect Reverend Shuttlesworth, Johnson reflected with a wry smile, "With my nonviolent .38 police special."

The potential violence that surrounded the movement at every moment exploded into sobering reality during the Freedom Rides. Setting out from Washington, D.C., on May 4, 1961, a group of seven blacks and six whites sponsored by the Congress on Racial Equality (CORE) headed south determined to desegregate interstate bus travel. When their bus entered the Deep South, the Freedom Riders refused to follow the rules relegating blacks to the back of the bus. Taunts, threats, and blows met them at the bus stations in small towns where, as historian Taylor Branch observes, "the Supreme Court and Gandhi were rarely discussed." Outside Anniston, Alabama, fifty carloads of Ku Klux Klansmen overtook one bus, forcing it off the highway. As the Freedom Riders scrambled for their lives, the assailants set the bus ablaze. Reboarding a replacement bus, the Riders rolled on to Birmingham, where a howling mob swarmed around them with iron bars, lead pipes, and brass knuckles. Most of the original Freedom Riders were unable to continue. Loath to back down in the face of violence, Diane Nash intervened, organizing a new round of Freedom Rides that helped overturn Jim Crow in interstate travel.

The images of flaming buses and raging mobs imprinted themselves in the minds of the Motown stars as they embarked on their marathon journey the following year. As a group of northern blacks traveling by bus, they ran real risks; Martha Reeves worried that they would be mistaken for Freedom Riders. Her fears were not unfounded. Early on during the southern leg of the tour the Revue bus pulled up to a roadside gas station so riders could use the restroom. The group was greeted by a man holding a double-barreled shotgun, who growled, "Don't you niggers step one foot off that bus, or I'll blow your asses to kingdom come." Shortly thereafter, Wonder recalled, "down in Alabama somebody shot a gun at the bus and just missed the gas tank." Wonder also remembered another stop where Motown management team member Gene Shelby confronted a promoter about a Confederate flag hanging above the stage. " 'Our big star Marvin Gaye ain't gonna like that flag,' Shelby said, to which the promoter responded, 'Hey, boy, see the way that flag's blowin' in the breeze? If you don't get your tail out of here, your tail's gonna be up in a tree blowin' just like that flag.' "

Ted Hull, who was usually the only white aboard the bus, received a crash course in the Jim Crow blues. Hull described his feelings about what they encountered in Memphis: "Holy smoke, that was really humiliating. We would have to go in the back entrance of restaurants and eat in the kitchen and go to hotels that had booked us, and you know, when they find they've got black people coming in, suddenly they can't find your reservations. I was generally the only white man on the bus, so I had to do what I could to make it work, but I didn't have a lot of experience. If you didn't laugh at it, you couldn't endure it."

A wonderfully symbolic moment occurred when the Revue reached Louisville. As the bus pulled into the parking lot at the motel, it was greeted by a young boxer still known by the name of Cassius Clay. Fresh from his victory over Archie Moore, Clay entertained the entertainers with his quick wit and winning personality. "He and Little Stevie Wonder remained alone and talking on the bus, long after we had gone in," Martha Reeves recalled. "We finally had to go and get Stevie so that he might dress and make his show time." For Wonder, Muhammad Ali would become a symbol of the encompassing demand for respect and dignity. "So many of us have to demand respect," Wonder told an interviewer when Ali was allowed to return to the ring after being exiled for his stand against the war in Vietnam. "Do you know how much noise he had to make before he was respected? It's ridiculous, it's absurd. At his age—and he is old in the fighting world—he had to prove himself. Those are the things which hurt—me, you. And that is where freedom begins. You have to seize that for yourself and then demand that kind of freedom for others."

For the most part, however, Wonder remembered the Motown Revue tours as times of self-discovery and adventure. The normal seating arrangements on the bus had tour musicians sitting in the back in a section informally dubbed "Harlem" while Gordy and the stars rode up front in "Broadway." Stevie started out "sitting unhappily in the middle," noted a Revue veteran, but inevitably drifted back to Harlem. Especially on the second and third tours, Stevie eagerly soaked in the aura of sexual adventure that accompanied the Revue. Despite the presence of company-hired chaperones, the attractive young men and women found ways of circumventing the strict rules against hanky-panky. Dismissing legends that present Motown singers as "young, bright-eyed people—waiting for Berry Gordy to come along and discover us and make us famous," Betty LaVette countered: "It really was not like that at all. None of these people were young or bright-eyed. They were never young almost. All these people were grown by the time Motown started. They weren't virgins, and they had all been drunk at one point. I don't know anybody that came over there with a smidgin of innocence but Stevie Wonder. And we soon corrupted him."

Not that Wonder resisted. Junior Walker, whose gutbucket saxophone on "Shotgun" represented the "blackest" pole of the Motown spectrum, smiled at his young friend's frustration over curfews: "I was on a lot of the Motown tours with Stevie. We used to joke around all the time.... I would always joke with Stevie when I'd be going out at night. I'd come by his room and knock on the door, and he'd open the door, and I'd say, 'I seen a little chick out there dug you.' He said, 'You get her and bring her back to the room.' I said, 'Yeah, okay, Stevie.'" Although Wonder never confirmed the story, there's a certain believability in a Revue band member's report that one night the denizens of "Harlem" decided to initiate the young star into the mysteries of sex. "Stevie comes by and says, 'You're having a party, ain't you? Sounds like a lot of pretty girls in here ... Man, I need one.'" The band got Hull out of the way and paid the fee. "They were gone about an hour, and she came back and said, 'Wow.' About a half hour later Stevie's knocking on my door again. 'You going to do that for me again?' Band member answered, 'I ain't paying for your pussy. You're making more money than I am. You pay for it.'" It was probably just as well that Hull still had "Little" Stevie on an allowance of less than ten dollars a week.

Wonder's most important moment on the tour came at Chicago's Regal Theater, where he recorded the song that established his reputation— "Fingertips, Part 2." The feelings of exuberance and uncontrolled energy that make the record something special are real. By the time the Revue rolled into the Windy City, "Fingertips" had emerged as the highlight of Stevie's set. "When Stevie got to 'Fingertips,' the closing tune, people jumped up and down, clapped their hands, and stomped their feet," Brian Holland reported. "They just went wild. The atmosphere was pure electricity, that's how great Stevie was.... At the end, it seemed, they were more exhausted by all the hand-clapping stuff they did than Stevie was."

The Regal performance surprised even those familiar with Stevie's ability to electrify the crowd. That night Stevie had just finished his set when he felt the spirit and ran back out onstage. The band had already begun to change personnel for the next act. "It was never planned," Wonder recalled. "Mary Wells was next on the bill, and it was time for her to go on, so what happened is that her bass player Larry Moses was getting situated and he came out, and we were going into another encore thing. Larry didn't know what to do. He was standing with his bass in his hand, and he said, 'What key? What key?' He said a few other things, but I guess they didn't get it on tape 'cause he said a few bad words, too."

"Fingertips, Part 2" represented a breakthrough not only for Wonder but also for Motown as a whole. It was the label's second number-one song (the first was the Marvelettes' "Please Mr. Postman"), and *Little Stevie Wonder/The 12 Year Old Genius* was Motown's first chart-topping LP. Loosely based on Jackie Wilson's "Baby Workout," the follow-up single, a call-and-response rave-up that crackled with an incoherent gospel energy, "Workout, Stevie, Workout," peaked at number thirty-three. Motown took advantage of "Fingertips" to book Little Stevie onto most of the important pop music television shows, including *American Bandstand, Where the Action Is,* and the variety shows hosted by Mike Douglas and Tom Jones. During his 1963 tour of England, he performed on the British TV showcases *Ready! Steady! Go!* and *Thank Your Lucky Stars.*

Stardom was not an unmixed blessing, especially for Stevie's family members, who continued to live in the East Side ghetto. The problem stemmed from the fact that, as Wonder observed, "whenever an artist had a record in the Top Ten, people automatically assume that he's got plenty of cash. That isn't necessarily so." Stevie's friend Lee Garrett elaborated: "It was neither easy for Stevie nor for his parents or sisters that he was a star. Like, some people in the neighborhood got really nasty. They envied Stevie and his family so much that they would try anything to make them unhappy. Especially the young ones, Larry, Timothy, and Renee, who were then twelve, ten, and four years old, had to suffer from neighbors' hate. They did not have a chance to grow up like other kids. They either found themselves surrounded by children who wanted to get to Stevie through them, or they would have vicious neighbors or even their kids say really terrible things to them. And believe me," Garrett continued, "it did get to him. He wished so much that he could do something about it. But he knew that for the time being his hands were tied and the only thing he could do was to set his aims high, so that one day he would really have enough money to get his family out of all this hassle and away from those people who hurt their feelings." In 1964 Gordy arranged to have the entire family move into a comfortable home in a newly integrated neighborhood on Detroit's Northwest Side.

On the road Wonder enjoyed a more relaxed relationship with the black community. During a visit to Los Angeles, Wonder, Ted Hull, and Stevie's hostess Elaine Jesmer wandered into the heart of Watts. "We pulled up at 103rd Street and we just let him out," Jesmer recollected. "He just stood there and people started coming over. Stevie was like a magnet. People would go up to him and they would touch him and he would touch them back. They didn't talk a lot, it was more like 'Oh my God, this is really Stevie Wonder.' The feeling from them to him and the other way round was just like magic. I remember one little boy who was walking around the street corner and when he saw Stevie he stopped dead. He just looked at Stevie and his mouth fell open and his eyes got really big and then he looked at me and he wanted to say something but he couldn't. And I just nodded my head. That very second the boy turned around and took off. But then, about five minutes later he came back and he must have brought about twenty-five other kids with him—all between twelve and fourteen years old. And they were all over Stevie. It was an incredible scene. Everybody wanted to touch Stevie or take his hand."

Stevie's adoring fans, many of them his own age, deluged him with fan mail and recorded messages. "You would not believe how much love the kids put into their tapes." Clarence Paul smiled. "Black or white—it didn't make no difference at all. They just loved Stevie and they also admired him for the courage that he had." Lee Garrett said Wonder took special pleasure in messages from disabled children who were inspired by his example. "It wasn't necessarily anything that had to do with music but all sorts of stuff. Like a guy who had spent years and years in a wheelchair after an accident and through Stevie had found the will power to want to learn to walk again. Or a young girl who was born with crippled arms but had begun now to learn to write and even paint with her feet."

While Wonder's charisma was obvious, Motown failed to follow up on "Fingertips." Although Motown executives staunchly deny that the label ever considered releasing Wonder, his career quickly reached a clear impasse. Berry Gordy was upset at the failure to follow up on the breakthrough hit. "We hadn't taken advantage of it," Gordy recalled. "That was a no-no for our company. As far as I was concerned, that was a sin. As hard as it is to establish an act, once you do, once you open that door, you just have to march right through. With Stevie we hadn't, and now it seemed we couldn't."

Casting about for the right way to develop their young star, Motown released two more albums—*With a Song in My Heart* and *Stevie at the Beach.* The first resembled something Clyde Otis might have cooked up for Aretha. Wonder's biographer John Swenson rightly dismissed the amalgamation of supper-club chestnuts and middle-of-the-road standards as "Stevie at the dentist's office." Compared with the concept behind *Stevie at the Beach,* however, having him record "When You Wish Upon a Star," "Put On a Happy Face," and "The Sunny Side of the Street" might not have been such a bad idea. Motown's doomed attempt to reach out to the teenybopper crowd by arranging cameo appearances in *Bikini Beach* and *Muscle Beach Party* deserves a special exhibit in the Museum of Bad Ideas. To be fair, some of the music on *Stevie at the Beach,* notably his soulful harmonica playing on "Beyond the Sea," "Ebb Tide," and "Red Sails in the Sunset," isn't bad. But the tepid commercial reception of the singles "Castles in the Sand," "Hey Harmonica Man" (a gospel-goes-to-the-beach disaster), and "High Heel Sneakers" (a live cut recorded in Paris with French musicians) did nothing to soothe Gordy's fears.

Those fears were exacerbated by worries that, as Stevie moved from childhood to adolescence, his voice would change for the worse. Fortunately, Gordy observed, "that young, undeveloped high-pitched sound that I hadn't loved when I first met him turned into a controlled, powerful, versatile instrument." And despite the absence of a hit single, live audiences never stopped responding enthusiastically to his stage show. On New Year's Eve

1964 Stevie, who had jettisoned the "Little" back in July, received an over-whelming reception when he replaced the Supremes, who were taping an appearance on *The Ed Sullivan Show*, at Motown's annual Detroit gala. Aware that "he had become wildly popular with the audience," Gordy decided to see whether a new support team would be able to translate the fire into record sales.

After considering several alternatives, Motown assigned him to the songwriter/producers Henry Cosby and Sylvia Moy, who would collabo-rate on the hits that reignited his career, "Uptight (Everything's Alright)" and "I Was Made to Love Her." According to Moy, Mickey Robinson, the head of Motown's A&R department, held regular meetings at which "they would go through the list of artists and give assignments to the various pro-ducers. In 1965 no one wanted Stevie." Clarence Paul confirmed Moy's memory: "I had exclusive production on Stevie, but we were cold. I didn't have no hits. I couldn't think of nothing, and he couldn't think of nothing." Stevie embraced the new arrangement eagerly. He'd been writing songs for as long as he could remember, but as he entered his midteens, he was "becoming more and more myself. I would get ideas for tunes and spend a lot of time just making my music, messing around with a tape recorder and experimenting. There were a lot of things that I wanted to do musically that I wasn't doing."

Moy and Cosby had no problem letting Stevie set the creative course. As Cosby said, "We kind of clicked. Sometimes we'd come up with the idea. And then sometimes we'd come up with the music first, 'cause Stevie's full of tunes. Oh man, he's got tunes. The stuff he would throw away, another producer would go crazy to get." Wonder was delighted to be in a situation that encouraged him to explore his overflowing imagination. "What would happen," Wonder explained, "is Henry Cosby would do some writing with us, he would come up with a chord pattern for my melody, then maybe he'd help Sylvia Moy with the lyrics to the tune. Sylvia did a lot of writing on the early things. I would come up with the basic idea, maybe a punch line, and she would write the story. I would give her a tape of it. I write so many tunes in bits that I really don't get the time to finish them all up, so I just give 'em to somebody to do." Still serving as Wonder's musical director on the road, Paul savored his young friend's revitalization: "That music wanted out. He'd be making up those tunes all the time. He just sang whatever came straight from his head. And boy, did we dig it. It was like kind of a parlor game. We'd fall about laughing like we were crazy. But then that was a kind of brainstorming, if you know what I mean. Something always came out of the 'sessions' we did."

Like "Fingertips, Part 2," the song that resurrected Wonder's career came about almost accidentally. Moy recalled sitting down with Wonder to consider the future: "I had a bag of songs at the time, but I told Stevie, 'I want you to play everything, all of the little ditties you have, play them for me.' He went through everything. He said, 'That's all I have,' and I thought I was going to have to start working from my bag. I asked him, 'Are you sure you don't have anything else?' He said, 'No, not really, although I have got this one thing.' He started singing and playing 'Everything is alright, uptight,' and that was as much as he had. I said, 'That's it. Let's work with that.' "

When they finished working and released the record in December 1965, "Uptight" exploded with a funky, exuberant expression of the gospel vision. Paying Stevie's debt to Ray Charles in full, the song's celebration of redemptive love rang out in a stirring call and response with the chorus of voices that was transforming the American soundscape. The Beatles, whose early albums included covers of Motown hits "Money," "You Really Got a Hold on Me," and "Please Mister Postman," had demonstrated they were much more than a passing pop fad with "Ticket to Ride," "Help!", and "Yesterday." But in 1965 the Supremes were matching the Fab Four hit for hit, and the Temptations had finally broken out of the R&B ghetto with "My Girl" and "Get Ready"; Sam Cooke's haunting response to Bob Dylan, "A Change Is Gonna Come," mournfully testified to what might have been, while Dylan himself threw down the gauntlet to the folk-revival poets and his own past by plugging in his guitar and ripping out the "Subterranean Homesick Blues." On "Satisfaction," the Rolling Stones combined their roots in Chicago blues and Memphis R&B with a fierce existential anger.

Wonder loved it all and said he'd based "Uptight" in part on "Satisfaction." As Mick Jagger and Keith Richards had done, Wonder placed an insistent rhythmic figure at the center of his summertime classic. But the contrast between the Stones' declaration of disaffection and Wonder's hosanna to the power of love speaks to the central importance of the gospel vision in African American culture. Most white rockers set themselves up in defiant opposition to the stifling worlds where they'd grown up. Wonder never gave a thought to rejecting his elders and ancestors. Backed by James Jamerson's pulsing bass and Benny Benjamin's thunderous drums, Wonder joyously declares himself a poor man's son from the wrong side of the tracks. The tattered shirt on his back may be the only one he owns, but none of that matters as long as his love stays true. In a single line Wonder crystallizes the philosophy of the movement at its best: "No one is better than I, I know I'm just an average guy." That's "average" in a sense that Walt Whitman, bard of democracy and singer of his common extraordinary self, would have understood perfectly. Everything's gonna be all right, Wonder assures his people. The affirming chorus of *woos* as the song fades out bears witness to the undying determination of the people who were shifting the center of the movement from the dusty backroads of the Delta to the concrete jungles of Newark, Watts, and the Motor City.

IN THE MID-SIXTIES, as the civil rights movement mantra "Freedom Now!" began to give way to uncompromising demands for "Black Power," Curtis Mayfield reminded anyone within range of his gentle voice that calls for black autonomy and militant action were nothing new. If you're looking for a three-word summation of what the gospel vision had to say, it's hard to do better than "Keep On Pushing." That's why more than one veteran of the struggle has called the Impressions' music "the soundtrack of the movement," a title Mayfield appreciated but declined. "Somehow I've been getting a lot of credit for being the one who more or less laid the soundtrack for civil rights," he said two years before his death. "I don't know who even gave me that title. It's not totally true, but I'm honored that some of my music could lock in with what was happening." A central part of Mayfield's ongoing soul sermon, "Keep On Pushing" infused the movement with the sounds Mayfield remembered from his grandmother's Traveling Souls Spiritualist Church. "Gospel was your foundation," he reflected, "and there's been many a song coming from the black church. All you had to do was just change some few lyrics. With 'Keep On Pushing,' all I needed to do was change 'God gave me strength, and it don't make sense not to keep on pushing' to 'I've got my strength, and it don't make sense.' I've got my strength. Nothing else needed to be changed."

No one fighting the good fight in Mississippi or Alabama or Chicago had any doubt what Mayfield was talking about in "Keep On Pushing" or "People Get Ready." When he urged his people to "get ready for the train to Jordan," he tapped in to the same energy that had powered the Underground Railroad's sweet chariot. "I've Been Trying" and "You Must Believe Me" were vivid reminders of what tied the different strands of the movement together: love, the determination not to give in, a profound sense of connection, and the belief that somehow things would work out. That was why stalwart civil rights organizers Guy and Candie Carawan ended their songbook, *Sing for Freedom*, with the Chicago movement's versions of Mayfield's "Meeting Over Yonder," "Keep On Pushing," "Never Too Much Love," and "People Get Ready." Mayfield spoke equally clearly to proponents of Black Power. Overflowing with the joy of self-acceptance, "I'm So Proud" quietly affirmed the Black Power movement's slogan "Black Is Beautiful." In an essay demanding that black artists commit themselves to an explicitly revolutionary agenda, Black Power guru Amiri Baraka acknowledged that Mayfield's songs "provided a core of legitimate social feeling though mainly metaphorical and allegorical."

Mayfield hadn't set out to compose musical manifestos. In the early sixties, he was primarily concerned with stabilizing his career. Attempting to follow up on the success of "Gypsy Woman," the Impressions released a series of singles, all of them recorded in New York, all of which failed to chart: "Minstrel and Queen," "Never Let Me Go," "Sad, Sad Girl and Boy," "I'm the One Who Loves You," and "Grow Closer Together." Providing a taste of the sweet soul of Mayfield's mature work, the last two deserved a better commercial fate. Frustrated with the lack of popular success, founding members Richard and Arthur Brooks left the group in 1962, leaving a trio consisting of Mayfield, Sam Gooden, and Fred Cash. The new format fit Mayfield's needs perfectly. Returning to their original recording base in Chicago, the Impressions recorded the first of their movement classics, "It's All Right." Mayfield's friend and music historian Johnny Meadows provided a perfect description of the group's classic sound. "You've got this background with Sam and Fred, high voices and happy trumpets, every instrument used elaborately in addition to Curtis's left-handed guitar," Meadows said. "It was the happy horns over the rhythms on 'Amen' and 'It's All Right.' It was a very bright happy sound." Okeh's Carl Davis pinned down the appeal that guaranteed the Impressions' R&B success even when the crossover audience stayed away: "I always felt we were a little bit of the South and a little bit of the North combined." Eddie Thomas hit the next point hard: "And *lots* of gospel."

The gospel elements shone through in part because of arranger Johnny Pate, one of the unsung heroes of Chicago soul. Mayfield fully appreciated Pate's contributions: "He was a musician's musician. He wrote great blues from way back, was an upright bass player, and an arranger. That was my first introduction to arranging; everything prior to that, we'd just try to nail the rhythm and get it through. But Johnny gave me my first encounter with real arranging, and along with Riley Hampton, who I used on the first *Curtis* album, he was the love of my life as far as real arrangers go." After Mayfield provided the melody and chord changes, Carl Davis recalled, Pate would take over: "I would sit there and would say I wanted such and such beat. Basically I was following Curtis's lead on his guitar. I wouldn't write it; I would play back the song as written and then we would take the guitar parts and turn them into various instruments—this might be horns, that might be something else. You gave Pate the basics and let him do it." No song showcases Pate's arranging brilliance better than "Amen," which had originally been sung by Sidney Poitier in *Lilies of the Field*. Featuring a majestic horn introduction, Pate organizes the song around a series of call-and-response patterns, between individual voices and harmonizing group, between horn section and vocal lines. When Mayfield calls out "Keep On Pushing" as the song begins to fade, Pate's arrangement offers a clear "Amen."

Complementing the call-and-response arrangements, the Impressions' vocal style set Chicago soul apart from the sounds coming out of Motown or Memphis. Describing the switch-off singing that made the new three-man Impressions' sound so distinctive, Mayfield reflected on the style's origins. "There was nothing original about it if you ever sang gospel," he said. "In gospel, you knew how to sing lead and also how to incorporate yourself into the group, how to blend in. Sometimes everyone would come out and sing harmony with a portion of the lead. It made us [as] a three-man group stronger than we were as a five-man group. It locks everybody in; you really know where the voices are. When you have four or five men, if one moves up, the other doesn't know where to go."

The elements of the style first assumed their classic form on "It's All Right." Built on a deep gospel foundation, "It's All Right" radiates with the love and reassurance that held the movement together even when it seemed like nothing was working out right. Mayfield credited Fred Cash with the inspiration for the song. "We were in Nashville, Tennessee, at a gig; we'd already done the first set, and we had about an hour before the second," Mayfield recounted. "It was a nice warm night, and we went out front of the club and were sitting in our station wagon—myself, Fred, and Samuel Gooden. I got to talking and running off at the mouth and just dreaming about ideas and things that might happen to us in the future. Fred kept answering back to me, 'Well, all right, well, that's all right,' you know. Before I knew it, it rang in my head. We had a real hook line, 'It's All Right,' so I said, 'Say it's all right.' Before we knew it, we had actually written two-thirds of that tune right there in the car! We could have gone onstage for the next show and sung it." "It's All Right" demonstrated both the group's crossover appeal and its special connection with black audiences, reaching number four on the pop charts and giving them their first R&B number one. The follow-ups, "Talking About My Baby" and "I'm So Proud," reached the Top Fifteen on both charts. The romantic glow of the Impressions' break-through hits reflected the change in Mayfield's personal life. Following his breakup with his first wife, he began a long-term relationship with his future wife Altheida Sims, the mother of six of his ten children. He was proud, happy, and looking ahead.

If the singles mapped a clear path, the group's first albums reflect an uncertainty about creative direction and marketing strategy that would continue throughout their years with ABC-Paramount. Released in 1963 to capitalize on the success of "It's All Right," their self-titled debut album collects their singles from "Gypsy Woman" up to "I'm So Proud." *The Never-Ending Impressions,* released in early 1964, suggests that the Impressions, like the Sam Cooke who could release the uninspired *Live at the Copa* at the same time he was writing soul classics like "Bring It On Home to Me," aspired to the Las Vegas lounge circuit. "I'm So Proud" strikes a discordant note in a set that includes Duke Ellington's "Satin Doll," Kurt Weill's "September Song," and a cover of the Trini Lopez hit "Lemon Tree."

The next two albums, *Keep On Pushing* (August 1964) and *People Get Ready* (March 1965), became Chicago-soul classics. Like Motown, Mayfield was primarily concerned with hit singles at the time, but he was delighted with the records' success on the album chart, where they reached numbers eight and twenty-three respectively. Inexplicably, ABC-Paramount followed up in September 1965 by releasing *One by One*, another doomed lunge for the Vegas market. Introduced by a trumpet fanfare worthy of an Academy Awards gala, the album opens with a remake of the Platters' "Twilight Time" and lurches through a set of Tony Bennett, Bobby Darin, and Nat King Cole covers that would have bored Dean Martin's dullest fans. As long as the Impressions stayed with ABC-Paramount, the problem with mediocre material would remain. *The Fabulous Impressions* (1967) and *We're a Winner* (1968) serve up a confusing combination of current singles, songs from Mayfield's back catalog, many of which had been recorded by other Chicago artists, and supper-club fare like "Up, Up and Away." An uncharitable, if insightful, observer might well have wondered whether Mayfield was merely playing out the string waiting for the ABC contract to expire.

Keep On Pushing and *People Get Ready* had established that Mayfield was capable of making albums that were more than showcases for hit singles. Together those two albums sum up the state of Chicago soul at the fateful moment when the movement was plotting its campaign in the city Martin Luther King called "the Birmingham of the North." Setting up a chorus of responses to the calls of the title cuts, both albums explore the emotions that ebbed and flowed with the movement's breakthroughs and setbacks. Each album side opens with a popular hit—"Keep On Pushing" and "Amen" on the first, "Woman's Got Soul" and "People Get Ready" on the second. But what makes them memorable albums is the way the songs echo and comment on one another in ways that erased the line between personal and political concerns. Listeners were free to respond to the romantic lyrics in their own terms, but they could also hear them as masked commentaries on the relationship between black and white America. Mayfield's plea for "some kind of answer" in "Sometimes I Wonder" and his weary vow to "keep on trying" in "I've Been Trying" echoed the feelings of black integrationists frustrated by their untrustworthy white allies. Similarly, "Woman's Got Soul" made sense as a message from the ghetto to the black elite. Casting himself as a regular fellow who "don't need much," Mayfield issued a gentle corrective to his compatriots who had trouble distinguishing between superficial "class" and real soul.

It wasn't necessary to hear the songs as political allegories to feel their political impact. Aware that the meaning of songs came as much from the audience's response as from the artist's call, Mayfield addressed the feelings that flowed through the souls of the movement's foot soldiers as they went about the mundane details of everyday life between marches and rallies. Echoing "It's All Right," "Get Up and Move," "We're in Love," and "Talking About My Baby" affirmed that as long as you kept faith with the gospel vision, it was all right to let the good times roll. But he also spoke to the doubt and despair that could destroy the movement as surely as they could rip apart a romance. "I Made a Mistake" acknowledges that it's not enough to point your finger at someone else when things go wrong. Comes a time, Mayfield sings sadly, when all you can do is come correct and do your best not to keep on making the same mistake. Looking at a similar situation from a different angle, "You Must Believe Me" warns against the doubters and liars and urges those who have fallen away to come back to the fold. It was as if Mayfield had found a way to bring the feel of his grandmother's church into a pop format. Like the members of the congregation, each song tells a personal story and commands interest on its own. But just as the individual voices combined into something more powerful at Traveling Souls Spiritualist Church, the strength of the albums comes from the way the songs coalesce into a portrait of a community that is both determined to move ahead and aware that the journey will not be easy.

Mayfield's reminder that it *was* a shared story resonated deeply in his hometown, where the intractable resistance to the movement was bearing out the wisdom of Bayard Rustin's warning to King. When King first told Rustin of his plans, the movement elder responded sharply: "You don't know what Chicago is like. You're going to get wiped out." Although King declared a face-saving victory in August 1966, the words of Hosea Williams, who had been rebuffed in efforts to establish neighborhood voter registration centers, provided a grimly fitting epitaph for the Chicago movement: "They wouldn't even give us what we got in Birmingham."

King's difficulties began almost immediately. Mayor Richard Daley met the movement with soft words and Machiavellian maneuvers. Welcoming King to Chicago, he solemnly intoned, "All of us are trying to eliminate slums." But as Adam Cohen and Elizabeth Taylor report in their magnificent *American Pharaoh: Mayor Richard J. Daley, His Battle for Chicago and the Nation,* the movement severely underestimated Daley's ability to divide and conquer. The Southern Christian Leadership Conference (SCLC) had not anticipated "the opposition it would face from significant parts of the black community," Cohen and Taylor write. "Chicago was the first city that we ever went to as members of the SCLC staff where the black ministers and black politicians told us to go back where we came from," recalled SCLC staff member Dorothy Tillman. "Dr. King would frequently say to me, 'You ain't never seen no Negroes like this, have you, Dorothy?' I would reply, 'No, Reverend.' He said, 'Boy if we could crack these Chicago Negroes we can crack anything.' "

They couldn't. Supported by the black political submachine, Daley simply employed the machine's standard tactics. If a minister offered anything more than rhetorical support to the Chicago movement, the city would dispatch inspectors with the power to condemn church property. If a businessman backed King, city permits or garbage collection would become a problem for him. Faced with a choice between supporting King and accepting grants to continue their programs, most neighborhood activists took the money. When the Chicago movement announced plans for mass marches targeting open housing, Daley got a court order restricting it to one march a day with no more than five hundred participants. At the height of tension in Selma, the Alabama courts had denied Governor George Wallace's request for a similar injunction. As Cohen and Taylor observe, "The streets of Alabama, it turned out, were freer for civil rights demonstrations than the streets of Chicago." When King joined Andrew Young and Mahalia Jackson on a march into the Marquette Park neighborhood, he was met by a crowd waving Confederate flags and "Wallace for President" signs. George Lincoln Rockwell's American Nazi Party never found itself so close to the mainstream. When a fist-sized rock dropped King to the pavement, many black Chicagoans took it as conclusive evidence that civil rights had failed. Some shifted their allegiance to the Chicago-based Nation of Islam or charismatic militant leaders like Stokely Carmichael. Others, in Chicago and elsewhere, took to the streets. The summer of 1966 was long and hot in America's cities. Nineteen sixty-seven would be longer, hotter, and even more violent. Redemption seemed a long way off.

Through it all Curtis Mayfield kept faith with the gospel vision. No song bore witness to the movement's trials with greater depth than "People Get Ready," which Mayfield said he wrote "in a deep mood, a spiritual state of mind." As close to pure gospel as anything that ever made the pop charts, "People Get Ready" brought the call-and-response voice of the movement to the Top Twenty in 1965. From the opening bars—a gospel hum carried along by bells, Pate's beautiful horn chart, and Mayfield's delicately syncopated guitar chording—the song pours a healing vision over a nation poised on the brink of chaos. Even as it singles out "the hopeless sinner who would hurt all mankind just to save his own," the song welcomes anyone willing to do the right thing onto the "train to Jordan." Casting his lot with "those whose chances grow thinner," Mayfield warns that "there's no hiding place against the kingdom's throne." Within months of the song's release, the Chicago movement was including a reworked version in the songbooks it distributed at churches and neighborhood centers throughout the city. Proclaiming "there's no hiding place when the movement comes," the new version dismissed the "Toms or any sorry Negroes, comin' to me saying they won't go." The Impressions ended the song with the soothing promise, "You don't need no ticket, you just thank the Lord." The movement rephrased it, "Everybody wants freedom, this I know." Either way, when the final strains of "People Get Ready" faded to silence, you could almost believe that, despite what was happening on the streets of Chicago and Detroit, the promise of the movement would be fulfilled.

CHAPTER THREE

"Spirit in the Dark"

**Music and the
Powers of Blackness**

$\mathbb{A}$RETHA FRANKLIN'S BAND LEADER King Curtis, a saxophonist who
created some of the most memorable riffs in soul music history, glanced
toward his crackerjack band, the Kingpins, and nodded to guest organist
Billy Preston. Decked out in a black leather jacket with an embroidered
horseshoe and a white leather horse's head on the back, King Curtis
caressed his horn and looked out over San Francisco's Fillmore West
Auditorium. It was the eve of the epic Muhammad Ali–Joe Frazier fight,
and the multiracial crowd packing the West Coast counterculture's musical Mecca buzzed with excitement. Tie-dyed Fillmore regulars accustomed to hallucinatory light shows and the psychedelic blues of the
Grateful Dead and the Jefferson Airplane now found themselves side by
side with Black Power radicals who'd donned sharply creased slacks,
African gowns, and glistening leather jackets for their foray into unknown
territory. King Curtis signaled Preston, the grizzled soul veterans in the

Memphis Horns, and the angelic vocalists in the Sweethearts of Soul—and delivered the invocation.

As the band punched out the opening riff of "Respect" and applause thundered through the cavernous hall, the spotlight danced across the rainbow crowd and settled on the woman who'd called the congregation together on that early spring Sunday in 1971. Dressed in a floor-length white gown with gold accents, Aretha Franklin looked her very best. Poised and radiant with her hair in a tight Afro, she affirmed what the crowd already knew: "What you want, baby, I got it." Brimming with confidence for the last show in her three-night stand, Aretha swept the crowd up in a wave of love, and it responded with long-stemmed red roses and Black Power salutes. Joints and bottles of wine passed freely between black and white hands as Aretha invited her listeners to join her in a gospel world where the counterculture and the Black Power movement could glorify creation together. First Aretha reached out to the hippies with the rock side of her repertoire—"Eleanor Rigby," "Satisfaction," "Bridge Over Troubled Water," and two songs she'd prepared specially for the occasion, Stephen Stills's "Love the One You're With" and Bread's "Make It with You." Following a sultry version of her number-one R&B hit "Don't Play That Song," she took the Fillmore to church with "Dr. Feelgood," building up to a fervent call-and-response exchange of "Oh yeah"s. "Every now and then you gotta sit down, cross your legs, cross your arms, and say, 'Yes, Lord,' " Aretha shouted out, as Preston eased into the organ chord announcing the gospel-soul rave-up "Spirit in the Dark." Lifting the crowd to heights familiar only to those who'd grown up in gospel churches, Aretha brought the song to its familiar climax and, while the Kingpins continued to lay down the groove, walked off the stage.

A moment later she was back, Ray Charles by her side. As Aretha guided him to the piano, Brother Ray bobbed his graying head toward the audience and flashed his signature crooked smile. While the band kept on vamping, Aretha took a few more choruses of "Spirit" while Charles tested the groove. Before long the two legends were warming the counterculture with their sanctified fire. Declaring the duet "a moment of perfect beauty, brief, and impossible to re-create," rock critic Michael Lydon was swept up in the frenzied response: "We danced, clapped, hugged, kissed, and finally wept." Reflecting on the album that preserved the magic, *Aretha Live at Fillmore West,*

Franklin agreed that the duet was something special. "Between the two of us, soul oozed out of every pore of the Fillmore. All the planets were aligned right that night, because when the music came down, it was as real and righteous as any recording I'd ever made."

The Fillmore concert represented a high-water mark for the gospel vision as it reached out beyond black America, and Aretha's duet with Charles provided a fitting climax. Atlantic Records producer Jerry Wexler, who'd guided Aretha out of the wilderness of her Columbia years, observed that "Aretha was continuing what Ray Charles had begun, the secularization of gospel, turning church rhythms, church patterns, and especially church feelings into personalized love songs. Like Ray, Aretha was a hands-on performer, a two-fisted pianist plugged into the main circuit of Holy Ghost power."

The Fillmore gig almost hadn't happened. Even at a time when "Respect," "Chain of Fools," and "Natural Woman" had made Aretha a real crossover star, Wexler admitted that he "considered the musical tastes of the Flower Children infantile and retarded." Although Aretha liked the hippies' "colorful garb and their love-the-world philosophy," she shared Wexler's apprehensions. The audience's response surpassed her wildest hopes. "What overwhelmed her—and surprised me—was the musical intelligence of the hippies. They picked up on her every shading and nuance; they were attentive, appreciative, and hip to exactly what was happening, technically and emotionally. The response," he concluded, "was as evolved and as well defined as though it had been an entirely black audience."

At the time it was reasonable to hope that Aretha's triumph at the Fillmore would help usher in a truly desegregated era in American music. There was plenty of supporting evidence for the theory that the generation of white Americans who'd grown up on Fats Domino, Elvis, and Motown was ready for something new. Otis Redding's straight-out-of-Georgia set at the Monterey Pop Festival whipped the flower children into a frenzy of call and response they definitely hadn't learned in Haight-Ashbury. Sly and the Family Stone had taken the torch to Woodstock, where their soaring "I Want to Take You Higher" left no doubt that Sly remembered his origins in the family gospel group that cut "On the Battlefield for My Lord" when he was four years old. The cultural call and response went both ways. Inspired by both Bob Dylan and the Beatles, Marvin Gaye, Stevie Wonder, and Curtis Mayfield cast off their pop masks and began preaching straight soul sermons on Vietnam, the inner cities, and the path to redemption.

Judging by the sounds, and the charts, Sam Cooke's dream of bringing "real gospel" to the Top Ten seemed to be coming true. But even as a new cultural era blossomed, there were disquieting signs—in the White House and on the streets—that the political battle was being lost.

༖

WHEN ARETHA FRANKLIN SAT DOWN at the piano at the Fame Studios in Muscle Shoals, Alabama, on January 27, 1967, her first notes heralded that new era. Spooner Oldham, who'd been hired to play piano for the session, called it a "magic chord," and amens echoed from every corner of black America. When Atlantic released "I Never Loved a Man (The Way I Love You)" in early March, crowds gathered outside record stores in black neighborhoods demanding to hear Aretha's gospel love song again and again. When Aretha followed "I Never Loved a Man" with "Respect," *Ebony* magazine declared 1967 the summer of " 'Retha, Rap and Revolt."

Aretha's transformation from frustrated chanteuse to the voice of black pride happened nearly overnight. The key was her decision to sign with Atlantic Records. "I took her to church, sat her down at the piano, and let her be herself," Jerry Wexler explained. "To say we took her back to church, that merely means we were trying the same recording context we were already using with Ruth Brown and LaVern Baker. Atlantic Records was like the West Point for rhythm and blues. We just applied what we knew about rhythm and blues to a rhythm-and-blues artist instead of trying to make her a pop artist like Judy Garland or Peggy Lee." For her part, Aretha appreciated Wexler's desire "to base the music around me, not only my feeling for the song but my piano playing and basic rhythm arrangement, my overall concept." The result was "raw and real and so much more myself."

Wexler had contacted Aretha at the urging of Louise Bishop, a Philadelphia DJ familiar with Aretha's gospel background and her frustrations with Columbia. Bishop's call reached Wexler in the Fame Studios, where he'd just finished breaking up a fistfight between Percy Sledge and Wilson Pickett. After brief negotiations Aretha agreed to what Wexler called a "handshake contract"—"no lawyers, managers, or agents in sight. It was beautiful," he beamed—variously reported at between $25,000 and $35,000.

John Hammond immediately offered Wexler his congratulations and predicted they'd make good records, but he warned that Aretha could be "enigmatic and withdrawn." In his autobiography Hammond wrote, "I was not unhappy to see her go to Atlantic. I knew Jerry Wexler, who would produce her records there, and was sure he would return her to the gospel-rooted material she should be recording. Her career since leaving Columbia has fulfilled every confidence I had in her. She had every musicianly quality I thought she had. All she needed was to hold to her roots in the church." Bob Althuser, who'd become Columbia's PR director after working for Atlantic, pinpointed the differences between Aretha's new and old homes: "At the end of the day, when people were listening to music at Atlantic Records, they were listening to Otis Redding or Rufus Thomas or Ray Charles. At the end of the day, when people listened to music at Columbia, they would be listening to Doris Day and Ray Conniff and Percy Faith." It was a long way from Percy Faith to Percy Sledge.

Wexler's first instinct was to assign Aretha to the Stax Studio in Memphis, which by 1967 was firmly established as the capital of southern soul. Unconcerned with the crossover strategies pioneered by Motown and Sam Cooke, Stax churned out a mesmerizing mix of gospel vocals and funky R&B that guitarist Steve Cropper called a "below-the-Bible-Belt sound. It was righteous and nasty. Which to our way of thinking was pretty close to life itself." Aware of the great tracks Booker T. and the MGs, the Stax house band, had laid down behind Sam and Dave, and Otis Redding, Wexler considered Aretha and Stax a perfect match. So he offered her contract to Stax president Jim Stewart. "Stax was steaming and no one figured to produce her better than those good folks in Memphis," Wexler wrote. "I told Jim that if he went for the $25,000 advance, Aretha could be a Stax artist with Atlantic promotion and distribution, the same arrangement we had with Sam and Dave. Stewart passed." Looking back with the knowledge of what followed, Wexler concluded, "Thank you, Jesus." Stewart, who may be forgiven for not joining in on the hosannas, made the decision for straightforward financial reasons: "Twenty-five thousand dollars cash, that was nonrecoupable to a man who was just starting to sell records and thought five thousand dollars was a lot of money."

When Stax stumbled, Wexler looked down the highway to Muscle Shoals and Rick Hall's Fame Studios. Like Booker T. and the MGs, the Muscle Shoals rhythm section enjoyed universal respect in the soul world for the solid sound it laid down for soul singers like Wilson Pickett. No one who made the call with their ears would have guessed the band was all white: keyboard player Spooner Oldham, guitarists Jimmy Johnson and Chips Moman, bass player Tommy Cogbill, and drummer Roger Hawkins. And once they'd hooked up with Aretha, no one who loved music cared. As Jerry Butler observed, "Nobody knew those were white guys playing behind her. They just knew it sounded good. They didn't care if it was white or black. That was sanctified and holy. It didn't have anything to do with color. It just had to do with the groove." Obviously, that didn't mean that color didn't matter in Muscle Shoals, Alabama. But it did highlight the enduring paradox of American music: despite a history shaped by an unabashed commitment to white supremacy, the South had always provided a laboratory for black-white cultural miscegenation. Witness Beale Street in Memphis, where "black" and "white" clubs stood next to one another and where more than a few folks wandered back and forth across the line. Anyone who mistook Beale Street for the promised land was headed for serious trouble. But being white in Memphis meant something different from being white in Chicago or New York. As the music out of Muscle Shoals demonstrated, Elvis wasn't some kind of freak of nature. Jerry Lee Lewis and Little Richard were working different sides of the same street. Growing up in a region where R&B and country mingled with the sounds coming out of black and white churches, Elvis simply listened hard and understood what he heard.

When Rick Hall told the Muscle Shoals players they'd been booked for the January 27 session, no one took special note. Songwriter Dan Penn, however, had heard Aretha's Columbia records, and he warned the musicians they were in for something special. "I knew about Aretha way before she got there. Rick contacted me about the session, but he didn't know who in hell was coming in," Penn told southern soul historian Peter Guralnick. When Hall identified the vocalist as Aretha, Penn warned the band, " 'Boys, you better get your damn shoes on. You getting someone who can sing.' Even the Memphis guys didn't really know who in the hell she was. I said, 'Man, this woman gonna knock you out.' They're all going, 'Big deal!' When she come in there and sit down at the piano and hit that first chord, everybody was just like little bees just buzzing around the queen. It was beautiful, better than any session I've ever seen, and I seen a bunch of them."

Spooner Oldham shared Penn's awe: "She hit that magic chord when Wexler was going up the little steps to the control room, and I just stopped. I said, 'Now, look, I'm not trying to cop or nothing. I know I was hired to play piano, but I wish you'd let her play that thing, and I could get on organ and electric.... It was a good, honest move, and one of the best things I ever done—and I didn't do nothing."

Two hours later "I Never Loved a Man (The Way I Love You)" was complete, and Aretha was on the path to immortality. "It was a killer, no doubt about it," Penn recalled. "The musicians started singing and dancing with each other, giddy on the pure joy of having something to do with this amazing record. That morning we knew a star had been born." Roger Hawkins said simply, "I've never experienced so much feeling coming out of a human being." Despite two decades in the music business that included classic sessions with Ray Charles, Ruth Brown, Clyde McPhatter, and Big Joe Turner, Wexler didn't trust his ears: "I couldn't believe it was that good. I said, 'That's my first record with her, and it can't be this good. I'll cool out in the morning. It will sound different in daylight.' I had to get used to that kind of greatness." Exhilarated by what they'd achieved on the first day of the scheduled week of sessions, Aretha and the band sketched out a second song—Dan Penn and Chips Moman's "Do Right Woman—Do Right Man"—and called it a day.

At which point the shit hit the fan. Within a few hours the joy over "I Never Loved a Man" collapsed into what Wexler described as "Walpurgisnacht, a Wagnerian shitstorm, things flying to pieces, everything going nuts. Back at the motel it was footsteps up and down the hall, doors slamming, and wild cries in the night." The next morning Aretha and Ted White were on a plane back to New York.

The problem began with what Jimmy Johnson called "the most fucked-up horn section you ever heard." Aware of White's reputation for creating difficulties, Wexler had attempted to forestall the problem of racial tension in advance. "A little anxious" at the prospect of "presenting Aretha and Ted with a wall-to-wall white band," Wexler asked Hall "to hire a black horn section—either the Memphis Horns or a section led by Bowlegs Miller. Hall goofed and hired an all-white section. Aretha's response was no response. I never should have worried—about her. She just sat down and played the music." While Aretha, Wexler, and the rhythm section were putting the finishing touches on "I Never Loved a Man," however, White and a white trumpet player sat down to share a celebratory bottle. Apparently the trumpeter used a casual racial slur, setting off a free and frank exchange concerning each of their heritage and character. Wexler observed sadly, "A redneck patronizing a black man is dangerous camaraderie."

What happened next isn't exactly clear. Hall remembered firing the trumpet player on the spot; other (probably apocryphal) versions feature gunshots fired by parties unknown and/or White beating the trumpet player up and dangling him over the balcony back at the motel. Rick Hall, who admitted to being "a lot drunker than I thought, evidently," provided what seems a reasonably likely report on the events precipitating Aretha's departure. Hall went to Aretha's motel room, where "Ted began to point his finger at me, and I guess I pointed my finger back at him. We went from 'redneck' to 'bluegum' to 'whitey' to 'nigger' and back again." The situation developed into a "real slugfest." Hall went to the lobby, where a wedding reception was in progress. "I get on the house phone and yell, 'You motherfucking son of a bitch, you better get your ass out of this fucking town.' And I just made a complete ass of myself."

The whole chain of events spoke to the paradox of race in the South. It was the real-life evidence of the story the music told: when you started messing around with the truth, you could go from heaven to hell overnight. One moment, you were listening to the sweetest sounds gospel had to offer; the next you were hoping to live till dawn. Aretha had been born in Memphis, and she'd traveled the black South on the gospel highway. But the Muscle Shoals debacle shook her to her shoes.

Back in New York, Aretha secluded herself from the men, black and white, who had appointed themselves guardians of her interests. Rumors swirled that she'd broken up with White and gone into hiding, maybe in New York, maybe in Detroit. Meanwhile Wexler had a gospel soul classic but no flip side. He released a demo version of "I Never Loved a Man" to his network of black DJs, who immediately began clamoring for its release. After two weeks of growing anxiety, Aretha and her sisters finally showed up at Atlantic's Broadway studio. Returning to the song she'd whipped up near the end of the ill-starred Alabama session, Aretha overdubbed the piano and organ parts that make "Do Right Woman—Do Right Man" a worthy companion for "I Never Loved a Man." Erma and Carolyn contributed the finishing touches with their haunting background vocals.

Wexler, who'd already released acetates of "I Never Loved a Man" to the DJs, could finally exhale.

The response to "I Never Loved a Man" surpassed anyone's hopes. From the first line—"You're no good, heart-breaker, you're a liar, and you're a cheat"—Aretha bears witness to the dark nights of the soul where you can't tell the difference between your agonies and the love that can redeem you. Mingling the aching reality of the deepest love she could imagine with a haunting knowledge that in this world at least nothing is sure to last, Aretha's voice explodes with an emotional complexity more like William Faulkner than Diana Ross. Taking her cue from Mahalia Jackson and Marion Williams, Aretha blows away the standard verse-verse-chorus structure of most pop hits, including those that had previously come out of Motown and Chicago. Spooner Oldham's organ and Jimmy Johnson's guitar punctuate Aretha's piano runs with responses even more sensitive than she would have heard back home at New Bethel Baptist. Hawkins and Cogbill nail every delayed beat. Nothing like it had ever graced American popular culture. Ray Charles had laid the track; Aretha rolled into the station. The record shot into the pop Top Ten and to the top of the R&B charts, where it remained for seven weeks. It was a firecracker start, but the follow-up was pure dynamite.

"Respect" burst like a howitzer shell over a nation braced for another round of summertime riots. Angry over the failure of the movement's southern victories to translate into meaningful change in their own communities, rioters had taken to the streets in dozens of cities in the North and West the previous two years. The defeat of Martin Luther King's Chicago campaign transmitted an unambiguous message to the residents of Newark, Watts, and Paradise Valley as well as those manning the front lines on the south shore of Lake Michigan. Many turned their backs on the civil rights movement's nonviolent and interracial ideals in favor of the emerging Black Power movement. But even many who weren't impressed with Black Power's ideology responded powerfully to the emotional punch of slogans like "Black Is Beautiful" and "Power to the People." "R-E-S-P-E-C-T" spelled the same thing to them, without the ideological baggage and with a gospel call to freedom on the backbeat.

That was part of the reason black journalist Phyl Garland declared "Respect" a "new national anthem," and the fledgling women's movement adapted the song as the battle hymn of their decidedly new republic. Aretha's definitive take on Otis Redding's song spoke to anyone who, as Mahalia sang, had ever been " 'buked and scorned." "I don't make it a practice to put my politics into my music," Aretha demurred. But she understood clearly that she had touched "the need of a nation, the need of the average man and woman in the street, the businessman, the mother, the fireman, the teacher—everyone wanted respect. It was also one of the battle cries of the civil rights movement. The song took on monumental significance. It became the 'Respect' women expected from men and men expected from women, the inherent right of all human beings." When Redding himself heard the record, he could only shake his head in admiration. "I just lost my song," he told Wexler. "That girl took it away from me."

Its success guaranteed by the two singles, Aretha's first Atlantic album, *I Never Loved a Man the Way I Love You,* marked her acclamation as the "Queen of Soul," a nickname bestowed upon her by politically active Chicago DJ Purvis Spann. Loath to return to Alabama to record the album, Wexler did the next best thing—he flew the Muscle Shoals band to New York, where he supplemented them with King Curtis's horn section and a trio of backup singers consisting of Aretha's sisters and Cissy Houston. Over two amazing days in mid-February 1967, they cut nine more tracks, including the hit singles "Baby, Baby, Baby" and "Dr. Feelgood (Love Is a Serious Business)." Staking Aretha's claim to greatness, the first album side distills the elements of the gospel vision perfectly. Following the clarion call of "Respect," Aretha plumbs the depths of her burdens in Ray Charles's "Drown in My Own Tears" and bitterness in "I Never Loved a Man." In her remake of King Curtis's 1964 hit "Soul Serenade," she pulls the sweetness out of the ache with one of her most lyrical piano lines. Echoing Dr. King's most famous speech, "Don't Let Me Lose This Dream" completes the stunning sequence by knitting personal love into a larger redemptive vision. The heartfelt sequence that closes the second side, the bluesy "Save Me" and Aretha's paean to her old sweetheart Sam Cooke's "A Change Is Gonna Come," retraces the path from burden and bearing witness to redemption. Like the voices in the choir, the songs mean more together than they do alone, combining to provide a soul-deep chronicle of the story Aretha shared with the countless others who left their southern homes only to find themselves knocked to their knees on the streets of the promised land.

Ironically, Aretha's new sound, which critics repeatedly identified as "unmistakably black," attracted the white audience that Columbia had failed to reach with its self-conscious crossover strategy. She would remain a constant presence on the charts for the next decade. By 1975, when she won her eighth consecutive Grammy in the Best Female R&B Song category, the award had been informally rechristened "the Aretha."

White critics frequently underestimated Aretha's brains and diligence, reverting to stereotypes of "instinctive genius" and "natural ability" to explain her success. Even Jerry Wexler fell into the trap when he described her talent as emerging "like Minerva, full-formed from Jupiter's head." When he turned his attention to the details, he came closer to the truth, underlining Aretha's combination of "head, heart and throat.... The head is the intelligence, the phrasing. The heart is the emotionality that feeds the flames. The throat is the chops, the voice," he mused. "Aretha, like Sam Cooke, has all three qualities."

So while her voice might have sounded like it came straight from the soul, Aretha and Wexler worked hard to make sure it came through on wax. Aretha was never passive in the process. "She remained the central orchestrator of her own sound," Wexler observed, "the essential contributor and final arbiter of what fit or did not fit her musical persona." Aretha knew that that persona was based on study and preparation. "When it comes to the ABCs of music, I am no dummy," she announced. "I always worked on my sound, my arrangements, *before* I went into the studio with a producer." Wexler agreed: "Nobody bothered us in the control room. In general, the sessions went like cream. She'd take the song—she found most of them— or she'd write it. And she would work out a layout, working at home with her little electric piano and the girls. So you had three major ingredients: First of all, you had the arrangement implicit in the piano bars, you had her lead vocals and you had the vocal background leads. She brings all this into the session. She'd sit at the piano and start to line it out, and the girls might not be there. So she might sing their parts, too. Then all we did was start to shade in drums, bass, guitar. We might make small changes, but it would always be by agreement with her.... Those records were so damn good because she took care of business at home."

Aretha's head, heart, and throat coalesced to make her second and third Atlantic albums, *Aretha Arrives* and *Lady Soul,* worthy successors to *I Never*

Loved a Man the Way I Love You. Backed by a King Curtis–led horn section and a rotating roster of all-star guitarists including Joe South, Eric Clapton, and Bobby Womack, the Muscle Shoals stalwarts execute their licks flawlessly. There's no letdown from the hits—the sublime "Baby, I Love You," "Since You've Been Gone (Sweet Sweet Baby)," and Carole King's "(You Make Me Feel Like) A Natural Woman"—and a typically eclectic set of covers that draw on the blues (Howlin' Wolf's "Going Down Slow"), R&B (James Brown's "Money Won't Change You," Ray Charles's "Come Back Baby"), Vegas fare (Sinatra's "That's Life"), country (Willie Nelson's "Night Life"), blue-eyed soul (P.J. Proby's "Niki Hoeky," the Rascals' "Groovin' "), and rock from the garage to the arena (? and the Mysterians' "96 Tears," the Stones' "Satisfaction"). The high points include two songs written by Aretha's sister Carolyn, "Ain't No Way" and "Ain't Nobody (Gonna Turn Me Around)," with its clear echoes of the movement standard "Ain't Gonna Let Nobody Turn Me Round." Set against an angelic choir singing "I believe, you know I believe," Aretha's "People Get Ready" takes the song that Curtis Mayfield wrote all the way back to church.

Even in that gallery of marvels, "Chain of Fools" stands out. Between Joe South's opening guitar riff, consciously modeled on gospel great Pops Staples's vibrato-heavy style, and the sanctified shout that lingers as the song fades to silence, "Chain of Fools" unfolds a two-minute-and-forty-five-second epic of love, betrayal, and determination. It was a black women's anthem, a reminder that Aretha meant what she said in "Respect." But the response wasn't limited to scorned women determined to survive. From South Vietnam to south Georgia, "Chain of Fools" reverberated with resolve. For the foot soldiers of the movement, it issued a challenge to cast off the chains of mental slavery and move on ahead.

And even though songwriter Don Covay said he'd been thinking of field hands when he wrote "Chain of Fools," Vietnam vets claimed it as their own. The song resonated especially deeply with black veterans aware that through the early years of the war they'd suffered a sharply disproportionate number of casualties. One black vet broke down what the song meant to his brothers slogging through the elephant grass and rice paddies of Southeast Asia for a cause no one could explain: "We had been fucked over and we knew it, right off. This woman, Miss Ree, saved some of us, I swear. My CO had Aretha on his tape cassette. And after one of those suicide

missions—you know, defusing booby traps with your own ass—after we fitted as many pieces as we could find into the body bags, we put on that tape.
'Chain of Fools,' I remember. And this may seem weird, but we danced. Like
the fuckin' *fools* we were. We danced until we puked our guts out and
laughed and cried. And I tell you, if we hadn't have done it, I might have
lost my mind. I might have gone and died." In Vietnam as in Detroit,
Aretha's music sounded the blues-gospel pulse of the unfolding history.

The intensity of the black response to Aretha can't be overstated. She
dominated *Jet* magazine's weekly "Soul Brothers Top 20 Tunes" poll. When
she performed at the Randall's Island Jazz Festival in the summer of 1967,
she drew a bigger ovation than Ray Charles. Phyl Garland described the
"frenzied hand-clapping and foot-tapping" that erupted when Aretha,
resplendent in a pink brocade gown, arrived in a chauffeur-driven black
Cadillac limousine: "It was a resounding 'amen' to all the words and emotions she had projected in her later records." In October 1967 Aretha sang
at Lincoln Center, offering a mix of her Columbia and Atlantic material,
listed in order on a elegantly printed program. In December she made her
national TV debut on *The Kraft Music Hall.* The next month on *The Jonathan
Winters Show* she appeared in a silver-spangled miniskirt surrounded by the
go-go-dancing Sweet Inspirations decked out in neon pink minis and dazzling white shoes. A surprisingly tepid album shaped largely by Ted White's
lingering desire to position Aretha for the Vegas circuit, *Aretha in Paris* documented her 1968 European tour. It was the only misstep of her early years
with Atlantic.

For Aretha, the greatest honor came when the city of Detroit declared
February 16, 1968, "Aretha Franklin Day." At a Cobo Hall ceremony Martin
Luther King presented her with an SCLC Leadership Award. Although he
was suffering from laryngitis and couldn't speak, the crowd responded in a
way that put ideological frictions between King and proponents of Black
Power in their proper perspective. The Black Panthers, the Republic of
New Afrika, the Dodge Revolutionary Union Movement, and the Shrine of
the Black Madonna might be gathering strength in Detroit, but even their
staunchest backers understood that King had helped create the world that
made Black Power possible. A writer for the African American newspaper
the *Michigan Chronicle* described the scene: "This was a 'love wave.' Everyone
just stood on their feet. He never said a word, because he couldn't. But you

could just feel the impact his presence had—just him being there.... At the time, people were said to be wishy-washy about King, that he wasn't militant enough. Well, all twelve thousand people in that room cared for him—you could feel it."

Two months later, on April 4, 1968, King was gunned down as he stood on the balcony of the Lorraine Motel in Memphis, where he had gone to support striking sanitation workers. While Aretha grappled with the sudden loss of her friend, riots erupted in dozens of cities. Less than two weeks after a mule-driven cart carried King to his martyr's grave, Aretha recorded "Think." Although she had written the song before the assassination, it rang out as a desperate plea to a nation that seemed to have surrendered to the violence and hatred that King had given his life to overcome. "You better think, think about what you're trying to do to me," she pleaded. Aretha clearly understood the anger expressed by black Vietnam vet Don Browne when he heard of the assassination at the U.S. base in Tuy Hoa. "My first inclination was to run out and punch the first white guy I saw," he admitted. With King's voice silenced, the prospect of race war wasn't a paranoid fantasy. In the days after the assassination troops huddled in the basement of the White House, and machine-gun nests ringed the Capitol. Against that, "Think" clings desperately to the gospel vision. Pouring her soul into her cries of "Freedom," Aretha demands that the nation and her people consider the future they're creating for each other. "You need me and I need you," she shouts, "without each other, there ain't nothin' we can do."

As usual, Curtis Mayfield was thinking hard. As always, he had his mind set on freedom. While Black Power moved to the center of the African American political stage, Mayfield probed the problems and potential of a movement fueled equally by revolutionary vision and undirected rage. The series of songs he released between 1968 and 1971—"We're a Winner," "We're Rolling On," "This Is My Country," "Choice of Colors," and "(Don't Worry) If There's a Hell Below We're All Going to Go"—charts the confused and sometimes contradictory constellation of thoughts and feelings he shared with countless citizens, black and white, struggling with Vietnam, the King assassination, and the election of Richard Nixon, who rode a "southern strategy" rooted in racial antagonism into the White House.

Profoundly political but never dogmatic, Mayfield's music responded to the call of the movement. "When you're talking about songs such as 'We're a Winner,' that's locked in with Martin Luther King. It took something from his inspiring message. I was listening to all my preachers and the different leaders of the time. You had your Rap Browns and your Stokely Carmichaels and Martin Luther Kings, all of those people right within that same era." Mayfield's embrace of leaders who often differed sharply reflects a basic truth about African American political life: uncompromising commitment to freedom matters more than ideological purity. Few responding to Aretha's thundering demand for "Freedom!" quibbled about whether she preferred the revolutionary transformation of a racist capitalist system to a bigger slice of the capitalist pie.

Mayfield understood the point perfectly. When the Impressions released "We're a Winner" in January 1968, they weren't taking sides in the sometimes-heated arguments that threatened to fragment the freedom movement. Mayfield saw no intrinsic contradiction between supporting Malcolm X and supporting Martin Luther King. He dismissed militant criticism of King as an "Uncle Tom" with a pitying smile at the same time that he savored the memory of Malcolm rapping and flashing his extraordinary smile to the ordinary brothers on the block. As tensions between civil rights and Black Power dominated media coverage of racial politics, Mayfield was content to pay tribute to the local people he called the "invisible heroes of the movement." Like "I'm So Proud," "We're a Winner" reaffirmed the gospel vision and anticipated James Brown's "Say It Loud (I'm Black and I'm Proud)," which wouldn't be released for another eight months.

Unlike "People Get Ready" and "Keep On Pushing," "We're a Winner" didn't mask the message, which is probably why, despite its distinctly upbeat feel, it was banned on several Chicago radio stations, including top-rated WLS. Mayfield attributed the ban to the song's "social conscience; it was about a mass of people during the time of struggle, and when it broke, it was so much out of the ordinary. It had a little gospel feeling, and it sort of locked in with the movement of equality. It wouldn't be what you could call a crossover record during those times, but the demand of the people kept it struggling and happening." The song opens with the sound of voices, like those that would introduce Marvin Gaye's *What's Going On* a few years later. An opening trumpet flourish in the classic Johnny Pate style gives way to a funky groove that points the way to Mayfield's musical future. Accompanied by background cries of "All right now" and syncopated hand claps, the song lays down a message that's pure Curtis. Urging his listeners to wipe away their tears, pay heed to their leaders, and "keep on pushing," he ushers in the "blessed day" when he and his people will move on up to the higher ground. "Our purpose is to educate as well as to entertain. Painless preaching is as good a term as any for what we do," he told an interviewer at the time. "If you're going to come away from a party singing the lyrics of a song, it is better that you sing of self-pride like 'We're a winner' instead of 'Do the boogaloo!' "

Though plenty of people danced to Mayfield's music, "We're a Winner" and the follow-up "We're Rolling On" entered a heated debate on the meaning of Black Power that would rage on through the seventies. Whether Black Power was a slogan, a program, an impulse, or even a disaster wasn't always clear. You could read about it in *The Autobiography of Malcolm X,* Eldridge Cleaver's *Soul on Ice, The Prison Letters of George Jackson,* and the fiery poems of Amiri Baraka, Sonia Sanchez, Etheridge Knight, Haki Madhubuti, and spiritual elder Gwendolyn Brooks. In the early seventies Black Power advocates generally subscribed to a set of precepts including "Power to the People," "Self-determination," and "Black Is Beautiful." The problem, as Mayfield knew, was trying to figure out exactly what the slogans meant. For the Nation of Islam, Black Power demanded an Islamic theocracy; for Coleman Young, it meant control of Detroit's Democratic Party; for some black Vietnam veterans, it meant applying the lessons they'd learned in the Mekong Delta to the Mississippi Delta; for the Dodge Revolutionary Union Movement, it meant equal access to supervisory positions on the assembly line; for the Republic of New Afrika, it meant a communal society founded on allegedly African principles; for the Black Panthers, it meant an international revolution against capitalism. A lot of black men and women just demanded what Aretha spelled out: respect.

For reasons both commendable and dubious, Black Power emphasized the recovery of black manhood. But many black women cautioned against confusing that with the whole story. Ann Peebles's "I'm Gonna Tear Your Playhouse Down" and Laura Lee's "Women's Love Rights" were keynotes of a collective sermon on the theme of black women's liberation. Freda Payne's debut single, "The Unhooked Generation," was a celebration of life as a single woman; the Honey Cone assured straying husbands and boyfriends that "One Monkey Don't Stop No Show"; Jean Knight issued a hilarious putdown of "Mr. Big Stuff"; and Lyn Collins, aptly nicknamed the "Female Preacher," ripped through "Think (About It)" over an infectious groove set down by James Brown's band. And no one could conclude that Chaka Khan, who had adopted her African name while working for a Black Panther breakfast program, would be satisfied washing the dashikis or stirring the grits.

While a growing number of blacks, male and female, agreed with Black Power's assertive stance, there was no general consensus concerning the notion of racial separatism. Building on undeniable historical facts—the white man may not be the devil, but his track record could lead to confusion on that point—groups like the Republic of New Afrika spun out a compelling, if flawed, chain of logic. For too long blacks had been denied any voice in public deliberations over their legal condition. Even the fifties and sixties movement leaders had compromised their words and actions to appease their white liberal allies. The time had come for real self-determination. White people could no longer define black possibility.

Mayfield understood Black Power as a change in style rather than a movement away from the underlying values of the gospel vision. A dedicated follower of Black Power fashion, he eagerly embraced the chance to put away the suits and ties that the Impressions had adopted during their ABC years. "It was a great opening," he recalled. "The style, the clothes, the wide pants, and the long German coats. Everything sort of fell in, and it hit a real nice fashion. To be fly was to *be*." In her book *Black Feeling, Black Talk/Black Judgement,* poet Nikki Giovanni celebrated the new Impressions as part of the musical mix that defined Black Power more clearly than any manifesto. Entranced by the "beautiful beautiful beautiful outasight black men," Giovanni placed Mayfield in the company of Jerry Butler, Wilson Pickett, the Temptations, and Sly Stone. Decked out in hues of fire red, lime green, burnt orange, and royal blue, Giovanni wrote, the soul princes walked the street in "the same ol danger" while embodying a "brand new pleasure."

More concretely, the Black Power movement's emphasis on economic autonomy resonated with Mayfield's determination to control his music. His decision to join Eddie Thomas in founding Curtom Records helped fulfill that desire. As early as 1966 Mayfield had begun exploring the possibility of establishing an independent label. His first two attempts—the "Windy C" and "Mayfield" labels—went under as a result of distribution problems. Nonetheless, the partners obtained invaluable experience with the business and production aspects of the music industry. By 1968, when the Impressions' contract with ABC-Paramount was about to expire, they were ready to devote themselves wholly to Curtom. Mayfield again ventured into the front office because "I wasn't a quitter. Sometimes these things are like marriages. You don't give up wanting to be in love and having the best you can expect, just because your marriage fails."

For more than a decade Curtom provided an emblem of the real potential of Black Power, financially and artistically. "The only power of blackness we thought of was being equal," Thomas explained, "being able to do what others do, being able to stay where others stay, being able to have our records played on the pop stations if they had the sales force behind it. We were trying to equalize things, not take over, just equalize it. That was our whole policy cause we were not equal, we were stuck down at the bottom, and no matter what happened, we stayed there. That's why we were fighting to get up." As far as politics was concerned, Thomas said he and Mayfield were aware of how "Jesse Jackson was putting his stamp on Chicago with Operation PUSH and Operation Breadbasket," but the Impressions' main contribution to the movement came in the form of music. "We did a couple of things for PUSH," Thomas reported, "but basically it was just that people appreciated what we were saying. It was an inspiration to them, to buckle their shoes up, and they thought, 'Hey we can do something.' As Curtis said, the black boy's drying his eyes and movin' on up, lord have mercy, movin' on up."

Musically, Mayfield accepted the Black Power movement's commitment to black pride, while insisting that it remain grounded in the gospel vision. The covers of the first two Impressions albums released on Curtom reflect the changing social currents. Their ABC-Paramount covers show the group dressed in suit jackets and ties; on their 1968 album, *This Is My Country*, they wear turtlenecks and stand in the rubble outside a ghetto tenement. On *The Young Mod's Forgotten Story*, released the following year, they pose in stylish leather jackets and sailors' caps favored by the Black Power set. More important, Mayfield agreed with Black Power's demand for uncompromising confrontation with the history of racism and oppression. In "This Is My Country" Mayfield points to a "hundred years of slave driving, sweat and welts on my back" as evidence of his unquestionable right to claim America as his own. Riding Johnny Pate's soaring horn charts and the Impressions' harmonies, Mayfield issues an uncompromising repudiation of anyone—Elijah Muhammad as well as Mayor Daley or George Wallace—who would deny blacks full participation in American society: "Some people think we don't have the right to say it's my country." His response is a simple pledge that the deaths of Malcolm, Dr. King, and the many thousands gone before them will not be in vain. "Too many have died," he testifies, "for me to go second class." Stripping away the lush arrangement that might distract from the point, he frames the question as clearly as it can be framed: "Will we perish unjust or live equal as a nation?" Similarly, the first cut on *This Is My Country* calls on the "invisible heroes of the movement" to fill the vacuum created by the assassinations. Backed by an arrangement that combines blues guitar and bass with gospel tambourine and organ, "They Don't Know" reassures those who feel despair over having "lost another leader" that they aren't alone. Holding on to his belief that "our love is going to help the world be free," Mayfield counsels his people that when they feel alone, wondering how much more they can endure, the answer is in themselves: "Every brother is a leader." Ella Baker, though she would have been careful to add "and sister," meant the same thing.

Keeping the faith, Mayfield knew, wouldn't be easy. The cuts that frame *The Young Mod's Forgotten Story*—the title track, "Choice of Colors," and "Mighty Mighty (Spade and Whitey)"—deal with the practical complications of holding to the gospel vision in the face of increasing racial tensions. "The Young Mod's Forgotten Story" promises to tell it like it is in a world where the blind battle the blind. "Mighty Mighty" details the problems in a country that's killing off its leaders and envisions a world where "black and white power" unite to do what's right. But the keynote comes in "Choice of Colors." Playing off one of Pate's finest string arrangements, the song shimmers like a dream slipping ever so slowly away. Mayfield calls his brothers to account, observing wryly that some would rather make a fuss than work for a better world. It doesn't make sense to hate white teachers, he says, and turn a blind eye to the backbiting within black communities.

Riding a slow, almost somber, drumbeat, Mayfield asks his listeners to step back from the heat of the moment and think about how they really feel. True love of black people flows from self-acceptance, not from rage against the oppressor. "We shall overcome someday," he sings, "if you'll only listen to what I say."

As the sixties came to an end, Mayfield knew it wasn't quite that simple. One of his almost-forgotten classics, the title cut of the last Impressions album on which he sang, *Check Out Your Mind* (1970), pleads with his listeners to take responsibility for resisting the divisive forces. The songs that Mayfield wrote for that album and for the first post-Curtis Impressions album, *Times Have Changed,* range from vintage ballads ("Can't You See," "Only You") and funky love songs ("(Baby) Turn On to Me") to uncompromising social commentary ("Stop the War," "Times Have Changed"). Repeatedly, Mayfield urges the community to hang on to the hope within the chaos. But, whatever the call of his music and whatever the promise of Black Power, conditions in the poor black communities of the North continued to disintegrate. As the implications of life in the world of high-rise projects became clear, a mood of desperation settled over Curtis's old stomping ground, Cabrini-Green. Although he was no longer living in the projects where he was raised, he was fully aware that the community that had provided him with his foundation was no longer a decent place for a black child to grow up.

Focused on the immediate demands of trying to hold their families and neighborhood together, many female residents of Cabrini-Green identified the riots that followed King's assassination as the point of no return. Chicago had known riots before; in 1919 white mobs had raged through the streets, leaving dozens dead and hundreds homeless. And the summer before the assassination a three-day series of guerrilla skirmishes on the West Side had killed two people. But until King's death, Chicago had avoided the full-scale conflagrations that in the sixties had shaken Watts, Detroit, Newark, and numerous other cities. When news of the slaying broke, Chicago passed an uneasy night with the police on high alert. The next day the situation escalated when black students poured out of their schools and gathered in Garfield Park, where speakers turned their rage against local landlords and business owners. As snipers fired from rooftops and arsonists set new fires faster than they could be put out, troops patrolled the streets in jeeps. By the time the riot was contained, eleven were dead and more than three hundred arrests had been made. Business districts near the projects had been reduced to rubble; on West Madison most of a twenty-eight-block stretch had been burned to the ground. Cabrini resident Rochelle Satchell said sadly that "after the riots there was a lot of things just burned down. It didn't affect [the residents] physically, but mentally they were affected. It affected everybody here. Not only was it the prices going up, it was the fear now. We were surrounded by whites, and now you had to shop outside the community and didn't know what was going to happen. You could see the transition, and the riots were the icing on the cake." For Zora Washington, King's death sapped the will of the community and ushered in a future that couldn't have differed more starkly from the Black Power movement's Afrotopian dreams: "It made you want to cry. It did because you knew a neighborhood that you lived in, and that black people had torn it up and the powers that be were not going to fix it up.... It was a scary time, it gave you a scary feeling.... It was like we lost hope. The person that could do it for us was gone. It was a terrible time. Those stores never came back.... You felt isolated because you had nowhere to go."

The ominous rolling bass at the start of Mayfield's first solo single, "(Don't Worry) If There's a Hell Below We're All Gonna Go," introduced a new side of his sensibility. The bass rumbles on beneath a montage of fragmented voices and a doom-laden reflection on the Book of Revelation, then explodes into a reverb-laced jeremiad directed at everyone from the "niggers and the crackers" to the "police and their backers." Coming from a man who fully deserved his title the "Gentle Genius," "If There's a Hell Below" stunned almost everyone who heard it when it was released at the end of 1970. Calling out to the "sisters," "niggers," "whiteys," "Jews," and "crackers," Mayfield cast an angry eye on a world run by "educated fools from uneducated schools," where everyone's "fussin' and cussin'," running away from their worries into stoned-out dream worlds. The vision harkened back to the apocalyptic warnings that had always sounded alongside the gospel vision's redemptive dream. As Dorothy Love Coates thundered, there was no hiding place down here. Or as Martha and the Vandellas put it, there was nowhere to run, nowhere to hide. As "(Don't Worry)" faded into an aural tapestry of swirling strings and an unrepentant growling bass,

Mayfield's warning was clear: together, and increasingly alone, we were descending into a uniquely American abyss.

↶

N INETEEN SIXTY-SEVEN WAS A LONG, HOT SUMMER of discontent in black America, but for Stevie Wonder it was also the "Summer of Love." Straining against the Motown formula, he felt as much affinity with white contemporaries like Bob Dylan and the Beatles as he did with black elders like Ray Charles. Splitting the difference between Paradise Valley and Haight-Ashbury, Wonder steadfastly resisted little boxes of whatever hue. "People ask me what soul is," he explained, "but all people have soul. Soul is what you feel. So anybody can have soul, and you can call it whatever you want. Psychedelic music has got soul because the people have got soul." Wonder spoke with particular vehemence concerning the impact of racial categories on musicians. "Categorization can be the death of an artist. It's that whole thing—the concept of a black artist. All that 'Oh Stevie—he's a soul man.' That kind of thing. It can kill an artist."

When Wonder cited his influences, he listed an eclectic group: Dinah Washington, Johnny Ace, Bobby "Blue" Bland, Simon and Garfunkel, the Coasters, the Dixie Hummingbirds, Jimmy Reed, Crosby, Stills, Nash and Young, the Staple Singers, B.B. King, Dylan, the Byrds, and Jesse Belvin, the silky-smooth West Coast balladeer Wonder named his favorite singer because of "a certain magic about his voice." He singled out Burt Bacharach, in whose music he heard a strong African American influence. "I've really followed him for a long time—since Chuck Jackson's record of 'I Wake Up Crying,' " Wonder said. "I've always wondered was his life influenced by a black person, because his tunes—they caught on more with black people because they could associate the mood of his chords."

As he began to map his musical future, however, Wonder increasingly embraced iconoclastic musicians who strained against pop conventions. He praised Cream, for example, in the breathless tones of the predominantly white hippie counterculture: "Some of that psychedelic music is really fantastic. It shows the creativeness of young people. I believe that music is bringing younger people closer together. Young people are expressing themselves through music, and that's bringing countries closer together." A high point in Wonder's exploration of the new sonic world occurred in October 1967, when he was in London to tape an episode of *Top Gear*, a BBC equivalent of *American Bandstand*. Arriving at the studio a bit early, he happened across Jimi Hendrix, who was scheduled for a session in an adjacent studio. BBC engineer Peter Ritzema described the duo's brief jam on "I Was Made to Love Her" and "Ain't Too Proud to Beg": "Stevie wanted to play the drums, to calm down before his interview. Jimi and [Experience bass player] Noel [Redding] played along with a bit of 'I Was Made to Love Her' for about a minute and a half, and then about another seven minutes of mucking about. It's not that wonderful, but it's one of those legendary things. Stevie Wonder did join with Jimi Hendrix, and it's there on tape."

But the strongest rock influence on Wonder's developing sound came from the Beatles. "When I think of the sixties," he would reflect later, "I think of two things: I think of Motown and I think of the Beatles. Those are the major influences. The Beatles made me feel that I could do some of the ideas that I had. Every time one of their records came out, I wanted to have it, particularly after 'Eleanor Rigby.' But we all really influence each other. That's really what it's all about." Like black musicians from Otis Redding to George Clinton, Wonder was especially fascinated by *Sgt. Pepper's Lonely Hearts Club Band*. "I just dug the effects they got, like echoes and the voice things, the writing, like 'For the Benefit of Mr. Kite.' I just said, 'Why can't I?' I wanted to do something else, go other places." One thing Wonder learned from the Beatles was the importance of the studio as a musical instrument. Especially after he began working with the brilliant engineers Robert Margouleff and Malcolm Cecil in 1971, Wonder crafted aural tapestries that appealed to audiences that mellowed out yellowly on Donovan or wandered the dark side of Pink Floyd's moon.

For the moment, however, Motown insisted that Stevie churn out hit singles. However much the label's reluctance to take albums seriously as a form of self-expression grated on Wonder, his apprenticeship had put him in an ideal position to enter the musical dialogues of the late sixties on his own terms. At age seventeen he was on the verge of pop superstardom. From the time "Uptight" hit number three in 1965 until Wonder assumed full control of his career in 1971, he remained a constant presence near the top of the charts. "Blowin' in the Wind," "A Place in the Sun," "I Was Made to Love Her," "For Once in My Life," "My Cherie Amour," "Yester-Me, Yester-You, Yesterday," "Signed, Sealed, Delivered, I'm Yours" and "Heaven Help Us All" all hit the pop Top Ten in those years.

Wonder's hits demonstrated his ability both as a ballad singer and as an R&B shouter. Although the ballads exemplified by "My Cherie Amour" were generally more successful with the pop audience, the real highlights were the funky up-tempo showpieces best represented by "I Was Made to Love Her." One of several hits cowritten with Moy and producer Henry Cosby ("I'm Wondering," "Shoo-Be-Doo-Be-Doo-Da-Day," "For Once in My Life"), "I Was Made to Love Her" features a stunning James Jamerson bass line, and a lyric line that slyly ties the love song to the freedom movement. In the first line Wonder proclaims that he was born in Little Rock, which, especially for black listeners, wasn't just another American city. It doesn't even rhyme with *sweetheart*. But the real triumph of the song was Wonder's intense gospel-tinged vocal that the producers worked hard to achieve. Cosby remembered taking Wonder to a Baptist church in Detroit and asking him to imitate the preacher's vocal attack. Back in the studio, Wonder had trouble finding that gospel intensity. "Stevie wanted people in the studio," Cosby remembered. "He had to feel the presence of people. If there were none around, his vocal was just dead. I had to go outside and just stop people who were passing to bring them in, so Stevie could feel their presence. Once we got that, he could fire into that feeling."

But the record that revealed most tellingly the forces stirring in the young man's soul was "Blowin' in the Wind," which had been a number-two hit for folk trio Peter, Paul and Mary in 1963. Like Dylan's lesser-known "Masters of War," "Oxford Town," and "Only a Pawn in Their Game," "Blowin' in the Wind" crystallized the values of the early-sixties folk revival. Although Dylan never accepted the role of movement guru, thousands of potential activists heard his music as a call to action. More than a few of the earnest guitar-strumming students who joined black organizers to register black voters during the Freedom Summer of 1964 had been inspired by Dylan's meditation on the eternal questions of suffering and endurance. The fact that Dylan, Joan Baez, Phil Ochs, and their folkie cohorts backed up their words by playing at benefits and rallies in support of SNCC earned them the respectful attention of black listeners (who often found themselves bemused by the folkies' apparent lack of interest in minor musical details like rhythm and good singing).

Accompanied by Clarence Paul's soulful vocal responses, Wonder transformed "Blowin' in the Wind" into a call-and-response engagement with African American history. The question of how many roads they'd have to walk before they'd gain recognition as men wasn't abstract to Wonder and his mentor. A riot ravaged Detroit the same month "Blowin' in the Wind" topped the R&B charts, suggesting one answer to how many more years might have to pass before their people would be "allowed to be free." A riot, Dr. King remarked, is "the language of the unheard." The question, and the note of yearning in Wonder's voice, recurred in the follow-up singles "A Place in the Sun" and "Travelin' Man," but his answers were still years down the road.

While Wonder had established himself as one of Motown's most consistent hitmakers, he was not yet making memorable albums. Audiences attuned to the Beatles' *Sgt. Pepper's Lonely Hearts Club Band* and Bob Dylan's *Highway 61 Revisited* justifiably viewed *Up-Tight Everything's Alright, Down to Earth, I Was Made to Love Her, For Once in My Life,* and *My Cherie Amour* as showcases for Wonder's singles. By the time Stevie reached twenty-one, he had had one number-one hit, two number-twos, and two number-threes. He'd placed an additional six in the Top Ten, and four more in the Top Thirty. On the R&B charts he'd done even better, with six chart-toppers, three runners-up, and four more Top Twenty hits. So it's not all that surprising that many listeners went directly to the two volumes of *Greatest Hits* released in 1968 and 1971 rather than buying his albums.

That wasn't entirely fair. Wonder released four albums between November 1966 and the end of the decade. A fifth album, the instrumental *Eivets Rednow*—read it backward—remains the weirdest moment in his career. Stevie had wanted to make an album with jazz guitarist Wes Montgomery, who had broken into the pop market with a heavily orchestrated set of rock and pop standards, *A Day in the Life*. Fascinated, Wonder wrote several songs for Montgomery, but the guitarist died of a heart attack before they could be recorded. While not adventurous in jazz terms, "How Can You Believe," "More than a Dream," and "Which Way the Wind" provided a few interesting musical moments when Wonder recorded them on harmonica, backed by overblown orchestral arrangements. The album's title, and the absence of Wonder's name on the jacket, fooled at least a few fans. Stevie enjoyed telling the story of a fan who came up to him in an airport complaining, "Those whites takin' over everything. Look, I heard a kid today, man, played 'Alfie' just *like* you."

Each of the other four albums offers glimpses of Wonder's rapidly maturing and many-faceted sensibility. *Down to Earth* (1967) combines soulful covers of folk-rock hits by the Byrds ("Mr. Tambourine Man") and Sonny and Cher ("Bang Bang") with tastes of Ray Charles–style country and western ("That Lonesome Road") and the topical R&B scorcher "Be Calm (And Keep Yourself Together)," a direct plea to the enraged brothers and sisters tearing up their own communities. *I Was Made to Love Her* (1967) showcases Stevie as a southern soulman who would have been at home in Memphis or Muscle Shoals. A fine if obscure Holland-Dozier-Holland song, "Baby Don't Do It," complements a strong set of covers including Sam Cooke's "Send Me Some Lovin'," Ray Charles's "A Fool for You," Bobby Bland's "I Pity the Fool," James Brown's "Please Please Please," Marvin Gaye's "Can I Get a Witness?", the Temptations' "My Girl," and "Respect." While both *For Once in My Life* (1968) and *My Cherie Amour* (1969) veer toward middle-of-the-road standards apparently directed toward Las Vegas promoters, the opening sequence of the former—"Shoo-Be-Doo-Be-Doo-Da-Day," "For Once in My Life," and "You Met Your Match"—offers glimpses of the sonic flow of the great albums to come.

Despite the high points, the album situation was a source of frustration for Wonder. His musical interests were gravitating toward album-oriented musicians who enlisted popular styles in the service of creative and cultural exploration, among them Jimi Hendrix, Roland Kirk, and Sly Stone. And he was acutely aware that some Motown acts, most notably those produced by Norman Whitfield, were successfully challenging the Hitsville formula. "Have you heard the Temptations' 'Cloud Nine'?" he asked one interviewer. "It's more or less what we call funkadelic. It's a combination of R&B, psychedelic, and funky African-type beats. I'm experimenting. A lot of things I've done recently are funkadelic." One of the songs Wonder had in mind was "Shoo-Be-Doo-Be-Doo-Da-Day." He was particularly happy with the clavinet solo, one of his first experiments with the new technology that would define his seventies work. "I had the confidence something good was gonna happen," he said, "but I didn't know when. And then it began to happen."

Increasingly, Wonder perceived himself as a Beatles-style artist rather than simply as an entertainer. He immersed himself in songwriting and record production. In 1971 he reflected on the process that would characterize his great work of the seventies: "Writing is my thing. Writing is me—letting my inner thoughts out. I think this all comes from meeting certain people, experiencing certain things, going to certain places. I believe a song has to have a strong melody. When you want to get into the beat, you gotta get that thing going. In writing I'll put the melody on tape, do the background voices or whatever I want. Then I get it together—like, go into the studio and do this and do that, and it's like I want it."

Hints of Wonder's future could be seen on *Signed, Sealed, and Delivered*, which featured "Never Had a Dream Come True," the gorgeous gospel lament "Heaven Help Us All," and a funky cover of "We Can Work It Out" that paid tribute both to the Beatles and to Motown's rivals in Memphis: "I had the desire to move out of the one little thing that Motown was in. If Stax did something I liked, I did it myself." The album's title cut featured an electric sitar, reflecting Wonder's increasing contact with rock musicians, like onetime Yardbirds guitarist Jeff Beck, who had begun experimenting with new instruments and Eastern sounds. The two met when Beck rented the Motown studio to lay down some tracks. Beck's willingness to pursue musical ideas and experiment with song form appealed to Wonder, who continued to strain against the limits of the hit-single format. Commenting on the difference between Beck's sessions and the Motown dynamic, Wonder said, "This is the kind of freedom I didn't want way back when. But becoming aware of different music, you need this freedom."

Soon after Wonder graduated from the Michigan School for the Blind in January 1968 with his mother beaming at his side, his drive for creative freedom brought him into near open conflict with Motown. Live recordings from 1969 and 1970 cast the problem in stark relief. Performing with the Motown Revue, Stevie blazed through funky versions of "For Once in My Life," "Shoo-Be-Doo-Be-Doo-Da-Day," and "Uptight." But Motown continued to groom him for Las Vegas; his company-assigned music director, Gene Kees, envisioned him as a young Sammy Davis Jr.: "By the time he's 21, he will have become Stevie Wonder, the entertainer, and not just Stevie Wonder, the maker of pop records." The dreadful *Stevie Wonder Live* LP released in March 1970 showcases the entertainer crooning his softer hits—

"My Cherie Amour," "Yester-Me, Yester-You, Yesterday"—along with the standard lounge-act fare of "Everybody's Talkin'," "I've Gotta Be Me," "Pretty World," the "Love Theme from Romeo and Juliet," and "By the Time I Get to Phoenix."

Aware that Wonder would soon turn twenty-one and be legally able to redefine his relationship with the label, Motown reluctantly allowed him to produce his next studio album. Although it included the hit single "If You Really Love Me" and the aching "Never Dreamed You'd Leave in Summer," the first album produced under the new arrangement, *Where I'm Coming From,* was less consistent and focused than *Signed, Sealed, and Delivered.* Taking his cue from Dylan and the Beatles, Wonder tried his hand at socially explicit songs like "I Wanna Talk to You," which addresses the racial and generation gaps; "Think of Me as Your Soldier," a tribute to his contemporaries fighting in Vietnam; and "Sunshine in Their Eyes," a slice of ghetto realism that concludes, "Most of the news is bad." Admitting that the album was "kinda premature," Wonder looked back on it as a rough draft for the vision he would soon begin to realize: "I had to find out what my direction and my destiny was. And there was no way that I could just go on from where I had stopped at Motown. It was a completely different thing that was in my head. This time it wasn't so much a question of where I was coming from but where I was going to."

I F STEVIE WONDERED WHERE he was heading, Curtis Mayfield knew where he'd been and had a clear idea of where he wanted to go. In the midst of the haunting version of "Mighty Mighty (Spade and Whitey)" that opens *Curtis/Live!,* Mayfield pauses to ask the crowd at the Bitter End Café, where the album was recorded, if he can "get a bit deeper." With the crowd behind him, accompanied by pattering bongos and funky vamps, he meditates on the racist "stupidness we've been taught" and asserts that there "really ain't no difference, if you're cut you're gonna bleed." Responding to James Brown, who himself was calling back to "We're a Winner," which was echoing Mahalia Jackson and thousands of angry, brokenhearted protesters, Mayfield broke down what it meant to him that night in 1971: "I got to say it loud, gotta say it loud, I'm black and I'm proud."

For Curtis, as for Stevie and Aretha, there was no contradiction, not even much tension, between Black Power and universal humanism. If the songs Mayfield wrote in the seventies sounded different, the shift reflected the new questions Mayfield was asking himself. "I was writing songs when I was maybe twelve," he said. "Some of them were gospel, and even though the later ones were different, it really stayed the same. My songs always came from questions that I need answers for, even for myself. I was observing things, what happened politically, what was in the paper, what was on television. Asking what things were wrong that oughta be right. It was just straight from the heart, and I didn't have answers all the time."

Increasingly, Mayfield's songs challenged his audience to think about the escalating problems of racial polarization and inner-city black neighborhoods. His solo albums confronted the blues realities of drug addiction ("Stone Junkie"), racial paranoia ("Mighty Mighty (Spade & Whitey)"), and the continuing theft of land from American Indians ("I Plan to Stay a Believer"). Mayfield's balancing of black self-assertion and racial openness reaches deep into the gospel tradition, which recognizes that the ability to accept others, to live out the democratic vision, requires self-acceptance. The same array of perceptions recurs in the two singles from the *Roots* album, "We Got to Have Peace" and "Beautiful Brother of Mine." A masterful combination of Mayfield's gospel and funk styles, "Beautiful Brother" holds out a vision of a community coming to terms with the real meaning of the slogan "Black Is Beautiful": "Together we're truly Black Power, learning to love by the hour."

The complexity of Mayfield's political vision comes through most powerfully in a triad of songs from his debut album, *Curtis*, perhaps the best album he ever made. Together "The Other Side of Town," "We the People Who Are Darker than Blue," and "Move On Up" explore the origins, problems, and promises of Black Power. A report from the urban war zone, "The Other Side of Town" paints a generation deprived of education, hope, and guidance. Mayfield's mournful cry wasn't what white America wanted to hear, but he refused to turn away from the spiritual despair of poor black communities waking up to find themselves even more isolated than they had been nearly two decades earlier, when the *Brown vs. Board* decision promised an end to segregation. The isolation had its roots in political decisions and economic forces that were already in place in the fifties. Seen from the outside, the high-rise projects in Chicago and the abandoned factories in Detroit served as emblems of the dreams deferred. Lived from the inside, the situation was even worse. Black-on-black violence, spiraling drug use, and the breakdown of community organizations mocked the vision he'd learned in his grandmother's church. Mayfield didn't disagree with the militants who confronted white hostility and hammered black pride as a necessary response to white supremacy. But as "We the People Who Are Darker than Blue" suggests, something more needed to be said. "Pardon me brother as you stand in your glory," he sang softly, "I know you won't mind if I tell the whole story." Zeroing in on the growing nihilism in ghetto life, he insisted that black people take responsibility for stopping the violence that was part genocide, part suicide. The blues didn't get any darker or deeper. And, Mayfield reminded his people, the blues didn't negate the possibility of redemption that yoked "Move On Up" to "People Get Ready" and "We're a Winner."

The changing sound and less conciliatory messages on *Curtis, Curtis/ Live!* and *Roots* reflect the rapidly changing political and social landscape. But they also speak to the creative independence Mayfield enjoyed at the Curtom label. For Mayfield and partner Eddie Thomas, Curtom marked a fulfillment of a dream. "We'd been thinking about it for a long time," Thomas reflected. "We went in together. That's why on the label you'll see a Gemini in the yellow and a Scorpion, Curtis and I. I'm the Scorpio in the yellow hot sun. We had June Conquest, we had Donny Hathaway on the label, we had the Impressions." And for the first half of the seventies they had one of the most successful black independent labels this side of Detroit. Curtom's financial success resulted from a series of astute decisions Mayfield had made first in collaboration with Thomas and then with Marv Stuart, a young white promoter who'd previously concentrated on rock acts.

One of the best decisions they made involved Curtis's career. Although the Impressions' first three Curtom albums made the charts, none rose into the Top One Hundred. Stuart recalled the crucial moment: "I told Curtis, 'Everyone makin' it is a singer-songwriter. You're an artist, you should go out on your own.' " Looking back, Thomas has no regrets about the choice: "All of your outstanding vocalists, performers, singers, players generally go solo, it's like a trend. Groups can last for so long, the Miracles, then it's Smokey Robinson and the Miracles, then just Smokey Robinson. Jackie Wilson,

Clyde McPhatter, Frankie Lymon, Michael Jackson. They all take off on solo flight. I heard Smokey say on the radio, 'I love the group, but I find it easier to make a decision, and it's final, easier to travel, I can just get on the plane. All of the things that had to be four or five other decisions made, I only make one. It gets easier for me. That was the way to go at a certain point." Chicago-soul historian Johnny Meadows believed that Mayfield's departure from the Impressions allowed him to write "more for himself than for the group. He usually wrote with an artist in mind, he didn't just write a song to write a song. He was writing with Gene Chandler in mind on 'What Now?' and 'Just Be True,' the same thing with Jerry Butler, the same thing with the Impressions. When he went solo, he wanted to showcase himself where he'd been showcasing the Impressions. He didn't want to be Curtis Mayfield without the Impressions, he wanted to be Curtis Mayfield."

The decision paid off immediately. Mayfield's solo debut, *Curtis*, made the Top Twenty. Each of his first five solo efforts made the Top Forty, capped by the *Superfly* soundtrack, which reached number one. Mayfield recalled his initial surprise at the success of his solo projects. He'd struck out on his own, he recalled, because he was "just spreading myself too thin, trying to do everything at Curtom and still going out on gigs with the Impressions. I never really intended to leave permanently. But when the *Curtis* album came out, we all of a sudden discovered we had two hit acts."

In fact, it took the reconstituted Impressions several years to reestablish themselves as a hit act. Leroy Hutson, Donny Hathaway's college roommate, replaced Mayfield as lead singer. Hutson never really clicked with the group, though he later had two Top Forty Curtom hits with "All Because of You" and "Feel the Spirit." When Hutson left the group late in 1973, he was replaced by two new tenor leads, Ralph Johnson, who had a strong gospel voice, and Reggie Torian, whose forte was soft ballads and who could handle Mayfield's parts on the Impressions' sixties classics. After two more unsuccessful albums, the new Impressions finally broke through with the number-one R&B hit "Finally Got Myself Together" and follow-ups "Sooner or Later" and "Same Thing It Took," both of which peaked at number three.

Alongside its two showcase acts, the Curtom roster boasted a number of solid artists, many of whom had been discovered and developed by Mayfield. The songs he wrote during the late sixties and early seventies uphold the high standards he established in writing for Butler, Chandler, and the Impressions. Mayfield devoted a great deal of attention to the Five Stairsteps, a pre–Jackson 5 family group whose hits included Curtis's compositions "Don't Waste Your Time," "Don't Change Your Love," and "Stay Close to Me." The most promising of the label's acts, however, was without question Donny Hathaway. Before he left Curtom for Atlantic, Hathaway recorded his first two minor hits, the Mayfield Singers' "I've Been Trying" and "I Thank You," a duet between Donny and June Conquest.

Mayfield first met Hathaway, whom he considered "a young genius," when the Impressions were performing at Washington's Howard University: "Donny was originally out of St. Louis, and he was at Howard studying music. He'd come out of the church too, but his family got him into the university. So he went back to the long-haired classical music and learned to play that piano any way you could imagine. So I was playing at Howard, and he came to the theater with a couple of his singers. They were all majoring in music." Hathaway impressed Mayfield with both the breadth and depth of his musical knowledge. "He had a lot of learning in him, but he was instilled with a lot of depth of the religious feeling of black music. This fella, you could just talk to him over the phone and play him a piece of music, and he could call out every chord and every movement and where the fifth was and the augmented and tell you what key it was in. He really baffled me. I always admired people that could do that because I never had that kind of learning. It was just amazing."

Flattered by Hathaway's request for permission to name his group the Mayfield Singers, Curtis attended a campus performance and immediately signed them to a contract: "They were singing like the Fifth Dimension before there ever was one. So of course I signed them up, and we got a chance to make a couple of recordings. That's how I came to know Donny. Of course he was an arranger, and he just wiped the studio musicians out. He was so intellectual with the music. We got some of our people for the records out of the Chicago Symphony, and oh, he had them kicking. All those little new ideas he'd learned in his writing. It was just a delight for the old-timers to come in and hear this new kind of music and to see this youngster just making his way. He was destined to be somebody big."

For a short time Hathaway worked alongside Mayfield as a Curtom arranger, songwriter, and staff producer. But the collaboration never really clicked. Eddie Thomas attributed the problems to the clash of two strong personalities: "Donny Hathaway is a genius by himself, and it's so difficult when two geniuses are together. A great great great musician, and I'm so sorry his life was so short. We tried to do something with him as an artist, but there was a little friction. I think what happened is Donny and Curtis just clashed. Donny proved later on how good he was. It's hard to tell a guy, 'Hey, this guy's great too.' There wasn't enough room for two of them. We only put out one Donny Hathaway single [the duet with June Conquest], and it just hit the bottom of the R&B charts."

Curtom released Hathaway from his contract, enabling him to sign with Atlantic. The music he created during the first four years of the seventies fully justifies Mayfield's "genius" assessment. Like Stevie Wonder, Hathaway could slide smoothly between penetrating social commentary ("Little Ghetto Boy"), delicate soul balladry ("Je Vous Aime (I Love You)"), driving funk ("The Ghetto" with its memorable interpolation of "We Shall Overcome" two minutes and thirty-seven seconds into the groove), deep blues ("Giving Up"), and pure gospel aspiration ("Someday We'll All Be Free"). His duets with Roberta Flack on "Where Is the Love?" and "You've Lost That Loving Feeling" reverberate with the sensation that somehow the once-bright beacons of reconciliation were dimming, in the world and in our hearts. Soul music may never suffer a greater loss than it did the day in 1979 when Hathaway, disoriented and depressed, plunged to his death from the fifteenth-floor ledge of New York's Essex Hotel.

Despite the problems with Hathaway, collaboration played a much larger part in Mayfield's music during the early years at Curtom. One of his favorite albums, *Curtis/Live!*, provides a tantalizing glimpse of what might have happened if the Impressions had developed a rapport with a regular rhythm section. Drummer Tyrone McCullen and bass player Joseph "Lucky" Scott lay down sinewy rhythmic patterns while Mayfield and second guitarist Craig McMullen frame Curtis's vocals with tasty guitar licks. The center of the sound, however, comes from master percussionist Henry Gibson, who alternates between bongos and congas to add a polyrhythmic West African feel to new versions of Impressions classics like "Gypsy Woman" and "People Get Ready" as well as more recent funk compositions "We People Who Are Darker than Blue" and "(Don't Worry)."

Curtis/Live! spent thirty-eight weeks in the Top One Hundred, by far

Mayfield's most successful album to date. Part of the success resulted from Mayfield's increasing appeal to an audience attuned to the psychedelic rock coming out of San Francisco. On both *Curtis* and *Curtis/Live!*, Mayfield's guitar playing took on a more aggressive edge, reflecting both his influence on and his response to Jimi Hendrix. Hendrix credited Mayfield with having a significant impact on his guitar playing, a connection that comes through clearly in the delicate phrasing and distinctive harmonies on "Little Wing" and "Electric Ladyland." Mayfield, who experimented with feedback and distortion on his early-seventies solos, saw Hendrix's explorations as part of a shared attempt to free music's connecting energies. "Jimi's approach to music transcends racial barriers," he said. "His imagination spoke to people on a deeper level than that. With the psychedelics and what have you, he was almost like a scientist, studying the effects."

Mayfield felt a special affection for the music Hendrix made with the all-black Band of Gypsies: "Every once in a while I have a need to hear that, Jimi and Buddy Miles and Billy Cox, just those three musicians lock in so well. I love 'Machine Gun.'" Elaborating on Hendrix's appeal, Mayfield emphasized his technical virtuosity. "Jimi of course could break out into lead and do tremendously creative things with his wah-wah," he said. "However, there were movements sometimes that he brought to his music that would make you immediately think of Curtis, where he actually does a little falsetto with his voice and makes a few Curtis Mayfield chord structures." Funkmaster George Clinton agreed: "You can hear a lot of Curtis in Jimi Hendrix. In the sixties every guitar player wanted to play like Curtis." Hendrix reciprocated Mayfield's admiration: "I like the Impressions. I like that touch; I like that flavor; that type of music. It's like an enchanted thing."

Mayfield's growing interest in the funky explorations being carried out by Hendrix and Clinton's recently formed Funkadelic gave his music a more distinctive sound. "I just had another way of coming off with my music, and it did appear to be just a little bit different," he said. "I'd never taken any music lesson, so I didn't really know the forms, eight bars, sixteen bars, this, that. So I played and wrote as I felt it." Less conventionally structured than the songs Mayfield wrote for the Impressions, the new sound challenged his musicians. "I did get slack from the musicians, but even they would make comments that 'gosh this is a terribly strange key to play in, what did he do?' They just had to follow as I wrote it, and I wouldn't dare let them change it. Always at the end it would turn out, and everybody would say, 'Wow, that's happening.' "

At the beginning of 1973 Mayfield and Eddie Thomas parted ways. The decision involved Mayfield's increasing reliance on Marv Stuart. Mayfield credited Stuart with helping fulfill Curtom's economic potential. "As green as he was, he was very ambitious," Mayfield said. "I taught him the record business and how to relate to people. Through his own know-how and his own go-gettingness, he learned. He was able to find weak spots in Curtom, and he turned them around." Thomas maintained a deep love for Mayfield and blamed the racial climate in the record industry for separating them. Despite Mayfield's Black Power philosophy, commercial realities led him to jettison his black partner. "After so long, I'd been doing a lot of promotion. Curtis felt that Marv could help him more in his career because he was white," Thomas reflected. "I admit my limitations being a black executive even to go that far. So we shook hands on it, and I said, 'I'll start my own studio. I'll stay South and start my own thing, Thomas Associates.' It was like two giants, one giant and a half." Thomas laughed. "Decided hey you gotta go this way and I'll go that way. Curtis set up a studio on Lincoln Avenue in Chicago, and that's where he did 'Superfly' and all the gutbucket stuff."

Even though Mayfield continued to advance his vision of love and acceptance, his emphasis on Black Power and social problems may have contributed to the difficulty he had crossing over to white audiences as a live performer. His solo albums sold well to white listeners. Surprisingly, attempts to book Mayfield into rock venues elicited little response from audiences who eagerly embraced other artists experimenting with combinations of rock, funk, and soul. In 1969 Mayfield played the Fillmore West on a bill with Santana and Ike and Tina Turner. In 1972 he was booked into Chicago's version of the Fillmore, the Aragon Ballroom. Neither crossover attempt worked. Chicago promoter Jerry Mickelson offered an explanation that rings hollow in light of the success of Sly Stone and Jimi Hendrix with similar crowds: "You learn the market. Take Curtis Mayfield. He was hotter than a pistol, and he died in the Aragon. So we learned that you can't do a black act up there."

Mayfield's failure to cross over as a live performer seems particularly baffling in light of the massive success of his movie soundtracks, beginning with *Super Fly*, which stayed at the top of the album charts for four weeks during 1972. Mayfield jumped at the chance when producer Sig Shore asked him to write the soundtrack for what would become one of the definitive films of the blaxploitation genre. "I can recall having received the *Super Fly* script from Sig Shore and [screenwriter] Philip Fenty at the Lincoln Center in New York," Mayfield recalled. "I was performing there and they brought this script in between shows and wow, was I so excited. I'd written a song just flying back home from New York. It took me hardly no time to prepare the songs and that's how it began. It was different, it was wearing a new hat. I was just elated to have a chance to do something of that manner. I began writing immediately upon reading the script. I was making notes and coming up with the songs already. That was just a fantastic adventure for me."

The songs Mayfield wrote in that burst of creative activity, especially the title cut, "Pusherman," and "Freddie's Dead," earn *Super Fly* a place alongside Isaac Hayes's *Shaft*, which defined the blaxploitation-soundtrack market when it was released in 1971. For Mayfield, *Super Fly* represented a chance to communicate the realities of urban life to a large audience. "Of course I could relate with a lot of it, because I knew what a 'Priest' and what a 'Superfly' was," he said, referring to the movie's leading characters. "It allowed me to get past the glitter of the drug scene and go to the depth of it—allowing a little bit of the sparkle and the highlights lyrically, but always with a moral."

From almost the moment the movie was released, however, audiences recognized a dissonance between the film's celebration of drugs and sex and the message of Mayfield's soundtrack, which clearly identifies the "Pusherman" as community enemy number one. Mayfield remembered his surprise at the way director Gordon Parks Jr.'s treatment transformed the meaning of Fenty's script. "For me when I first was reading it, it read very well. Here's this guy that may have been a nice guy and could have been totally positive, but he got caught up in the wrong group of people. I didn't put Priest down. He was just trying to get out. His deeds weren't noble ones, but he was making money and he had intelligence. And he did survive. I mean all this was reality." The script was one thing; the movie was something else. "Reading the script didn't tell you 'and then he took another hit of cocaine' and then about a minute later 'he took another hit,' " Mayfield lamented. "So when I saw it visually, I thought 'This is a cocaine infomercial.' "

Some would argue that Mayfield should have bolted. But rather than backing out of the project, he set about creating what amounts to a masked statement undercutting the surface message. "I made the commitment, and of course I wasn't going to let go of my chance to do a movie. Yet I didn't want to be part of that infomercial. So it was important to me that I left the glitter and all the social stuff and tried to go straight in the lyrics. I tried to tell the stories of the people in depth and not insult the intelligence of those who were spending their money. That was an actual effort on my part." In addition, Mayfield countered the infomercial by releasing a vocal version of "Freddie's Dead" in advance of the movie. The song leaves no doubt about the message: "Remember what I said, 'cause Freddie's Dead." "I released it three months prior to the movie coming out so when the kids got in there they knew the music." The strategy meant that even though the film includes only an instrumental version of "Freddie's Dead," audience members familiar with the single could juxtapose the film's images with Mayfield's sober reminder that it all leads to meaningless violence and community destruction. Mayfield emphasized the point by concluding the title song with a moment that could be described as gospel funk. While Pate's orchestration fades out over one of the decade's catchiest rhythmic grooves, Mayfield repeats the line "trying to get over" again and again, bringing "Superfly" into dialogue with the gospel classic "How I Got Over."

Mayfield may not have succeeded in resolving the contradictions at the heart of *Super Fly*, but he'd put his finger on the malaise that was rapidly changing the tone of life in black America. On his next album he turned his attention to the most obvious manifestation and source of the malaise: Vietnam. One of Mayfield's most consistent albums, *Back to the World* (1973) reworks the basic concept of Marvin Gaye's 1971 classic *What's Going On*. Like Gaye, Mayfield tells the story of a black veteran returning home from Vietnam to a community on the verge of collapse. The inspiration came from a set of performances at military bases. "I wrote *Back to the World* because we'd played some bases in France, England, Germany and that was a very popular common saying. 'I'll be glad when I get back to the world,' which meant to them coming back home to America. And so I wrote that song as my own interpretation of what the war was all about." Ruminating on the song's picture of soldiers crawling through the mud wondering why the Lord had abandoned them, Mayfield reflected on what the vets found when they returned home: "Then you get back to the world and you wonder what it's all for. You can't get a job. You're being robbed. Your woman that was there two or three years, your woman's long been gone. And of course, all these different things were part of the times. So all you could do was deal with the questions and answers of how you might try to reasonably work it out so you could live with it."

The concern with finding a way to live with it—to reconnect with your woman, your community, your spirit—differentiates *Back to the World* from *What's Going On*. Injecting gospel intensities into the dense orchestral textures and funk rhythms, Mayfield focuses on the vets' changing psychological responses. In contrast, part of what makes *What's Going On* an unquestioned masterpiece is Gaye's concentration on the social cross-currents sweeping through the inner cities and the country as a whole. Mayfield acknowledges the social forces in "Back to the World" and "Future Shock" but concentrates on the vet's personal struggles with despair ("Right On for the Darkness") and the renewal of hope he finds when he turns to his "heavenly father" in "Future Song (Love a Good Woman, Love a Good Man)." Where Gaye concludes *What's Going On* with the near-desperation of "Inner City Blues"— "makes me wanna holler"—Mayfield resolves *Back to the World* with the upbeat "Keep On Trippin'." As always in Mayfield's music, what black intellectual Cornel West calls the "audacious hope" of the gospel vision shines through the darkness.

⌣℗⌣

THAT HOPEFUL AUDACITY COMFORTED Stevie Wonder on his twenty-first birthday as he moved to make his vision of creative independence a reality. Taking advantage of his client's legal right to disavow agreements signed as a minor, Wonder's lawyer informed Berry Gordy that Stevie was no longer under contract to Motown. Wonder explained the decision primarily in creative terms: "My contract was made when I was very young. And I didn't know the significance of having my own publishing. But I basically wanted to do more. I felt I didn't want to slide into one bag. Music changes, and if you're in the line of change and don't move, you get trampled."

The news shocked Gordy, who had hosted Wonder for an early birthday dinner the night before. When Gordy asked him why he hadn't provided advance warning, Stevie indicated that his lawyer had acted without his permission, and dismissed him. His replacement, a scruffy-looking hardball player named Johanan Vigoda, was, Gordy sighed, "ten times tougher." First Vigoda hired accountants to examine Motown's previous financial dealings with Wonder. Finding the accounts in order, Vigoda conducted a grueling round of negotiations with Motown, Atlantic, and Columbia that culminated in Wonder's decision to re-sign with his old label. The key to the agreement was Motown's somewhat reluctant willingness to surrender most of its accustomed control over its acts. "It was a very important contract for Motown and a very important contract for Stevie, representing the artists of Motown," Vigoda reflected. "He opened up the future for Motown. That's what they understood. They never had an *artist* in 13 years. They had single records, they managed to create a name in certain areas, but they never came through with a major, major artist."

Motown president Ewart Abner had been aware of Wonder's creative dissatisfaction and was less surprised by his move. "He was about 19 then," he recalled. "He used to remind me that his day was coming, that when he turned 21 he was going to do what he wanted to do. I used to ask him—or tell him—to do things, and he'd say, 'Okay, but when I'm 21 I'm going to have things my own way. I don't think you know where I'm coming from. I don't think you can understand it.' " Still, Abner reported, when Stevie "came to me and said, 'I'm 21 now. I'm not gonna do what you say anymore. Void my contract,' I freaked." After Gordy recovered from his initial shock, he reconciled himself to Wonder's unprecedented deal. The package included a greatly increased share of revenues for the artist, and it established Taurus Productions and Black Bull publishing, both staffed by employees under Wonder's direct control. In his autobiography, *To Be Loved*, Gordy described Wonder's creative emancipation with a mixture of regret and admiration. "I had some misgivings when he asked for total creative control," Gordy acknowledged. "I thought of the progression he had made from an eleven-year-old high-pitched singer banging on bongos to a full-voiced vocalist, writer, and now producer. So I agreed to the creative control. Stevie was ready to fly."

While the negotiations took place, Wonder was already testing his wings. Collecting the million dollars he'd earned under the terms of his original contract, he checked into a room at a West Side Manhattan hotel and went to work at the Electric Lady Studio, which Jimi Hendrix had assembled on Eighth Street in Greenwich Village. For Wonder, the move marked his emancipation from Motown's production-line creative process, as well as from his own past. "I knew I couldn't forever jump up and down and do 'Fingertips,' " he told *The New York Times Magazine*. "I basically wanted to stay with Motown. I've been with them since the beginning, and I felt that I would like to be one of the pioneers of seeing it change, get into a new direction. I knew the company, and I knew the people, and all I had to do was somehow convince Gordy, and part of my convincing had been done when I split. I knew that a lot of the emotions that existed were because of the fact that I was young, as opposed to looking at me as being a *man*. They were looking at the past, when I was Little Stevie Wonder running up and down the street. So they had another kind of attachment, and it was sort of an insult or hurt to them when I did split, because they could only relate back to the beginning." Looking back at his period of transition, Wonder said that while Motown had been upset at first, "they began to understand—later. Whatever peak I had reached doing that kind of music, I had reached. It was important for them to understand we were going nowhere. I wasn't growing. I just kept repeating the Stevie Wonder sound, and it didn't express how I felt about what was happening out there. I decided to go for something besides a winning formula. I wanted to see what would happen if I changed."

The changes involved Wonder's personal life as well as his music and finances. Eight months before his twenty-first birthday he married Syreeta Wright, a Motown secretary and talented singer who would record two fine albums bearing her husband's unmistakable musical imprint. Syreeta taught transcendental meditation, and the couple's relationship sparked Stevie's interest in Asian philosophy and mysticism. From the start, however, the marriage ran into problems, including Syreeta's lack of interest in behaving in accord with Stevie's belief—recall he was barely out of his teens—that "a woman's supposed to take care of a man domestically and spiritually." When the marriage came to an end the following year, Stevie first attributed the split to the stars. "She's a Leo, and I'm a Taurus," he told several interviewers. "They're both fixed signs, and they both want to lead." Later, he would reflect that "I just wasn't ready to get married. I think the beauty of going together and being close is so beautiful that sometimes when you get married you feel that you blow it. There were hassles and other things that involved me finding myself."

The real problem was Stevie's total immersion in his music. According to Jim Giltrap, a backup singer who worked with Wonder throughout the period, "He'd be in the studio most of the time, and then when he comes home, first thing he does is sit at the piano. And his woman, she wants to be with her man. Not just listen to his tapes and him playing music all the time. How can a woman cope with that, day after day? And also when he finishes work, he's tired and out. Steve only sleeps a few hours per day, and when he's awake, he makes music. A woman needs more attention than that." Whatever forces led to its dissolution, the marriage inspired at least two first-rate songs: Syreeta's beautiful rendition of "Cause We've Ended as Lovers" and Wonder's heartfelt eulogy for a sweet love lost, "Superwoman."

A seductive ballad built around the constantly shifting rhythms and sound textures that would become a signature of Wonder's mature work, "Superwoman" emerged from a series of marathon sessions at Electric Lady. Reveling in his newfound sonic wonderland, he opened his creative floodgates. "I recorded 40 tunes in about two weeks," he said. "They weren't totally finished, I just did piano basics or whatever. I would just lay down what came to mind, on the piano or on the clavinet, usually one of the two instruments. Depending on the instruments the songs do come out differently, 'cause an instrument is like a color, it puts you in a certain mood." The synthesizer brought out Wonder's mystical side. Often he described his experience of sound in visual terms: "When I hear music, I can *see* it, each instrument has its own color. The piano for instance is brown, and I can see each instrument playing its own part. It's like a puzzle, and when I fit all the pieces together, that's my high."

His interest in sound colors coalesced around his newly purchased state-of-the-art Moog synthesizer, an elaborate sound processor that had been assembled to his specifications. He'd liked Walter Carlos's use of the instrument on *Switched-on Bach* and was entranced by its possibilities. "It really isn't so much to imitate a particular instrument as to make the horizon for an instrument even wider," he said. "The sound has to be created because it's just another electrical impulse. With it you have the ability to shape the melody into any form you desire, attack, sustain, delay, release, or the combination of those can be done any way you want, to create the sound."

Wonder owed much of his success with synthesized sound to Robert Margouleff and Malcolm Cecil, who helped him realize his ideas from *Music of My Mind* through *Fulfillingness' First Finale*. Margouleff and Cecil had attracted Wonder's attention with the album *Zero Time*, an electronic extravaganza they'd released under the name of Tonto's Expanding Headband. African American troubadour Richie Havens introduced Wonder to the duo, which soon joined him at Electric Lady. Cecil told Motown chronicler Nelson George, "Stevie showed up with the Tonto LP under his arm. He said, 'I don't believe all this was done on one instrument. Show me the instrument.' He was always talking about seeing. So we dragged his hands all over the instrument, and he thought he'd never be able to play it. But we told him we'd get it together for him."

The trio went to work immediately, exploring the possibilities of numerous Manhattan studios, including Mediasound and Electric Lady. Margouleff remembered that they entered the studio at the start of the Memorial Day weekend. "By the end of that Monday—it must have been two or three in the morning—we had seventeen songs in the can," Margouleff said. "We never stopped working from that moment, night and day. He'd do the playing, we'd do the programming, and we started to accumulate a huge library of songs. Sometimes he'd just go into the studio and work on a groove, and four weeks later, it was a song."

The result was Wonder's first fully realized album, *Music of My Mind*. As the title indicates, Wonder was engaged in a period of introspection. The album jacket suggests the cavalcade of thoughts coursing through Wonder's mind as he prepares to create his greatest work to date. The front and back covers present a serious-looking Stevie wearing sunglasses that reflect a panoply of counterculture icons: the face of an American Indian, Buddha, the Earth as seen from outer space, the silhouette of Taurus, strange geological formations, a rainbow. If the montage situates Stevie in a fairly conventional hippie matrix, the music on the album was directed equally to his core R&B audience and to listeners who had grown up on *Sgt. Pepper's Lonely Hearts Club Band*. A shimmering sequence of beautiful textures spiced with funky R&B, the album's highlights include "Love Having You Around,"

"Happier than the Morning Sun," and "Keep On Running." The album's best cut, which curiously failed to crack the Top Thirty when released as a single, "Superwoman (Where Were You When I Needed You)," charts the changing emotions surrounding a collapsing love affair, shifting from self-justifying dismissal of the woman who "wants to boss the bull around" to wistful lament. While the album attracted positive critical comment, it wasn't a major hit, partly because it lacked a big hit single and partly because fans of progressive rock still had Wonder conveniently filed away in the parts of their brain labeled "Top Forty" or "soul."

A desire to break out of these categories lay behind Wonder's decision to accept the Rolling Stones' invitation to open for them on their 1972 North American tour. For Wonder, the tour proved aggravating. The press and promoters paid almost no attention to the Stones' "opening act," and especially during the early parts of the tour, the overwhelmingly white audiences greeted Wonder with indifference and inattention. The Stones, who had opened for Little Stevie Wonder on their first American tour back in 1964, had a good track record supporting black artists; their previous opening acts included Howlin' Wolf, Tina Turner, Billy Preston, and B.B. King. In 1972, however, they were in the midst of their most decadent period, as richly documented in the cult documentary *Cocksucker Blues.* From the start of the tour Wonder had trouble finding a place in the Stones' bacchanalian circus. Keith Richards broke from the drugs and debauchery just long enough to issue disparaging remarks about Wonder to the press. Stevie responded with sharpness. "I thought at the very beginning it was going to be good vibes," he told *Rolling Stone.* "But, you know, I could see that we were on two different levels. I never went and got high with them because I don't get high. So maybe that had something to do with it. I don't know. I went a few times to get a drink, some beer or something, but I never really hung out with them."

It didn't help that Wonder was just learning how to handle the demands of directing his own band, Wonderlove. One of the positive aspects of Motown's paternalism was that it spared the singers some of the responsibilities that accompanied personnel management. Amid the tensions between Wonder and the Stones, the first incarnation of Wonderlove never coalesced into a real band. Tensions boiled over midway through the tour when Wonder canceled a set in Houston after his drummer walked out. It was a classic rock 'n' roll moment. "My drummer had a nervous break-down," Wonder recollected. "I told him he rushed the tempo and the tempo was messed up, and he said, 'I didn't rush it too much,' and I said, 'Yes, you did.' He said, 'I'll tell you what. *You* play the goddamn drums,' and he split. He said, 'You play the drums, you're a drummer, you play the drums and sing at the same time and play your harmonica too.' He was very upset. I didn't believe that he would, but he did leave."

Nonetheless the tour generated some memorable musical moments. On most of the final stops, Wonder joined the Stones onstage for a medley of "Uptight" and "Satisfaction" that developed into a real showstopper. "It was spontaneous," Wonder remembered. "We did it once, and it was so exciting that we decided to just keep it in. From then on we fit it to the show." On the final stop of the tour at Madison Square Garden, which coincided with Jagger's birthday, an impromptu pie-throwing contest broke out during the medley. Undeterred by his blindness, Wonder dove in. "I got me some of that," he laughed. "Gimme that pie, baby. Somebody threw one at me, and I said, 'Oh, wow,' y'know. Poor Steve. Then I picked it up and *did* it. I was picking them up where I could find 'em and giving a fling. One of my singers picked up a piece, and we were smearing it all over each other's face. All these people, horn players and everything just sliding around, stepping in pies and chucking them, stuff flying all over, and meanwhile everybody's still playing." Despite the problems Wonder understood that the exposure he received was crucial to his larger vision. "No matter how many hassles we had, the good vibes have more than offset the bad ones," he admitted. "Music is like a religion to me, and the more sharing that takes place between the musicians and the audience, the more spiritual the music becomes. We've still managed to make a lot of people have soulful experiences."

Wonder followed up on the tour by reaching out to the counterculture audience that had responded so strongly to Aretha at the Fillmore. Writing in *Rolling Stone,* Ben Fong-Torres provided a fascinating portrait of Wonder's 1972 appearance in the Bay Area. After sold-out concerts at San Francisco's Winterland and Berkeley's Community Theater, Wonder traded in the African gown and shark-tooth necklace he'd performed in for a champagne gold suit complete with plaid bow tie and metallic copper platform shoes with four-inch heels. Fong-Torres described Wonder's attractively quirky style: "He establishes rapport on the basis of astrological signs and otherwise talks in black hippie fashion, zigzagging, sometimes from Pollyannish to apocalyptic." For all the countercultural trappings, Wonder insisted that he had no interest in drugs. "I smoked grass one time, and it scared me to death," he told Fong-Torres. "Things just got larger. It was something new and different, but I found I'm so busy checking things out all the time anyway that I don't really need it. If I were high it would destroy the character of my music because I would be tripping out so much on myself as opposed to the things around me."

The flashy dress and philosophical musings coexisted with Wonder's unflagging dedication to Martin Luther King's vision of interracial harmony. Translating the "I Have a Dream" speech into the argot of Woodstock, Wonder said, "If you think of blacks and whites in separate terms, you're feeding off something that's dying every day." Like Curtis Mayfield, he saw no contradiction between black pride and universalist humanism. "If I can do anything to help my people in respect of black pride, help the black people, then I'll do it," he emphasized. "Black people have a serious problem because we are not united. Everybody else is together. We must learn to appreciate ourselves. We have to learn to appreciate the accomplishments of our forefathers, like Nat Turner and Frederick Douglass." At the same time, Wonder sounded an ominous note: "I hate to sound pessimistic, but it will take people many years to realize the true meaning of Malcolm X's message. I may sound pessimistic, but we have serious problems that have to be dealt with. Nixon is cutting off all these programs and holding back funds. Who do you think it's hurting? The black man. We have always been the last to get and the first to have it taken away." As he would continue to do with increasing frequency, Wonder devoted himself to an eclectic array of progressive causes. Those that drew his attention included Kenneth Gibson's campaign to become the first black mayor of Newark; the Freedom Rally for John Sinclair, the White Panther leader jailed for possession of two joints; and the "One-to-One" benefit for a New York hospital for the mentally retarded. While Wonder clearly believed in the causes, the benefit appearances established his approach to political activism—rhetorical support backed by financial contributions—that would continue throughout his career. Although the approach made sense as part of the broader movement of the sixties and seventies, the limitations of symbolic politics would become increasingly clear in the eighties and nineties.

For Joe Billingslea, who had accompanied Wonder on the early Motown Revue tours as a member of the Contours, Wonder's political explorations grew directly out of tensions inherent in the Motown artists' peculiar relationship with their white contemporaries. "Motown got caught in some funny crossfire," Billingslea reflected. "Here's a bunch of black kids going flat-out after the American dream, you dig? The nice house, the clothes, the car. Just what everybody else has always gone for. But with what was going on, the riots, the Vietnam mess, it was the *down* side of the dream. And so just when some cat gets enough to afford the Continental—*bang*—it's not *cool* to drive it, disrespectful to the movement or whatever. Just when you're making it in the company, maybe, like Diana Ross, you see your brother pack off to Vietnam, when all them kids you play to in the theaters, baby, you know they gonna have college exemptions from the draft. In your own home, you *whipsawed*. You get your mama out of the projects first. *Then* you buy the car. Still, somebody got somethin' to say."

Judging by the success of the 1972 album *Talking Book,* both Stevie's new and old audiences liked what he was saying. The album's hit singles, "You Are the Sunshine of My Life" and "Superstition," certainly didn't hurt, but as Wonder stated, the singles were "only one page in the book. An album is a book." Combining to form a talking book in both the African and blind-culture senses, the chapters in the full volume came equally out of *Sgt. Pepper's Lonely Hearts Club Band* and Hitsville, U.S.A. As he would throughout the seventies, Wonder wrote and produced the songs and played most of the instruments himself. But he welcomed guest appearances such as Deniece Williams's vocals on "Tuesday Heartbreak" and Jeff Beck's guitar solo on "Looking for Another Pure Love." Each track on the album—"You've Got It Bad Girl," "Maybe Your Baby," "Blame It on the Sun," and "I Believe (When I Fall in Love It Will Be Forever)"—contributes to its status as Wonder's first fully realized artistic statement.

The complementary facets of Wonder's maturing genius come through most clearly in the triad of "You Are the Sunshine of My Life," "Big Brother," and "Superstition." Picking up from "My Cherie Amour" and "Yester-Me, Yester-You, Yesterday," "You Are the Sunshine of My Life" fulfilled the expectations of those who shared Motown's image of Stevie as the new Sammy Davis Jr. A number-one hit and million seller, the gentle lyrics perfectly complement a hook that only had to be heard once to be remembered. It didn't take long for Frank Sinatra, Andy Williams, Engelbert Humperdinck, Liza Minnelli, Perry Como, and Johnny Mathis to scramble to the front of the ever-growing ranks of stylists and crooners who have made "You Are the Sunshine of My Life" a fixture in the supper-club repertoire. That does not change the fact that, like "My Cherie Amour," "You Are the Sunshine of My Life" is a delightful song; nor should Wonder be blamed for any number of bad covers.

"Big Brother" was the political keynote of the album, suggesting that Wonder's political awareness was deepening alongside his musical intelligence. Striking out angrily at the cynical politicians who came around the ghetto only at election time, the song, in historian Brian Ward's words, "conjured up images of Orwellian state surveillance around the same time that the FBI's COINTELPRO operation against the Black Panther Party and other radical black groups was at its wretched peak." Wonder linked the song to his growing interest in history. "The most interesting thing to me was about civilizations before ours," he reflected, "how advanced people really were, how high they had brought themselves, only to bring themselves down because of the missing links, the weak foundations. So the whole thing crumbled, and that's kind of sad. And it relates to today and what could possibly happen here, very soon. That's basically what 'Big Brother' is all about. I speak of the history, the heritage of the violence, or the negativeness of being able to see what's going on with minority people. We don't have to do anything to [the people in power] 'cause they're gonna cause their own country to fall."

Less explicit but more compelling, "Superstition" joined the Stones' "Gimme Shelter," Buffalo Springfield's "For What It's Worth," Sly and the Family Stone's "Family Affair," and Creedence Clearwater Revival's "Bad Moon Rising" in capturing the raging paranoia that settled over the nation during the Nixon years. The lyrics swirl with nightmare images out of Robert Johnson or Bob Dylan. The devil's on his way and the writing's on the wall, but no one can read it. If you can get out with seven years of bad luck, take the deal. "Superstition's not the way," Wonder growls to the accompaniment of a horn line that splits the difference between Memphis and Duke Ellington. But if he has a better idea, he ain't letting on what it is. Wonder means every murky word, and the music backs him up; he said he'd built the song around the clavinet because "it's a funky, dirty, stinky, *nasty* instrument."

The song's aura of bad vibrations extended into real life around Jeff Beck's desire to record "Superstition." Beck had wanted to record "Maybe Your Baby" on his upcoming *Beck, Bogert & Appice* album, but Wonder reserved the song for himself and offered to write a new song in its place. Beck's version of what happened next seems to be substantively accurate. "I was sitting at the drum kit, which I love to play when nobody's around, doing this beat," Beck reported. "Stevie came kinda boogying into the studio. 'Don't stop.' 'Ah, c'mon, Stevie, I can't play the drums.' Then the lick came out: 'Superstition.' That was my song. I thought, he's giving me the riff of the century." Recognizing what he had, Wonder laid down his own version, originally intending to include it as a cut on *Talking Book.*

When Motown heard Stevie's version, they rushed it onto the market as a single. Wonder recalled the sequence of events leading up to the trouble: "I told Motown, 'Don't release 'Superstition.' And they said, 'Man, are you crazy?' They have control of releasing the singles. I knew there would be trouble. If his single had come out before mine and mine had flopped, it would have been cool. Or if both of ours had flopped, it would have been cool." The chances of which were zero. Realizing that competing with Stevie's first number-one hit since "Fingertips, Part 2" was pointless, Beck issued a bitter statement to the rock press: "Bastard. What can we say? He wrote it, that's the frustrating thing about it. He's got an incredible ear for small combo material. It fitted us like a glove. Stevie, you screwed up." Wonder would later atone by providing two songs, "Thelonious" and "Cause We've Ended as Lovers," for Beck's 1975 *Blow by Blow* album.

However difficult his interactions with the Stones and Beck might have been, Wonder was clearly following his own advice and connecting with every corner of the popular-music scene. He jammed with Edgar Winter and Elton John, with Sly Stone and Bob Marley, with Bob Dylan, Chaka Khan, and Jackson Browne; he sang duets with everyone from Prince to Frank Sinatra. And as *Music of My Mind* and *Talking Book* made clear, he wasn't about to surrender his roots in black music. Yet another of Stevie's collaborators, B.B. King, had one of his biggest hits in 1973 with "To Know You Is to Love You," which was written by Stevie and Syreeta Wright. The great bluesman summed up the reason that, however far he extended his musical horizons, Wonder would always maintain the love and respect of the people back in Paradise Valley: "Stevie understands R&B. Stevie *is* R&B."

❧

As THE MYTHIC SIXTIES—not to be confused with the ten years between 1960 and 1970—neared their belated end, Stevie and Aretha had become central symbols of Black Power. Funk trickster George Clinton echoed King when he anointed Stevie "Minister of Culture" for the "Chocolate Cities" where black people were beginning to claim the political power bequeathed them by white flight to the vanilla suburbs. Aretha Franklin was simply the "First Lady." When Aretha herself reflected on the movement's meaning, she concentrated on its effect on her self-image: "The black revolution certainly forced me and the majority of black people to begin taking a second look at ourselves," she commented. "It wasn't that we were all that ashamed of ourselves, we merely started appreciating our natural selves, falling in love with ourselves *just as we are.* So I suppose the revolution influenced me a great deal, but I must say that mine was a very *personal* evolution—an evolution of the *me* in myself." For Aretha, "the whole meaning of the revolution" was tied up in self-acceptance. "I know I've improved my overall look and sound," she reflected. "I've gained a great deal of confidence in myself." Responding to a question about Amiri Baraka's view of black music as a potentially revolutionary force, Aretha shifted the focus from the streets to the spirit: "Soul music is music coming out of the black spirit. A lot of it is based on suffering and sorrow, and I don't know anyone in this country who has had more of those two devils than the Negro."

By all accounts, Aretha knew the devils all too intimately. If she was known publicly as the "Queen of Soul," those who knew her used other nicknames. Donald Walden, who played saxophone in her road band, called her "Mona Lisa," while Jerry Wexler sympathetically referred to her as "Our Mysterious Lady of the Sorrows." "Sometimes she'd call me at four in the morning and we would talk—*long* talks," Wexler wrote in his autobiography. "If the call came then, it would usually be about her troubles." Aretha's troubles had many sources and symptoms: her ongoing battle to control her weight; her strained and deteriorating relationship with the mainstream press; charges of reckless driving and disorderly conduct against her in Detroit; erratic performances and canceled concerts, including an engagement at Caesar's Palace in Las Vegas; her father's problems involving the IRS and a gun battle between police and the Republic of New Afrika that left a policeman dead outside his church; and, most consuming of all, the collapse of her marriage with Ted White amid persistent, and widely believed, rumors of domestic abuse. The blues were, as Bessie Smith once sang, all around her bed and up inside her head.

In the midst of it all Aretha sought refuge in the havens black women had turned to for generations: music and the church. As she told her old friend Mahalia Jackson, "I'm gonna make a record and tell Jesus I cannot bear these burdens alone." "I don't think she's happy," Mahalia added. "Somebody else is making her sing the blues." Mahalia's remarks were quoted in a June 18, 1968, *Time* magazine cover story that Aretha vociferously condemned as a source of the "false and thoughtless lies" that her mother had abandoned the children. While she didn't deny having referred to herself as "an old woman in disguise, 25 going on 65," she complained that the article exaggerated her depression. "Things can never be that bad," she responded. "For the blind man, there is always the fellow with no feet. I've been hurt. You can't get over it all, but you can go on living and keep on looking. I'm not free yet, but I will be." In the offending article she had outlined the basic blues approach to dealing with the brutal experiences of everyday life: "Everybody who's living has problems and desires just as I do. When the fellow on the corner has something bothering him, he feels the same way I do. When we cry, we all gonna cry tears, and when we laugh, we all have to smile."

The most sensational passages in the *Time* article concerned Aretha's marriage. As *Rolling Stone* observed, "The story said her husband beat her up and that is the one sentence that anybody remembers." Many of Aretha's friends and associates confirmed that the marriage had been, at the least, tumultuous, but Aretha downplayed her suffering. "Oh, I've had my bad times," she told an interviewer, "but they're the same problems, aches and pains other people have; relationships that don't work and relationships that begin not to work. Okay. That causes pain, but when I think back on my marriage, I only think of how beautiful it was...and then came the time when it wasn't." By the middle of 1969 Aretha and White had separated, and shortly thereafter they filed for divorce.

While it would be several years before Aretha made the gospel record she promised Mahalia, she released her pent-up emotions in her music. Donald Walden, who worked in her band throughout the most difficult period, advised, "String the titles together, and that's the story of her life." Jimmy Johnson of the Muscle Shoals band recalled that at the time of the final breakup Aretha had been "highly depressed" and failed to show up for several sessions. When she did appear, however, she turned her sorrows into overpowering art. Describing the session where she recorded "Call Me," Johnson said, "I think she may have cried doing the lyrics of that song— because she definitely had us crying."

Jerry Wexler took a more philosophical approach to Aretha's art. "The songs she chose or wrote were loosely but significantly autobiographical," he reflected, contemplating the cathartic power of her songs. "If she couldn't feel it, forget it; if she didn't live it, she couldn't give it. And although I'm sure five-and-dime psychologists could write volumes on her reliance on unreliable men, she actually broke the chain of songs of self-pity, those poignant but somewhat masochistic lyrics sung by her mythic soul sisters like Bessie, Dinah, and Billie. Aretha would never play the part of the scorned woman: she wouldn't beg her man to come back no matter what. Her middle name was Respect." Aretha said matter-of-factly, "I sing to the realist. People who accept it like it is. I express problems. There are tears when it's sad and smiles when it's happy. It seems simple to me, but for some people, I guess feeling takes courage."

Although *Aretha Now* and *Soul '69* mark a slight decline from her first three Atlantic albums, both are moving testaments to her courage. The titles of the songs she wrote and chose to cover—and even more the ache in her voice—refract the emotional complexity of her dying marriage: "Today I Sing the Blues," "I Say a Little Prayer," "If You Gotta Make a Fool of Somebody," "I Can't See Myself Leaving You," "Think," "The Tracks of My Tears," "See Saw." As Wexler said, there's no point in reducing any of them to strict autobiography. What's important is the way Aretha delves into the indigo moments when something that felt right goes wrong. Even as she promises to keep her love alive in Burt Bacharach's "I Say a Little Prayer," she can hear the whispering waters of blues poet Percy Mayfield's

"River's Invitation" calling her away to death's promised peace. Her remake of "Today I Sing the Blues," the song that caught John Hammond's attention and gave her her first R&B hit, shows how far she'd come since taking her first steps away from the gospel highway. And her majestic reading of old friend Smokey Robinson's "The Tracks of My Tears" is damn near enough to make a ghetto real estate vulture consider the state of his soul.

Soul '69 lacks the collective impact of Aretha's best albums, but it remains an underappreciated landmark in her career. The title is, as Wexler admitted, a misnomer forced on her by Atlantic's overzealous marketing department. "It should have been called her jazz album," he observed. In fact, the album beats her Columbia LPs at their own game, presenting a variety of jazz, blues, and pop standards in tasteful jazz settings. Supplementing the Muscle Shoals rhythm section with top-flight jazz musicians including guitarist Kenny Burrell, bass player Ron Carter, and pianist Joe Zawinul, Aretha flawlessly executes a set that seems designed for fans of Nancy Wilson or Sarah Vaughan. Along with old chestnuts "So Long," "I'll Never Be Free," and Sam Cooke's "Bring It On Home to Me," Aretha insisted on covering two wistful folk-rock ballads, Glen Campbell's "Gentle on My Mind" and Bob Lind's "Elusive Butterfly." "Her taste could sometimes be very mainstream," Wexler observed. "That's part of her genius. When it went off a bit, it went off in its own way."

As Aretha's marriage disintegrated over the final years of the sixties, events in the outside world offered little relief. When she first returned to Detroit after the 1967 riot, she was "shocked and saddened to see the bullet-ridden house a few doors from my dad's, the National Guard still set up at Central High School with tanks and guns." Still stunned by King's April 1968 assassination, she accepted an invitation to sing at the opening session of the Democratic National Convention in Chicago that August. For many of those battling Mayor Daley's police in the bloody streets, it was a mistake for any black person, especially one who seemed to voice the aspirations of the revolution, to offer even indirect support to the establishment. But as Aretha prepared in a small dressing room with "just a curtain, chair, and mirror," she had "no idea pandemonium had erupted outside."

Aretha's position just outside the political firefight raging between radicals and liberals as well as conservatives and anyone committed to racial equality was complicated by her father's high visibility in black Detroit. In

April 1969 Reverend C.L. Franklin found himself near the center of the storm. From the dawn of the Black Power movement, Detroit had been a hotbed of black nationalist sentiment. One of the more visible nationalist organizations was the Republic of New Afrika (RNA), which the year before had issued a statement calling for the establishment of an independent black nation located in the Deep South. Although Reverend Franklin would never even have considered membership in the RNA, and in fact would have disapproved of many of its policies, he understood its appeal to some of his parishioners. Viewing his church as an active part of the dialogues going on in the community, he granted the RNA's request to hold a conference at New Bethel. Shortly after the conference ended, a confrontation between Detroit police and armed security guards escalated into a full-scale firefight. One officer was killed, and five people, including another policeman, were seriously wounded. Responding to the calls for backup, dozens of police converged on the neighborhood, arresting anyone unfortunate enough to be caught on the street.

When African American judge George Crockett, a friend of Reverend Franklin's, received word of the mass arrests, he rushed to the precinct station and set up court. Challenging police to justify their actions, he set most of the detainees free, setting off a firestorm that would rage in the Detroit press for weeks. Meanwhile, the janitor at New Bethel had located C.L. and told him of the shootings. When he arrived at the church, he encountered police "gathering the bullets that had lodged in the benches." Noting that "there wasn't any physical sign of shots going out of the church," he reached the obvious conclusion that "the policemen were doing the shooting." Reentering New Bethel, Franklin found the church's music director, Thomas Shelby, sitting with his head in his hands. Franklin did his best to reassure his colleague, saying, "We are in the throes of a revolution, a social revolution. Some people have lost their lives in this revolution, and we have lost a little glass. I think we got out cheap."

Nonetheless, Reverend Franklin was far from a revolutionary. As a part of the city's black political elite, he had friends in the Democratic Party who were making real advances in their quest for political power, especially after the riot kicked white flight into high gear. Deprived of their voting majority and forced to choose between fighting and running, the white supremacist opposition fled for the suburbs. If not exactly empty, the victory of the black politicians led by Coleman Young made infuriatingly little difference to those stranded in the inner city. The problem was simple if intractable. Finishing the process initiated by auto industry executives after World War II, the white exodus deprived Detroit of anything resembling a sufficient tax base. The economic deterioration accompanied the seismic shift in national politics reflected by the widespread support for George Wallace, who won the 1968 Michigan Democratic primary, and the election of Richard Nixon. Against the larger backdrop, it mattered little that a coalition of black Democrats and white liberals had routed the white supremacist opposition in Detroit proper. Deprived of the funding promised by Lyndon Johnson's Great Society programs, they lacked the resources to deal with the festering problems in education, housing, and employment. Responding to claims that Detroit's problems resulted from the new leadership's incompetence, Young angrily replied, "The same people who left the city for racial reasons still want to control what they've left. It starts with economic pressure, and the first economic pressure was slavery. It reminds me of something Martin Luther King said. 'How do you expect us to pull ourselves up by our bootstraps when we don't even have boots?' " Young concluded bitterly, "The motherfuckers *stole* our boots."

Even when things seemed bleakest, there was a flip side. For all its failings and foibles, Black Power had transformed American culture. At least when the motherfuckers stole their boots, now black folks could say so, plainly. There might be times when you put a smile on your face to cover your hurt, but it was no longer required. The change signaled a real triumph, one that presaged a truly desegregated democratic conversation that never quite materialized. Still, for the next few years American music would tell messy, complicated truths in a messy, complicated, and often transcendentally beautiful way. Even as the skies continued to darken, the airwaves carried the gospel vision in its soul incarnation to every corner of black America and to anyone else seeking shelter from the present and coming storm. Life might be hard, but the soundtrack was never better.

Which is why the early seventies really were the "Age of Aretha."

The phrase was coined by Aretha's new beau, Ken "Wolf" Cunningham, and Aretha held it to her heart: "I loved that phrase, by which he meant people were growing up to my music, getting married, having babies, defining their youth." A dapper member of a group of independent black businessmen who marketed Afro styles and called themselves the "New Breeders," Cunningham helped Aretha "appreciate myself as a beautiful black woman. Wolf was also interested in African poetry, art, and sculpture. He loved jazz and music of all kinds. And he had friends who, like Wolf, were intellectual and positive people." Exhaling after her stormy relationship with Ted White, Aretha lost weight, took dancing lessons, and basked in the quiet joys of family life with her sons and Cunningham's daughter Paige, who, Aretha said, "stole my heart."

The positive vibrations—tempered by Aretha's deep understanding that life's burdens were never-ending—shone through on the five great albums she released between 1970 and 1972: the studio sets *This Girl's in Love with You, Spirit in the Dark,* and *Young, Gifted and Black,* along with the fascinating pair of live LPs, *Live at Fillmore West* and *Amazing Grace.* Reaching out to the white counterculture and back to her gospel roots, Aretha charted the path that was leading the nation ever closer to a dangerous crossroads. There had to be a way to make it through with our spirits intact, Aretha seemed to say, and together we could find it.

That was the vision that shone through on Aretha's version of "The Dark End of the Street," her soul-deep testimony to the difficulty and the glory of holding on to each other and the dream. When she traveled to Miami to complete *This Girl's in Love with You* in October 1969, she was emerging from a postdivorce hibernation of some six months. Backed by the Muscle Shoals regulars, the Sweet Inspirations, and white southern guitarists Duane Allman and Eddie Hinton, Aretha ripped through a phenomenal set: "Son of a Preacher Man," "Eleanor Rigby," "This Girl's in Love with You," her original composition and R&B chart-topper-to-be "Call Me," and "Dark End of the Street," which had already received two near-definitive treatments. The original, by star-crossed Memphis soulman James Carr, dropped listeners into an unrelenting blues hell. Huddling in the shadows at the end of a godforsaken city street, Carr's lovers don't even have each other. Choking back his sobs, Carr tells his lover to walk on by, and it's easy to imagine him as the black half of an interracial liaison staring into an abyss of fire and rope. Clarence Carter's remake-qua-response, "Making Love (At the Dark End of the Street)," couldn't conceivably differ more. If the blues, to paraphrase Langston Hughes, is laughing to keep from crying, Carter transforms Carr's tears into ribald chuckles. Assuming the persona of a Delta bluesman imitating a down-home preacher for the amusement of the patrons lounging in the parlor of a Memphis whorehouse, Carter delivers a wry sermon on the intricacies of procreation. Transfixed by the universal spectacle of cows, horses, human beings, and mo-ski-toes in earnest pursuit of sexual communion, Carter pinpoints the enchanting absurdity of sex and desire. Suddenly, however, the comedy metamorphoses into incisive, but still good-humored, social commentary. "Some of us ain't ever had nothin', we ain't gonna get nothin', and don't ever expect to get a doggone thing," Carter preaches, before wrapping the song up with a straight-from-the-soul chorus that reminds his listeners that Carr's bleaker version tells a big part of the complicated truth.

Incredibly, Aretha found something absolutely original to add. At first her version of "Dark End of the Street" seems destined to retrace Carr's tormented path. After Jimmy Johnson introduces the song with a sparse solo guitar line, Aretha's piano and Barry Beckett's organ take the sound to church. As the texture gradually thickens, Aretha fingers the jagged grain of her troubles. When she cries out that "time's gonna take its toll" and that the lovers are bound to "pay for the love we stole," the intensity builds in her voice. The images call upon countless midnight hours. As Carr had sung, it felt like too much to bear. But then Aretha and her soul sisters in the Sweet Inspirations find the strength to bend midnight toward morning. The musical crescendo relaxes and Aretha calls out the line that marked the end for Carr: "They're gonna find us." When Carr sang the line, it was the end. For Aretha, the same words signify a determination to stand together against the darkness. Where Carr heard only silence, the Sweet Inspirations refuse to let Aretha fall. As they respond to each repetition with cries of "together" and "you and me," Aretha's voice gathers strength. The street may be dark for now, but when Aretha sings, "Baby, hold me," and the musical community around her promises it will, you can believe that the suffering may someday give way to a brighter day. The connection between gospel, blues, and pop genius may never be clearer.

During the early seventies Aretha recorded, by a very conservative count, at least a dozen songs as powerful as "Dark End of the Street." The trilogy of albums that provide the foundation for her second great period— *This Girl's in Love with You*, *Spirit in the Dark*, and *Young, Gifted and Black*— stands alongside *I Never Loved a Man*, *Aretha Arrives*, and *Lady Soul* as her lasting contribution to American secular music. The best way to experience all of those albums is to let them rain down on you, playing them over and over until they've soaked down into your soul. But for purposes of classification, you can break Aretha's achievement into three sometimes overlapping categories: the hits; the covers; and the original compositions that should have earned her recognition as a crucial figure in the female singer-songwriter movement of the early seventies.

In retrospect, it seems curious that almost no one at the time seemed to recognize the quality of Aretha's writing. Over the next two years she wrote enough songs to fill an album on their own, including four hits, "Day Dreaming," "Call Me," "Spirit in the Dark," and "Rock Steady." Complemented with album cuts like "All the King's Horses," "First Snow in Kokomo," "Pullin'," and "You and Me," the hits qualify Aretha's imaginary "personal" album as a formidable rival for Carole King's *Tapestry*, Carly Simon's *Anticipation*, Joni Mitchell's *Blue*, and Laura Nyro's *Eli and the Thirteenth Confession*.

There were probably quite a few singers who secretly wished that Aretha *had* concentrated on her own songs. King Curtis stated the reason in his half-gleeful observation, "When Aretha records a tune, she *kills* copyright. Because once she's worked out the way to do it, you're never going to be able to come up with a better approach. And it's damn sure you're not going to be able to improve on how she's done it her way." Aretha chose an eclectic set of songs to cover. She felt equally comfortable with R&B hits, pop confections, counterculture standards, and Burt Bacharach–Hal David compositions like "This Girl's in Love with You" and "April Fools" that would have fit in with her Columbia sets. She knocked her overlapping audiences out with B.B. King's "Why I Sing the Blues," Otis Redding's "I've Been Loving You Too Long," Lulu's "Oh Me Oh My (I'm a Fool for You Baby)," and Delaney and Bonnie's "When the Battle Is Over." Twice Aretha set down covers of Dusty Springfield hits ("A Brand New Me," "Son of a Preacher Man") that even Dusty considered definitive. When she demolished and rebuilt "Border Song (Holy Moses)," Elton John and Bernie Taupin's cryptic piece of hippie ennui sounded like it had grown up in the Mississippi Delta. Aretha often drew from the Beatles' songbook, transforming "Eleanor Rigby" from a chamber piece into an R&B declaration of female independence and testifying that she too had traveled a "long and winding road." Her soulful version of "Let It Be" lent credence to the unfounded rumors that the song had been written with her in mind. Paul Simon claimed that he had in fact been thinking of Aretha when he wrote "Bridge Over Troubled Water." When she sang the song on the Grammy telecast when Simon and Garfunkel's version won Song of the Year, everyone involved recognized it as an instant classic. The single version, featuring Aretha trading piano licks with Donny Hathaway's organ, went straight to the top of the R&B charts.

Quickly establishing himself as a prized collaborator, Hathaway played on a half-dozen songs on Aretha's 1972 album, *Young, Gifted and Black,* recorded at the Criteria Studio in Miami. Like "Dark End of the Street," the title cut had already been blessed with two stunning renditions: Nina Simone's original and Hathaway's thoughtful response on his marvelous *Everything Is Everything* album. Introduced with an extended call and response between her voice and Hathaway's sustained organ lines, Aretha's version would have fit perfectly in a Baptist service. Paying tribute to Hathaway as an "introverted musical genius, a friendly person with a deep musical personality," Aretha credited him with making "Rock Steady" into "one of my greatest hits." "It was Donny who added the high organ line that gives 'Rock Steady' such extra added flow," she reflected. "Like Ray Charles and me, Donny came out of the sanctified church as a singer and pianist. His grandmother was a minister, and he had gospel written all over him. Also like Ray and me, he was multi-musical the way some folks are multilingual." Like Aretha's tribute to *"black* and Spanish Harlem" on her R&B chart–topping remake of Ben E. King's hit, "Rock Steady" affirmed the movement in a time of need.

More a unique creation than a remake of B.B. King's blues hit, Aretha's reconstruction of "The Thrill Is Gone (From Yesterday's Kiss)" weaves together the personal and the political, the nightmare and the dream. Clearly addressing her recent divorce, the song issued into a parallel political universe where very little seemed to be working out right. As the song fades to silence, the backing vocalists echo the climactic words of Dr. King's greatest speech: "Free at last, free at last, great God almighty, free at last." But they're singing in a minor key, testifying to how much things had changed in the few short years since King and Mahalia Jackson had electrified the nation from the steps of the Lincoln Memorial. Where King's words resounded with the assurance that, given faith and courage, the battle would go to the just, Aretha expressed the growing fear that, yet again, the dream would be deferred.

"Spirit in the Dark" evokes the sense of political community that seemed to be slipping away. The song opens with Aretha's quiet gospel moan but rapidly settles into a steady rock beat as she asks her sisters and brothers how they're feeling. When she invites them to get up and dance, it's as much a call to political renewal as "People Get Ready" or "Respect." The groove that carries the first half of the song explores the feel of the beloved community in unified motion. If the song had ended halfway through, it would still be a classic. But Aretha refuses to accept the rock and soul groove as the best of all possible worlds. Almost three minutes into the song, when most singles would be fading out, she inserts an emphatic gospel piano run. Joyously responding to their sister's sanctified call, the Sweet Inspirations shout out, "I think y'all got it." The rock groove explodes with a sanctified energy as powerful as Mahalia's "Walk in Jerusalem" or the Five Blind Boys of Mississippi's "Jesus Gave Me Water." The Stones never rocked harder. For another minute and a half, Aretha and the Sweet Inspirations take the secular audience to church. The spirits they call down vibrate with a clearer sense of shared purpose than anything ideology had to offer.

The live albums recorded at San Francisco's Fillmore West and the New Temple Missionary Baptist Church in Los Angeles demonstrate Aretha's newfound vitality as a performer. After she came to terms with her bitter divorce from Ted White, Aretha returned to the stage in September 1970 backed by a crack soul band consisting of King Curtis on sax, Cornell Dupree on guitar, Richard Tee on piano, Jerry Jemmott on bass, and Bernard Purdie on drums. It was the first time outside church that she'd had a band that could both inspire her and follow where she led. The audiences that greeted her let her know she'd been missed. As C. Gerald Fraser wrote in a *New York Times* review of her New York "homecoming": "The thousands of black people who saw and heard Miss Franklin were more than an audience. They were part of a black interaction—they came not only to see and hear 'Lady Soul,' 'Soul Sister Number One,' 'The Queen of Soul' and all those other labels she bears, but also to participate with her in an exultation of blackness."

Ray Charles had once said that Aretha sang "the way black folk sing when they leave themselves alone." The overwhelming response to Aretha's performances at the Fillmore West suggested that a growing number of whites were willing to listen to the real thing. As *Live at Fillmore West* rose into the Top Ten—her best album chart showing yet—Aretha began to fulfill her dream of making a gospel album that would speak both to those who remembered her from the gospel highway and to those who had come to the gospel vision by way of soul. Working with her musical mentor James Cleveland, now widely recognized as the greatest living gospel composer, she made plans to realize that dream with a set of recorded performances at the New Temple Missionary Baptist Church in the heart of Watts.

But before she could do so, she was saddened by the death of King Curtis, stabbed to death on the stoop of a New York City apartment building in August 1971. "King Curtis could make me laugh *so* hard," Aretha wrote of the man whose saxophone could kick from driving funk to whispering ballads so effortlessly. "King Curtis was a soul superhero and I miss him still." Aretha sang "Never Grow Old" at Curtis's funeral, the first of three times she would perform such duties over the next two years. In February 1972 she sang "Precious Lord (Take My Hand)" at Mahalia Jackson's funeral in Chicago, and less than a year later "The Day Is Past and Gone" when Clara Ward was laid to rest in Philadelphia.

If Aretha's Fillmore duet with Charles on "Spirit in the Dark" had given the counterculture a taste of her uncut gospel soul, *Amazing Grace* delivered a sumptuous feast to anyone willing to join her at the welcome table. Aretha had long wanted to pay tribute to her musical elders and ancestors, but she refused to call *Amazing Grace* a "return" to gospel. "I never left the church," she told numerous interviewers. "The church went with me. Church is as much a part of me as the air I breathe. I expanded, but I never abandoned." When Aretha entered the New Temple Missionary Baptist Church on South Broadway in Watts in January 1972, James Cleveland and Reverend C.L. Franklin at her side, the congregation washed her in a wave of love befitting a prodigal daughter. From the first notes of Marvin Gaye's half-secular spiritual "Wholly Holy," she let them know she was with them all the way. Driven on by ecstatic shouts from the audience and by Cleveland's swaying, hand-clapping Southern California Community Choir, Aretha soared and swooped through a program of songs that had been "the original source of my musical inspiration": "Precious Lord," "Old Landmark,"

"What a Friend We Have in Jesus," "Give Yourself to Jesus," and "How I Got Over," the signature song of Clara Ward, who was there to share her musical daughter's moment of glory. When Aretha wrapped her voice around Rodgers and Hammerstein's "You'll Never Walk Alone" and Carole King's "You've Got a Friend," it was impossible to doubt that they'd been talking about Jesus all along.

Having long ago claimed his place in the pantheon of gospel arrangers, Cleveland urged his choir on to ever-greater heights. It helped that Atlantic sound engineer Ray Thompson performed wonders under difficult acoustic circumstances. And not even the church mothers and deacons regretted that Wexler had managed to sneak "the devil's rhythm section" into the sanctuary. Guitarist Cornell Dupree, organist Ken Lupper, conga player Pancho Morales, bass player Chuck Rainey, and master drummer Bernard Purdie performed flawlessly, fueling the fire when Cleveland's arrangements called for flames and banking down to the faintest of glows in the moments of quiet reflection. Collectively, they gave Sister Ree a fierce "amen."

When Aretha, Wexler, and Arif Mardin sat down with the tapes from those two nights of spiritual communion, they extracted a two-LP set that remains the gold standard for popular gospel. Achieving the more than slightly unlikely feat of placing a gospel album in the Top Ten—it had never been done before and may never be done again—*Amazing Grace* quickly became the best-selling gospel album ever and continues to reward tens of thousands of new listeners every year. Aretha never sang with greater passion, conviction, or subtlety. Her ten-minute versions of "Never Grow Old" and "Amazing Grace" weave epic tapestries of sound and spirit. Retelling a story African Americans had made their own since their first encounter with the Christian Bible, "Mary Don't You Weep" renews the call at the heart of the gospel vision. Immersed in a sea of hand claps, shouts, and pure spirit sound, Aretha wraps her voice around the tale of exile and bondage and triumph and makes it new. When she tells Mary not to weep and Martha not to moan, she echoes her father's exhortations and renews the message of her very first recordings. As the song reaches its breathtaking climax, Aretha and the choir urge each other on toward the higher ground with chants of "Right on, right on" that yoke the age-old story to the one unfolding on the streets of the nation where Pharaoh still walks.

By the time Aretha reached the stage of the New Temple Missionary

Baptist Church, she had traveled many a weary mile. She had wandered the corporate wilderness of midtown Manhattan and initiated audiences from Paris to the Fillmore West into the mysteries of the gospel spirit. She had communed with the tormented spirits of Billie Holiday and Dinah Washington and wept over the murders of Sam Cooke and Martin Luther King Jr. In times of torment and triumph, she continued to raise up her voice in the service of the movement and the Lord. And like the members of the congregation at New Temple that Friday evening, she knew that however far they might have come, many a mile stretched out ahead. The ache in her voice when she sang of Pharaoh's demise to the syncopated responses of the Southern California Community Choir bore witness to the bitter reality that the battle had not yet been won, that Pharaoh and his modern-day minions, a few of them black, continued to live in a luxury squeezed from the poor and downtrodden. The devil had gotten more than his due. And somehow, despite it all, Aretha summoned the strength to renew the gospel vision. Threatening to blow down the walls of the church and take the battle to the streets, her song warned that the fight would be a long one. But with faith and strength, Aretha called out with assurance, it might yet be won.

CHAPTER FOUR

Songs in the Key of Life

The Gospel Vision
in Changing Times

B Y THE FALL OF 1974, THE TEMPTATIONS' "Ball of Confusion" should have been the national anthem. Richard Nixon had fled from office in disgrace, only to receive a full pardon from Gerald Ford. The year's best films, *Chinatown* and *The Godfather, Part II,* hinted that Watergate might be the rule rather than the exception. South Boston erupted in violence over school busing. One of the most telling photographs of the period showed a white Bostonian trying to impale a black attorney with an American flag. The Ohio National Guardsmen on trial for killing four student protesters at Kent State were acquitted of all charges; no one seemed to even remember the black students gunned down by the Mississippi Highway Patrol at Jackson State a week later. American Indian Movement leader Dennis Banks faced the possibility of a long prison term on charges connected with the protests at Wounded Knee.

Whatever the calendar said, the seventies had finally arrived. By the time the election of Ronald Reagan signaled their end, about all the president and his detractors could agree on was that the sooner we forgot about the immediate past, the better. For seventies-bashers on the right, the decade represented the culmination of sixties hedonism. The arrival of what Tom Wolfe labeled the "Me Decade" simply confirmed what Spiro Agnew and then–California governor Reagan had been saying all along. The counterculture wasn't really about saving the soul of America. It was simply a flight from the harsh realities of adulthood. The left's version of the story played a set of variations on the same theme. The revolution had disintegrated into materialistic hedonism, and visionary commitment had lapsed into cynical self-indulgence. Drugs, which had once promised to cleanse the doors of perception, now fueled the mindless motions of disco robots. It just wasn't *serious*.

It was hard to shake the lingering images of a world gone wrong: blank faces and vacant words at the Watergate hearings; American helicopters lifting off the roof of the Saigon embassy; Gloria Steinem confronting unrepentant legions of male chauvinist pigs; endless lines at the gas pumps; blindfolded hostages being paraded through the streets of Tehran; Jimmy Carter's saintly smile withering into a perplexed grimace. In much of black America things looked even worse. Black Power had promised more than the civil rights movement and delivered much less. The urban industrial economy had completed its agonizing collapse into a nightmare of stagflation. The Supreme Court's *Bakke* decision began the formal dismantling of many of the freedom movement's gains. As the seventies stumbled to an end, few Americans would have refused to join *Doonesbury*'s Zonker Harris in toasting the demise of "a kidney stone of a decade."

In time—very quickly, in fact—a new seventies appeared in popular memory. A different set of images bubbled up from the depths of our collective memory. The grim reality reflected in the decade's best movies—*Taxi Driver, A Clockwork Orange, The Deer Hunter,* and *Apocalypse Now*—was gradually superseded by a Day-Glo world illuminated by a smiley-face sun. The new, improved seventies were enough to make even a stout-hearted fashion designer weep. It was a world of polyester, platform shoes, and gold medallions; exploding sideburns, towering Afros, and celebrity skin at Studio 54. For those too young to remember the actual seventies—and for many who just wanted to forget them—the nostalgic remix edited down to a single image: John Travolta, decked out in a blinding-white three-piece suit, striking the classic disco pose. Soundtrack by the Bee Gees and the Village People. No one ever went to a seventies revival party dressed up as Aretha Franklin or Stevie Wonder, but their music defined the decade as surely as Berry Gordy and the Beatles had defined the sixties.

Both seventies happened—kind of. Speculating on the connection between the glittery surface and the malaise it masked, Curtis Mayfield would later examine the good-time messages that dominated the disco soundtrack. "So many of the lyrics were just, 'Dance, dance, dance, let's get the hell outta here, cause it's rough on the bottom,' " he reflected. "At times escape means you're closing your eyes and ears to what's going on. Then when you open them up, it's even more screwed up than before you closed them. You wish you had just gone on and lived through it."

The line separating the real decade from its self-parody isn't easy to pin down. Case in point: pro sports. Suspended between a past dedicated to Vince Lombardi's crew-cut ideal of discipline and a future defined by global marketing and $100 million contracts, the most interesting seventies athletes were wilder, freer, and a hell of a lot more fun. The Oakland As' dazzling green and gold uniforms thumbed their nose at baseball's gray and white past, while the team parlayed its merry mutiny into three straight world championships; Lombardi would have shot them all at dawn and then made the corpses run laps. The Pittsburgh Pirates, whose star African American pitcher once threw a no-hitter on LSD, closed out the decade with "We Are Family" tearing the roof off a clubhouse where even the white guys had nicknames like "Scrap Iron." In football, the Dallas Cowboys embodied the cultural battles of the decade, pitting Duane Thomas, the pot-smoking tailback who scampered through NFL defenses with inimitable artistry, against Tom Landry, their dour, computer-operated coach, whom Thomas derided as a "plastic man." It was emblematic that Thomas dazzled the fans but disappeared while Landry kept the power. The American Basketball Association—original home of Marvin "Bad News" Barnes, George "Iceman" Gervin, David "Skywalker" Thompson, and the immortal Julius Erving—served notice on the NBA and the nation that it could ignore black American style only at the risk of rendering itself irrelevant.

In the midst of it all rose Stevie Wonder, reflecting on a nation plunging from visionary hope to sour narcissism. If you're looking for an emblem of what the seventies were really about, Stevie beats the hell out of Disco Duck. No musician has ever had a better decade. Paul Simon summed Wonder's stature up best in accepting the 1975 Grammy for *Still Crazy After All These Years*. "But most of all," Simon concluded with a wry smile, "I'd like to thank Stevie Wonder for not making an album this year." It surprised no one when *Songs in the Key of Life*, which topped the album charts for fourteen weeks in 1976 and 1977, completed the trifecta that began with *Innervisions* and *Fulfillingness' First Finale*.

Reaching out across America's rapidly re-forming racial and musical lines, Wonder offered a sound that rendered the distinctions between (soon-to-be "white") rock and (black) soul meaningless. As the sixties did a slow dissolve into the eighties, Wonder held to his belief in the compatibility of the sixties counterculture and the black church. The hippies might have arrived at their vision of universal love by way of the head shop rather than the choir loft, but their response to Aretha at the Fillmore West demonstrated a willingness to respond to the gospel vision. No matter how desperate things might seem, Wonder told us, we could still come together in ways that forged differences into strengths. People would keep on lying and soldiers would keep on warring, "Higher Ground" observed, but it wasn't going to stop the world from turning or the preachers from preaching. Driving his point home with a relentless groove, Wonder echoed the movement's central message—"Don't you let nobody bring you down, they'll sho 'nuff try"—and vowed to keep on pushing till he, and we, reached the higher ground.

Wonder's first concern was with the rapidly changing conditions in black America. Some of the changes reflected the weariness that descended in the wake of Watergate and Vietnam. But several disturbing trends had been set in motion, ironically, by the successes of the freedom movement. The first generation of R&B artists had grown up and played their music in a world where the vast majority of black people lived, worked, and played in the same communities. Duke Ellington, Louis Jordan, and Ray Charles knew their audience included black surgeons and insurance executives as well as women who spent their days scrubbing the white folks' floors and men who woke at dawn to empty the white folks' garbage. Brothers and sisters scratching out a living on the streets shared bus stops with postal workers and schoolteachers. The idea of a "black community"—which came in different flavors depending on whether you were in the North, South, or West—wasn't entirely an abstraction.

When the freedom movement began to open areas of American society that had formerly been reserved for "whites only," many blacks jumped at the chance to raise their children in a better world. Ironically, the movement's success in breaking some racial barriers helped shatter the gospel dream of communal redemption. Given the desire for universal brotherhood, it *should* have been a good thing when some blacks moved into white spaces. The reality was more complicated and disturbing. As more black college graduates entered the professional world and moved to suburbs or integrated middle-class neighborhoods, the inner cities became more and more isolated. The collapse of the industrial economy and an increasingly hostile political climate made it ever more difficult for those who remained behind to follow their fortunate kinfolk out of the ghetto.

Released in August 1973, *Innervisions* was Wonder's attempt to wrest a measure of hope from a social situation where the ideals of the sixties seemed to be slipping away. Wonder considered alternative titles for the album, including *The Easter Album* or *The Last Days of Easter*. Plans called for a cover picturing an elder who "can now sit and look at the confusion" with "wisdom and contentment." "It's the last days of life, of beauty," Wonder reflected before the album's release. "All the horrors and hypocrisy in the world today. People neglecting other people's problems. It's what needs doing, socially, spiritually and domestically. I can only do it through song, and I try to be positive about it."

Like *Music of My Mind* and *Talking Book, Innervisions* emerged from intense working sessions involving Wonder, synthesizer gurus Malcolm Cecil and Robert Margouleff, and guest musicians including guitarist David "T" Walker and conga virtuoso Larry "Nastyee" Latimer. A former Wonder staffer described his employer's demanding work habits: "Stevie is someone who goes into the studio at seven o'clock at night and comes out at ten o'clock the next morning. Time doesn't mean anything to him while he's creating. He just goes on and on and on. He would stay in the studio even longer if the people who worked with him could keep up with it. Only when we say 'Hey, Steve, it's nine o'clock in the morning,' then he'd say 'Okay, let me just get these two more tracks down' or something like that.' " Backup singer Deniece Williams, an R&B star best known for her exuberant remake of Curtis Mayfield's "I'm So Proud," lamented Stevie's ability "to stay in the studio for 48 hours without crashing." Wonder shrugged it off, saying simply, "My rhythms go by my moods."

Responding to reports that he'd created between two hundred and six hundred unreleased songs since he began working in New York, Stevie demurred, "No, we do have a lot of material but a lot of it isn't finished." Trying to keep track of Wonder's ideas wasn't easy. Cecil and Margouleff compiled a legendary "Blue Book" listing all of the songs-in-progress in alphabetical order. The problem was that when Stevie picked out a song to complete, he was likely to sketch out three or four more at the same session. At one point Clarence Paul said he was going through back material to put together an anthology that would include two unreleased songs from every year of Stevie's career. We can dream.

Wonder unveiled the masterpiece he'd sifted out of the possibilities with a truly memorable album-release event. Music critic Dave Marsh describes what happened: "They put a whole batch of us on a bus in Times Square and blindfolded us. Then they drove us around for what seemed like a long time—it was probably in the neighborhood of ten minutes, but it felt like half an hour. They pulled up in front of some place and shepherded us off the bus and into a cool, air-conditioned space. Each of us had a guide. (Mine turned out to be Patti Smith, a good friend of Stevie's, as it turns out.) Then they played us the record. It was an amazing thing. Totally disorienting. The music had a clarity, a lucidity, and a flat-out *power* that was greatly increased by the limitation of the visual sense; no distraction, or complete distraction, but in the end, it really focused the whole experience, and *not* only because the music was unforgettable, although of course it was. It was one hell of a way to experience 'Living for the City' for the first time."

A searing meditation on the brutal realities of black life that bears comparison with Robert Johnson's "Hellhound on My Trail" and Grandmaster Flash and the Furious Five's "The Message," "Living for the City" presents an unsparing image of how hope dies when confronted with economic hardship and personal betrayal. "I think the deepest I really got into how I feel about the way things are was in 'Living for the City,'" Wonder observed. "I was able to show the hurt and the anger, you know. You still have that same mother that scrubs the floors for many, she's still doing it. Now what is that about? And that father who works some days for 14 hours. That's still happening." As defiant as it was mournful, "Living for the City" reflected the blues tradition of looking a vicious world straight in the eye and vowing to endure.

A series of vignettes tracing a southern migrant's odyssey from hopeful arrival to a ten-year jail sentence, "Living for the City" issues a blistering condemnation of empty materialism and impersonal institutions that reduce us to mutually distrustful individuals out for what we can get for ourselves. The problems Wonder described would worsen for at least the next twenty years; in 1980 a survey of fourteen major metropolitan areas revealed that, despite the growth of the black middle class, *all* had black poverty rates of at least 23 percent. Chicago provided the case study of the origin and implications of the problem. In *The Truly Disadvantaged* black sociologist William Julius Wilson examined the changing relationship between housing segregation and economic conditions in Chicago during the seventies. The patterns Wilson discovered are stunning. In 1970 only one of Chicago's seventy-seven neighborhoods had a poverty rate as high as 40 percent. In only one district was the unemployment rate as high as 15 percent. By 1980, a radically different pattern had emerged. In two over-whelmingly black neighborhoods over half the residents now lived in poverty. In seven others the rate was above 40 percent; in ten more above 20 percent. Not surprisingly, the concentrations of poverty were *all* centered on the South and West Sides.

At street level the changes savaged the futures of black children, who were now isolated not only from whites but from black mentors who could teach them how to negotiate the economic system without denying their blackness. On the same street where the young Curtis Mayfield had received the attention of a loving community, a child growing up in Cabrini-Green in the seventies was facing a concrete wilderness with few guides. Wilson describes the vicious cycle set in motion by the demographic changes: lacking contact with regularly employed elders, teenagers are unlikely to develop the type of work habits valued by employers; tardiness and absenteeism contribute to low retention rates. "Since the jobs that are available to the inner-city poor are the very ones that alienate even persons with long and stable work histories," Wilson concludes, "the combination of unattractive jobs and lack of community norms to re-enforce work increases the likelihood that individuals will turn to either underground illegal activity or idleness or both." Which is precisely the cycle that musical sociologist Stevie Wonder describes in "Living for the City."

That uncompromising blues backdrop adds to the power of Wonder's call to recapture the gospel vision. The album's opening sequence of "Too High" and "Visions" establishes the tension between the urge to escape, if only into a drugged-out haze, and the need to imagine something new and better. Love, Wonder insists, is the answer, but love isn't simple; "Golden Lady" affirms human devotion as a path to spiritual fulfillment, but "All in Love Is Fair" reminds you that a long road stretches out before you, and there's no guarantee you'll make the right choice when you reach the crossroads. One minute you're grooving to "Don't You Worry 'Bout a Thing," next thing you know, the hellhound's howling at your heels.

And for all that, you can't quit. Along with Mahalia's "Move On Up a Little Higher," the Impressions' "Keep On Pushing," and Bob Marley's "Redemption Song," Stevie's "Higher Ground" defines the heart of the gospel vision. Wonder wrote the song in a burst of inspiration. " 'Higher Ground' was a very special song," Wonder recalled. "I wrote it on May 11. I remember the date. I did the whole thing—the words, the music, and recorded the track—in three hours. That's the first time I ever finished a song so fast. It was almost as if I had to get it done. I felt something was going to happen. I didn't know what or when, but I felt something." "Higher Ground" simplifies nothing. The liars keep on lying, the believers keep on believing, and for Wonder and the community he was trying to sing into being, the only thing to do was feel the power in the music and ride the driving rhythm that lets you know that however weary you may be, you're not alone.

As *Innervisions* climbed the album charts, eventually stalling behind Jethro Tull's *A Passion Play*, the Allman Brothers' *Brothers and Sisters*, the Stones' *Goat's Head Soup*, and Elton John's *Goodbye Yellow Brick Road*, Wonder and his band, Wonderlove, embarked on a tour of the South. The response, especially from black audiences, was lukewarm. For a southern audience accustomed to the showbiz shtick of the soul revues, Wonder's flirtation with the looser rock concert format elicited bemused shrugs. "The people couldn't feel me," Wonder observed, "and I didn't know if it was because of me, or because of the way we were presenting the show." On the evening of August 6, 1973, Wonder set out from Greenville, South Carolina, to Durham, North Carolina, where he was scheduled to give a benefit concert in support of black activist radio station WAFR (Wave Africa). Before departing, Wonder announced to the band that there would soon be a meeting to consider possible changes in the concert format.

He never made it to Durham. Just outside of Salisbury, North Carolina, Wonder's car pulled up behind a log truck that was weaving from side to side on the two-lane Highway 85. When Stevie's driver, his cousin John Harris, pulled up to pass, the truck driver slammed on the brakes. A dislodged log smashed through the window, striking the sleeping singer in the head.

At three A.M. Berry Gordy's sister Esther woke him with news of the accident. Informing Gordy that Stevie had been rushed to the emergency room at Rowan Memorial Hospital in Salisbury, Esther reported, "It's a madhouse down there. I couldn't get many details. Berry, it doesn't look good." Suffering a broken skull and severe brain contusions, Wonder lapsed into a coma. Wonder's longtime friend and staff member Ira Tucker described Stevie's condition after he was transferred to North Carolina Baptist Hospital in Winston-Salem: "Man, I couldn't even recognize him. His head was swollen up five times normal size. And nobody could get through to him."

Wonder remained in a coma for a week. Tucker described the turning point in his recovery: "I knew that Stevie likes to listen to music really loud, and I thought maybe if I shouted in his ear, it might reach him. The doctor told me to go ahead and try, it couldn't hurt. The first time I didn't get any response, but the next day I went back and I got right down in his ear and sang 'Higher Ground.' His hand was resting on my arm, and after a while his fingers started moving with the music. I said to myself, 'This cat's gonna make it.'" After two terrifying weeks, Gordy wrote in his autobiography, "I heard he was playfully grabbing at nurses and entertaining the whole medical staff with his antics. I knew he was well on his way to recovery." When Wonder was transferred to the UCLA Medical Center, Tucker arranged to have his clavinet brought to the hospital. "You should have seen Stevie's face," he recalled. "For a while he was afraid to touch it. He didn't know if he had lost his musical gift. And then he finally started playing. And you could actually see the relief and happiness all over his face."

When Wonder awoke, he had only a vague recollection of the accident. "The only thing I know is that I was unconscious," he recalled later, "and that for a few days I was definitely in a much better spiritual place that made me aware of a lot of things that concern my life and my future and what I have to do to reach another higher ground." Reinforcing his already strong mystical leanings, the accident confirmed a sense of foreboding that had been building in the weeks before the accident. Shortly before he left on the southern tour, he'd told *Rolling Stone* that he thought he was going to die soon despite the fact that "I don't have any reason to kill myself and I don't know anyone who would want to kill me."

Wonder returned to life with a strengthened sense of purpose. "I would like to believe in reincarnation," he mused. "I would like to believe that there is another life. I think that sometimes your consciousness can happen on this earth a second time around. I wrote 'Higher Ground' before the accident, but something was going to happen to make me aware of a lot of things, and to get myself together. This is like my second chance for life, to do something or to do more, and to face the fact that I am alive. God was telling me to slow down, to take it easy."

The more relaxed pace forced on him by his convalescence gave Wonder time to develop his relationship with Yolanda Simmons, who would become the mother of his three children. Wonder met Simmons when she called Wonder's production company seeking a secretarial position. Picking up the phone on a whim, Wonder fell under the spell of Yolanda's melodious voice. "I can usually tell a woman by her conversation," he claimed. "Her voice and the way she carries herself. Some women can have a very beautiful outer face and a very ugly inner face." Although they announced their engagement, the couple never actually married. "We didn't have to do a 'marry me' and 'I marry you' thing," Stevie said in classic counterculture mode. "Love is free—it's not about possession." Never making a pretense of fidelity to any one woman, Wonder elaborated on the free-love philosophy he endorsed in "All in Love Is Fair." "You cannot demand love. I for myself am very glad to know that my woman loves me today and when I feel that there is a chance that she might still love me tomorrow. But to expect any more than that is crazy. It only means that you are more possessive than in love. Love is something you have to be grateful for and which you have to treat tenderly. Very, very tenderly. But it is nothing that you can take for granted."

When Wonder returned to the stage after his convalescence, he radiated intensity and commitment. On September 25, 1973, Elton John dispatched his private plane to fly Stevie from New York to Boston, where he would join Captain Fantastic in a medley of "Superstition" and "Honky Tonk Woman." When Wonder walked out onto the stage at Boston Garden, the crowd overwhelmed him with a fifteen-minute standing ovation. In January he played four shows at the Rainbow Theater in London before returning to New York in March for a triumphant homecoming concert at Madison Square Garden. Opening with a half-hour version of the not-yet-released jazz-funk instrumental "Contusion," Wonder presided from behind a three-tiered ARP synthesizer that allowed him to conjure up visions of Count Basie one moment and *Sgt. Pepper's* the next. Exhorting his audience to keep the frenzy up "so that maybe our Father, our Maker can hear us," Stevie sizzled through a set crowned by "Superwoman," "Keep On Running," and "Living for the City," which he dedicated to the unborn son of nine-months-pregnant flute player Bobbi Humphrey. By the time it was over, reviewer Robert Christgau wrote, "the only act who could have topped Stevie Wonder was Jesus Christ."

Feeling an unaccustomed serenity since the accident, Wonder returned to the studio to assemble *Fulfillingness' First Finale.* The title and idea for the album, originally conceived as a double set, came to him in a dream where he'd seen one stage of his life coming to an end while another began. As he'd been doing since he gained his creative freedom, Wonder poured money into equipment and studio time, developing an intensely idiosyncratic working process. His personal valet Charlie Collins described the creative ferment: "Sometimes he'll call me at two in the morning and he'll say, 'Charlie, come to the room right away!' I ask him is there anything wrong, and he tells me, 'No, but I just got this song and you gotta hear it.' He's just waked up, you know, and a tune is in his head. It doesn't come from a dream necessarily; he just wakes up and it's there." The process created an amazing amount of wonderful music, but some close to Wonder were beginning to worry that he was losing touch with the communal sources of his inspiration. Longtime friend Lee Garrett told Wonder biographer Constanze Elsner that Stevie was "overprotected." "Steve has seeing-eye people that go with him all the time," Garrett said. "It lets all the energy that he has go into his music. On the other hand, though, he is at the mercy of the people he is with." From the mid-seventies on Wonder would attain near-legendary status for his inability to meet deadlines or show up for appointments on time; numerous journalists wrote stories detailing their lengthy waits for promised interviews. Once Stevie did arrive, however, his cheerful demeanor and magnetic personality unfailingly dissipated the bad vibrations.

Propelled by the seething grooves of "You Haven't Done Nothing" and "Boogie On Reggae Woman," *Fulfillingness' First Finale* became Wonder's first number-one album since his 1963 breakthrough *Little Stevie Wonder / The 12 Year Old Genius.* The album's mixture of social insight, spiritual aspiration, and musical textures typified the sound that had been maturing since *Music of My Mind. Fulfillingness'* sequel to "Living for the City," "You Haven't Done Nothing," insists on blues reality, but the album cover is pure gospel, centering on a piano keyboard reaching up toward the heavens. Like "Higher Ground," the opening cut, "Smile Please," echoes the gospel vision's fundamental belief that "there are brighter days ahead." His exhortations to "feel the spirit" on the fadeout of "Heaven Is Ten Zillion Light Years Away" confirms his place in the tradition linking Dorothy Love Coates and Archie Brownlee to Curtis and Aretha.

But where Mayfield and Franklin were most comfortable taking it back to New Bethel Baptist or the Traveling Souls Spiritualist Church, Wonder once again lit out for territories usually controlled by the "white" counterculture. Without losing black listeners raised in the church, he renewed his attempt to reach young whites whose sense of spirituality might come from transcendental meditation or the Grateful Dead. One of the most beautiful cuts on *Fulfillingness',* "They Won't Go When I Go," flows into a meditative conclusion that draws on everything from Islamic prayer to Gregorian chants while echoing the lyrics of Mayfield's "People Get Ready." Wonder's explanation typifies his idiosyncratic spiritual vocabulary: "That'll tell you where I'm going—away from sorrow and hate, up to joy and laughter. I feel everyone should be able to grasp what you're doing. It shouldn't be so complicated that it's beyond everyone's capabilities, nor should it be so simple that you cannot use your mind to think about it."

Not everyone was impressed with Wonder's insights, especially when he cluttered them with New Age jargon. As Robert Christgau observed in an essay that celebrated Wonder as a "sainted fool": "If you were to turn on a talk station and hear an anonymous Stevie rapping about divine vibrations and universal brotherhood, especially with the inevitable dash of astrology, you would not be impressed by his intellectual discernment." Yet Christgau understood that the New Age elements reflected Wonder's ability to transcend categorization. Pinpointing the difference between Wonder, whose career was very much on the ascendant, and Sly Stone, who was in the process of succumbing to the contradictions of his tortured genius, Christgau observed: "The split between Stevie's embrace of oneness and Sly's union of opposites extends to their audiences; Stevie's is genuinely integrated, while Sly's is simply biracial."

Once Wonder began to play, it wasn't hard to forgive the occasional lyrical awkwardness. Very few resisted the power of "Boogie On Reggae Woman" or the blistering rage of "You Haven't Done Nothing," probably the most uncompromising expression of black anger ever to reach number one. The exuberant "doo doo wop"s provided by the Jackson 5 contributed to the song's catchy appeal, but Watergate made sure it resonated across the color line. When questioned about the tension between the song's biting content and the catchy music, Wonder explained, "The best way to get an important and heavy message across is to wrap it up nicely. It's better to try and level out the weight of the lyrics by making the melody lighter. After all, people want to be entertained, which is all right with me. So if you have a catchy melody instead of making the whole song sound like a lesson, people are more likely to play the tune. They can dance to it and still listen to the lyrics and hopefully think about them." Wonder underlined the political point in a statement distributed to the press when the song was released shortly after Nixon's resignation. "Everybody promises you everything but in the end, nothing comes out of it," Wonder observed. "I don't vote for anybody until after they have really done something that I know about. I want to see them do something first. The only trouble is that you always hear the president or people say that they are doing all they can. And they feed you with hopes for years and years. I'm sick and tired of listening to all their lies."

Backing up his words with actions, Wonder refused an invitation from President Gerald Ford to participate in a UNESCO benefit. "I would have been the only black person there other than ambassadors from various African countries," he explained. "A woman from UNESCO called me on behalf of President Ford to invite me, and I said, 'Oh no, miss!' And she said, 'But this is from the President of the United States.' 'I know, miss, I know who he is, I know exactly, and *that's why* you're getting this opposition.'" Choosing his performances with their political symbolism in mind, Wonder played at the 1975 Human Kindness Day concert at the Washington

Monument, a 1976 Night of the Hurricane II benefit for Rubin Carter at the Astrodome, and several benefits with John Lennon, while adding his voice to the background choir on "Give Peace a Chance" from John and Yoko's *Shaved Fish*. Better yet, he sat in on electric piano with Lennon, Paul McCartney, and Ringo Starr at a Santa Monica studio in 1975. Although nothing from the session was released, it was the last time John and Paul recorded together.

As *Fulfillingness'* climbed the charts, *Time* magazine announced, "Today the color line in music is almost completely erased." While that overstated the case and ignored the color line in society still bright as blood, Wonder had clearly arrived at the musical mountaintop. When informed that *Fulfillingness'* had been nominated for four Grammys, he paid tribute to his peers and ancestors: "I definitely feel that Marvin Gaye should have received a Grammy. And Al Green should have gotten an award. If they say Stevie's music is *black music*, it's up to us black people to create a situation that others will not have to go through this, because this is supposed to be the Land of the Free. I hope that the person I'm about to mention will receive a Grammy because he has given so much to the music industry. I hope he receives it before he dies. Hope it's not like Mahalia Jackson or Louis Armstrong. That person is Ray Charles." When Stevie won four Grammys, he ran out of thank-yous and entertained the crowd at the ceremony with a sequence of improvisations. As writer O'Connell Driscoll observed, "Anyone who can stand up on national television and accept a Grammy award in the memory of Elijah Muhammad and Jack Benny can do anything at all."

Increasingly, Wonder saw his music as part of a larger social mission, but he wasn't sure how to define it. "It became very clear to me that it wasn't enough just to be a rock 'n' roll singer or anything of that nature," he said but went on to stress that "regardless of what a lot of people think, I'm not a politician or a minister." The issues facing black America in the mid-seventies couldn't be resolved in a three-minute song or, for that matter, in a two-and-a-half-album set like the one Wonder was beginning to work on. And the situation for musicians had changed since the sixties when their music played an active role in inspiring and supporting a vital movement. Even as Wonder's mid-seventies albums tried to take the gospel vision to the heart of American pop culture, the movement fell into profound disarray, relieved only briefly by Jimmy Carter's populist-tinged presidential campaign. The symbolic climax to the drive came when Carter invited a host of civil rights luminaries to join him in singing "We Shall Overcome" at the Democratic National Convention.

Even as he praised Carter's appointment of Andrew Young as ambassador to the United Nations, Wonder could, and did, remind his vast audience of its shared burden and the struggle for communal redemption. He condemned media distortions that fueled racial tension. "I remember in Boston seeing a news item on television," he said. " 'Twelve black kids jumped on one little white boy today.' What happened, I later found out, was that a black kid got beat up by a gang of white kids first. But if I were a middle American and I'd seen that on TV, I'd be angry as hell and I'd want to go kill every nigger that ever existed. Things like that pull people apart and make conditions ripe for mass violence." In addition, Wonder devoted time and money to charity and progressive causes. "It's good to do something for sickle cell anemia," Wonder reflected, "or for the Black Panther Party if they want to give clothes to kids or food to the community, if it's really a sincere move on one's behalf to do something for people and I can contribute my services, I will do so." For Malcolm Cecil, the fact that Wonder was in a position to make a financial difference was itself a significant improvement over the past. "His songs do more than sell millions and millions of copies," Cecil observed. "For one, they reach other people, and also quite a lot of money the records make Stevie uses to help underprivileged groups of people. So all of a sudden you find money going from white people to black people even if it's only for their bloody music." Although Stevie had less and less direct contact with his hometown, he was a strong supporter of Mayor Coleman Young and played at a benefit for Young's program for busing children to cultural events outside the ghetto.

The limits of Wonder's effectiveness were inherent in his underlying premise that the root of racial problems lay in correctable ignorance. The idea had a long liberal pedigree. But two decades of education and the largely successful desegregation of American musical culture had failed to eradicate white supremacy. Young whites were no longer forced to go underground for relief from Patti Page and Pat Boone, but most of them were still living in a different universe from the children of Paradise Valley and Cabrini-Green. Education seemed capable of teaching most Americans of European descent not to use the word *nigger,* but it didn't stop them from acting white. It would soon be next to impossible to find even a mildly respectable white person who would publicly endorse white supremacy, but it would be even harder to find a white politician who would spend political capital in support of those living on the other side of town. It seemed clear that something more than liberal protest over injustice would be needed to deal with the worsening situation, but no one was sure what that something might be.

Increasingly, Wonder imagined that an answer might lie in the African diaspora. Inspired by the Black Power movement's invocation of a homeland that was part history and part myth, Wonder began dressing in dashikis and African robes and wearing his hair in cornrows. In 1975 he made his first pilgrimage to Africa, where, greeted as a long-lost relative, he fell under the spell of the dignitaries and common people alike. In 1976 he announced plans to retire from music and move to Ghana to work with handicapped children. "America doesn't make people aware of what's happening in other parts of the world," he said, adding that he hoped "to bring back an alternative way from Africa." When he changed his mind, Wonder commented, "I wanted to go to Ghana but then I made up my mind not to. There are people here I would like to help. America makes me very angry at times. It's the closest to being right—but it could be out of sight." Over the next quarter century Wonder would visit the mother continent regularly and donate substantial sums to educational and relief efforts. (An amusing side note to his African excursions occurred in 1977, when he accepted the Grammy for *Songs in the Key of Life* via a remote feed from Nigeria. The connection didn't work very well, leading host Andy Williams to commit a faux pas that would be repeated with minor variations by President George W. Bush in 2002. "If you can't hear me," an obviously flustered Williams asked Stevie's flickering image, "can you at least see me?")

Wonder's "retirement" announcement was widely viewed as part of a ploy involving contract negotiations. When Motown relocated from Detroit to Los Angeles in 1972, most of the magic vanished. By 1976 many long-time hit-makers—singers, songwriters, producers—had left the label, and Gordy desperately needed the cash flow generated by Wonder's albums. Outbidding Epic and Arista, Gordy guaranteed Wonder $13 million over seven years. It was the most lucrative contract in music industry history.

The royalty rate, reportedly 20 percent, surpassed standard superstar norms by 5 to 7 percent. The contract also included an unprecedented clause giving Wonder the right of approval over any buyer if Gordy should attempt to sell Motown. At the time, Gordy considered that as likely as "my going back to work on the Lincoln-Mercury assembly line, singing 'Mary Had a Little Lamb.' " In fact, Wonder would exercise that right, nixing the deal when Gordy attempted to sell the Jobete publishing company in the early eighties. When Gordy presented the deal to the buyers without Wonder's catalog, negotiations collapsed. Although he was angry at the time, Gordy eventually came to appreciate his protégé's business acumen. Gordy wrote in *To Be Loved,* "Thank God for Stevie."

After he signed the new deal, Wonder reflected on Motown's economic and cultural significance. "There are faults at Motown, but they can be corrected," he told a reporter for a black newspaper. "If you went somewhere else, there'd be other problems—probably a lot worse ones. I'm staying at Motown, because it is the only viable surviving black-owned company in the record industry. If it were not for Motown, many of us just wouldn't have had the shot we've had at success and fulfillment. It is vital that people in our business—particularly the black creative community, including artists, writers and producers—make sure that Motown stays emotionally stable, spiritually strong, and economically healthy."

Looking beyond an American music industry concerned more with marketing than with spiritual or musical renewal, Wonder gravitated toward reggae, which was just beginning to attract attention as a major voice in the African diaspora. Bob Marley became a political ally. Like most reggae pioneers, Marley had grown up in Jamaica listening to American soul music on the Miami radio stations that blanketed the Caribbean. Combining soul melodies and harmonies with the rhythmic drive of Jamaican ska, Marley and the Wailers forged a specifically Jamaican version of the gospel vision. A more aggressively black nationalist response to the vision of the American freedom movement, reggae combined an inclusive vision of "Jah love" with a revolutionary politics centered on icons Marcus Garvey and Haile Selassie. Musically, Marley's closest affinity was with the Impressions. One of his most stirring anthems, "One Love / People Get Ready" revoices Mayfield's gospel testimony as an apocalyptic promise to "fight this holy Armageddon." Like the Impressions, the Wailers merged their distinctive voices in a three-part harmony that perfectly expressed the communal energy of "I and I," the reggae phrase underlining the unbreakable bond between self and community. When Wonder embraced Marley, the influence came full circle.

Wonder began listening to reggae during a 1969 trip to Jamaica, and he gradually came to hear the music as a fresher, less compromised expression of the spiritual politics of the best soul music. He had developed a friendship with the roots reggae band Third World and expressed admiration for Johnny Nash's sunny "I Can See Clearly Now" and Lee Perry's sonic experiments on "Revolution Dub." But his interest sharpened when the Wailers began touring America. Still recovering from his accident, he had been unable to hear them on the 1973 tour, where they opened for Sly and the Family Stone. When Marley returned in 1975, Wonder felt an immediate spiritual affinity and suggested they play a benefit for the Jamaican School for the Blind. On October 11, 1975, the summit meeting took place in Kingston. Third World opened the set followed by a reunion between Marley and the Wailers, who had recently split up. After Wonder performed a set capped by "Boogie On Reggae Woman," the Wailers joined him for a jam on "I Shot the Sheriff." By all accounts, the jam never really ignited, and the Jamaican audience responded to Wonder with more respect than enthusiasm. But the image of Wonder and Marley blending their voices would take on great symbolic power as the years wore on, reaffirming the healing power of black unity *and* universal love in a world that valued neither.

WHILE STEVIE WAS EXPANDING his musical, political, and spiritual horizons, Curtis Mayfield was finding it harder and harder to look beyond the walls of the Curtom studios. Especially after Marv Stuart replaced Eddie Thomas as his primary business partner, the details of running the company consumed more and more of his time. "That was probably no good for me, the company, and for the customer that had so much expectation for me," Mayfield admitted. "The whole name of the game was to make money. The investors want to hear one thing—'I want to make money.' Probably what people should have done, and I probably should have done myself, was just laid back and kind of watched things for a while." A changing social and musical scene in which the spotlight was shifting rapidly to disco compounded the problem. "As far as my doing songs with messages, disco interrupted it very much," Mayfield said in the early eighties. "The name of the game these past few years has been escape. People have been going off and doing their thing since time began. But it's important that they remember themselves and who they are. They've got to stay in touch with the earth."

Still, Mayfield continued to play a central role in Chicago's changing soul music scene. Working in the city presented him with problems that his rivals in Detroit never had to deal with. Eddie Thomas put it succinctly: "We had it all; labels, studios, record plants. But it was never important to Chicago to be associated with its music industry. When they put Chicago forward, it was the steel industry, the Loop. We were just a little cottage industry to them. It was different in Detroit and Memphis." Johnny Meadows agreed: "You think of Detroit, you think of Motown. You think of Chicago, you think of the museums, the Bears, the Bulls." In an alternate universe, it would make sense to find statues of Mahalia Jackson, Muddy Waters, Sam Cooke, and Curtis Mayfield lining McFetridge Drive between the Field Museum and Soldier Field. In real life, the closest Mayfield came to official recognition from his hometown was a 1973 special on Chicago station WTTW. With *Super Fly* playing to capacity audiences in Windy City theaters, the special reunited most of the original Impressions, including Jerry Butler, with the members of the group who had succeeded the classic trio. The *Curtis in Chicago* album, released to celebrate the special, consists primarily of remakes of Mayfield's classics, topped by an ensemble finale of "Swing Low Sweet Chariot" and "Amen."

Although Curtis was active as a producer, his efforts yielded few commercial triumphs beyond his solo albums, which remained primary sources of Curtom's visibility and cash flow. His performance as a songwriter yielded better results. The two-CD British box set *The Curtom Story* provides an overview of Mayfield's late-sixties and early-seventies songwriting. The highlights include vintage compositions recorded by Holly Maxwell ("Suffer"), Baby Huey and the Baby Sitters ("Mighty Mighty Children"), Love's Children ("Soul Is Love"), the Staple Singers ("Let's Do It Again"), Mavis Staples on her own ("A Piece of the Action"), and younger acts including the Natural Four and the Notations. Sadly, his attempts to revive the careers of old friends Major Lance, Gene Chandler, and Billy Butler met with little success; only Lance's "Stay Away from Me" reached the R&B Top Twenty. Mayfield's most satisfying creative efforts beyond his own albums focused on the Five Stairsteps and Cubie. A family group that set the stage for the Jackson 5 and the Osmonds, the Five Stairsteps had recorded several minor hits on Mayfield's Windy C label in the mid-sixties, most notably the catchy "You Waited Too Long" and "Come Back." When Curtom began recruiting, Mayfield re-signed the group and produced the *Love's Happening* album, which ranks alongside his work with Major Lance and Gene Chandler as the best of his nonsoundtrack collaborations. Mayfield wrote and produced most of the songs, including the title track, a weirdly appealing combination of flower-power musings and gospel-bubblegum production. With a melody reminiscent of the Impressions' mid-sixties hits, "Love's Happening" offers a gentle smile that only the most committed cynic would bother to resist. Despite three minor hits—"Don't Change Your Love," "Baby Make Me Feel Good," and "We Must Be in Love"—the Stairsteps failed to break through commercially.

Mayfield's solo albums provided the primary relief from the commercial disappointments. No Mayfield album from *Sweet Exorcist* in 1974 to the demise of Curtom in 1980 withstands comparison with *Curtis, Roots, Superfly,* or even *Back to the World.* But it would be a serious mistake to overlook the best songs on the ten albums he released during that period. Obviously, that's way too many albums, especially in light of his production, film scoring, and songwriting duties. *Sweet Exorcist* (1974), featuring the driving "Ain't Got Time" and "Kung Fu," wasn't a sharp dropoff from *Back to the World.* Mayfield viewed it as a reaffirmation of the power of love after a series of albums that emphasized the evils loose in the world. "The album allowed me to say some things I'd wanted to say for quite a while, things that were in my mind which I wanted to get out," he said. Mayfield's favorite tracks were the number-three R&B hit, "Kung Fu," and the title cut, a meditation on good and evil inspired by the horror classic *The Exorcist.* But the most compelling cuts provide a picture of an artist nearing the limits of his political patience and physical energy. "Ain't Got Time" probes the breakdown of trust within and between black communities, while "To Be Invisible" knits together personal and political experience as deftly as "I'm So Proud" or "I've Been Trying." After *Sweet Exorcist,* however, only *Never Say You Can't Survive, Something to Believe In,* and the soundtrack to *Short Eyes* come close to standing up on their own. Still, in the luxury of retrospect, it's easy to imaginatively distill two or three first-rate albums from the raw material. (You can do it yourself, or you can go directly to disk three of Rhino Records' *People Get Ready! The Curtis Mayfield Story,* which could legitimately be retitled *The Great Lost Curtis Mayfield Album.*)

Mayfield's late-seventies work features a set of yearning love songs including "Only You Babe," "So in Love," "Show Me Love," and two duets with Linda Clifford, "Between You Baby and Me" and "Sweet Sensation." Worthy additions to Mayfield's explicitly political songbook, "To Be Invisible," "Mr. Welfare Man," "Mother's Son," and above all "Do Do Wap Is Strong in Here" chronicle the conditions that made it increasingly difficult to reconcile the gospel vision with what was happening in the inner cities. "Back Against the Wall," "Got to Find a Way," Mayfield's version of "Suffer," and the title cuts from *Never Say You Can't Survive* and *Something to Believe In* cling to the gospel vision as the only shelter against the gathering storm.

While his film soundtracks added immensely to the drain on Mayfield's energy, he took great satisfaction from his achievements for Hollywood. He could pinpoint the moment when he realized the degree of his success as a soundtrack writer: "I was standing in Chicago right on State Street, the main street in the Chicago theater district, right there in the Loop. And I looked out, and right there I could see the marquee for three of my movies at the same time, *Super Fly, Let's Do It Again,* and I think it was *Claudine.* Right there in my hometown. So you know I felt like a big man."

Between 1972 and 1977 Mayfield wrote the music for a half-dozen soundtracks, performing the music himself on *Super Fly* and the underrated *Short Eyes,* one of the better films in the prison-movie genre. Varying widely in quality, Mayfield's collaborative soundtracks included *Claudine* (1974) and *Pipedreams* (1976), both performed by Gladys Knight and the Pips; *Sparkle* (1976) with Aretha Franklin; *A Piece of the Action* (1977) with Mavis Staples; and *Let's Do It Again* (1975) with the Staple Singers. Like Motown, Curtom took an active financial interest in the films as well as their soundtracks. Mayfield applied the lessons he had learned from "Freddie's Dead" to his new projects. "We were now setting up the film by releasing an album two, three months prior, and the audience would come in with a familiarity as to what they were about to visualize," he said. "If it was a good movie, everything just came together, and you have two hits coming out of it."

Sadly, the best of the movies, *Short Eyes,* failed commercially. Based on a prize-winning play by Miguel Piñero, the movie provides an unsparingly realistic look at the "codes of wrath" ruling New York's infernal Tombs Detention Center. At a time when rates of incarceration for young black men were spiraling upward, *Short Eyes* sketches a gallery of individuals attempting to maintain some hope in a hopeless world. Divided into mutually suspicious camps of blacks, Latinos, and a white minority, the prisoners focus their rage on the title character, a middle-class white man accused of child molesting. Refusing to sugarcoat the obscenity at the core of prison life, Mayfield's soundtrack and Pinero's brilliant dialogue reaffirm the prisoners' beleaguered humanity.

While the *Short Eyes* soundtrack shares the erratic quality of all Mayfield's late-seventies albums, several songs—especially "Back Against the Wall" and "Do Do Wap Is Strong in Here"—would have been at home on *Curtis* or *Super Fly*. The latter crystallizes the gospel-blues call and response between "Living for the City" and "Higher Ground" into a five-and-a-half-minute meditation on a world where there "ain't no heaven." Left all alone, the prisoners get stoned, scramble to stay alive, and hold on to the sound that keeps the hope of something better alive in their hearts. "We got great recognition and real good write-ups," Mayfield remembered. "However, it was probably too real. When we did it, it was during the times of escapism and *Star Wars*."

The rollicking *Let's Do It Again* and *A Piece of the Action* fit the times much better. Mavis Staples loved working with her old friend on the soundtracks. "When I got one of his songs, I would just be grinning in my sleep," she beamed. "When he sings, his voice just calms you down. I've always admired the stories in his songs. He paints such a clear picture of what he's writing about. I remember when Curtis called me to work on *A Piece of the Action*," Staples continued. "He'd run into some kind of trouble, and he was on a tight deadline. So he called and said, 'Mavis, I'm in a bind,' and I said, 'Okay, Curtis, I'm on the way.' All of the musicians ended up spending the night in the studio, sleeping over two nights to get the album done. He had a deadline, but it was real comfortable there. When you're in the studio with him, there's never a moment when you're not relaxed. No tension, no rushing."

The Staples' gospel background created problems when Mayfield presented them with the title cut from *Let's Do It Again*. "They started out with the church music, gospel music, and they'd already built a great following and name for themselves. So they of course made their crossover," Mayfield said. "But they always wanted their music to be inspirational. So their style didn't really change too much. They simply found a music that spread them out, allowed them to make a better living." The problem lay in the song's obviously sexual lyrics. Mavis Staples remembers her father's reluctance to record a song that "was definitely more explicit than anything we'd ever done before. Pops didn't want to sing it at first." Fortunately, Mayfield's humor combined with Pops's affection for his young friend to win him over. Mavis recalls the crucial conversation. "Pops would say, 'Curtis, I ain't gonna say that *funky* stuff. You know me, Curtis, I don't sing songs like that.' Curtis said, 'Oh Pops, please, Pops, it's just a movie score. It ain't like your regular stuff. You're just doing it for a movie.' When Daddy said all right, I said, 'Lord, Curtis, you have done something ain't nobody but you could do. Ain't no way Pops was gonna say 'funky.' '" When the single sold over two million copies, everyone concerned was happy that Mavis and Mayfield had carried the day.

~⑤~

ARETHA FRANKLIN'S BEST DECISION of the late seventies also involved Mayfield. After *Young, Gifted and Black* and *Amazing Grace* lifted Aretha and her audience to sublime heights, her career entered a dry spell that sputtered for the rest of the decade. Along with a few first-rate songs scattered over the last eight albums she recorded before leaving Atlantic in 1980, the Mayfield-produced *Sparkle* was the only significant oasis in the creative desert. The timing of the project was right for both Mayfield and Aretha, whose long-term collaboration with Jerry Wexler had run out of gas. Casting about for a way to reverse the creative and commercial malaise that began in 1973 with *Hey Now Hey (The Other Side of the Sky)* and had most recently coughed up the generally dismal *You,* Wexler's partner Ahmet Ertegun provided Aretha with a list of possible producers for the follow-up. She chose Curtis.

When Ertegun contacted Mayfield in late 1975, Mayfield was concentrating on the soundtrack for *Sparkle,* a rags-to-riches ghetto story. The movie opens with a church choir singing Thomas Dorsey's "Precious Lord (Take My Hand)" and soon takes its young protagonists to a chitlin circuit–style revue, where they encounter the full range of fifties R&B styles: Ruth

Brown–style gospel soul; a Coasters/Clovers novelty number; dreamily romantic doo-wop; and stylish soul testifying *à la* Clyde McPhatter. From there the movie walks a fine line between realism and stereotype as it follows the fortunes of a girl group struggling to break into the music business. Mayfield had lived the basics of the story, and its archetypal qualities reminded him of *Super Fly*, this time without the "cocaine infomercial." He responded with an extraordinarily soulful set of songs for the movie's then-unknown stars, Philip Michael Thomas, Lonette McKee, and Irene Cara, who would go on to star in *Fame*. Dissatisfied with the renditions included on the actual soundtrack, Mayfield jumped at the opportunity to work with Aretha on new versions. The movie's stars reacted with dismay when they were told the actual soundtrack would not be released. "The next thing I knew, Curtis Mayfield was giving an interview saying he couldn't understand how they could cast unknowns when they should have gone with black stars like Diana and Aretha," McKee said with understandable bitterness. "He made it hard, deliberately setting the keys of the songs in uncomfortable registers for all of us. And I guess his spite, coupled with Warner's lack of faith, brought about the soundtrack arrangement with Aretha. I don't think she was aware of the politics." Musically at least, the switch to Aretha was the right move. The actresses' versions of "Jump," "Run to Me," and "Look in Your Heart" incorporated into the film don't do the songs justice, and there was simply no way McKee or Cara could capture the combination of confidence and vulnerability that makes "Giving Him Something He Can Feel" a deep soul standard.

Industry and family politics aside, the not-quite-soundtrack of *Sparkle* released in August 1976 was the best album Curtis or Aretha would produce for at least five years, and one of the best either released after 1975. The key to its success was its adherence to a straight gospel-soul sound reminiscent of *Curtis* or *Aretha Arrives.* "It proved the permanent power of rootsy rhythm and blues," Aretha observed. Curtis agreed: "It was a sound that never grows old. The songs speak to the yearnings and hopes. I was working on several projects at that time, but to work with Aretha was a true honor." Behind the mutual satisfaction with the outcome, however, there were creative tensions. Aretha was uncomfortable with Mayfield's work habits but in general deferred to his judgment. "It took us about five days to record the album because he likes to work pretty fast," Aretha told interviewer David Nathan. "He pretty much let me have a free hand, but there were a few differences. Our only real disagreement was over one note—he wanted me to sing one way, but I had another way in mind. So we recorded both versions, and what you hear on the album is his concept. He was the producer, so I let him produce."

The period between *Amazing Grace* and *Sparkle* had been difficult for Aretha commercially, creatively, and personally. The problems began when Aretha, who'd become friends with Quincy Jones and his wife Peggy Lipton of *Mod Squad* fame, suggested that Quincy produce the studio follow-up to *Young, Gifted and Black*. Realizing that it had been a couple of years since Aretha's last major hit, Wexler approved of Jones, a major player in the world of movie music and smooth jazz. "When she told me that Quincy was interested in coproducing a jazz album," Wexler recalled, "I jumped at the idea." Soon, however, tensions began to develop. The problems concerned Jones's desire to move the album in a pop direction. Always a fan of Aretha's best Columbia work, Wexler imagined something more like her work with the Ray Bryant combo or *Soul '69*. He'd never liked Aretha's treatment of abstract counterculture-style lyrics, singling out her covers of the Band's "The Weight" and Elton John's "Border Song (Holy Moses)" as "mistakes." So he couldn't have been happy with the title cut of *Hey Now Hey (The Other Side of the Sky)*, which invoked an otherworldly goal that didn't seem to have much to do with the black Baptist heaven. The best cuts on the album hinted at what the abandoned jazz project might have achieved. The hit single "Angel," written by Aretha's sister Carolyn, gave Aretha a well-deserved number-one R&B hit, and "Moody's Mood" showcases her as a stylist capable of matching Ella Fitzgerald or Sarah Vaughan.

But the rest of the album wandered aimlessly, and the cover art was nearly unspeakable: a psychedelic portrait on the front followed by a street-life cartoon featuring Aretha as a thin Egyptian princess complete with wings and exposed breasts. Over the next two years Aretha produced three albums, *Let Me in Your Life, With Everything I Feel in Me,* and *You,* which Wexler, who coproduced cuts on each, dismissed curtly, saying, "I don't want to talk about those albums. I'm not happy with them, except for an occasional isolated song." Despite the presence of ace musicians Cornell Dupree, Richard Tee, Bernard Purdie, and Donny Hathaway, the trio of albums produced only a smattering of memorable cuts: Bobby Womack's "I'm in Love"; two of

Aretha's own compositions, "With Everything I Feel in Me" and "Mr. D.J. (5 for the D.J.)"; two Stevie Wonder songs, "I Love Every Little Thing About You" and the number-one R&B hit "Until You Come Back to Me (That's What I'm Gonna Do)"; and two more Carolyn Franklin songs, "Sing It Again, Say It Again" and the achingly beautiful "Without Love," which she cowrote with R&B elder Ivory Joe Hunter. The most telling cut on the three albums, however, may be Aretha's version of James Cleveland's "All of These Things," which sounds the sadness that was reasserting itself in her life. Aretha continued to take home Grammy awards, for "Master of Eyes (The Deepness of Your Eyes)" and "Ain't Nothin' Like the Real Thing," but until she connected with Mayfield, it seemed that the magic was slipping away.

Even during her fallow period, Aretha's music didn't vanish. Those who'd grown up in the "Age of Aretha" kept right on living their lives to the rhythms of "Baby, I Love You," "Since You've Been Gone (Sweet Sweet Baby)," "Spirit in the Dark," and "Respect." That was especially the case for black women, who'd always seen Sister Ree from a slightly different angle than anyone else. While feminists, revolutionaries, and Vietnam veterans all responded to the metaphorical possibilities of Aretha's music, the ghetto women whom black novelist Paule Marshall called "poets in the kitchen" understood her as one of their own—if not quite a ghetto girl, certainly the voice of the girls in the ghetto. Aretha's struggles for self-acceptance, her fiery insistence that her man do the right thing, her melting sensuality, her never-easy knowledge that at the end of the day Jesus would give her the strength to weather the storm: all of it remained as real for Aretha's African American sisters in the late seventies as it had been five or ten years earlier.

As the black feminist (or womanist, to use Alice Walker's preferred term) movement emerged in the late seventies, Aretha became an icon. The first generation of black women to articulate womanism's aims and values was Aretha's. They'd grown up with the civil rights movement and benefited from the movement's assault on Jim Crow. Most of them had been the first in their families to earn a graduate degree. Patricia Hill Collins, who articulated the new black feminism as well as anyone, places Aretha at the center of the tradition of black women's resistance. Writing on "Respect," Collins observes, "Even though the lyrics can be sung by anyone, they take on a special meaning when sung by Aretha in the way that she sings them. On one level, the song functions as a metaphor for the condition of African Americans in a racist society. But Aretha's being a Black *woman* enables the song to tap deeper meanings. Within the blues tradition, the listening audience of African American women assumes 'we' Black women, even though Aretha as the blues singer sings 'I.' " Poet Sherley Anne Williams, who wrote a wonderful homage to Bessie Smith titled "Some One Sweet Angel Chile," agrees: "Aretha was right on time, but there was also something about the way Aretha characterized respect as something given with force and great effort and cost. And when she even went so far as to spell the word 'respect,' we just knew that this sister wasn't playing around."

Aretha certainly wasn't playing around, but she wasn't happy either. She consistently denied reports that she was moody or depressed but admitted to spending a lot of time sitting at home watching soap operas and boxing on television. "I was part of the first generation of kids addicted to the small screen," she explained. She also loved going out to see old movies. One of the reasons she'd miss New York, she told interviewers after she and her boyfriend Ken Cunningham announced plans to relocate to Los Angeles in 1975, was that "you can see a lot of old movies here. Sometimes at four in the morning, the kind with Joan Crawford, Barbara Stanwyck, Ingrid Bergman." After her relationship with Cunningham ended in 1976, reportedly as a result of conflicts concerning Cecil Franklin's role as Aretha's manager, Aretha was once again facing her old friend the blues. "The end of the seventies and much of the eighties," she said, "would be the most challenging period of my life."

The music Aretha made as she shouldered her sorrows deepened her bond with her black female audience. Embracing their power and demanding respect didn't negate the fact that, as Aretha reflected, "on any given day, any of us can have the blues. We don't control fate or destiny, and we can't control the circumstances of our lives." While "Respect" and "Rock Steady" blaze with confidence and determination, "Angel," "Until You Come Back to Me," and "Break It to Me Gently" burn with a quiet desire. "Angel" begins with a spoken-word introduction describing a conversation between Aretha and her sister Carolyn, who wrote the song. Reaching out for a love that's part human, part divine, the song calls out achingly to the larger community of sisters who don't need the details spelled out for them. "The song had wings," Aretha said. "It combined loneliness and hope in a way that spoke directly to the heart." When she sings, "Got to get me an angel in my life," she caresses the last word, touching the depth of the sorrow and the yearning for something better. The combination of realism and sadness speaks to anyone who's had hard times, but at its core it reaffirmed Aretha's place as the Queen of the Black Women's Blues.

In 1976 her eight-year streak of Grammy awards for best R&B female vocal performance ended when Natalie Cole won "the Aretha" for "This Will Be." When Natalie had first begun to perform, Aretha had sent flowers to her openings and called with holiday greetings. But a set of circumstances surrounding "This Will Be" contributed to a break in what had seemed to be a developing friendship. The problems began when songwriters Chuck Jackson (Jesse's brother) and Marvin Yancy brought a set of songs to Aretha, who turned them down. Subsequently they offered them to Natalie, who decided to record "This Will Be" and "I've Got Love on My Mind." Aretha wasn't happy with what she heard as Natalie's unoriginal approach to the song: "At one point, Natalie called me to say that it was Chuck Jackson's idea—not hers—for her to try to sound like me," Aretha wrote in her autobiography. "Later, every time I opened a publication, it seemed like Natalie was telling journalists something about our fantasy feuds." Natalie remembered things differently. "Someone told her I went around bragging about the fact that she had called me and that she must have been scared of me," the younger singer reported. "Then I'm calling her, and she wasn't returning any of my calls, and the next thing was the Grammys. I went up to her, and she broke my face," the street term for a particularly sharp snub. It would be the first of many reported conflicts pitting Aretha against other black women singers, including Gladys Knight, Patti LaBelle, Mavis Staples, and Whitney Houston.

After the landmarks of *Live at Fillmore West* and *Amazing Grace,* Aretha entered a bizarre period in her performing career. A highly publicized concert at Radio City Music Hall in November 1974 turned into a surreal disaster when Aretha entered wearing a clown suit, complete with red nose, singing "That's Entertainment." A beautiful version of Stevie Wonder's "All in Love Is Fair" wasn't enough to rescue the evening. A month later she opened at the Apollo in a sequined lavender suit and top hat singing "Rock-a-bye Your Baby with a Dixie Melody," which probably wasn't what the followers of Malcolm X and Angela Davis expected from Sister Aretha.

Responding to bemused and sometimes hostile reviews in both the black and white press, Aretha said only, "I thought it was a nice change of pace. Maybe the public just doesn't know me."

∽⧽

ʙ Y THE TIME ARETHA THRILLED the crowd at Jimmy Carter's inaugural gala with a stirring a cappella "God Bless America" on January 19, 1977, American pop culture was entering the disco era. Even as *Sparkle* testified to the beauty and brilliance of gospel-based soul, Aretha and Curtis Mayfield found themselves scrambling to adjust to a rapidly changing musical scene. At first the challenge wasn't obvious. When disco first appeared, it was just another part of the black dance mix that made no distinction between funk, soul, and the imported novelty records that took their name from the European discotheques where they had first been played.

But before long, it became clear that disco represented a deliriously illogical extension of the fundamental premise of gospel soul. Gospel music sang about salvation through God; soul music sang about the power of love. Taking the progression another step into the secular world, disco translated "love" as "sex." Churchgoers who shook their heads when Ray Charles and Sam Cooke testified to the redemptive power of romantic love howled in dismay over Donna Summer's orgasmic marathon "Love to Love You Baby" or transvestite diva Sylvester's "Save My Soul." The fact that Sylvester sang with sanctified fervor didn't impress the respectable African Americans who shared Jesse Jackson's angry dismissal of disco as "garbage and pollution which is corrupting the minds and morals of our youth." After *Saturday Night Fever* sparked the disco craze, even disco's staunchest defenders were forced to admit that the music had receded into a bacchanalian dream of cocaine, poppers, and promiscuity. As upscale clubs like Studio 54 opened their doors to interracial coteries of celebrities and thrill-seekers, disco stars found it lucrative to cater to an audience dedicated to narcissistic hedonism rather than communal uplift. While local disco scenes—most notably the house music communities of Chicago and New Jersey—maintained their vitality, disco culture gradually lost contact with black clubs and audiences in the rural South and the urban ghettos, where hip-hop would soon fill the cultural vacuum.

The best disco, much of it created by black women who looked to Aretha as their elder sister and role model, underlined the music's gospel roots. Gloria Gaynor's "I Will Survive" and Sister Sledge's brilliant trilogy—"He's the Greatest Dancer," "Lost in Music," and "We Are Family"—reasserted the gospel vision of unity at the precise moment Jimmy Carter's dismissal of UN ambassador Andrew Young ended his administration's honeymoon with black America. Music critic Iain Chambers described the disco tradition as an extension of ideas that had been developing in post–World War II African American secular music: "In disco the musical pulse is freed from the claustrophobic interiors of the blues and the tight scaffolding of R&B and early soul music. A looser, explicitly polyrhythmic attack pushes the blues, gospel and soul heritage into an apparently endless cycle where there is no beginning or end, just an ever-present 'now.' Disco music does not come to a halt. Restricted to a three-minute single, the music would be rendered senseless. The power of disco lay in saturating dancers and the dance floor in the continual explosion of its presence."

Despite disco's genuine connection with the communal aspects of the gospel vision, the fragmented reflections glittering in the facets of the mirror balls provide a fair symbol of its relation to gospel. On one hand, black women occupied a central place in disco culture. Many had learned to sing in church and shared Chambers's sense of the music as an extension of soul. On the other, disco pounded out from the clubs on New York's Christopher Street and in San Francisco's Castro district, where a sexually exuberant gay culture had burst out of the closet in the wake of the 1969 Stonewall riots. San Francisco gay diva Sylvester voiced the aspirations and suffering of the brave new world of bathhouses and one-night stands in powerful gospel disco hits like "Power of Love," "(You Make Me Feel) Mighty Real," and "Sell My Soul." While many saw that culture as a logical and fitting fulfillment of an egalitarian dream with its roots in the civil rights movement and the counterculture, many others—including a fair number of black churchgoers—recoiled in puritanical horror.

The centrality of gays and black women in disco culture contributed to a ferocious antidisco backlash. The backlash was driven by a bizarre coalition of feminists uneasy with women's role as sexual playthings at disco palaces like Studio 54; angry young white men like the ones who turned an antidisco rally between games of a Chicago White Sox doubleheader into a full-scale riot with clear homophobic and racist overtones; and morally conservative Christians, black and white. Nile Rodgers of the disco super-group Chic, the idiosyncratic musical genius at the center of the disco mix, pinpointed the source of the problem in disco's evolution away from its gospel-soul roots. "It was definitely R&B dance music," Rodgers observed. "That was where it originated. Then it took on more blatant sexual over-tones because of the gay movement. It seems to me that disco—from when I first recognized it as a musical form—was the most hedonistic music I had ever heard in my life. It was really all about Me! Me! Me! Me!" For Rodgers, that made disco a welcome relief from the pretensions of the countercul-ture he had lived in as a self-identified black hippie. "When I was political and a hippie," he said, "we talked about freedom and individuality, and it was all bullshit. You could tell a hippie a mile away. We conformed to our nonconformity. Whereas disco really *was* about individuality. And the freakier, the better."

Whatever soul artists felt about disco, they couldn't ignore it. Some adjusted easily; the Jacksons and former Temptation Eddie Kendricks quickly established themselves as disco favorites. James Brown trumpeted his claim to the title of the "Original Disco Man." But for Curtis and Aretha, the new sound presented seemingly intractable problems. It wasn't that they disliked the music or, for the most part, the scene. Looking back at his involvement with disco tracks, Mayfield concluded, "It was definitely a good experience. You're always walking that tightrope of what is commer-cial to the fans and then whether you're expressing yourself independently as a creative person. Sometimes you have to..." The fact that he was unable to finish the sentence speaks volumes. Always enamored of innovative styles, Aretha felt right at home with disco's sometimes outrageous fashion sense. She appeared in public wearing LaBelle-style silver lamé. During the King Tut craze she appeared on a television special with gold wings attached to an Egyptian-styled dress. In a 1978 interview she told David Nathan that she enjoyed disco both as music and as milieu. "I didn't think it would be as big as it is and I was kinda surprised that it was more than just a fad," she said. "I've been to Studio 54 in New York and the Speakeasy in L.A. and a disco down in Acapulco. It's good for us girls who want to shed a few pounds."

Despite their interest in disco, neither Aretha nor Curtis could consis-tently create dance-floor hits. Aretha's attempts to cash in on what she called

"America's love affair" with disco were halfhearted. In 1977 she turned to Lamont Dozier of the Holland-Dozier-Holland team responsible for most of the classic hits by the Supremes and the Four Tops. The resulting *Sweet Passion* album is rivaled only by 1979's *La Diva* as the low point of her Atlantic years. Aretha's failure to solve the disco puzzle resulted in large part from her ambivalence about moving away from her roots. "A song, like a person, must have soul," she reflected. "I realized that my voice would have worked with disco tracks. But I was determined not to be labeled a disco artist. No matter how much the radio stations were shoving rhythm and blues back in the corner, I still believed and I believe today in the permanent value and staying power of soul music." In fact, she'd been offered several first-rate cuts—"Upside Down" and "I'm Coming Out"—by Nile Rodgers and songwriting partner Bernard Edwards. While she recognized them as "good songs" with "in-the-pocket grooves and cute lyrics," she clashed with Rodgers and Edwards over how to produce her singing. "Their idea for me was 'Just come in and sing impromptu and we'll take it from there,' " she said. "Well, I hadn't worked that way. I'm an interpreter, and I need to be involved with the total musical environment." Both songs wound up as smash hits for Diana Ross.

Aretha's failure to split the disco difference can be seen in the fact that the four-CD retrospective of her Atlantic years, *Queen of Soul*, contains only one song from her three late-seventies albums, *Sweet Passion, Almighty Fire*, and *La Diva*—the beautiful deep soul ballad "Break It to Me Gently." In fact, when Aretha embraced her R&B roots during the disco period, black audiences responded eagerly. "Break It to Me Gently" topped the R&B charts in 1977, while both "When I Think About You" and the Mayfield-produced "Almighty Fire (Woman of the Future)" made the R&B Top Twenty. Where it had been a stroke of genius to pair Aretha with Curtis Mayfield for *Sparkle*, the attempt to revive the collaboration on *Almighty Fire* floundered, in large part because Curtis had no more idea how to respond to disco than she did.

Mayfield began to experiment with disco on *Give, Get, Take and Have* (1976) and *Never Say You Can't Survive* (1977) and followed up with a pair of disco-dominated albums, *Do It All Night* (1978) and *Heartbeat* (1979). In retrospect, Mayfield found the late seventies almost amusing: "Those were some strange times for me. I had done so well for myself for such a long time. You know I was spoiled." Neither Mayfield's music nor his sensibility was well suited to the hedonistic aspects of disco culture. The polyrhythmic textures of "Move On Up" or "Underground" resisted the thumping backbeat that made it easy for DJs with only a minimal sense of rhythm to keep the mix in monotonous motion. When Mayfield tried to play the game, as he did on "Do It All Night" and the minor British dance hit "No Goodbyes," he succeeded only in erasing his personality. Even more basically, Mayfield never had much interest in a world where the here and now demanded all the attention and love took a back seat to sex. Even when his lyrics celebrate sensual fulfillment, his voice sounds wistful. It wasn't what most of the dancers really wanted to hear.

The most symbolically interesting, if not musically compelling, stage of Mayfield's flirtation with disco came with *Heartbeat,* which was produced by Norman Harris, Bunny Sigler, and Ronald Tyson, who had contributed to the success of the Philly International label. Mayfield explained his decision to surrender production duties on his records for the first time since the early sixties. "You're somewhere in there trying to express yourself in order to prove yourself," he mused. "To show your own value, you must make hit records. It just can't be me me me. That always fails. Every once in a while even the best of the best have to say, okay maybe I better let somebody who's proven themselves with a new track record do something to keep me going."

The truth may simply have been that Mayfield didn't belong in disco, and any attempt to make him fit was doomed from the start. At first glance, the idea of matching Curtis with Philly International seemed promising. Philly International was the brainchild of Kenny Gamble, Leon Huff, and producer Thom Bell, the maestro of "symphonic soul." The label's slogan— "The Message in the Music"—signaled its goal of picking up the gospel-soul legacy by creating a socially uplifting music that would appeal to everyone in the black community and reach out to anyone else who would listen. It was a bold gesture at a time when the freedom movement had faded. Philly International held a special place in the hearts of many black musicians who saw it as a perfect expression of the underlying spirit of R&B. Stevie Wonder praised Gamble and Huff for mixing "the joy of love with the pain of oppression. They let it marinate, and it was sweet." Mayfield saw them as "young, proud black men" who went into righteous battle with the increasingly hostile "powers that be." "They walked a tight line in many directions," Mayfield said, "but you always knew Gamble and Huff were steering that ship."

Although *Heartbeat* and *Do It All Night* sounded like Mayfield was lost at sea, he claimed that he didn't regret the disco experiment: "It wasn't so bad. I liked the music. It was strange how *Heartbeat* worked out. The hit record from that album, 'Between You Baby and Me,' that I did with Linda Clifford, was the one track that was my own creation. So I felt good about that." But Mayfield's assessment sounded at least a note of regret. "Other people's styles could never express me the way I expressed myself. I learned from that that all my life the music I made only sold when I was being me, when I was just being Curtis," he concluded, acknowledging the failure of his attempts to adjust to the new fashion. "When I tried to be other than what I was, you could forget it. I had to be me to be a singer at all. I wasn't knocking down anything, but it was just that little style and just from the heart, that high vocal. Thank God I had microphones 'cause I wasn't a strong singer. But everybody seemed to like that falsetto."

In retrospect, Mayfield saw his late-seventies floundering as symptomatic of the larger problems facing Curtom. Money dictated many of Curtom's questionable decisions during the period. No longer involved with the label, Eddie Thomas believed that many of the difficulties stemmed from a failure to focus on Mayfield as a songwriter and singer. "To be honest," he said, "I blame some of it on Marv Stuart. Curtis had earned the right not to spend his time on so many different things. He should have been able to do his work without worrying about everything else." For Mayfield, the fragmented focus came with the turf. "Of course you have to look at it as a business. It is a business," he said. "And those who actually spend the money and invest, the stockholders and the people like that, they may not even listen to the music. The bottom line is what do I get out of it. But what was happening was that I was wearing too many hats."

The quality of Mayfield's albums declined, as did his popularity, for several reasons. His soundtrack work demanded an increasing amount of attention, and many of his best songs—"Let's Do It Again," "Giving Him Something He Can Feel"—were recorded by other artists. In itself that was nothing new. But Mayfield believed that the multiple pressures of running Curtom hurt his music: "I was going on the road, doing movies, trying to keep my career going strong, making decisions in the studio for many a person. I was trying to handle all my personal affairs and watch out for the money. Thus I began to allow other people with bad decisions to influence me."

Signs that Mayfield had overextended himself began to affect his performance as a producer. While many sessions went smoothly, others disintegrated. When Mayfield approached Gene Chandler about making a record with Curtom, Chandler jumped at the chance to rekindle the fire of their magical sixties collaborations. Unfortunately, Mayfield failed to appear for the scheduled session. "It was weird, awfully weird," Chandler reflected. "I love the brother, but Curtis did not show up. Don't ask me what happened. I don't know." Chandler went ahead and recorded as scheduled, but Mayfield misplaced the tapes, and Chandler gave up. Some speculated that Mayfield had fallen into the common traps of life on the fringes of late-seventies drug culture, but few who knew him doubted that the ultimate source of his problems lay in pure exhaustion.

The final albums of the Curtom years—*Something to Believe In* (1980) and *The Right Combination* (1980)—abandon the disco wonderland for Mayfield's soul and gospel roots. A collection of duets with Linda Clifford, *The Right Combination* attempted to capitalize on their old-school soul duet "Between You Baby and Me" as well as Clifford's 1978 disco hit "Runaway Love." Even when Clifford was marketed as a disco singer, her vocals revealed her origins as a soul singer, which is probably why she was saddled with the unenviable task of recording a disco version of "Bridge Over Troubled Water." The fact that that could ever have seemed like a good idea goes a long way toward defining the cultural moment. Anyone who wants more clarity need only listen to Al Green's quasi-disco version of "Love and Happiness," included on the *Live in Tokyo* LP. Some things just shouldn't happen. Both musically and lyrically Mayfield's duets with Clifford wander. The effective moments are almost all intensely personal. In late 1979 the duo went on tour in support of *The Right Combination*, the first time in five years that Mayfield had gone on the road.

Although it received little attention, *Something to Believe In* provides a fascinating and frequently moving sense of Mayfield's response to the changing times. The weariness at the heart of the album had accumulated over two decades of hard work, decades during which Mayfield helped define the cultural feel of two distinct eras in black politics. Carried along by the energy of the freedom movement during his years with the Impressions, Mayfield engaged the promise and problems of Black Power as creatively as any musician of his generation. The first cut on the album, "Love Me, Love Me Now," opens with the sound of a police whistle over a string-washed dance beat that recalls the disco of *Heartbeat* and *Do It All Night*. Even as Mayfield repeats the line "come dance with me," however, his repeated cries of "Love me baby" communicate a depth of isolation unlike anything in his earlier music.

The fascinating remake of "It's All Right" on *Something to Believe In* underscores the changes in Mayfield's energy since the high point of the movement. The Impressions' version of the song radiates an energy of connection, especially when the three voices come together at the ends of lines. The 1980 recording accentuates the distance between the lead singer and the female backup singers, who sound like they're located in a different room. You can feel the call and response falling apart. But if "It's All Right" suggested that Mayfield had lost control, the best songs on the album—"People Never Give Up," "Never Stop Loving Me," and the searching "Something to Believe In"—demonstrated his profound understanding of the gospel vision. Even as he stood alone on the dance floor, contemplating the inevitable collapse of the disco community, Mayfield testified to the power of love. But whatever the lyrics might claim, the sound warned forebodingly of the coming world in which nothing was going to be all right.

A S AMERICA CELEBRATED ITS BICENTENNIAL, Stevie Wonder contemplated the state of the union with a mixture of tenderness and ferocity. Polishing the material that would make *Songs in the Key of Life* a definitive moment in African American cultural history, he wore the robes of New Age Guru and Old Testament Prophet. Alternating between gentle prodding and thundering denunciation, Wonder challenged America to live up to its professed ideals. The keynote of Wonder's musical sermon was "As," which in a more truly democratic world would join Woody Guthrie's "This Land Is Your Land" on the ballot for a new national anthem. The song starts out as a strange New Age gospel love song. Conjuring up visions of flying dolphins and parrots living in the ocean, Wonder promises a love that will last until that visionary day when "you are me and I am you." But after a soaring instrumental break, he slams us down in a blues world where the hard times drive many to wish they'd been born in another place or time. Reasserting the core of the gospel vision, a vision honed during four centuries of slavery and segregation, Wonder assures the community that their burdens are part of God's larger plan. He drives home the point of the sermon in a voice that can only be described as astonishing in its intensity and conviction. Those who say they're "in it but not of it," Wonder warns, are helping to create the very hell they're trying to escape. His conclusion celebrates the vision that unites the great black singers and the activists who insisted on turning their visions into reality. If we change our words into truth and our truth into love, we'll have something worth passing down the generations.

Songs in the Key of Life attained the mountaintop Wonder had been climbing toward since "Blowin' in the Wind." After Margouleff and Cecil's departure, Gary Olazabal assumed primary studio duties, and Wonderlove emerged as a more active part of Wonder's creative process. Although the band had existed in some form since 1972 and appeared on the Rolling Stones tour, the *Songs*-era Wonderlove was the first relatively stable line-up. Consisting of bassist Nathan Watts, drummer Raymond Pounds, keyboardist Greg Phillinganes, and guitarists Ben Bridges and Mike Sembello, the *Songs*-era Wonderlove was the first group to play an important part in shaping Wonder's music since the Funk Brothers. Watts's fluid bass and Sembello's virtuoso guitar playing meshed perfectly with Wonder's increasing interest in the jazz dimensions of the African American musical tradition. Ralph Ellison had defined a jazz impulse in African American culture that focused on innovation, envisioning new possibilities that would transform the burdens and brutal experiences of life into something better. "True jazz is an art of individual assertion within and against the group," Ellison wrote. "Each true jazz moment (as distinct from the uninspired commercial performance) springs from a contest in which each artist challenges all the rest; each solo flight, or improvisation, represents (like the successive canvases of a painter) a definition of his identity; as individual, as member of the collectivity and as a link in the chain of tradition."

Wonderlove allowed Wonder to redefine his individual voice and sense of tradition while maintaining an active dialogue with a concrete musical community. Sembello, who'd joined the road band at about the time of *Innervisions,* played a crucial role in supporting Wonder's musical evolution. Preferring the experimental music of Pat Martino, John Coltrane, and Igor Stravinsky to R&B or rock, Sembello hadn't even intended to audition for a position in Wonderlove. "When I got the gig with Stevie, I was completely unaware of his music," Sembello admitted. A friend had talked him into going to a "jam session" in Philadelphia, Sembello said, without mentioning to him that the session was in fact an audition for Stevie's band. "Halfway there he said, 'Oh by the way, Stevie Wonder's gonna be at this jam session.' He failed to tell me it was an audition because he knew I wouldn't have gone." When they arrived, they encountered a swarm of two hundred guitarists, most of whom knew Wonder's music intimately. As it turned out, that wasn't an advantage. "He started playing all this off-the-wall shit, and obviously all these guys are waiting for 'Fingertips' or 'Superstition,' and he starts going into all this jazz stuff," Sembello recalled. "It was kind of like a game show for guitar players.... I lasted there about three or four hours, and it came down to me and this other guy, and Stevie started playing all this off-the-wall bebop and modulating keys, and it was no problem for me."

Through most of the period when they were creating *Songs in the Key of Life,* Wonder and his band worked intensively. Originally titled *Fulfillingness' (Second) Finale* and then *Let's See Life the Way It Is,* the two-and-a-half-disk masterpiece would take him two years to complete. While the two-year gap between *Fulfillingness' First Finale* and *Songs in the Key of Life* would occasion little comment today, then it was considered extreme. Bass player Nathan Watts recalled that "there were times when he'd stay in the studio 48 hours straight. You couldn't even get the cat to stop and eat." As usual, Wonder viewed the marathon sessions as an extension of his natural rhythm. "If my flow is goin' "—he smiled—"I keep on until I peak." The marathon sessions were fueled by the improvised banquet stocked by musicians, friends, and Stevie's mother, whom he'd rewarded for her love and support with a house in the San Fernando Valley. Backup singer Gypsie Jones told Wonder biographer Constanze Elsner about a session that turned into a culinary extravaganza. "I'd made Stevie a huge blackberry cobbler—because I know that he's got such a sweet tooth," Jones began. "Anyway, I get down to the studio, and five minutes later in walks Lula with a peach cobbler as big as the blackberry cobbler. And macaroni and cheese and baked chicken and broccoli and pizza and God knows what. Another two minutes later this guy walks in, and he brings the health-food trip. So the whole thing is like a feast. There was food and plates all across the studio."

As the sessions passed the one-year mark, Wonder took to wearing a T-shirt that answered the question before it was asked: WE'RE ALMOST FINISHED! Motown employees had their own STEVIE'S NEARLY READY shirts. As a series of announced release dates in early and mid-1976 receded into the past, rumors circulated blaming Stevie's uncertainty about the album's reception and his unwillingness to stop tweaking the production. Others speculated that he was waiting for the propitious astrological moment. When the long-awaited day finally arrived, Stevie hosted a lavish release party for press, musicians, and music industry mavens on a farm in rural Massachusetts. The white-fringed cowboy outfit he wore was something out of a George Clinton dream. Consisting of two full albums and a four-song EP, *Songs in the Key of Life* debuted at number one on October 16, 1976, and remained there for the rest of the year. Its fourteen-week stay at the top of the chart was bettered during the seventies only by Fleetwood Mac's *Rumors* (thirty-one), the *Saturday Night Fever* soundtrack (twenty-four), and Carole King's *Tapestry* (fifteen).

Songs in the Key of Life weaves the threads of gospel, jazz, and the blues into a tapestry that defines the breadth and depth of the African American tradition as clearly as any record ever made. Expanding on the blues realism of "Living for the City" and the gospel aspirations of "Higher Ground," the album denies neither the reality of suffering nor the power of love. The fact that it struck a profound chord in millions of white listeners simply underlines the inclusive potential of the gospel vision. Wonder frames the album with gospel statements, opening with the explicitly spiritual "Love's in Need of Love Today" and "Have a Talk with God" and closing with the communal celebration of "Easy Goin' Evening (My Mama's Call)." Celebratory moments spice the set in the glorious number-one hit "I Wish" and "Isn't She Lovely," Wonder's gift to his daughter Aisha Zakia. But he never denies the brutal experiences that threaten to drag people under. "Village Ghetto Land" and "Ordinary Pain" express the social and individual levels of the blues, while "Joy Inside My Tears" revoices Langston Hughes's classic definition of the blues as "laughing to keep from crying."

One of the album's two number-one singles, "I Wish" walks a fine line between sunny and sentimental. Part blues nostalgia for days spent hustling with his "hoodlum friends" and part warm memory of a ghetto community where the joys of family could outweigh the burdens of poverty, the song provides an emotional touchstone for the album as a whole. Wonder wrote it after attending a Motown company picnic. "I had such a good time at the picnic that I went to Crystal Recording Studio right afterward, and the vibe came right to my mind: running at the picnic, the contests, we all participated. It was a lot of fun. And from that the 'I Wish' vibe. And I started talking to [engineer] Gary [Olazabal] and we were talking about spiritual movements, 'The Wheel of '84' and when you go off to war, and all that stuff. It was ridiculous. Couldn't come up with anything stronger than the chorus, 'I wish those days would come back once more.' Thank goodness we didn't change that."

The core of *Songs in the Key of Life* is Wonder's improvisational vision of a new and better world. The jazz impulse elements on the album are unmistakable. Thematically, "Saturn" imagines a world where people live for hundreds of years, while stylistically, "Contusion" explores the jazz fusion style developed by Miles Davis's seventies groups. Building on his interests in reggae, Wonder forges new links in the chain of the diasporic tradition. Sung in Zulu, Spanish, and English, "Ngiculela/Es una Historia/ I Am Singing" calls for a broader sense of black unity, while "Black Man" celebrates Native American, Asian American, and Latino heroes alongside their black and white counterparts. The album's other number-one hit, "Sir Duke," pays joyous tribute to the jazz elders: Sir Duke Ellington, Louis Armstrong, Count Basie, Ella Fitzgerald, and—in a nod to the interracial aspects of the tradition—white swing band leader and trombonist Glenn Miller.

The most profound synthetic serendipity on the album occurs on "Pastime Paradise." The song starts out as straight blues. Wonder meditates on the damned souls who flee into the past or into fantasies of the future to escape a hopeless social morass. But Wonder isn't content with the blues goal of simply finding the strength to get up and face another day. Near the end he segues into a haunting minor-key rendition of the movement classic "We Shall Overcome," reminding us of the need for reconnection and renewal. No single aspect of "Pastime Paradise" derives obviously from jazz.

Yet the combination of the choirs from the Hare Krishna Temple and the West Angeles Church of God redefines Wonder's spiritual tradition as surely as Ellington's *Far East Suite* or John Coltrane's meditations on the relationship between Hindu, Islamic, and black Baptist spirituality in *Ascension* and *A Love Supreme*. By rearranging the fragments of the traditions he inherited, Wonder embraces the improvisational possibilities of life in the inner city. His jazz-inflected juxtaposition of blues moments transforms the song into a hymn to human possibility.

The response to *Songs in the Key of Life* from the mainstream media was less enthusiastic than might have been expected. Many rock-oriented critics preferred *Talking Book* or *Innervisions*. *Village Voice* critic Robert Christgau called *Songs in the Key of Life* a "flawed masterpiece" with a list of "identifiable mistakes," including awkward phrasing, forced rhymes, and the excessive length of "Isn't She Lovely" and "Black Man." John Rockwell noted Wonder's "distressing predilection for cosmic meanderings and soupy sentimentality. . . . The man is obviously no giant ideologically, but he does have a reasonably accurate idea of what's going down." The liner notes to the album did little to appease the doubters. Combining sixties-style free love with New Age mysticism, Wonder announced, "My mind's heart must be polygamous and my spirit is married to many and my love belongs to all," adding that "love plus love minus hate equals love energy." Waxing psychological, he continued, "An idea to me is formed through in the subconscious, the unknown and sometimes sought for impossibles, but when believed strongly enough can become reality." All of which was pretty lucid compared to what was coming soon, in *Journey Through the Secret Life of Plants*.

For the moment, however, none of that mattered, especially on the streets and in the living rooms of black America, where *Songs in the Key of Life* was, and is, almost universally recognized as Wonder's finest achievement. *Talking Book* may have been more revelatory; *Innervisions* and *Fulfillingness' First Finale* were leaner and more consistent. Anyone arguing for any of them as Wonder's greatest album can make a case. But context can't be ignored. When Wonder released *Innervisions*, the Black Power movement could still lay a marginally believable claim to the future. When *Fulfillingness* appeared, it was one of dozens of albums, including Aretha's *Spirit in the Dark* and Curtis's *Roots*, competing for the attention of an attentive interracial audience. By 1976 things had changed. The movement's slogans no longer carried the visionary moral authority they had a few years earlier. And blacks and whites were headed in different directions in a hundred different ways.

In the face of the gathering doubts, *Songs in the Key of Life* stood firm. Wonder refused to surrender an inch of the hard-won turf. Taking the central conceit of the movement classic "This Little Light of Mine" to a higher level, "Another Star" challenged the beloved community to rekindle the fire that had illuminated the way. Refusing to let his blindness obscure the beauty of blackness, Wonder assured his people that they were, in the eyes of man and God, lovely. Wonder had once volunteered to judge a beauty contest, and the idea wasn't as silly as it might have sounded. There's probably never been a more moving celebration of black beauty than "Isn't She Lovely," though the short list of runners-up would include his own "Ebony Eyes," "Golden Lady," and "Dark 'n Lovely." Maybe Wonder simply couldn't be distracted by the different shades of "black" that threatened to undercut the shared vision that had made the movement possible. In 1976 that was exactly what black America wanted and needed to hear.

The follow-up to *Songs in the Key of Life, Journey Through the Secret Life of Plants,* surprised almost everyone when it was released late in 1979. A meditative jazz tapestry organized around the analogy between the growth of plants and the nurturing of children and the future, the album reflects Wonder's interest in a dazzling array of musical traditions. Bits of Japanese and traditional African music mingle with jazz-inflected funk, synthesized strings, and classical guitar. Lacking the sharp social edge of Wonder's previous seventies albums, *Journey Through the Secret Life of Plants* intimates the elusive mysticism that Wonder would express more fully, if not necessarily more clearly, on the liner notes to *In Square Circle. Journey's* strongest defenders usually echo Janet Jackson, who identified it as "one of my favorite Stevie Wonder albums, the one that made me feel like I was drowning in beauty. When I'd get home from school, I'd pop this puppy on the stereo, slap on the headphones and just soak up the gorgeous melodies. Escaping."

While very few would join Jackson in placing *Journey* alongside the five great albums that preceded it, it offers fascinating glimpses into Wonder's personal evolution, especially his refusal to accept his blindness as a limitation. The three-year gap between *Songs in the Key of Life* and *Journey Through the Secret Life of Plants* drove Berry Gordy to the brink of despair. With Motown cash strapped by ill-conceived film ventures, Gordy was hoping that Wonder's next album would alleviate the problem. Stevie "was forever telling us, 'Next month,' " Gordy reported. "We would gear up, gear down, gear up." When Wonder finally delivered the masters, Gordy wrote in his autobiography, "I got a sinking feeling it might not be the smash we needed. But because he was such an innovator, influencing a generation of music makers, I was hopeful." Faye Hale, Motown vice-president in charge of manufacturing, quickly disabused him of his delusion: "I have no ear as you always remind me and I may be missing something, but a record about plant life with elephants stepping on glass?" Poised to press two million, Gordy reluctantly cut back to one million. "And still," he lamented, "that turned out to be around nine hundred thousand too many."

If *Journey Through the Secret Life of Plants* was a commercial disappointment of epic proportions, it was certainly interesting. Long fascinated by the spiritual vibrations knitting together the natural world, Wonder had immersed himself in the mystical New Age sounds of Vangelis, Rick Wakeman of Yes, and the German band Tangerine Dream. At the same time he learned to play a variety of Japanese and African instruments. The new interests came together around director Michael Braun's plans to make a film based on the book *The Secret Life of Plants* by Peter Tompkins and Christopher Bird.

Which raised the question of how a blind man was going to compose a soundtrack for a movie that relied neither on plot nor character. Wonder gleefully accepted the challenge. "The more I heard people ask, 'How will Stevie, being blind, be able to write music for a film?' the more of a challenge it became," he recollected. "I just knew I'd have to figure out some way to do it." Wonder, Braun, and engineer Gary Olazabal contrived an ingenious solution using the two channels on Stevie's headphones. While Braun explained the visuals in the left headphone, Olazabal counted off the timing of the frames in the right channel, allowing Wonder to internalize the cinematic rhythm. "He would tell me the starting time of a sequence and count the frames till it would end," Wonder explained. "They put it all on this four-track tape; the sound of the film, the sound of Michael explaining, and the sound of Gary counting on three of the tracks; the fourth would be used for the music... they made me a copy, I'd take it home, listen to it a few times, and work the music out on a tape cassette. I would play along with it and get the time signature I felt was conducive to the sequence.

That's how we did it." It was complicated, creative, and at its best gorgeously evocative.

From the thick orchestral introduction of "Earth's Creation," *Journey Through the Secret Life of Plants* drops the listener into a world of curling tendrils, lush underbrush, and thick leaves undulating in the sonic breezes. Strange sounds generated by Japanese instruments, a sitar, tiny tinkling bells, and toned African percussion surround intentionally childlike snippets of melody. "Ai No, Sono," a lovely melody, conjures a moment of peace in a Japanese garden; "Black Orchid" flowers into exotic beauty. Motifs sparkle in and out of hearing, reappearing full-blown later in the suite. Playing with languages including Bambara and Japanese, Wonder imitates the natural world where stunning new shapes mingle with forms found everywhere. The spiritual and philosophical seed of Wonder's shadowy green world emerges in "Kesse Ye Lolo De Ye," Bambara for "A Seed's a Star." Adapting an African proverb concerning the way plants revitalize Earth's connection with cosmic energies, Wonder carefully nurtures the musical and lyrical motif until it blooms in "A Seed's a Star." Wonder probably intended the English version as a clarifying epiphany, but to put it mildly, not everyone felt spiritual enlightenment. The album has aged better than most sixties and seventies forays into orchestral mysticism. (It's been years since the last reported sighting of the Moody Blues' *To Our Children's Children's Children* or the Stones' *Their Satanic Majesties Request.*) The album spun off one hit, "Send One Your Love," which, for a seventies Stevie Wonder single, made a terrific florist's commercial.

The baffled response to the album, which reached number four on the charts largely on the strength of Wonder's name, highlights the risks associated with the jazz impulse. While he had imagined a beautiful new world, few rushed to join him in it. Anyone seeking to radically redefine his tradition has a much better chance of succeeding when working with raw material familiar to the audience. When a concert version of the album failed to sell out in Detroit, Wonder admitted that he'd been hoping for a more enthusiastic reception. "It would have been nice to see Cobo Hall full," he told an interviewer. He seized on the situation to reassess his feelings about the balance between jazz explorations and the need to communicate with his communities. "The true meaning of an artist is to be expressive of his art and to be innovative. But a lot of things have been afforded me by the people, so I have to share with them the experiences I have had and am having. When I listen to my work and I realize that certain things are too out, too abstract, I try to make it so that everyone will be able to understand it, whether they're young or old. But if you don't take a chance in life, then you really cannot move forward. If you're going to sit yourself in one thing that you know is going to work and just do it over and over, then ultimately people are going to get tired of it anyway. And so if you don't make the change, then there will be a change that someone else makes." While some accepted the challenge of following the changes Wonder imagined on *Journey Through the Secret Life of Plants,* many others, as Gordy had feared, simply waited for him to return to more familiar ground.

꿍

By THE END OF THE SEVENTIES the changes seemed to have passed Curtis Mayfield by. Curtom's sales had peaked in 1976; by 1979 Mayfield, Linda Clifford, and the funk-disco group TTF were the label's only remaining successful acts. Tired and burned out, Mayfield lacked the energy or inclination to break the slide. When RSO bought Curtom's distribution rights in 1979, it marked the effective end of the label, which formally ceased operation in 1980. At the same time Mayfield decided to move permanently to Atlanta, where he had maintained a second residence since 1967. He explained the move in terms understandable to anyone who's ever survived a Chicago winter. "That Chicago weather. Man, man. That hawk'll get you," he said, using the local nickname for the Arctic wind that blows off Lake Michigan. "The music scene was kind of drying up in Chicago. Of course, you know Chicago is my home. I love it, but my needs and my desires were quite different. I guess after coming up in the city all your life, you can appreciate a little bit of ground around you. Atlanta had trees, space, some of those things you want to have. It was a good place for the children." Curtis Mayfield had certainly earned the right to relax, but the world would miss his voice.

For Aretha, things were more complex. After moving to Los Angeles with Ken Cunningham, she shopped on Rodeo Drive; immersed herself in decorating her home, complete with rose walkway; spent time with old friends like Smokey Robinson, James Cleveland (who had a church and a soul food restaurant), and Berry Gordy, whose home featured black velvet paintings of Aretha and Diana Ross. In times of need she could commune with the soul food spirits at Mr. Jim's Ribs, whose motto was "You don't need no teeth to eat our meat." Although she was aware that her fashion choices had not met with universal applause, she dreamed of a line of clothing creations that would be marketed by a major designer. "I like what I wear, and I design a lot of the clothes myself," she told interviewer David Nathan. "Sometimes I test things out for my family. And, yes, I have tested a few things that didn't work so I don't wear them in public." But despite living in a neighborhood alongside Motown's Jacksons, actor Mike Connors, and the Walt Disney estate, Aretha never really settled into the West Coast lifestyle. "Los Angeles was not the easiest time in my life," she wrote in her autobiography. As her relationship with Cunningham collapsed, she told Smokey Robinson she was homesick for Detroit.

Her romantic life took an unexpected turn for the better when she met the actor Glynn Turman at a benefit for Rosey Grier's Giant Step program. Aretha's son Clarence knew that his mother had admired Turman's performances in *A Raisin in the Sun, Cooley High,* and Ingmar Bergman's *The Serpent's Egg,* so he brought the actor to his mother's dressing room. "I told him that I was interested in drama, in acting, and he said he was an instructor at an inner-city cultural center," Aretha recalled. "And I said, 'Oh, really?' I took the information down and told him I'd come to some of his classes. And I did. I stayed the whole session." Aretha invited Turman, who was four years her junior, to her thirty-fifth birthday party, and soon *Ebony* featured the couple under the headline "Older Women / Younger Men: A Growing Trend in Love Affairs." To which Aretha responded sassily, "I want everyone to know that I'm a *young* woman with nothing but young ideas. There's *nothing* older about Aretha." In April 1978, with Reverend C.L. Franklin officiating, the couple were married at New Bethel Baptist Church. As Aretha walked down the aisle in an eggshell-colored silk gown trimmed in mink with 17,500 seed pearls and a seven-foot train, the Four Tops sang Stevie Wonder's "Isn't She Lovely."

Despite the auspicious start, the marriage never really had time to settle in. The couple's Encino mansion on a three-acre lot complete with a large swimming pool provided plenty of room for their combined family. But Turman was a nonsmoking vegetarian, and Aretha had no intention of giving up either meat or cigarettes. In addition, cooking for their total of seven children made it difficult for her to watch her weight. The effort of keeping slim, she said, made her weak and irritable. "I couldn't bear to deny myself all my life all the good foods I like to eat, just to keep a slim, birdlike figure," she said. Cooking did have its compensations; she enjoyed dazzling company with the soul food specialties that she contemplated collecting in a cookbook to be called *Switchin' in the Kitchen*. Any chance of a successful adjustment to the marriage was ended by tragedies outside either partner's control.

On June 19, 1979, Aretha was in Las Vegas rehearsing for an upcoming engagement when she heard the news that her father had been shot at his home in Detroit. At first Aretha and her brother Cecil, who took the emergency phone call from Pops Staples, thought C.L. had died after being shot twice, in the knee and groin. It turned out he was still alive, but he would never regain consciousness. Apparently he had surprised intruders attempting to steal a leaded-glass window. The assailants were apprehended and convicted, but as Aretha said, "That didn't help my father."

As Franklin lingered in his coma, Aretha and her sisters assumed responsibility for his long-term care. Carolyn, who had been living with Aretha in Encino, moved back to Detroit. Aretha paid for around-the-clock nursing. Now smoking over two packs a day, she visited her father's bedside at least twice a month. The financial and psychological burdens put tremendous stress on her marriage. When Aretha decided to move back to Detroit, her third marriage came to an end. Aretha was grateful for the absence of arguments or recriminations. At the time her primary concern was for her father. "A man of enormous energy and boundless vitality, a man of high eloquence and burning intellect," Aretha wrote later, Reverend Franklin "was now without speech or the ability to move." At the time she rarely spoke to the public or interviewers about what she was going through. "There was no way I could express the pain," she wrote. "I merely went on." Still, when Aretha burst into tears after dedicating George Benson's "The Greatest Love" to her father, it testified to the weight of the cross she had been given to bear.

IN 1978, FOR THE FIRST TIME in two decades, no record by Aretha Franklin, Stevie Wonder, or Curtis Mayfield appeared in the Top One Hundred. Juxtaposed with the growing power of a conservative movement intent on reversing the gains of the freedom movement, the silence delivered a deafening eulogy for the gospel vision that had reshaped American life since World War II. The movement fueled by that vision had achieved meaningful victories. Blacks could enter into most public spaces, north and south, with legal protection if not always psychological and physical safety. The growing black middle class no longer found itself confined to the traditional ghettos. Black athletes and entertainers enjoyed a much greater degree of recognition and remuneration than they had a generation earlier. On the surface, all of that looked like the partial fulfillment of African American aspirations that, as Martin Luther King intoned, were "deeply rooted in the American dream." Like their white compatriots, black Americans had long envisioned a world where they could succeed on the basis of their individual merits. By the start of the eighties, for a lucky few, something resembling that world had come to be. Literally and figuratively, it would be a world without soul.

CHAPTER FIVE

"Who's Zoomin' Who?"

Megastars, Monuments, Elders

A HARSH WIND WHIPPED ACROSS Stevie Wonder's face as he stood before the crowd huddled on the National Mall on January 15, 1982. It had been a terrible week in Washington, D.C. Earlier in the day a subway car had smashed through a wall, killing two and injuring dozens; two days before, an airliner had crashed into the Fourteenth Street Bridge. The freezing weather simply confirmed the feeling of the city. Even so, nearly fifty thousand people had braved the icy streets to help Wonder and a cast of civil rights icons celebrate Martin Luther King's birthday and support the campaign to make it a national holiday. Diana Ross, Gil Scott-Heron, and Gladys Knight sang; Coretta Scott King, Michigan congressman John Conyers, Washington, D.C., congressman Walter Fauntroy, and Jesse Jackson extolled King's virtues. But the crowning moment came when Wonder moved to the microphone. "I know you've been standing in the cold for a long time, but I hope your spirits are warm," he called out. With

Jackson nodding in encouragement, Wonder continued, "Many times in life things happen and we question God as to why. These are not easy times, yet they are not hopeless times. We must refresh our souls and uplift our spirits and harmonize with our brothers and sisters. Dr. King left an unfinished symphony which we must finish. We must harmonize our notes and chords and create love and life. We need a day to celebrate our work on an unfinished symphony, a day for a dress rehearsal for our solidarity. I hope your spirits are hotter than *July*!"

The crowd burst into applause and joined Wonder in singing "Happy Birthday," the jubilant song he'd written in honor of the fallen leader. As their voices battled the bitter wind blowing through the capital, Wonder served notice that despite King's death his vision would not be forgotten. In October 1983 Wonder capped a concert at New York's Radio City Music Hall with a sing-along version of "Happy Birthday" celebrating the signing of the bill establishing the King holiday. "Every time we did that song, it was a celebration of that day." Wonder beamed. "I was living its reality every time we performed it."

The successful campaign for the King holiday provided a symbolic victory at a time when those who held to the gospel vision had little else to celebrate. In a political climate increasingly predicated on raw self-interest, the communal call of the soul music that had grown up alongside the movement no longer resonated as it had for the past three decades. It was as if the larger forces expressed in and unleashed by Reaganism had reduced soul's vision of suffering love and redemptive community to a quaint and outmoded dream. Stevie, Curtis, and Aretha all made new music that reasserted the need for spiritual connection, but it no longer shaped people's day-by-day experience. As rap music gradually assumed a central place in the self-proclaimed hip-hop generation's worldview, the changes went deeper than the shift from R&B to soul or from soul to funk. Created largely in communities cast adrift during the seventies and eighties, hip-hop emerged as a blues form fixated on the age-old problems of money and sex. Although it didn't exactly abandon the gospel vision, hip-hop certainly had strong materialistic and individualistic tendencies, reinforced by MTV and overemphasized by the mass media. One of the primary challenges facing both the soul survivors and the hip-hop artists who shared their vision was finding a way to engage the post–civil rights generation in a meaningful call and response on the nature of the burden and the meaning of redemption.

Even at the height of the Reagan era, there was a lot of activity swirling around Stevie and Aretha, most of it connected with good causes. You could track the soul legends through the eighties with a montage of news clips and videos: Stevie campaigning on behalf of the King holiday; Aretha serenading Jesse Jackson with "Look to the Rainbow"; Stevie and Paul McCartney joining ebony and ivory in song; Aretha and Annie Lennox touting the sisters who could do it for themselves; Stevie accepting an Oscar in the name of Nelson Mandela; Aretha gliding down the freeway of love in a plush pink Caddy; Stevie trading verses with Bruce Springsteen on "We Are the World"; Aretha singing the national anthem as the Democratic National Convention prepared to nominate a successor to George Bush the First.

The press kit for the montage would come with a scrapbook full of invitations to fund-raisers and a trophy room or two. The pictures on the walls would show Stevie performing at benefits for the Give Kids the World foundation; the Hale House program for Harlem babies born with AIDS or addicted to drugs; Special Olympics Africa; the Los Angeles Inner City Foundation for Excellence in Education; the Welcome Home concert for Vietnam veterans; the Peace Sunday: We Have a Dream rally; and the Eiffel Tower Centenary. Wonder was inducted into the Songwriters Hall of Fame; received the key to the city of Detroit; and won a list of honors including the Whitney Young award from the Los Angeles Urban League; the Nelson Mandela Courage award; and the National Academy of Songwriters Lifetime Achievement award. Aretha's gallery could begin with pictures of her command performance for Queen Elizabeth and the street sign designating part of Washington Boulevard in Detroit "Aretha Franklin's Freeway of Love" and lead up to the Aretha Franklin Appreciation Day ceremony at which the state of Michigan proclaimed her a "natural resource." Framed photos would show her leading union workers in a birthday serenade for Jesse Jackson and greeting Mandela when he visited Detroit in 1990 after his release from prison. Presiding over it all would be the robes designating Wonder an Honorary Courtier of traditional Cameroonian ruler Fon Agwafor III and the wax statue of the Queen of Soul on loan from Madame Tussaud's. (Pictures of Stevie and Aretha at the White House would have to wait for the election of baby boomer Bill Clinton.)

Meanwhile Curtis Mayfield drifted into unjustifiable obscurity. While politicians and celebrities cultivated Stevie and Aretha, Mayfield logged tens of thousands of miles hopping back and forth between his family retreat outside Atlanta and Europe and Japan, where fans clamored for him to play their old favorites from *Super Fly* and his days with the Impressions. While Mayfield genially obliged them, his introductions often linked the "oldies" to current problems, and he continued to write new songs in hopes that someone still cared. Only after a tragic 1990 accident suffered at an outdoor concert left him paralyzed did the music industry seem to realize he'd been gone.

For singers who'd grown up along with the freedom movement, the eighties posed personal as well as political problems. Reaganism and its collateral damage were only a part of it. The celebrity culture of the eighties and nineties was as congenial to the gospel vision as the surface of Neptune. The bursting of the disco bubble ushered in hard times for soul music commercially. The rise of MTV forced established artists to redefine their relationships with their audiences. Hip-hop created a major generational split in African American musical taste. While both Aretha and Stevie made hit records, including the biggest-selling album of Aretha's career, *Who's Zoomin' Who?*, neither artist occupied a central position in the consciousness of the nation, black or white. It wasn't that they'd abandoned their ideals. After Clinton's election in 1992, both would receive official recognition as national treasures. Ironically enough, however, that was part of the problem. Where the gospel vision thrived on call and response between the elders and their community, celebrity culture threatened to reduce Stevie and Aretha to statues in a moral hall of mirrors.

It didn't help that soul, which had emerged from R&B sometime in the sixties, had given birth to eighties R&B. As Nelson George observed in *The Death of Rhythm and Blues*, the eighties marked a watershed in African American music: for the first time the most popular forms of black music did not appeal to both young and old. The fragmentation of the African American community was clear in the unprecedented hostility directed against R&B by substantial numbers of hip-hop fans for whom the initials signified "Romance & Bullshit." All too often the musical conflict played out in terms of class, gender, and cultural identity. Venting antiwoman and antigay bigotry that scandalized those who shared the movement's commitment to universal human dignity, hip-hop impresarios claimed an authentic blackness (young, male, ghetto) while dismissing R&B as the feminized voice of middle-class wannabes. It didn't help that more than a few of the R&B stars who inherited the gospel-soul tradition from Stevie, Curtis, and Aretha seemed content to wrap themselves in a cocoon of silky ballads and new jack beats without paying much attention to the world outside the bedroom walls. In short, the rappers had a point—*and* missed the point.

Outside those walls, the blues realities were all too clear. As the Reagan administration drained resources from social programs, a voting majority embraced a political rhetoric organized around baseless anecdotes of welfare queens riding in Cadillacs to purchase porterhouse steaks. Originating in the South Bronx and spreading rapidly to other cities in the Northeast and on the West Coast, early hip-hop provided a blues chronicle of a community ravaged by deindustrialization and white backlash. The blues heart of hip-hop beat clearly in "The Message" by Grandmaster Flash and the Furious Five, a cinema verité report from the urban jungle. Sounding a warning of the bitter day dawning in Reagan's America, the song's chorus, "Don't push me 'cause I'm close to the edge," elicited choruses of amens.

If hip-hop was, as rapper Chuck D of Public Enemy called it, "Black America's CNN," the news reports portrayed a community that had lost its political bearings. While Public Enemy called for a renewed black revolution, Jesse Jackson's Rainbow Coalition and Louis Farrakhan's increasingly self-assured Nation of Islam competed for the support of a community divided along lines of class, gender, and generation. The root of the tensions lay in the social paradox that created a black middle class of unprecedented size at the same time many inner-city residents were dropping off the edge of the economic world. Feelings of political betrayal and nihilistic rage spread through the ghettos. Afrocentric identity politics attracted thousands who had little interest in academic critiques of a movement that rarely bothered to distinguish between history and inspirational mythology. Afrocentrism was only the most popular flavor of identity politics; by the midpoint of the eighties the conservative counterrevolutionaries had succeeded in dividing their opposition into warring camps divided by ethnicity and sexual orientation as well as the ideological hair-splitting traditional on the left.

All of which was anathema to Stevie Wonder. In 1980, as less than half of the eligible voters trudged to the polls to elect Reagan, Wonder's *Hotter than July* trumpeted a resounding "no" to the nation's abandonment of the gospel vision. Highlighted by the Bob Marley tribute "Master Blaster (Jammin')," the album reached number three on the charts, getting Wonder's decade off to a blazing start. Dedicated to Martin Luther King Jr., *Hotter than July* mixed the gentle vibrations of "Did I Hear You Say You Love Me?" and "All I Do" (featuring backup vocals by the O'Jays, Michael Jackson, and Betty Wright) with uncompromising bulletins from the political battlefront. Calling Jah's children from Zimbabwe to the corner park, "Master Blaster" envisions a renewed Pan-African liberation movement. If such a movement existed, "I Ain't Gonna Stand for It" could have been its battle anthem. Focusing on housing discrimination, "Cash in Your Face" reminded anyone who still cared that the problems that had inspired and plagued the northern movement for thirty years hadn't magically gone away. Linking the sixties movement with the sobering present, the photomontage on the album's inner sleeve portrayed a burning city, police in riot gear, a black man lying in a pool of blood, and Dr. King leading an interracial march.

As the contours of Reagan's America took shape, Wonder joined Jesse Jackson in attempting to make his vision of solidarity real. Wonder condemned America's failure to ratify the Equal Rights Amendment, rejected its hypocritical willingness to do business with South Africa, and attacked its growing militarism. "I'm concerned because I can see how Reagan can win lots of people over," he told an interviewer. "If you breathe the spirit of 'we've got to have more strength, we've got to have more missiles, we've got to have more sites, we've got to do this to be a strong America,' it only breeds for the other side to say the same thing." Meanwhile Jackson was doing his best to unify the Reagan opposition by focusing on the issues that should have united the frequently warring factions. "Mr. Reagan keeps asking us all to pray," Jackson intoned. "Well, I believe in prayer; I have come this far by the power of prayer. But then Mr. Reagan cuts energy assistance to the poor, cuts job training, cuts breakfast and lunch programs for children—and then says to an empty table, 'Let us pray.' Apparently Mr. Reagan is not familiar with the structure of prayer. You thank the Lord for the food you are about to *receive*, not the food that has just *left*. I think we should pray, but not pray for the food that's left. Pray for the man that took the food . . . to leave." While

Wonder shared Jackson's feelings, he did his best to maintain a constructive emphasis. In October 1984 he introduced "Happy Birthday" in a New York performance by talking about the upcoming election. When he mentioned Jesse Helms, who'd been attacking King, the crowd booed. Stevie cautioned them, "Every minute you allow yourself to hate, you've wasted one minute God has given you to love." Jackson himself made the point clearly when he proclaimed the gospel "the most revolutionary manifesto in history. Man, *think* about it. When you start dealing in terms like forgiveness and redemption and treating the least of these like they were you yourself, that's saying something that goes way beyond left-wing or right-wing. Homeboy, that's *witnessing.*"

Bearing witness to Wonder's convictions about redemptive unity, "Ebony and Ivory" and "We Are the World" attempted to counter the growing divisions. For Wonder, recording with Paul McCartney fulfilled a long-standing dream. Over the years, he had developed a friendship with the former Beatle and his wife Linda, who had written "WE LOVE YOU STEVIE" in Braille across the back cover of Wings' *Red Rose Speedway* album; in turn, Stevie wrote "What's That You're Doing" for *Tug of War*. Recorded at Montserrat in the Leeward Islands, "Ebony and Ivory" expressed a childlike belief in music as the path to "perfect harmony." So-called "realists" dismissed the song as naïve. Still, as the eighties battle lines solidified, it was hard to complain about any reminder that a better way was possible. Judging by the sound of their voices, Wonder and McCartney had slightly different ideas of what constituted perfect harmony, but it worked out fine. "Lots of times when things are said very clearly it is almost like speaking in the mind of a child," Wonder replied to the cynics. "I felt that for whatever significance we both have, both in multi-colored, multi-racial society, we're all many different colors and cultures, it would be good for us to sing something like that." His point came through clearly at Radio City Music Hall in October 1983. Before performing "Ebony and Ivory," Wonder invited eight children, chosen at random, to join him onstage. Black and white together, they all knew the words.

If "Ebony and Ivory" provided a breath of fresh air in 1982, "We Are the World" unleashed a hurricane of hype when the song premiered simultaneously on five thousand radio stations on April 5, 1985. Organized by Michael Jackson and Quincy Jones on behalf of the famine relief efforts of "U.S.A.

for Africa," the high-profile project raised over $44 million. While no one could question the cause, the media coverage meshed all too easily with the mid-eighties obsession with the rich and famous. The massive satellite linkup enabled a giant sing-along involving Stevie, Aretha, Paul McCartney, Johnny Cash, Whitney Houston, Diana Ross, Michael Jackson, and Jackson's date Liz Taylor. The televised images of the glitterati did nothing to lessen the disquieting sense that the event was really *about* the celebrities.

That's a comment on the culture, not the individuals involved, most of whom were there for the right reasons. From the title on, the song tended toward elephantine melodrama, but Stevie's duet with Bruce Springsteen added enough real fire to lift "We Are the World" far above the saccharine standard set by its British predecessor "Do They Know It's Christmas?" The all-night recording session spawned its fair share of amusing moments, topped by the vocal coaching that Wonder provided for Bob Dylan. Realizing that Dylan was having trouble with the phrasing on his lines, the onetime Berry Gordy–imitator stepped in and sang them in pitch-perfect Bob Dylan style. Dylan's performance followed Stevie's suggestions note for note. "I just basically was saying, 'I have a lot of respect for you,' " Wonder explained good-naturedly. "It was just to loosen things up, which it did."

Wonder's most successful attempt to harness the mass media to constructive causes centered on Los Angeles radio station KJLH-FM, which he purchased in 1979. A devoted radio fan since his childhood hours listening to Larry Dixon's *Sundown* show, Wonder had begun to conceive of radio as a political instrument in the early seventies. When Wonder bought KJLH from black funeral home director John Lamar Hill, who had built it into the top-ranked black FM station in the city, he modeled its approach on New York DJ Del Shields's WLIB-FM show *The Total Black Experience in Sound.* At the time KJLH was broadcasting from a storefront studio in the heart of South Central Los Angeles. Station manager Edward Abner explained Wonder's goal: "Stevie is a communicator, a fantastic communicator, and he understood that radio could be used to serve the community. He thought that it had a larger duty to the community than playing records. He thought that it owed the community something; it should be speaking to the issues, it should be informing and educating its listeners. So he thought that if he owned the station, in addition to the music that he would play, that he would be able to inform, communicate, enlighten, and participate with the community, and that's what he's done with KJLH." As black radio historian William Barlow observes, Wonder largely succeeded, beginning by upgrading the "the news and public-affairs programming. They added new informational and call-in shows, hired a team of reporters to cover local news events and opened up their airwaves to black community groups." Adding substance to the station's motto, "We Are You," an outreach program, *Survival in the Eighties,* helped poor community members pay electric and utility bills.

While Wonder remained in the public eye, the eighties as a whole disappointed him and his fans. Few musicians had ever been in a position to consider a decade during which they had four number-one pop singles and placed an additional four atop the R&B charts a letdown. It's true that none of Wonder's albums of the mid-eighties—*In Square Circle* (1985), *Characters* (1987), and the soundtrack to *The Woman in Red* (1984)—match the quality of *Talking Book, Innervisions,* or *Songs in the Key of Life.* But the same could be said of well over 99 percent of the albums released since Elvis Presley walked into the Sun Studios. Songs from Wonder's newer albums—including "I Just Called to Say I Love You," "Part-Time Lover" (featuring R&B star Luther Vandross on backing vocals), "You Will Know," "Overjoyed," "Go Home," and his most powerful political song of the decade, "Skeletons"—added to a line of hits that by the end of the eighties had moved him into third place (behind Elvis and the Beatles) on the list of artists with the most Top Ten singles.

Throughout the decade Wonder's music played a gospel counterpoint to the blues events dominating the news. The four new songs from the 1982 compilation album *Stevie Wonder's Original Musiquarium* would have been at home on any of his seventies masterpieces. "Front Line" confronts Reagan's revisionist myth of Vietnam as a "noble cause" with the voice of a black veteran; "Do I Do," featuring a guest appearance from Dizzy Gillespie, extends the jazz celebrations of "Sir Duke" and "Contusion"; and "That Girl" was a funky addition to his list of number-one R&B hits. But the song that gave the best indication of how Wonder would attempt to connect his past with his future was "Ribbon in the Sky." Riding one of his richest piano lines and a moaning vocal interlude, the ballad reaches down for the "strength in each tear we cry."

For Wonder, the strength that made it possible to survive tragedy couldn't be separated from spirit. The connection was reinforced in a haunting manner by a series of events connected with the death of Marvin Gaye, who was shot to death by his father in April 1984. The day before the murder Wonder had been visiting his mentor Clarence Paul in the hospital. He'd told Paul that he was worried about Gaye, and the two discussed their old friend's problems with drugs and depression. "I felt something was happening," Wonder reflected, "something was about to go wrong. I didn't know what it was." When Wonder returned home, he wrote a song, "Lighting Up the Candles," which expressed his hopes and fears about Gaye. Although it didn't appear on an album until the soundtrack to Spike Lee's *Jungle Fever* in 1991, the haunting ballad brought tears to the eyes of the mourners when Wonder sang it at Gaye's funeral.

Despite their quality, the songs Wonder was writing in 1982 and 1983 weren't coalescing into an album, even though a financially strapped Berry Gordy eagerly awaited Wonder's new work. While delays in the announced release dates of Wonder's albums had become commonplace, the five years between *Hotter than July* in 1980 and his next full studio album, *In Square Circle*, felt more like wandering in the wilderness than crafting a masterpiece. The music industry was changing rapidly, and Wonder seemed uncertain how to adjust. Contemplating the MTV-driven ascent of a new generation of megastars, Wonder mused on Prince's ability to articulate social realities through seemingly personal lyrics. "Prince has really been unique with the way he uses words. He's like the Bob Dylan of the eighties as far as what he's saying. Incredible lyrics. And the song, the melody, the music, is good too. It's kind of like Prince is an African storyteller, right? It seems like he's passing on what is happening in this time and place that we're living in right now. And he doesn't say specifically, 'Oh, this is horrible; this is wrong.' Which you know is what he's saying. He says, 'Hey, let's get married, have a baby, raise a family. Let's do something.' "

Wonder experimented with a parallel approach first on *The Woman in Red* soundtrack (1984) and in a more focused manner on *In Square Circle* (1985). When Dionne Warwick contacted Wonder in behalf of *Woman in Red* director Gene Wilder, Wonder agreed to contribute one song to the soundtrack. Wilder was shocked when Wonder listened to the film's dialogue on cassette. "Three days later he'd written two songs and played them over the phone to me," the actor/director reported. "Then he wrote one more, and

I thought that was it. I went to France to relax for a week. Then I got a call at two A.M. It was Dionne saying Stevie wanted to write more." By the time he was finished, Wonder had written all but one of the songs on the soundtrack, singing four of them himself and two as duets with Dionne Warwick, who also sang one herself. Hoping as he was that Stevie would help rescue Motown from its mounting financial problems, Gordy was stunned that his star had agreed to a side project. Despite the fact that it wasn't marketed as a Stevie Wonder album, *The Woman in Red* provided Motown with momentary financial relief. In addition to topping the U.S. charts for three weeks, the pop confection "I Just Called to Say I Love You" gave Wonder his first number-one hit in the United Kingdom and became one of the ten best-selling U.K. singles ever. With the exception of "Love Light in Flight," a Prince-esque paean to spiritual sexuality, the rest of the album settles into a generic R&B groove complete with vocoder and the processed drums that marred much of Wonder's most promising eighties work.

While not one of Wonder's worst albums—we pause here to remember *With a Song in My Heart* and *Stevie at the Beach*—*In Square Circle* was probably the most disappointing album of his career. The cryptic title and the intriguing cover image of Wonder smiling out from a magenta and purple alien landscape suggested that the music would extend the experiments he'd begun on *Journey Through the Secret Life of Plants*. The liner notes, written by Wonder and Theresa Cropper, meditated on the nature of love and spiritual politics via a dialogue between a philosopher known as "Songlife" and seven symbolic beings: the romantic, the insecure, the cynical, the optimistic, the curious, the bewildered, and the dreamer. "Their hearts were recalling cycles of love," the essay propounds, "while their minds were exploring the square root of the universe." Explaining the album to an interviewer in more prosaic terms, Wonder said, "The theme is that life and love are beautiful, but people have to work at making things happen all the time."

Unfortunately, the songs didn't differ all that much from typical mid-eighties R&B. "It's Wrong (Apartheid)" reiterated Wonder's political stance on South Africa. "Go Home" and "Overjoyed" withstood several listenings. But the most ambitious cuts, "Land of La La" and "Spiritual Walkers," Wonder's spirited defense of the Hare Krishnas and Jehovah's Witnesses, fell well short of the standard established by first cousins "Village Ghetto Land" and "Heaven Is Ten Zillion Light Years Away," let alone "Living for the City" and "Higher Ground." "Part-Time Lover" rode a catchy groove to the top of the pop, R&B, adult contemporary, and dance charts, the first record to have done so, and the album sold well, peaking at number five. But for the most part, *In Square Circle* sounded like a compilation of decent Stevie Wonder cuts that would have wound up in the recycling bin for *Talking Book* or *Fulfillingness' First Finale*.

Released in 1987 after only two years, *Characters* was a much stronger collection of songs. If someone had shot the little metal box that stole the drummer's job, it might have compared with *Music of My Mind* or *Hotter than July*. The album focused on "many characters, no one particular character," Wonder explained. "Characters in politics, the character of people in relationships...the different *moods* of people, bringing out their character." "There's a theme," he continued, "and I think you'll see part of it unfolding in the first single, 'Skeletons.'" Despite the intrusive mechanical percussion track, "Skeletons" strikes at the core of Reaganism. Wonder rails against the lies permeating the nation's political life, observing ironically that "a black one" can "turn into a white one." Dropping down into the gritty vocal register he used on "As" and "Higher Ground," he warns that the country's "getting ready to blow." With the Rodney King riots just a few years down the road, the song rings out with a prophetic power akin to James Baldwin's *The Fire Next Time*. The extended-play version of "Skeletons" pointedly splices in snippets of Oliver North's testimony at the Iran-Contra hearings and samples Reagan denying the arms-for-hostages deal that had helped put his 1980 campaign over the top.

"Skeletons" sounded the keynote of the album, but at least half the cuts surpassed anything on *The Woman in Red* or *In Square Circle*. The opening track, "You Will Know," promises resolutions to the problems that seemed to be worsening by the day; "Dark 'n Lovely" pays an indirect tribute to the South African people that communicates more deeply than the didactic "It's Wrong"; and "Free" earns a place on the ideal *Stevie Wonder Gospel Album*. Surrounded by the spiritual energy and musical beauty of those cuts, ballads and rockers like "With Each Beat of My Heart," "My Eyes Don't Cry," and "Get It"— an all-star collaboration with Michael Jackson, B.B. King, and Stevie Ray Vaughan—fill out an album that was easily Wonder's best of the Reagan era. The strength of those songs suggested that the closer Wonder hewed to the vision from which he emerged, the freer he was to do his best work.

Wonder backed up his beliefs with a seemingly unending series of benefits that made him a significant political symbol. On March 25, 1985, he accepted the Oscar for "I Just Called to Say I Love You" in the name of Nelson Mandela. The next day South Africa banned his music. "If being banned means people will be free," Wonder replied, "ban me mega-times." Two months later the United Nations Special Committee on Apartheid issued a special commendation for Wonder. Typically, he responded by emphasizing the connections among the various causes he espoused: "I'm very happy now that people are rallying around causes that are against things that have been sicknesses in the system of mankind. Look at AIDS. When people realize life is in jeopardy, all the prejudices go out the window. It's the same with color prejudice, the greed for political power, the nuclear question—they're all sicknesses. The only difference between a bomb and a disease is the time it takes to kill people."

Wonder's greatest symbolic triumph came with the signing of the King holiday bill in 1983. After the signing Wonder once again paid homage to his hero: "You can assassinate the man, but you cannot kill the values. I knew Reagan would sign the bill." For the first observance of the holiday a year later, Wonder organized celebratory concerts in Washington, New York, and Atlanta and hosted a television special with Bill Cosby, Quincy Jones, Yoko Ono, Diana Ross, Joan Baez, Dick Gregory, and Liz Taylor. In an interview with *Rolling Stone* Wonder stressed the breadth of King's importance: "As many whites as blacks have benefitted from having a man like Martin Luther King, Jr. I say this because there's a kind of consciousness that he raised among *all* people." He joined the boycott of Arizona, promising not to perform in the state until Governor Evan Meacham reinstated King's birthday as a state holiday. When Arizona finally joined the rest of the nation in 1993, Wonder welcomed the gesture by playing a breakfast concert in Phoenix.

The problem was that the King holiday was fundamentally symbolic in an era when symbolism too often substituted for reality. It was a game Reagan had mastered. To be sure, symbolism had always played a part in the movement. Jackie Robinson and Rosa Parks fully comprehended their symbolic importance. King directed the campaigns in Montgomery and Birmingham with a spin doctor's awareness of how the televised images would be received in the living rooms of America and in the eyes of the world. By the eighties, however, symbolism too often seemed an end in itself.

✌

A S ELLA BAKER RECOGNIZED, the problem was inherent in the leadership tradition that dominated most versions of movement history. Focusing on symbolic campaigns organized around charismatic leaders created a misleading notion of real political work. The eighties generation that had grown up with inspirational film footage of King at the head of an army of marchers understandably associated the movement with individual heroism and liberal romance. The "greatest hits" version of civil rights implied, with stunning inaccuracy, that the movement had enjoyed overwhelming public support. (It certainly didn't help that the songs that had drawn on and contributed to the movement's energy appeared as yuppie nostalgia in *The Big Chill*.) The myth of the movement, officially sanctioned by the King holiday, made it much harder to keep its fighting spirit alive.

The arc of Jesse Jackson's career illuminates the problem. Jackson had first encountered the movement while attending North Carolina A&T on a football scholarship. As the sit-in movement swept the region, Jackson received an up-close education in the effectiveness of SNCC's emphasis on community organizing. When Jackson moved to Chicago to attend seminary, he attracted the attention of the SCLC, which chose him to head Operation Breadbasket. Spearheading a series of effective "Buy Black" campaigns, Jackson combined the stylistic flair of the emerging Black Power movement with the grassroots focus he'd learned in the South. "We have a monopoly on rats in the ghetto, and we're gonna have a monopoly on killing 'em," Jackson warned Chicago. Proselytizing for black businesses, he enlisted his verbal brilliance in support of Mumbo barbecue sauce, Diamond Sparkle wax, and Joe Louis milk. "Now, Joe Louis milk does not come from a Negro cow," Jackson boomed. "Only difference is, your husband can make twelve thousand a year driving a truck for this company. Say it loud: I'm black and I'm proud, and I buy Grove Fresh orange juice. Say it loud: I use King Solomon spray deodorant and I'm proud I use Swift Out. Why, it's so strong, if you pour it in your sink, it'll open up the sewer down the block." The companies Jackson endorsed thrived, helping raise deposits in two black-owned banks from $5 million to $20 million, thereby increasing the amount of investment capital available for black neighborhoods. Campaigns to force the High-Low and A&P grocery chains to hire more black workers were the centerpiece of a series of Operation Breadbasket employment campaigns that by 1971 had opened at least four thousand jobs to black Chicagoans.

Although Jackson would become much more famous in later years, Operation Breadbasket was a high-water mark in his career. The founding of Operation PUSH (People United to Save Humanity) represented a crucial shift in his approach. While he continued to address the problems facing poor people and residents of the inner cities, he increasingly focused on nationally visible issues. Concentrating on fund-raising and serving as a moral conscience for a nation that needed one, he laid the groundwork for his future. This left little time for organizing people to follow up on the energy generated by his personal appearances throughout the nation. Uncharitable critics murmured that Jackson's political agenda had grown indistinguishable from his political ambition. "I'm a tree shaker, not a jelly-maker," he explained unapologetically. His 1984 and 1988 presidential campaigns became issues in and of themselves. If Jesse could make it, the logic seemed to go, his people could follow him into the promised land.

To be sure, no one spoke truth to power with greater passion. Jackson's sardonic dismissal of George H. W. Bush's promise of a "kinder, gentler America" sums up the legacy of Reagan's two terms with laser precision. "A kinder, gentler nation, yeah. Kinder and gentler for the corporations and merger-maniacs and mega conglomerates swallowing up the family farmer and taking factory jobs overseas," said the man biographer Marshall Frady dubbed the "High Sultan of Assonance and Alliteration." "Urban America looks like it's been bombed out, rural America abandoned like a plague's hit. Family farms gone, jobs out, drugs in, profits up, wages down, workers abandoned. And yet they playing us off one against the other, trying to make us think we different kinds of people, playing those ole race games with us when we *need* each other. Always some kind of scheme by the economic aristocracy to try confounding democracy. But lemme tell you, if the family farmer and urban worker, black and white, the good-hearted common people all over this country, if we should ever—watch out!—*get together,* then we sure 'nough *would* see a kinder, gentler nation; a fairer, freer, juster, stronger America all way round."

LIKE STEVIE WONDER, ARETHA FRANKLIN supported Jesse Jackson wholeheartedly. When she slid her voice around the song "Look to the Rainbow," it was both a tribute to her father and a musical response to Jackson's brilliant keynote address at the 1984 Democratic National Convention. Graciously supporting the party's candidate after a hard and sometimes bitter campaign, Jackson did his best to rally the gospel troops behind Walter Mondale. "America is not like a blanket—one piece of unbroken cloth, the same color, the same texture, the same size," Jackson called out. "America is more like a quilt—many patches, many pieces, many colors, many sizes, all woven and held together by a common thread. The white, the Hispanic, the black, the Arab, the Jew, the woman, the native American, the small farmer, the businessperson, the environmentalist, the peace activist, the young, the old, the lesbian, the gay, and the disabled make up the American quilt." His biblical cadence summoning memories of Dr. King's greatest speeches, Jackson thundered, "Our time has come! Our faith, hope, and dreams have prevailed. Our time has come. Weeping has endured for nights, but joy cometh in the morning. Our time has come. No grave can hold our body down. Our time has come. No lie can live forever. Our time has come. We must leave the racial battleground and come to the economic common ground and the moral higher ground. America, our time has come!"

If you could keep Jackson's words and "Look to the Rainbow" alive in your mind, you could almost hear "Freeway of Love," the hit that made Aretha an eighties megastar, as an update of "Rock Steady." The world might have changed, but Sister Ree was still moving ahead in a pink Cadillac fueled by high-octane gospel. While the connection might have looked like a stretch, producer/percussionist Narada Michael Walden's grooves challenged you to think again. But the sad fact remained that no individual voice—not Jesse Jackson's, not Stevie Wonder's, not Aretha's—could speak the vision into reality. With Reagan calling the shots and the economy in disarray, at least for anyone who didn't peddle arbitrage or ammunition, the gaps between black, brown, and white, rich and poor, men and women, suburbanites and city dwellers continued to grow.

Aretha experienced the fragmentation through its impact on musical styles. After signing with Arista in June 1980, it took her several albums to figure out how to navigate the R&B scene that was replacing sixties and seventies soul. Her contract with Atlantic had expired after the dismal *La Diva* album, and she was receptive when Clive Davis approached her about moving to Arista. Although their paths had crossed when they were at Columbia in the mid-sixties, Aretha was aware of Davis as the man who had "ushered the label into the era of hard rock and soul" with his signings of Janis Joplin, Sly and the Family Stone, and Earth, Wind & Fire. Davis had demonstrated his commercial acumen by signing Barry Manilow, Melissa Manchester, and later Ray Parker Jr., Patti Smith, Alan Parsons, Phyllis Hyman, and Angela Bofill. Aretha was even more impressed with how Davis had revived the careers of Melanie, Martha Reeves, Eddie Kendricks, Carly Simon, and especially Dionne Warwick, whose 1979 album, *Dionne,* became the biggest seller of her career. Davis had let Aretha know of his interest through mutual friends, including Stevie Wonder, whom he'd failed to woo away from Motown. "I'm certain she noted what happened with Dionne," Davis said, adding that his recruitment efforts included assurances of his personal involvement: "We said that we would work as a partnership. That's what she had missed since the Jerry Wexler days."

Aretha's first two Arista LPs, *Aretha* (1980) and *Love All the Hurt Away* (1981), reaffirmed her ability to make first-rate soul music but also made it clear that she was interested in making the transition to new-school R&B singer. Her debut album opens with an orchestrated soul ballad, "Come to Me," and showcases her in a variety of settings, ranging from straight southern soul to Vegas-style torch songs. Setting the pattern that would continue throughout his association with Aretha, Davis recruited established producers including her old Atlantic friend Arif Mardin and Chuck Jackson, who had produced Natalie Cole's seventies hits. Davis suggested songs, but Aretha wielded absolute veto power. The musical key to *Aretha,* however, was his decision to reunite her, on half the songs, with the Sweet Inspirations and the central figures in her great seventies band: guitarist Cornell Dupree, keyboardist Richard Tee, and drummer Bernard Purdie, supplemented by the king of bass players, Motown's James Jamerson. The result was certainly her most satisfying studio album since *Sparkle* and perhaps since *Young, Gifted and Black*. The highlights included her covers of the Doobie Brothers' "What a Fool Believes" and Otis Redding's "Can't Turn You Loose."

Although *Love All the Hurt Away* included a nice touch of southern soul in Aretha's impassioned Grammy-winning rendition of Sam and Dave's "Hold On I'm Coming," the album as a whole edged toward the eighties R&B mainstream. Backed by an all-star group of Los Angeles studio musicians led by bassist Marcus Miller and drummer Jeff Porcaro, Aretha assumed a central role in shaping the album's sound. She played her best piano in years and shared production duties with Mardin. She wrote two new songs ("Whole Lot of Me" and "Kind of Man") and cowrote the title cut. Along with her cover of the Rolling Stones' "You Can't Always Get What You Want," "Love All the Hurt Away" defined the emotional core of the album. Even in the Stones' original, "You Can't Always Get What You Want" cried out for the full gospel treatment provided by James Cleveland, who directed the choir on Aretha's remake. In the Reagan years the song's emphasis on a world of diminished expectations was closer to the center of eighties R&B than the sanctified spirit of "Hold On I'm Coming." Aretha's silky duet with George Benson on "Love All the Hurt Away" would have fit nicely on *Soul '69* or a compilation of the best jazz from her Columbia years.

While longtime fans welcomed *Aretha* and *Love All the Hurt Away*, neither album reestablished her as a major commercial force. By the early eighties R&B had shifted from live bands to producers adept at crafting gospel-tinged slow jams for the burgeoning Quiet Storm radio format. Romantic balladry had always had a place in the R&B-soul mix; Aretha herself had grown up swooning over dreamboats Clyde McPhatter and Sam Cooke, and younger women rarely resisted when Marvin Gaye and Al Green offered to soothe their souls. The problem, from the perspective of those nurtured on old-school soul, was that the format excluded the more assertive rhythms that had played alongside Cooke, Marvin, and Reverend Green's ballads. Drained of the political energy that had united personal desire with communal aspiration, eighties R&B settled for making it through the night. Those who responded to the thunderous anger of "The Message" or Run-DMC's "It's Like That" argued that it wasn't easy to distinguish turning down the volume from surrendering. That was part of what made the artificial separation between R&B and rap all too real.

The least convincing part of the split was the association of hip-hop with ghetto authenticity and R&B with bourgeois sellout. In reality, eighties R&B had a huge "street" audience, and not all of it was female. More than a few hardcore rap lovers were willing to overlook the cultural ideology and chill to the mellow sounds of Frankie Beverly, Phyllis Hyman, and Luther Vandross. You needed Anita Baker *and* Afrika Bambaataa if you planned on staying sane.

That's why Luther Vandross was an inspired choice to produce *Jump to It*, the album that returned Aretha to R&B stardom. Vandross had released his first solo album in 1976 but had really broken out with his 1981 *Never Too Much*. Splitting the difference between the sanctified church and the nightclub circuit, Luther's voice placed him in the lineage of Sam Cooke and Marvin Gaye. The song that gives the best sense of Vandross's affinity for Aretha is probably "Power of Love / Love Power," which updates "People Get Ready" and "A Change Is Gonna Come" for the eighties. As Aretha and Clive Davis recognized, Vandross's smooth production style was ideally suited to frame gospel vocals in the post-disco era. Aretha's cousin Brenda had suggested that the two would work well together; already a fan of *Never Too Much,* Aretha listened with a possible collaboration in mind, and the "similarity in stylings" convinced her.

Declaring himself an "Arethacologist," Vandross had already gone on record in *Rolling Stone* saying his dream was to produce Dionne Warwick, Diana Ross, and above all the Queen of Soul. He'd been a fan as long as he could remember. "My brother would get a bicycle for Christmas," he told an interviewer. "I would get records by Aretha Franklin. My mother knew instinctively that I would spend my life surrounded by music." When Clive Davis approached him, Vandross didn't make him ask twice.

Luther and Aretha hit it off at once. "When I first met Luther, he had me laughing like crazy," Aretha recalled. Reflecting on the sessions for their first album, *Jump to It,* Vandross emphasized that he "dealt with her as one singer to another. I sang her everything the way I heard it, and she took most of my suggestions. The vocals were put down in one take. Aretha is the one-take queen." Aretha reciprocated, saying, "Luther Vandross, a man of elegant taste. Big sense of humor. Serious musician, and someone capable of outrageous silliness." The similarity in their styles went beyond music, extending to their shared love for soul cuisine. A production assistant who worked on *Jump to It* described a fried chicken feast that became a minor studio legend: "They brought in industrial-size buckets of Kentucky Fried Chicken. There were bones everywhere, and there were gigantic cans of Wild Bee Honey. In the middle of all this hot tea and honey and chicken bones were Aretha and Luther."

Aretha's first number-one record in seven years, "Jump to It" was a classic summertime hit. A breathless celebration of romantic infatuation, the single starts off with a virtuoso display of Aretha's ability as a scat singer skittering on top of Vandross's bouncing beat. Midway through the song Aretha interjects a spoken interlude intended to appeal to the teen audience. Breaking down the "411" on "who drop-kicked who," Aretha ad-libbed the rap in the studio. *Today* show producer Barbara Shelley, who was filming a segment in the studio, reported that Aretha "had so much fun, it was like watching a little kid playing a game that she loved, for the first time."

The title single's exuberance and joy set the tone for the album as a whole. Prior to the sessions Cissy Houston, who sang backup on several cuts, reported that Aretha had recaptured her gospel spirit. "My good friend Miss Ree says she has some fine things ready to go. You can tell when she is ready," Cissy told journalist Gerri Hirshey. "She'll sit down at the piano and line it out for you—Reverend Cleveland taught Aretha to play a *fine* keyboard— and she'll have all the parts ready, all the harmonies. You know you understand gospel when you get a feel for the *wholeness* of the sound." *Jump to It* wasn't going to make soul fans forget about *Lady Soul* or *Young, Gifted and Black,* but it was consistently satisfying, combining up-tempo numbers like Vandross's "Love Me Right" and the Isley Brothers' "It's Your Thing" with quiet stormers including Luther's "This Is for Real" and her own composition "I Wanna Make It Up to You." Her romantic reading of Smokey Robinson's "Just My Daydream" approaches the standard of pop balladry that Aretha had set for herself on "Call Me" and "A Brand New Me."

While *Jump to It* seemed to presage a lasting musical partnership, tensions soon emerged between Aretha and Vandross. Their growing animosity threatened to derail the follow-up album, *Get It Right.* Aretha felt that Vandross had lost sight of the proper balance between singer and producer. "All of a sudden Luther wanted to tell me how to sing, when it was I from whom he had learned much about how to sing," she said. "My point was simple: If he wanted to tell the artist how to sing, why didn't he sing it himself?" She was unimpressed with Vandross's reminder of his role in revitalizing her career. "Well, Mr. Vandross wanted to know who had produced my recent number one, and I felt he should be reminded that I had enjoyed at least twenty gold records before I or the world knew his name," Aretha reported. "I picked up my coat and walked out of the studio as he and I continued shouting at each other." Clive Davis intervened, convincing Vandross to issue what Aretha called a "half-hearted apology." She reciprocated in kind and they completed the album in an uneasy truce. A few of the songs, most notably the bouncy title cut and a slow, soulful version of the Temptations' "I Wish It Would Rain," match the standard set by *Jump to It*, but the album disappointed everyone involved. After it was released, Aretha sued Arista, claiming Vandross had been hired without her consent. Nothing came of the suit, but it served as official notice that Aretha was seeking a new producer.

The ill will surrounding *Get It Right* contributed to a larger set of problems that made the early eighties a difficult period in Aretha's life. After the end of her marriage to Glynn Turman and her move back to Detroit, friends and family members worried publicly over what they saw as her retreat from the world. In her autobiography Aretha strenuously denied her sister Erma's depiction of her as an introvert who came alive only onstage. It was, Aretha wrote, "the biggest lie ever told about me. No one loves a party more than I; as I have said, I am a people person. When people are introverted, they may be unable to reach out and enjoy other people. They may suffer through their inhibitions and be deprived socially, which is the exact opposite of who I demonstrate myself to be on a daily basis."

Nonetheless, a series of highly publicized events suggested that Aretha was painting an overly sunny picture. In January 1981 Arista arranged a post-Grammy party for her on the forty-eighth floor of the Time-Life Building. Never comfortable with heights, Aretha made it only as far as the top of the first bank of elevators before turning back toward solid ground. Of greater importance to her career, her fear of flying became debilitating. After missing a scheduled flight from Atlanta to Detroit, she accepted a seat on a two-engine prop plane, which, she admitted looking back, was a "*big mistake.*" Caught between lines of thunderstorms, the small plane bounced across the sky, subjecting Aretha to "drastic drops" and "dipsy doodles." At one point, the traumatized passenger claimed, it turned completely upside down. Her subsequent decision to take a break from air travel was certainly understandable.

As it became clear that the fear of flying would not pass quickly, the travel issues proved more than an inconvenience. In 1984 Aretha agreed to play the title role in "*Sing, Mahalia, Sing!*," a Broadway musical honoring her old friend and mentor. A better match couldn't have been imagined. Fully intending to be in New York for the start of rehearsals in early May, Aretha immersed herself in the material, including "Move On Up a Little Higher" and "Didn't It Rain." "At that point," she recalled, "even though my traumatic flight from Atlanta was still recent, I figured I'd be flying by play time." When May arrived, however, Aretha found herself unable to even contemplate leaving the ground. Although she started to make the journey by bus, she couldn't handle the thought of the lengthy trip and turned back to Detroit. Her failure to appear cost her nearly a quarter of a million dollars in a court-ordered payment to the producers for breach of contract. The next year, still unwilling to travel outside Detroit, Aretha turned down an offer to star in another Broadway musical, this one based on the life of Bessie Smith. Further underlining the depth of the problem, she backed out of scheduled concerts with Stevie Wonder, Luther Vandross, and Smokey Robinson that were intended to help offset Jesse Jackson's campaign debts.

Life in Detroit offered some compensations. Aretha enjoyed frequent excursions to popular night spots like L'Esprit and Club Taboo, and she loved driving around town in her blue Rolls-Royce. Settling into her new house in suburban Bloomfield Hills, she indulged her passion for design, decorating the interior with birds in gold cages and glass cases proudly displaying the robe and crown she had been given as the Queen of Soul. She was involved in an on-again off-again romance with Dennis Edwards of the Temptations, who later told *Vanity Fair,* "I should have married Aretha. It was all in my court, and I think I'm the one that was so scared of marrying this superstar." Meanwhile a new romance with Detroit fireman Willie Wilkerson was society-page news. As always, Aretha devoted some of her creative energy to designing gowns and evening dresses, although she once again failed to realize her dream of having her own fashion line.

Through it all, Reverend C.L. Franklin remained the emotional center of Aretha's life. Until his death on July 27, 1984, after five years in a coma, Aretha returned to Detroit regularly to be with her father, and he was never far from her mind. Partly because of Reverend Franklin's political and social prominence, funeral arrangements generated several heated arguments over content and seating. At one point Jesse Jackson had to intervene to cool simmering tensions. On the day of the funeral Aretha was near paralysis; her knees buckled as she entered the church, where Pops Staples and gospel-star-turned-soul-singer Johnnie Taylor were among those delivering eulogies. Franklin's protégé Reverend Jaspar Williams delivered a stirring funeral sermon. "He was born in poverty, but poverty could not stop him. He was born in segregation, but segregation could not stop him," Williams preached. "When God wants a flower to bloom, no drought can stop it. His flower did blossom. And so we say thank you for a petal, for an insight, for a sermon." He concluded with an invocation of C.L. Franklin's best-loved sermon: "When the eagle stirreth its nest, the flower blossomed."

Those close to her worried that C.L.'s death would precipitate a total emotional collapse for Aretha. "We were all looking at her thinking she was going to fall apart," admitted her sister Carolyn. "She's had her own problems, so we thought she was going to go into a fit or go off, but she really handled it quite well." Just as she had clung tightly to her memories of her mother, Aretha cherished her undying love for her father. Even before his death, visitors to her house commented on the numerous candles and pictures dedicated to him. *Vanity Fair* described the house as a "virtual shrine to his memory." As with her mother's death, Aretha rarely spoke of her father's passing in public. Even after several years had passed, her sister Erma said, "You can't say the word 'death' around her. You have to say 'passed away' or find some other expression. She and my dad were very, very, very close."

In the shadow of her biggest loss, Aretha somehow transformed her personal and artistic struggles into the biggest-selling album of her career, *Who's Zoomin' Who?* Featuring six songs produced by Narada Michael Walden, the album let Aretha reassert her power as a woman and an artist. Walden initiated the project when he sent musical sketches for three songs to Clive Davis, who forwarded them to Aretha in Detroit. "She was delighted with what she heard—I sent her roughs on 'Push,' 'Freeway of Love,' and 'Who's Zoomin' Who?' " Walden recalled, emphasizing Aretha's role in their subsequent development. "I really came up with a lot of the ideas lyrically from talking with Aretha on the phone. I'd ask her about what she'd do at home, how did she spend her time. She told me one of the things she liked to do on occasion was go to a club and maybe she'd be checking out some guy who'd be checking her out too—that's where I got a lot of the ideas for *Who's Zoomin'*

Who? I discovered that Aretha had this great sense of humor, something I had no idea about before we started working together."

Walden was perfectly situated to help Aretha transcend the musical boundaries that shoved most black artists of the mid-eighties into the reseg-regated world of R&B. After establishing himself as the drummer for John McLaughlin's jazz fusion group, the Mahavishnu Orchestra, Walden had gone on to produce Whitney Houston, Stacy Lattisaw, Angela Bofill, and Phyllis Hyman, all of them R&B artists who attracted a sizable crossover audience. Walden appreciated Aretha's gospel roots, but he came to her with a commercial vision that went beyond R&B. "It's not like it's all church to me," he commented. "In the voice you feel a lot of gospel roots, it's true. But her expression of the church is very streetwise." Tuning in on Aretha's "hip class"—he called her the "black Mae West"—Walden observed, "She can be very gritty and ladylike at the same time.... She takes her fur coat off and she's got jeans and a sweatshirt underneath."

Encouraging Aretha to make use of both her church and her street sides, Walden helped craft a mid-decade masterpiece that earned a place along-side Prince's *Purple Rain,* Tina Turner's *Private Dancer,* Madonna's *Like a Virgin,* and Bruce Springsteen's *Born in the U.S.A.* Like Michael Jackson's *Thriller,* which had ushered in the era of the megastars, each album on the list mingled a deep seriousness about life in the eighties with a glossy, "streetwise" surface. As MTV reshaped the relationship between music and image, the challenge was figuring out how to bend the rules enough to do something worthwhile. In some ways it was a throwback to the problem Sam Cooke and Berry Gordy had encountered at the height of the Cold War: once again black artists found themselves required to adjust their styles to the preconceptions of an industry bent on forgetting most of what it had previously learned about black music. Where the crossover soul singers had carefully toned down the sexual content of their personas, the new breed plunged into a post-disco funhouse that made for an uneasy fit with the gospel vision. It was difficult to assert the values of sacrifice and commu-nity in a format predicated on conspicuous consumption and individual image. The best of the megastars found ways to play with, rather than into, the game. Madonna and Tina Turner took the sexual stereotypes to the top and kept on rising; Prince and Michael elevated androgynous indetermi-nacy into its own art form. MTV transmitted an unending series of updates from the strange new erotic city, but it was hard to imagine its citizens confronting Pharaoh on behalf of their less fortunate sisters and brothers.

Oddly enough, Aretha's closest affinities in the eighties wonderland were with Bruce Springsteen, an unreconstructed romantic at heart. Springsteen's vocal style came to him from gospel shouter Marion Williams by way of Little Richard. His spiritual politics grew directly out of gospel soul. Released a year before *Who's Zoomin' Who?*, Springsteen's *Born in the U.S.A.* screamed what should have been an unmistakable "no" to most of what was happening in Reagan's America. The fact that a whole lot of people somehow mistook his populist protest for jingoistic patriotism spoke to the perils of life among the megastars. Appropriately, "Freeway of Love," the opening track on *Who's Zoomin' Who?*, opened with a guest appearance from Springsteen's African American sidekick Clarence Clemons. Setting Aretha's biggest-selling album in motion with a straight-out-of-Memphis saxophone wail, Clemons sounded like he was determined to keep blowin' till the walls came tumblin' down.

Part of the success of *Who's Zoomin' Who?* no doubt reflected the fact that you *could* enjoy it without doing much thinking. Particularly in comparison with the overproduced norm of eighties pop, the album just plain sounded good. Driven by a mix of live drums, tambourines, and synthesized beats, "Freeway of Love" announces Aretha and Walden's intention of taking the eighties to church. Viewers fixated on the video images of Aretha in a glitzy Detroit club or the pink Cadillac that had originally been owned by Jayne Mansfield could shrug the song off as inoffensive fluff. But the polyrhythmic energy and the sequencing of songs on the album asked them to think again.

Following the gospel pop of "Freeway of Love," "Another Night" injects a note of bluesy realism while repudiating rumors of Aretha's psychological demise. One of Aretha's best eighties love songs, "Another Night" half-hides its emotional complexity behind the type of story line favored by disco divas like Yvonne Ellman and Gloria Gaynor. As she had in the semi-autobiographical song sequence that tracked the collapse of her marriage to Ted White, Aretha tries out a series of explanations of why, yet again, she's found herself alone. The past's past, it doesn't matter, she begins. A moment later she admits to wearing a mask, telling herself she'll be fine even if she has to fake it. The most convincing moments come when, echoing Springsteen's fierce refusal to give in to the forces out to destroy him, she pledges to stand her ground and shouts her defiance to the men who have tried to bring her down. The closing sequence of Walden's "Push" and Aretha's composition "Integrity," which she said reminded her of Curtis Mayfield's sixties work, restates the gospel-blues foundation. A duet between Aretha and J. Geils Band vocalist Peter Wolf, "Push" builds to a frantic call-and-response exchange on some of the most basic gospel vision phrases. "Break for the higher ground," Wolf calls out, "just a little farther till we see the light." "We got to keep on pushin'," Aretha responds, and Wolf answers, "We can get over." It wasn't exactly Mahalia, but you had to have heard Mahalia to get the point.

Aretha's duet with Annie Lennox of the Eurythmics on "Sisters Are Doing It for Themselves" ties the gospel vision to a feminist movement that, despite momentary setbacks and ideological disagreements, was no longer relegated to the margins of the political world. Lennox and partner Dave Stewart had originally conceived the song with Tina Turner in mind, but Tina decided that the feminist message clashed with her new punk-metal-sex-goddess image. Mindful of the freedom movement's nonnegotiable commitment to equality, Aretha requested that the line "the inferior sex are still superior" be altered to "the inferior sex have got a new exterior." But she had no real problem with the song's politics. She saw it as a more explicit articulation of songs like "Respect" and "Think" that had made her into a half-willing feminist icon. "It was my first musical declaration of clear-cut women's liberation," Aretha reflected. "I've always considered myself a progressive woman. And more and more in the eighties I saw women competing for jobs reserved for men—not just doctors and lawyers, but construction workers, traffic cops, Federal Express workers. My attitude was, You go, girl, if you've got the heart to do it. And if you do it, you sure deserve the same money a man makes." Lennox supported Aretha's interpretation, saying, "I suppose the song's feminist in the sense that it's women singing about women, but it's really just a song for people in a situation like mine, people who now do things through their own assertion, through their own power, that they would never have been able to do before."

Although Aretha and Lennox dutifully praised each other in the press, their styles weren't an ideal match. For many black women, the feminist movement appeared to be a "white feminist movement," leading writer Alice Walker to declare herself a "womanist" committed to a more inclusive political vision. Part of the problem concerned sharply divergent attitudes toward the church. While many individual white feminists held strong religious convictions, some of the most prominent feminist advocates openly repudiated Christianity as a patriarchal imposition. As the powerful performances of "Take Me to the River" in her live concerts demonstrated, Lennox herself had a deep appreciation for gospel music. In terms of public persona and personal style, however, the two women came from different worlds. Their initial attempts to accommodate each other led to an amusing situation at the recording session for "Sisters Are Doing It for Themselves." "I think we had a role-reversal there," Aretha said. "Because I showed up wearing the 'punk' look, and the Levi's jacket and the rhinestones—that look. And she showed up very chic, with a black pantsuit, and spectator shoes. I thought it was kind of cute." Lennox's version was a bit more subdued. "I got along alright with her, but we didn't have an immediate rapport," she remembered. "Aretha struck me as rather shy, a bit sad, a bit lonely. She had an entourage which I thought was a bit eccentric."

The video shoot raised more serious problems. According to director Jan Roseman, "Annie had just had a photo session, and the woman photographer was gay. Aretha has a thing about gays and assumed Annie was a lesbian. She more or less ignored her throughout the entire session. After the video Annie didn't want to talk to Aretha. The atmosphere was strained between them." Fortunately, the strain didn't come through on the video. Montaging Aretha and Lennox's spirited performances with images of women in roles ranging from nuns and swimmers to astronauts and martial artists, the video became a symbol of sororal unity that was proving elusive in real life.

The tension between the MTV hall of mirrors and the gospel values that grounded Aretha lifts "Who's Zoomin' Who?" from a clever relationship song to metaphorical commentary on the tensions at the heart of the decade. Aretha sketches a scenario in which the man thinks he has the power, only to turn the tables with the announcement, "You will remember my name, I'm the one that beat you at your game." Despite the confident assertion, however, the "Who's Zoomin' Who?" metaphor resists certainty. True, Aretha demanded that the man—and for the politically inclined, the white males who dominated the Reagan-era political process—"take another look." As she sang in "Integrity," "Put your daddy's ways behind you, things have changed." But even as the song tapped into women's power, which would soon be a political fact that not even the most unreconstructed Reaganite would be able to ignore, it wasn't at all clear how that power would express itself, personally or politically. If women—or any of the other groups flirting with political approaches grounded in some aspect of one's "identity"—really had the power, why did they still find themselves in situations where the roles needed reversing? If disagreements between groups kept them from joining their forces in something like Jackson's Rainbow Coalition, was it possible to imagine any real change in the policies that were killing children in the ghettos and feminizing poverty? Politically, "Who's Zoomin' Who?" was a damn good question.

Who's Zoomin' Who? placed five singles in the Top Forty and sold well over a million copies, giving Aretha her first platinum album in a decade that wasn't satisfied with gold. Over the next two years collaborations with George Michael and with Keith Richards and Ron Woods of the Rolling Stones would keep her in the public eye, but none of her other Reagan-Bush-era pop albums—*Aretha* (1986), *Through the Storm* (1989), and *What You See Is What You Sweat* (1991)—stood out. Her second self-titled Arista album of the decade, most of it produced by Walden, yielded two minor hits in "Jimmy Lee" and her collaboration with Woods and Richards on "Jumpin' Jack Flash," the title track from Whoopi Goldberg's movie of the same name. Marveling over the piano run Aretha used to ignite the latter, Richards said, "A lot of people forget that on top of an incredible voice, she's an incredible piano player. She comes up with amazing musical ideas. You never have to worry about the tempo because she just sets it."

The musical and conceptual highlight of *Aretha,* however, was Aretha's duet with George Michael on "I Knew You Were Waiting (For Me)." Like her earlier duets with Luther Vandross and Annie Lennox, the project with Michael helped both singers attract new listeners. As Clive Davis observed, Michael, who was seeking to shake the teen idol image he'd earned as front man for Wham!, "was looking to establish individual credibility, that he was not just a pop artist. And for her, she was able to reach a teenager audience." Michael was thrilled to sing with Aretha, whom he praised as "the best, quite simply. Much as I love a lot of other female artists, there's no one touches her." Although many R&B fans expressed their doubts about pairing Aretha with the red-hot heartthrob, "I Knew You Were Waiting (For Me)" surprised them by recapturing the gospel fire of her Atlantic classics as well as any of her eighties hits. Supported by a tasteful video that suggests a call and response between Aretha as live singer and Michael as video image projected on a large screen behind her, the lyrics are pure gospel: "When the river was deep, I did not falter. When the mountain was high, I still believed."

"I Knew You Were Waiting (For Me)" was Aretha's last truly memorable pop performance of the Reagan-Bush years. Although each contains a couple of good cuts, neither *Through the Storm* nor *What You See Is What You Sweat* finds a center. On *Through the Storm* Walden's rhythmic inventiveness seems to have atrophied into predictable electronic mush, while the featured duets with guest stars James Brown, Whitney Houston, Elton John, and Levi Stubbs lack the immediacy of "Sisters Are Doing It for Themselves," "I Knew You Were Waiting (For Me)," or even "Push." In the case of her duet with Brown on "Gimme Your Love," that's hardly surprising since the two were never actually in the studio at the same time. Assembled by a grab-bag of producers including Walden, Vandross, the team of Burt Bacharach and Carole Bayer Sager, and Aretha herself, *What You See Is What You Sweat* is a slightly stronger album than *Through the Storm.* Walden recaptures some of his polyrhythmic inspiration on the remake of Sly Stone's "Everyday People." Aretha rightly called her duet with Michael McDonald on Bacharach and Bayer Sager's "Ever Changing Times" a "gem." But several of the collaborations, notably those with Houston and Vandross, devolved into personal animosity. Yet again she clashed with Vandross over production of their duet on "Doctor's Orders." "I sounded like one of the background singers," Aretha complained. "He put the word out so strongly that other producers were reluctant to interfere." Although they originally compromised on what Aretha called an "acceptable mix," her relations with him remained strained.

As she had always done in times of trouble, Aretha again sought solace and support in the church. Thinking back on her childhood and her father's legacy, she felt a strong pull "to go all the way back to my roots." While she loved *Amazing Grace,* she formulated a plan for a gospel album to honor the world that had shaped her being. Carolyn recalled her sister's excitement as plans took shape for the 1988 album *One Lord, One Faith, One Baptism:* "She said she wanted to re-create her childhood like in the church with the candlelight service." Along with singing the Ward Singers' songs that the sisters had performed as children, Aretha wanted to experience the moment "when the choir walks down the aisle of the dark church, only the flickering flames illuminating their way."

Although Aretha never directly compared *One Lord, One Faith, One Baptism* with her pop albums of the period, her reflections on gospel music suggest her weariness with eighties gloss. "I am a traditionalist when it comes to gospel," she said, "and it doesn't mean I don't appreciate the modern forms. There are many ways to praise the Lord. Different generations hear different beats. I must say, though, when the bass lines are pure boogie and the beats are pure funk, I wouldn't call it gospel. When the performer's body language is funking so hard as to be religiously disrespectful, then I wouldn't call it gospel. Gospel is a higher calling; gospel is about God. Gospel is about beautiful and glorious voices and spirit-filled performances, and people who are anointed." During preparations for the album Aretha worked closely with Minister Thomas Whitfield, who supervised the choral arrangements. Aware that Aretha hoped to re-create the fire and feeling of the revival meetings and gospel shows of the fifties, Whitfield commented on the difficulties of recapturing the earlier era. "For singers today, it is hard to replicate how they sang back then, because they didn't really sing structured at all," he said. "The parts just kind of *felt*. You had to kind of catch on."

The services where *One Lord, One Faith, One Baptism* was recorded took place at the relocated New Bethel Baptist Church on three sweltering Detroit nights in July 1987. The services themselves, attended by a crowd of nearly four thousand, fulfilled Aretha's expectations. The receptive congregation welcomed the three Franklin sisters, their cousin Brenda, and their grandmother, who was confined to a wheelchair. Cecil Franklin addressed the crowd along with fellow ministers Jaspar Williams and Donald Parsons of Mount Cavalry Baptist Church in Chicago. Jesse Jackson served as master of ceremonies. Guest vocalists included Mavis and Yvonne Staples and Joe Ligon of the Mighty Clouds of Joy. The musical highlights included the Franklin sisters' treatment of Clara Ward's "Jesus Hears Every Prayer" and "Surely God Is Able," Mavis and Aretha's duet on "Oh Happy Day," and above all "I've Been in the Storm Too Long," on which Aretha and Ligon whipped the worshipers into a spiritual frenzy leading up to the altar call. The spiritual keynote of the album, however, comes on the church standard "Higher Ground." Meditating on the central image of the gospel vision, Aretha and Reverend Williams communed with the spirit of C.L. Franklin.

When Reverend Williams started shouting, "I'm pressing on!," Aretha recalled warmly, "I sang between his words, just as I had done with my dad." For those three nights she felt almost at peace. "We couldn't see the tragedies around the bend," she wrote looking back. "But for those three nights we were together as a family, singing and praying as we did as children. The spirits of our mom and dad were surely with us."

Unfortunately, the *One Lord, One Faith, One Baptism* album failed to communicate the power of the actual services. Part of the problem was the quality of the sound recording, which fell well short of the standard set by *Amazing Grace*. In addition, Aretha's decision to maintain the church service structure creates lengthy stretches when the listener has no way of sharing the responsive attentiveness of those wrapped up in the moment. Although the album won the Gospel Music Association's Dove award for best traditional gospel album, its lasting importance is as a reminder of gospel's centrality to everything Aretha did. "I need that old-fashioned, stick-to-your-ribs gospel, the kind that will carry you as far as you need to go," she said. "As Dr. King used to say after a dynamite dinner, 'I can go around the world on a meal like that.' "

Aretha needed more than Dr. King's favorite soul food to deal with the health problems that struck her family in waves beginning in the late eighties. As she wrote in her autobiography, the title of her 1989 album, *Through the Storm*, "describes what my family was going through during that time. The storm was tougher than I could have expected; it took a tremendous toll." Just as the family began to regain equilibrium after C.L. Franklin's death, Carolyn was diagnosed with breast cancer. As her health failed, Aretha's sister continued to work toward her degree from Marygrove College, which she received ten days before her death in April 1988. Less than two years later Aretha's brother Cecil died, also as a result of cancer. In 1990 C.L. Franklin's mother, Rachel, passed. Emotionally drained and heartbroken, Aretha paid homage to Big Mama's faith as "the backbone of the family." In 2002 cancer claimed her sister Erma, leaving Aretha as the only surviving Franklin sister at age sixty.

⤦

ARETHA WAS NOT THE only one visited by troubles in those years. On August 13, 1990, Curtis Mayfield was preparing to take the stage at an outdoor concert at Brooklyn's Wingate High School. He'd taken a few months off and was playing the free concert as a tune-up for his upcoming European tour. The sky was cloudy and the forecast included rain, but there was no reason to expect a real storm. As Mayfield reached the top of the steps and moved toward the microphone, a freak gust of wind blew in without warning. A light tower at the edge of the stage toppled and fell, pinning Mayfield beneath it. "I knew what had happened right away," Mayfield remembered. "The first thing I told myself was just to stay alive." The tower had crushed several vertebrae. When the ambulance arrived, the emergency medical crew that rushed him to Kings County Hospital wasn't sure he'd survive. Once his condition stabilized sufficiently, he was transferred to Atlanta's world-class Shepherd Spinal Center, where he received extensive therapy. The gospel traveler would never walk another step.

When Mayfield returned home after long months in the hospital, he faced the difficult adjustment to life as a quadriplegic. While he would never be free of pain, Mayfield's spiritual recovery provides an inspirational story that, if it weren't true, would seem like a made-for-television fantasy. The mere existence of his 1996 album, *New World Order,* represents a triumph of gospel spirit over fallible flesh. Its wisdom and beauty make it truly magical.

The path that would lead Mayfield back to the recording studio was hard. "At first I thought since I was paralyzed, there wouldn't be so much pain," he reflected. "But I found that aches come and go. I have a lot of complications, the effect of low blood pressure, chronic pain, things no one really could see or would even know unless you were around people with spinal cord injuries. I'm trying to maintain the status quo, but the hardships are many as are the complications. Sometimes you don't have answers." Speaking openly and honestly about his physical condition and the accompanying spiritual challenges, Mayfield said he generally avoided depression. "I think my spirits are maybe even higher. It's like I died and woke up to see this wave of love from so many people I knew and people I didn't know. Of course it doesn't mean you don't every once in a while find a tear in your eye. Your body does not allow you to do many things that your mind says. Your mind always says, 'I'm ready, let's go.' You have to deal with it; you have to learn patience. It's tough being a person who totally has to rely on someone else when you've been independent all your life."

The decade prior to the accident had accustomed Mayfield to disappointment. Although skillful handling of his own career had relieved him from the financial pressure to produce hit records, he'd certainly hoped for a stronger response to the four albums he released during the Reagan-Bush years: *Love Is the Place* (1981), *Honesty* (1982), *We Come in Peace with a Message of Love* (1985), and *Take It to the Street* (1990). Still, he responded philosophically. "Stars are made to burn," he reflected. "Does it matter whether there is a time when you're not number one? It only gave me time to put some of my main thoughts toward other important things, like being a father. It's the media that always asks, 'Why aren't you still as big as you were?' Well, why aren't I still twenty-two? Why aren't I just thirty-six?"

As the eighties began, Mayfield had been enjoying his release from the burdens of running Curtom. Free to concentrate on writing songs for himself, he had signed with Neil Bogart's Boardwalk label, where his music recovered some of its vitality. "At that time, I wasn't so hot so we were all looking for the right recipe to bring me back," Mayfield observed. Although *Love Is the Place* and *Honesty* are markedly uneven—"they didn't want to do an album that was a hundred percent Mayfield"—the Boardwalk albums reestablished Mayfield on the R&B charts with the gorgeous falsetto ballad "She Don't Let Nobody But Me." They also include Mayfield's strongest social commentary since *Back to the World* in the Impressions-style "Come Free Your People" and "Dirty Laundry," an incisive criticism of Reagan-era political corruption. A musical setting based on harmonica and steel guitar gives a deceptively soft, near-country feel to Mayfield's uncompromising condemnation of greed and hypocrisy: "Dirty laundry in the country / can't trust our Uncle Sam / broken link, future sinking, and no one gives a damn."

After Bogart's death in 1982, Boardwalk folded and Mayfield attempted to revive Curtom. Partially as a result of changes in radio formats, the climate for independent labels had changed drastically by the eighties. Chicago-soul-music guru Johnny Meadows analyzed the situation: "What happened was that fragmented radio came in where you got away from the Top Forty formats on pop stations and the black radio stations got very fragmented. You had some going to jazz, some going to gospel, the R&B format for some radio stations, you had some others doing disco. It was all cut up. You didn't have the concentration and saturation that was able to push these things in the pop direction. It didn't put the pressure on Top Forty radio." Attempting to revive Curtom, Mayfield signed a distribution agreement with Ichiban Records. Despite the diffuse musical scene, both *We Come in Peace with a Message of Love* and *Take It to the Street* hold fast to the ideals of love and unity. Like his Curtom albums of the late seventies, each includes first-rate songs, including the lovely ballads "Baby, It's You" and "Do Be Down." Two effective message songs frame *We Come in Peace with a Message of Love:* the title cut and a quirky but effective updating of "We Got to Have Peace" from Vietnam to the Reagan era. "Homeless," the first cut from *Take It to the Street,* issues a compassionate plea in behalf of the grow-ing numbers who had fallen to the lower circles of the urban inferno. As the eighties drew to a close, Curtis immersed himself in several projects, including a return to film. He contributed music to the soundtrack of *The Return of Superfly,* which includes a collaboration with rapper Ice-T on a remake of Mayfield's classic funk cut. In 1987 he collaborated with the English ska group the Blow Monkeys on "Celebrate (The Day After You)," a strong political statement criticizing the conservative policies of Prime Minister Margaret Thatcher.

Although none of the albums dented the American charts, Mayfield continued to enjoy great popularity with European and Japanese fans. "Curtis is an icon. You go over there to Europe, and that's all they want to talk about," Mavis Staples reported. "They just love him." Mayfield appre-ciated the reception. "You have to remember that when I was having all my hits in the States, my records really weren't being exposed properly in Europe," he told soul journalist David Nathan at the time. "So maybe this is like a catch-up situation. People seem more loyal in Europe. I see some of the same faces at my concerts each time I come over, and that's a com-fortable feeling." He was looking forward to another overseas tour when the tower fell on him.

As he underwent the interminable tests and round after round of physi-cal therapy, Mayfield looked back over the path he'd traveled. The thing he regretted most about life after the accident was that he could no longer play guitar: "For expression and harmony, my guitar was like another brother to me. I mourn my guitar to this day." In his first public interview after the acci-dent in 1993, Mayfield had given thanks that he possessed his full mental faculties, but he lamented his inability to realize his musical ideas. "I have lots of thoughts and visions and ideas," he said, "but that's all they are until they can become compositions and then finally be recorded to do the magic with somebody." That somebody would turn out to be Roger Troutman of the eighties funk powerhouse Zapp, who would introduce Mayfield to the computer technology that allowed him to create *New World Order.*

Mayfield took pride in his ability to provide for his large family despite the injury: "You just try to do the right thing for all that are immediate to you. My particular thing is how, within my limits, to still find ways to earn a decent living, just prove to myself that I'm doing the best that I can do. How many fifty-four-year-old quadriplegics are putting albums out? You just have to deal with what you got and try to sustain yourself as best you can and look to the things that you can do. So that's how I'm looking at things. I'm devoting what time I have to my children. I'm trying to get the rest of them out of here to college." He laughed, then paid tribute to his second wife, Altheida, whose strength helped see him through his darkest moments. "I got a very strong woman," he said. "You never know who's going to take that stand and say, 'Hey, I'll do it.' Nobody wants to do it, but she's been around all these years."

Mayfield's publishing ventures enabled him to withstand the financial stress caused by the accident. When Rod Stewart's version of "People Get Ready" and En Vogue's remake of "Giving Him Something He Can Feel" became smash hits, Mayfield collected substantial royalties. Similarly, he benefited when hip-hop producers enriched their records with samples from "Freddie's Dead" and "Superfly." He expressed satisfaction with the way the record industry came to terms with sampling: "James Brown's voice sort of taught everybody to work it out and get your credits. His 'owwwws' were the whole record, they were on everything. But now it's been standardized, and one must be given the proper credits. It becomes a residual for you even if it's not just but one beat. So it works out where you can make a decent living." Marv Heiman, who managed Mayfield through the later stages of his career, elaborated: "Sampling allowed him to keep his dignity and self-respect. He had health insurance, but his injury cost the insurance company over $1.5 million. Sampling let his family be financially secure."

Aware that the business acumen he had shown from the beginning of his career allowed him to support his ten children by three women—"you know I wouldn't do that to one woman," he laughed—Mayfield maintained deep empathy for the writers and singers who lost control of their material. Despite his own secure economic position, he joined in a 1995 class action suit filed to gain remuneration and a pension fund for soul acts exploited by unscrupulous labels. "Publishing was the foundation of large estates, I found out as I got older," he said with an uncharacteristically hard edge to his voice. "And learning the value of that, I found it's better to keep your song and bargain with them and try and be strong and resist taking the one hundred or five hundred or whatever it might be. The value is in you the person."

Mayfield supported the lawsuit as a gesture of respect for a community and a tradition. "That's why I did it," he said. "I'd always hear the old guys saying you gotta pay your dues. Yeah, I paid my dues; a lot of people paid their dues. It's true, you do have to pay your dues, but sometimes you pay so much out that you find you have to buy yourself back if you could afford to do so." He expressed particular concern for artists who had lost the rights to records sampled by hip-hop acts: "Not all of that is properly standardized, and anyone who uses a rhythm piece out of a song or something, whoever owns the masters has the right to collect residuals. Even if it's a voice, the money goes back to the label."

While Curtis never became a national icon like Stevie and Aretha, other musicians recognized what he had given them. Two 1993 tribute albums, *People Get Ready: The Curtis Mayfield Story* and *All Men Are Brothers: A Tribute to Curtis Mayfield*, featured performances of Mayfield songs by a who's who of the rock and soul worlds, including Bruce Springsteen, Jerry Butler, Stax guitarist Steve Cropper, B.B. King, David Sanborn, and Whitney Houston. Both Stevie and Aretha contributed to the latter, performing "I'm the One Who Loves You" and "The Makings of You," respectively. A third compilation, *I'm So Proud: A Jamaican Tribute to Curtis Mayfield*, includes recordings of Mayfield's compositions by Bob Marley and the Wailers, the Heptones, and Marcia Griffiths. VH1 produced an hourlong documentary on Mayfield as part of its "Legends" series. He was inducted into the Rock and Roll Hall of Fame in 1991 as a member of the Impressions and again in 1999 as a solo act, the NAACP Hall of Fame in 1994, and the Soul Train Hall of Fame in 1996. He received the Grammy Legend award in 1994, and the R&B Foundation Pioneer award in 1997.

As he contemplated the world and life from his wheelchair, Mayfield worried about the decaying conditions of life in inner-city neighborhoods like the one he'd grown up in. Although his physical condition prevented him from joining Stevie Wonder and the scores of musicians who lent their support to the Million Man March, he approved of the impulse driving it. Painfully aware of the self-destructive forces turning some urban areas into war zones, he expressed a deep sympathy for young people deprived of hope. He saw the march as a logical response to a growing sense of despair. "You might sense a mass of people wanting to find some answers," he said. "That's really what a lot of young blacks and young people in poverty want. They need answers. You're not the smartest person in the world. It don't look like with what's happening in the schools, you're going to be. You need answers. How do you get from here to there when you want to be a righteous person? I don't want to do crime, hey that's risky, and it takes smarts to even do that. So the young kids need something to believe and to prove and to be proven to that it works." Mayfield traces the problem to the divisive forces he had targeted at the outset of the Reagan era in "Dirty Laundry." "The bigotry, the discrimination and the selfishness and the greed. All these things really come from the top down. Those at the bottom of the totem pole don't have things. They have to carry the load by sweat and labor, cheap labor. Whether they're black or white, they're being manipulated by the higher powers that be."

B Y THE TIME ARETHA FRANKLIN SANG the national anthem to open the second night of the Democratic National Convention on July 14, 1992, black America was sick and tired of the powers that had occupied the White House for the last twelve years. The quarter century since the last time her voice had called the party's convention to order had thoroughly reconfigured the American political landscape. Presenting himself as the last, best hope of a liberal vision that had somehow lost the moral high ground to unabashed proponents of privilege, Bill Clinton had rendered himself electable by repudiating Jesse Jackson. Setting out to recapture the "Reagan Democrats," Clinton sent racially coded symbolic messages. He played golf at a segregated country club, creating a "scandal" that worked to his advantage. He executed a mentally retarded black man in Arkansas. The sobering reality is that Clinton's strategy—organized around the mantra "It's the economy, stupid"—was probably the only way of bringing the Reagan nightmare to an end.

Clinton's election signaled a major change in presidential style. Setting aside any feelings she might have harbored over Clinton's summary disregard for Jackson, Aretha supported the new administration's campaign to establish its credibility with black America. In turn, she credited Clinton with giving a boost to the music she loved: "The president let everyone know he loves straight-up soul. To have a fellow baby boomer—and a bubba and a saxophonist to boot—in the White House, well, let the party begin." Clinton was fully aware of Aretha's symbolic importance. On January 17, 1993, she performed at an event called "A Call to Reunion" at the Lincoln Memorial, the site hallowed by the voices of Marian Anderson, Mahalia Jackson, and Martin Luther King. Two days later she sang "I Dreamed a Dream" at the inaugural gala.

The Clinton inauguration ushered in a new era in the nation's public culture. African American artists, including a few R&B stars like Ray Charles, had previously received recognition from the White House, but when Clinton made Aretha a centerpiece of his administration's cultural presence, he meant it. Aretha and Stevie Wonder, both of whom sang at Clinton's second inaugural celebration, had become national icons, their status confirmed by a litany of awards and highly visible performances at events that weren't primarily about the music. They sang at Super Bowls, the NBA All-Star game, the World Series, and the closing ceremonies of the Olympics. They received honorary doctorates, humanitarian awards, and lifetime achievement awards from the Kennedy Center and the Grammys. They were inducted into every vaguely appropriate Hall of Fame. As they had in the eighties, they gave freely to charities, played at benefits, and made guest appearances with everyone from Prince to Frank Sinatra. A few of the events—notably the gospel version of "Blowin' in the Wind" that Wonder performed at Bob Dylan's 1992 birthday party—managed to transcend the photo-op feel that was so difficult to avoid in a media world where scores of cable stations demanded around-the-clock infotainment.

Aretha's performance of "Nessun Dorma" at a dinner honoring operatic tenor Luciano Pavarotti on February 23, 1998, set off a chain of events that resulted in even broader recognition from the cultural elite. Two days later

Pavarotti himself was scheduled to sing Puccini's aria as part of the Grammy awards telecast. Shortly before he was scheduled to go on, however, Pavarotti developed a minor throat ailment, and his doctor advised him not to sing. Scrambling to keep the show on track, the producers turned to Aretha. She described the last-minute preparations: "There were eight minutes to go, and they ran upstairs with the boom box and a tape of the rehearsal Mr. Pavarotti had done that afternoon, so I could hear the arrangement of the orchestra. I knew the aria because earlier in the week I had performed it for him at the Waldorf. But I had crammed for it then, and when you cram, you kind of forget it. So I had to scramble to put the pieces together." The music for the telecast was in Pavarotti's key and, Aretha noted, "someone was kind enough to remind me that 1.5 billion people throughout the world would be watching."

Aretha came through with a transcendent performance. Soaking in the accolades from the world press, she savored her triumph: "I did it. I sang the aria and the ovation from my peers was wonderful. I sang Puccini because I love Puccini. It was God who gave me the gift of song, and it is God who keeps me strong in that gift." Encouraged to pursue her interest in opera and classical music, Aretha presented a concert of what she called "symphonic soul" that November with the Detroit Symphony Orchestra. The program included orchestrated versions of "Freeway of Love," "Angel," "Think," "It Hurts Like Hell," and "Why Do Fools Fall in Love?" as well as "Vissi d'arte" from Puccini's *Tosca*. Commercially positioned to release an album of operatic arias if she chose to do so, Aretha emphasized, "No matter how far I may venture into other genres, my heart remains in soul and the soul of my people."

Keeping that connection alive presented real challenges to both Aretha and Stevie as the millennium neared its end. Soul music had allowed singers to tap in to the driving energy of the freedom movement and broadcast it to the world. The connection between the singers and their communities, forged in churches, nightclubs, and the theaters of the chitlin circuit, wasn't abstract. In their teens and twenties Stevie and Aretha regularly sang for audiences that included a cross-section of black America and an increasing number of relatively ordinary whites. Changes in politics, the music industry, and the cultural meaning of celebrity began to loosen those bonds during the seventies and eighties. Although the streets and churches of black

America continued to produce new singers on both sides of the R&B/hip-hop divide, it became increasingly difficult for even the most determined stars to maintain contact with the roots of their art.

Neither Stevie nor Aretha really figured out how to handle the problem; at times it didn't seem that they realized it existed. Surrounded by people charged specifically with shielding them from the swarms of fans and attention-seekers, both grew increasingly idiosyncratic. At a major New York concert in her honor, Aretha insisted the air conditioning be shut off, leaving her fellow musicians and the audience to swelter in the closed-in summer heat. She suffered through major fallings-out with many old friends and fellow singers including Patti LaBelle, Gladys Knight, Whitney Houston, and Mavis Staples. When her long-awaited autobiography *Aretha: From These Roots,* written in collaboration with ace music writer David Ritz, finally appeared in 1999, few readers or reviewers felt that she had provided the kind of deep insights and revelations they had hoped for.

Meanwhile, Wonder solidified his reputation for marching to the beat of his own rhythm section. On the increasingly rare occasions when his staff agreed to let him talk with outsiders, he invariably failed to show up on schedule, sometimes keeping reporters waiting for days. Both Stevie and Aretha found their private lives dragged into the tabloids. Besieged by reports of unpaid bills, heavy drinking, and her children's legal difficulties, Aretha issued angry denials, filed several suits, and withdrew further into her protective cocoon. Although he maintained a much more positive public persona, Wonder was forced to counter accusations concerning his sexual behavior and was hit with a huge palimony suit.

On one level it was all simply part of the price they paid for their celebrity. On a deeper level, the constant buzz obscured Stevie's and Aretha's potential role as elders for the emerging musical generation. The concept of "elder" has never fit comfortably into a popular culture that from fifties rock 'n' roll to the self-proclaimed "hip-hop generation" has celebrated youth for its own sake. Popular music, in a sense, has always served as a generational marker for the young. But in a world where the quality of education provided by most urban school systems remained unspeakable and a quarter of black children went to bed hungry, the voices of the elders were desperately needed. As the nineties unfolded, there was reason to hope they might be heard.

Stevie's and Aretha's music was easily accessible, if often in forms that presented the singers as celebrities, icons, or oldies acts. As she had done since moving from Atlantic to Arista, Aretha sought out vocal partners and taped a television special consisting of duets with Gloria Estefan, George Michael, Bonnie Raitt, Smokey Robinson, Rod Stewart, and Elton John, who joined her at a double grand piano to sing "Border Song" and "Spirit in the Dark." Both Aretha and Stevie contributed to Frank Sinatra's duet albums, although neither was actually in the studio with him. Aretha contributed the British dance hit "A Deeper Love" (produced by Robert Clivilles and David Cole aka C&C Music) to the *Sister Act 2* soundtrack. She offered up a moving blues "It Hurts Like Hell" to the multiplatinum soundtrack for *Waiting to Exhale*, which amounted to a multigenerational summit conference of black women singers including Patti LaBelle, Toni Braxton, Mary J. Blige, Whitney Houston, Chaka Khan, Brandy, Chante Moore, and Faith Evans. At the 1997 Grammys Aretha performed a medley from the soundtrack along with Blige, Houston, Brandy, Khan, and CeCe Winans. Like Aretha, Wonder contributed material to several movies, most notably *Jungle Fever* (1991), the first of several collaborations with black filmmaker Spike Lee. Apart from "Lighting Up the Candles," which Wonder had introduced in 1984 at Marvin Gaye's funeral, the *Jungle Fever* soundtrack album consists of pleasant but unremarkable material from one of Lee's least satisfying movies. For some reason the best song from the actual soundtrack, "Feeding Off the Love of the Land," which plays over the closing credits, was left off the album.

BEGINNING WITH THE BRILLIANTLY realized box set of Aretha's Atlantic years, *Queen of Soul*, a confusing array of compilations and retrospectives arrived in the Stevie and Aretha sections of the record stores. In addition to *Queen of Soul*, the best of the Aretha collections were *Jazz to Soul*, an excellent winnowing of her Columbia material; *The Delta Meets Detroit: Aretha's Blues*, which highlights the bluesy side of her Atlantic material; and *Greatest Hits, 1980–1994*, a collection of most of her Arista hits along with four new songs, two produced by Kenny "Babyface" Edmonds. One of the Babyface cuts, "Willing to Forgive," reached number five on the R&B charts. Wonder released a comparable number of retrospectives, beginning with an excellent live album, *Natural Wonder*, recorded in Osaka, Japan, and Tel Aviv. Presenting Wonder and his band in full orchestral settings, *Natural Wonder* introduced four new songs, including the mesmerizing funk fusion jam "Dancing to the Rhythm." In 1996, Wonder released a double-CD greatest hits compilation, *Song Review*, followed in 1999 by a four-CD box set, *At the Close of a Century*, and in 2002 by a single volume *Stevie Wonder: The Definitive Collection*, which, despite its title, wasn't. The most valuable Wonder compilation, however, was probably *Stevie Wonder: Early Classics*, which complemented his hits from "Fingertips" through "I Was Made to Love Her" with some of the best cuts from his early albums.

While the Stevie and Aretha compilations ranged from excellent *(The Queen of Soul, Natural Wonder)* to redundant (the overlapping *Song Review* and *At the Close of a Century*), Rhino Records' refusal to let Curtis Mayfield's work slip into obscurity deserves special commendation. The three-volume compilation *People Get Ready! The Curtis Mayfield Story* provides a near-flawless overview of his career with an appropriate emphasis on the later, difficult-to-find material. In addition, Rhino released a series of single CDs focusing on specific periods *(The Very Best of the Impressions, The Very Best of Curtis Mayfield)* and styles (gospel, love songs), along with enhanced versions of *Curtis, Curtis/Live!, Roots,* and *Superfly*. Greatest hits albums by Gene Chandler and Major Lance, a compilation titled *Curtis Mayfield's Chicago Soul,* and a series of British anthologies, *The Class of Mayfield High, The Curtom Story,* and the Grammy-worthy *Impressed! 24 Groups Inspired by the Legendary Impressions and Curtis Mayfield,* made it possible for dedicated fans to experience something approaching the fullness of Mayfield's genius.

The most significant recovery of Mayfield's music, however, took place in Spike Lee's film on the Million Man March, *Get on the Bus,* which uses four Mayfield songs—"People Get Ready," "New World Order," "We're a Winner," and "Keep On Pushing"—to open a cross-generational dialogue on the contemporary meaning of the gospel vision. The movie reaches its climax when a group of black men gather at the Lincoln Memorial in the shadow of the Great Emancipator. While Lee's camera explores their thoughtful faces, the music reminds us of the ancestors for whom the promise of equality before the law sometimes must have seemed an unattainable dream. It spoke volumes that for Lee, a cultural icon of the hip-hop generation, Mayfield's ancestral wisdom continued to point the way: "I've got my strength and it don't make sense not to keep on pushing."

During the first years of the new century, a growing group of African American intellectuals, including Bakari Kitwana and Todd Boyle, argued that the values and vision of the hip-hop generation represented a departure from, and to a lesser extent a repudiation of, the civil rights agenda. Still, there were signs that the hip-hop generation of the new millennium would be more responsive to the gospel vision than its immediate predecessors in the eighties and nineties. Drawing liberally on the music and message of the elders, the Fugees, the Roots, Common, Goodie Mob, Outkast, and gangsta-turned-ghetto-philosopher Scarface engaged in a dynamic call and response on the age-old questions at the heart of gospel and the blues. Many of the conscious rappers' best cuts drew their power from samples taken from the music of Stevie Wonder, Donny Hathaway, Curtis Mayfield, and Earth, Wind & Fire. Far from providing evidence of the collective failure of the African American musical imagination, then, hip-hop sampling encouraged communion with the spirits of the elders. When Outkast invited the movement to get crunk on "Rosa Parks" and Goodie Mob kicked off its brilliant *Soul Food* album with a gospel moan called "Free," they were embarking on some of those paths. "Hush" by Mississippi rapper Afroman, best known for his tragicomic hip-hop blues "Because I Got High," was a stunning example of the potential for cross-generational spiritual calls and responses. Speaking from the heart of the region that had given rise to the gospel vision that powered the movement, Afroman communed with the spirit of his grandfather and heard the voice of Jesus whispering that, someday, everything would be all right.

Frequently, hip-hop producers in search of spiritually resonant samples turned to Stevie Wonder and Curtis Mayfield. Two huge hip-hop hits, Will Smith's "Wild Wild West" and Coolio's "Gangsta's Paradise," clearly owed their success to samples from *Songs in the Key of Life*. Like "I Wish," "Wild Wild West" tapped in to the good-time summertime energy with a bit of nonthreatening social commentary mixed in for those who cared to hear it. Organized around a sample from "Pastime Paradise," Coolio's near-remake took a more serious approach to the situation in black America. Refusing to limit his awareness to the violence and confusion surrounding him on the street, Coolio traced the problem to a collective amnesia that cuts off contact with the past. Stevie's cut fades out with a haunting chorus of "We Shall Overcome," which remains just barely audible in Coolio's response.

Mayfield played an even more prominent role in the conversations between the hip-hop and the civil rights generations. "We're a Winner,"

"(Don't Worry) If There's a Hell Below We're All Gonna Go," "Freddie's Dead," "Pusherman," "Superfly," and "Right On for the Darkness" echo through dozens of cuts by artists representing every corner of the hip-hop nation. A partial list includes old-schoolers Biz Markie, Big Daddy Kane, L.L. Cool J, and Stetsonic; West Coast O.G.s Ice-T, N.W.A., and Above the Law; white rappers the Beastie Boys and Eminem; R&B crossovers Mary J. Blige and R. Kelly; as well as Too Short, the Geto Boys, Digable Planets, Snoop Dogg, Jay-Z, M C Hammer, De La Soul, Craig Mack, Brand Nubian, Gang Starr, and Eric B. and Rakim. It's probably simpler to list the acts who didn't sample Mayfield. His manager, Marv Heiman, emphasized that samples increase awareness of Mayfield's own music. "It's not even the financial thing that matters most. More important to me is that his name doesn't die out," he noted. "Maybe a lot of kids don't read credits on an album, but the ones who do say, 'Hey, Snoop Dogg sampled Curtis Mayfield. I like that cut. And oh, Tupac sampled Curtis Mayfield. Who the hell is Curtis Mayfield? Maybe I ought to go into a record shop and see if I can buy something on him.' "

Mayfield believed the rappers' interest in his music reflected basic human needs that didn't change from era to era. "I don't see any great differences between what people are expressing now and what we used to do," he commented. "There's observations on contemporary goings-on, personal freedoms, civil rights, and discriminations of minorities. Then of course, there's always love, the ins and outs and movements and the happenings of love." As both a parent and an elder, he sometimes worried about the violence in hip-hop, but he trusted his children to come to their understanding of the harsh aspects of reality, as he had done himself. "When we were children, we knew there was room for the future, to pursue all the beautiful dreams of love and happiness," he reflected. "Let's face it, that's not promised today. They see a weird jungle in the streets. It makes them have to live in the present. 'Now! I have to have it now. Give it to me now.' But the children understand the difference and still can be obedient and good. We sometimes forget their own ability to lay back and say no or 'Hey, I'm not into this.' "

∽◉∾

ARETHA'S MUSICAL CONVERSATION WITH the younger generation took a different, but equally significant, form. While hip-hop DJs rarely sampled her work, she provided inspiration and a creative role model for the parade of young female singers who dominated the charts from the mid-nineties on. Some of them were African American and a few were "white," but many were hard to file away in a clearly labeled racial box. Inspired by Aretha's musical daughters Whitney Houston, Natalie Cole, and the undervalued R&B singer-songwriter Jody Watley, Aretha's spiritual granddaughters quietly reintegrated the pop music charts during the Clinton years. Stylistically, the new R&B varied from Mariah Carey's pop confections and Faith Evans's gospel love songs to the streetwise hip-hop fusions of Mary J. Blige and the gospel-meets-the-girl-groups fusion of Mary Mary.

The impact of the church-trained singers both reflected and contributed to a resurgence in gospel music. Gospel had never gone away, of course, but from the mid-seventies on, it had rarely made a direct impact on the pop charts, and its political statements were heard almost solely by a churchgoing African American audience. Summoning memories of Sam Cooke, Kirk Franklin emerged as the most powerful force in gospel's reengagement with black secular music. Incorporating hip-hop beats and R&B production techniques into his gospel compositions, Franklin used his Gospocentric label to help reopen a crossover market that had been closed for the better part of two decades.

On the secular side of the black music scene, R. Kelly played a role roughly equivalent to Kirk Franklin's in gospel. Although Kelly's marketing team usually presented him as a cross between a thug and a blaxploitation lover man, his musical identity was pure gospel soul. When Kelly finished with the gangsta posing and bedroom boasting that scared most of the older generation away from his albums, he revealed himself as a sensitive storyteller who understood the connection between the romantic and spiritual quests. Beginning with his duet with Sparkle on "Be Careful," Kelly produced a sequence of male-female dialogue songs ("When a Woman's Fed Up," "Reality") in which he challenges both parties to accept responsibility for their actions. In "Bad Man" and the heartrending eulogy for a fallen homie, "I Wish," Kelly assumes the robes of a kind of street psalmist, tracking a self-reflective sinner as he wanders the moral wilderness. Raising his eyes above the tormented streets to the spiritual sphere, Kelly composed a set of gospel soul anthems that appeal to both sacred and secular audiences. "I Believe I Can Fly," "Storm Is Over Now," and "The Greatest" will be sung by church choirs and middle-school vocal ensembles long after Kelly's reprehensible tabloid exploits have faded into musical trivia.

Fortunately, many musicians who came of age in the late nineties heard the call and responded by forging a neo-soul movement that turned to the elders for inspiration and guidance. One of the most compelling of the neo-soul artists, India Arie, made the point explicit when she dedicated the first track on her *Acoustic Soul* album to the "remembrance of our ancestors." Invoking Sam Cooke, Marvin Gaye, and Donny Hathaway, she concluded with "You opened up a door, because of you a change gonna come." A second invocation midway through the album expands the list to include a pantheon of jazz and blues musicians, including Arie's female predecessors from Ma Rainey and Memphis Minnie on. The bonus track on the album, "Wonderful," a montage of lyrics and titles from Stevie Wonder's songbook, makes it clear Arie recognizes the elders as ancestors-in-training. The neo-soul singers' gentleness was both a strength and a weakness. A modern equivalent of Sam Cooke's crossover strategy, their smoothly soulful tones and laid-back beats helped define the neo-soul sound. At the same time the restraint sometimes seemed to mark a generational inability to really cut loose with a scream of anger, pain, or rage. Arie, Angie Stone, D'Angelo, and R. Kelly certainly knew the pain was there, and they dealt with it in their own quiet way. Unlike Aretha and Stevie, however, they rarely let their voices swoop and dive on the wings of the spirit.

One of the most talented musicians contributing to the hip-hop-gospel-R&B hybrids, Lauryn Hill understood the point. Rejecting the highly polished studio styles that had characterized black popular music since the eighties, she cast her music as a direct response to the emotional depth of gospel soul: "Look at someone like Aretha. She didn't hit with her first album, but she was able to grow up and find herself. I want to make honest music. I don't like things to be too perfect, too polished. People may criticize me for that, but I grew up listening to singers like Al Green and Sam Cooke. When they hit a high note, you really felt it."

So it made sense that Hill would help Aretha connect with an audience that knew her mostly through oldies radio and their parents' record collections. Hill had a firm grasp on what was happening musically and an equally clear idea of the political changes she wanted to help sing into being. First as a member of the Fugees and then as a solo artist, she paid homage to her elders, invoking Nina Simone as the antidote to gangsta misogyny and releasing the first classic gospel hip-hop album, *The Miseducation of Lauryn Hill,* the nineties' closest equivalent to *Songs in the Key of Life.* The only reason Stevie Wonder didn't write "Every Ghetto Every City" was that Lauryn beat him to it. As a child, Hill had been immersed in soul music via her mother's record collection. From the start she sensed the connection between music and politics: "Our podium, what we have to speak from, is the music. It's really important that we stay focused, because things become misconstrued in the media. So we have to stick firm to who we are, and stand our ground musically. We have to make sure the music and the message and the words and all the elements come through in our songs and every time we appear in public. A lot of us are too busy focusing on what we think people want to hear, as opposed to just saying what's in our hearts."

When Hill approached Aretha about recording her song "A Rose Is Still a Rose," the timing was ideal. About to re-sign with Arista, Aretha was seeking fresh material and a new approach for her first album in over five years. Aware that Aretha had never worked with a hip-hop producer, Hill anticipated a period of adjustment. But when she arrived in Detroit with her mother and infant son, Zion, she was pleasantly surprised. "The rhythm, the syncopation is definitely hip-hop," Hill observed. "I expected to have to really go through it with her. But she took the demo version, came in the studio, and it was done." Expressing her satisfaction with Hill's conscientious grasp of detail and positive attitude, Aretha praised her as "a young woman who knows what she wants; she's responsible and long on patience." An ideal vehicle for the cross-generational collaboration, "A Rose Is Still a Rose" presents an older woman's advice to a girl facing the end of a bad relationship. Aretha knew the story all too well. Responding beautifully to Hill's syncopated rhythms, Aretha's voice infuses the encouraging lyrics with sympathy and conviction. However battered she might feel, Aretha counseled, the young woman would go on to survive and bloom as long as she held on to the sources of her power, in herself and her God. "The song is about inner beauty," Aretha reflected, "women understanding that the deepest validation comes from God."

"A Rose Is Still a Rose" was an ideal opening number for Aretha's set when she joined Mariah Carey, Celine Dion, Gloria Estefan, and Shania Twain on VH1's *Divas Live* show from the Beacon Theater in New York City in April 1998. While Aretha enjoyed sharing the spotlight with the young stars, she viewed the "diva" label with amusement. Aretha preferred to reserve the title for the "real divas, ladies like Sarah Vaughan, Ella Fitzgerald, Judy Garland," along with her personal inspirations Clara Ward, Dinah Washington, Shirley Caesar, and the "supreme diva" Josephine Baker. By any standard Aretha had earned a place in their legendary company, and her performance on *Divas Live* dispelled any doubts about whether she was still the Queen. Throughout her set Aretha demonstrated that when she cut loose or dove down deep, no one could come close to matching her. In addition to her current hits "A Rose Is Still a Rose" and "Here We Go Again," Aretha welcomed Carole King for a duet on "A Natural Woman" and Mariah Carey, who mostly watched in awe as Aretha ripped through "Think." Along with the ensemble finale on the gospel standard "Testimony," "Think" made it clear that while the young divas might have surpassed Aretha as pop hit-makers, they had a lot—a whole lot—to learn from her about singing. Gracious in her triumph, Aretha reflected happily that it had been a pleasure to end the evening with a taste of "old-fashioned down-home, romping and stomping gospel."

The *Divas Live* performance followed the release of Aretha's second major comeback album, *A Rose Is Still a Rose*. (Depending on your criteria, the first had been either *Jump to It* or *Who's Zoomin' Who?*) The title song introduced the central concerns of one of Aretha's most female-centered albums. Working with many of the hottest producers remapping the border between hip-hop and R&B, Aretha revisited the disappointment and determination that had defined her life from her teenage pregnancies through her failed marriages. The sound had changed, but the themes and the vocal intensity remained the same. The affirmation of "Never Leave You Again" (produced by Sean "Puff Daddy" Combs) and the dreamy romanticism of "In the Morning" run up against the world-weary realism of "Here We Go Again" and "Every Lil' Bit Hurts" (both produced by Jermaine DuPri). Picking up the pieces and putting them together in a mosaic that expressed both the joy and the pain, "Watch My Back" and the final cut on the album, Aretha's own composition "The Woman," assure her musical daughters that, while the road will surely be hard, they have the strength within them to survive.

A Rose Is Still a Rose was the third in a series of messages from the elders that began with Wonder's *Conversation Peace* and Mayfield's *New World Order.* Together the albums amounted to a trilogy on the basic themes of the gospel vision. Wonder wrote many of the songs on *Conversation Peace* on an extended trip to Ghana in 1993. Mixing equal measures of political anger and spiritual uplift, Wonder brought a needed sense of balance to the musical mix just as rap and R&B began to reconcile their longstanding differences. Rage and redemptive love, he reminded his listeners, were equally necessary responses to the same world.

Jettisoning the mechanical percussion sound that had marred much of his work since *Hotter than July, Conversation Peace* was Wonder's strongest and most coherent album since *Songs in the Key of Life.* The album consists of three sequences: the first five songs focus on the various dimensions of redemptive love; the next five reconsider that ideal in relation to a world of random and senseless violence; and the final three reflect on the consequences of failing to heed the redemptive call. Picking up the central themes of his work since "Heaven Help Us All," the first sequence reiterates the connections between sexual, romantic, social, and spiritual love. Following the inspirational overture, "Rain Your Love Down," Wonder defines the album's conceptual center in "Edge of Eternity." "A really heavy union between two lovers can be a link to God just as surely as a monk praying in a monastery," he reflected. While his description echoed the mystical trappings of *Journey Through the Secret Life of Plants* and *In Square Circle,* the funky rhythms and appealing melodies of "Rain Your Love Down" and "Take the Time Out" had more in common with *Talking Book.*

Following a deceptively upbeat polyrhythmic opening, "My Love Is with You" shatters the mood. Intended both as eulogy for the innocent victims of street violence and a statement in support of gun control, the song recalls the ferocity of the second verse of "As" and redefines the emotional impact of the next four "love songs": "Treat Myself," "Tomorrow Robins Will Sing," the sultry "Sensuous Whisper" with a lovely backing vocal from Anita Baker, and "For Your Love," the latest addition to Wonder's collection of classic ballads. In a world where meaningless violence can take it all away in an instant, focusing on personal connection seems less like romantic naïveté than a realistic refusal to surrender.

The final sequence of *Conversation Peace* reiterates the reality of the threat. As he had done so often, Wonder tuned in to the half-conscious hopes and fears that defined the moment. Taking personal stories and transforming them into social metaphors, "Cold Chill" and "Sorry" communicate a deep sense of foreboding and regret that sets the stage for his concluding tour de force, "Conversation Peace." Without "My Love Is with You," "Cold Chill," and "Sorry," the song might have seemed like a sermon left over from the *In Square Circle* sessions. Heard as a response to the political lives of ordinary people, it rings true. The lyrics restate Wonder's longstanding concern with the many dimensions of human suffering—the Holocaust, Middle Passage, ethnic cleansing—and his belief in Christ's resurrection as the path to salvation. As always in Wonder's most effective songs, however, the sound communicates as much as the lyrics. The gospel call and response between Wonder and Sounds of Blackness, who provide the backup vocals, builds up to the concluding montage of voices offering the phrase "Conversation Peace" as a mantra for a world in need.

Curtis Mayfield's contribution to the elders' deep soul trilogy, *New World Order*, elicits a real sense of wonder. That's a dangerous word, hard to take without irony. But it's the right word. The creation of *New World Order* serves as a testament to advances in studio technology. Mayfield's health made it hard for him to sing more than a couple of lines at a time. Throughout most of the recording sessions he lay on his back to conserve energy. Nonetheless, he felt the album represented his true voice. "Mostly what I had to change was that I don't have the ability to sing the high falsetto nor do I have strength to really sing a song on stage as a performer," he said. The producers' collective mastery of sophisticated techniques for "punching in"—combining lines recorded at different times—leaves no audible evidence of the way the songs were recorded. Mayfield appreciated the advances in recording technology since he was last in the studio. "Two of the songs Roger Troutman did with me, he came right into my house with a little box of a console and a hard drive and I sang the two songs in bed. He ran it right in here into my speakers. I didn't have to move, he put a mike in front of me and I sang 'We People Who Are Darker than Blue' right here."

As consistent as any of Mayfield's previous albums—and it's only fair to remember that consistency was never the hallmark of an artist who created so much for himself and others—*New World Order* circles back to the clear-sighted gospel soul of the mid-sixties Impressions. Obviously written with his physical condition in mind, "Back to Living Again" spoke equally to the political needs of black America as it sought to renew its sense of purpose in the aftermath of Reaganism. "The Got Dang Song," "Ms. Martha," and the soulful remake of "We the People Who Are Darker than Blue" grapple with the continuing realities of poverty and despair. But images of rebirth resonate throughout the album, most notably in the title song. Happy with *New World Order* as a direct expression of his real voice, Mayfield viewed it as a reaffirmation of the faith that carried him through good times and bad: "Lyrically, my philosophy hasn't changed. The concept of peace, love, get it together, and maybe there'll be a new world order."

Mayfield was particularly happy with the way the album merged classic soul and contemporary sounds. "Fusing elements of hip-hop on this CD was not so much a concession to the times, as much as it was a connection to the times," he observed. "We all have to grow. You have to stay true to yourself while recognizing and acknowledging what's going on now." The album's contemporary feel results in part from the contributions of its coproducers, including Organized Noize, best known for their work with TLC, Roger Troutman, the guiding spirit of the eighties funk group Zapp, Narada Michael Walden, and hip-hop pioneer Daryl Simmons, whom Mayfield credited with convincing him to return to the studio. "Fortunately we had a lot of the young people who always admired my work," he said, "so they could put music together that was of the nineties and all I needed to do was just lay my signature down. They're all great producers and have great ideas but they were all very kind and always left the parts for Curtis."

On the soul side, guest appearances by Aretha and Mavis Staples deepened the spiritual feel, especially on "Ms. Martha," a bluesy response to the gospel standard "Mary Don't You Weep." After the sessions Mavis announced that she was trying to convince Curtis to go on the road despite his injuries. "Prince can have a big old bed up there on stage," she observed. "Why not Curtis?" More seriously, Mavis expressed her joy over Mayfield's ability to maintain his spiritual mind in the face of his burdens: "Curtis is so unique. There's a beauty about him, an angelic state. Everything he wrote had a whole lot of love. Curtis has influenced so many of these young people with his music and his guitar playing. Can't nobody play it like Curtis. Curtis's guitar will make you move. It's so soulful. Curtis is just one strong individual. You know his heart's got to be right with the Lord for him to be able to deal with what's happened. And he still has his sense of humor. His music is healing, that's the fact. He's just a great great person, and I love him and I always will love him."

Mayfield sensed his 1996 album, *New World Order*, would be his last: "At this point in my life I'm just glad that I was able to do it. That's not to say I might not do a little something with someone else. But I've been doing this since I was seven, professionally since I was fifteen. I turned sixteen in the Apollo Theater. I'm a fighter, but it's best at this point to go on and retire and be appreciated for whatever you have done. As I sum it up, I just want folks to say he didn't do bad with his life in inspiring others." Curtis Mayfield died the day after Christmas 1999.

Ancestors live in the voices and lives of their descendants.
Monuments command awe, but rarely matter.

As the new millennium began with a disputed presidential election and the horrifying attack on the World Trade Center and the Pentagon, those who remembered the way the gospel vision had shaped American life in the sixties and seventies struggled to keep the music that gave it voice from slipping into nostalgic inertia. It certainly wasn't that Stevie Wonder or Aretha Franklin slipped into the obscurity that Curtis Mayfield had lived through in the eighties. Even the new Republican president validated his baby boomer credentials by turning out to see Stevie Wonder, and the accolades continued to flow as they had during the Clinton administration. Black Entertainment Television aired a three-hour black-tie gala celebrating Wonder's enshrinement on the network's Walk of Fame. Before treating the audience with "I Can't Imagine Love Without" from his much-delayed new album, Wonder pointedly questioned the looming war in the Middle East and issued a moving plea for renewed commitment to community uplift. But despite the presence of neo-soul acolytes India Arie, Jill Scott, and Musiq, the evening felt more like a valediction than a call to arms.

Wonder joined Lauryn Hill, Eric Clapton, and the surviving members of the Impressions, Fred Cash and Sam Gooden, to celebrate Mayfield's legacy at the First African Methodist Episcopal Church in Los Angeles on

February 23, 2000. The First AME Freedom Choir backed the stars in joyous renditions of Mayfield classics including "Choice of Colors," "I've Been Trying," "I'm So Proud," "People Get Ready," and Hill's soulful recovery of "The Makings of You." Wonder added an affectionate version of "Gypsy Woman," which had captivated him as a child huddled by the radio in his ghetto bedroom. After Clapton joined the Impressions for "We're a Winner," Hill and Wonder returned for a euphoric version of "It's All Right" that shook the rafters. "I sort of went out there a bit"—Wonder smiled—"I was getting into it. But how can you sing it any better than Curtis did?" First AME pastor Steven Johnson delivered the closing eulogy, basing his words on what he called "the gospel according to Mayfield." "It's all right!" he shouted. "I've got to keep on pushing, I can't stop now."

At other moments, however, it seemed like the mass media could reduce even the most stirring event to a nostalgic sideshow in the celebrity circus. A striking example came following the fourth VH1 *Divas Live* special, "A Tribute to Aretha Franklin." On April 12, 2001, a star-studded audience and a cast of performers from all corners of the musical world gathered at Radio City Music Hall to reaffirm Aretha's place in the pantheon. Backed by a jazz ensemble headed by James Carter, Herbie Hancock, and Clark Terry, Aretha sang with the surviving members of the Ward Singers, Bishop Paul S. Morton Sr. of the Greater St. Stephen Full Gospel Baptist Church Ministries, a few of the Backstreet Boys, Caucasian rock rapper Kid Rock, Jill Scott, and Aretha's Cuban counterpart, the great Celiz Cruz. Mary J. Blige, who like Aretha had grown up in the unforgiving gaze of the public eye and whom many viewed as her heiress apparent, joined Aretha for a moving duet on "Do Right Woman—Do Right Man." When Stevie Wonder took the stage for the encore, he was greeted by a round of thunderous applause. After the taping ended, Aretha and Stevie stayed onstage for a medley of Ward Singers classics. More than half the audience filed out. Apparently they were interested in the hits, not the story.

Wonder had drawn attention to the underlying problem in the two songs he contributed to the soundtrack of Spike Lee's searing satire *Bamboozled*. Where Lee unleashed a ferocious barrage of images from America's violent and unreconciled racial subconscious, Wonder encouraged the younger generation to reflect seriously on the call embedded in the surreal nightmare. "Some Years Ago" reminded those who had benefited from the movement of the time when black people had "more hope than money." Musing over the movement's unrealized potential, Wonder meditates on the paths untaken, the ones leading to a world in which even those with wealth and power take the gospel vision seriously. More effective musically than "Some Years Ago," "Misrepresented People" identifies the first step toward reconstructing the movement. Restating the message of Black Power 101, Wonder exhorts his people to take control of their story, beginning with the stories they tell themselves about themselves when the white folks aren't around. "Where do those images come from?" Wonder muses. "How can we change them?" Unless you've got a decent image of yourself to work with, none of the rest matters. That's why the gospel vision insists that redemption begins at home. As both "Some Years Ago" and "Misrepresented People" suggest, the problem at the dawn of the new century was that most of us had forgotten what it felt like to really believe a change was still gonna come.

Change came to the United States on September 11, 2001. The portraits of the dead reflected the reality of twenty-first-century America. Black, brown, red, white, and yellow came together in shock, grief, and an anger that wasn't easy to direct or control. Ten days after the fall of the towers, with fires still burning and haunting images filling the media and our minds, all of the major television networks and dozens of cable outlets turned to music to help work through the anger and grief. Young divas and country singers joined rockers and rappers on the *America: A Tribute to Heroes* special to raise a collective voice of sorrow and survival.

Sorrow and survival had been defining elements of Stevie's, Aretha's, and Curtis's lives. Their lives and music told a story not of revenge but of redemption. Each had lived through experiences that would have crushed most people: Aretha's teenage pregnancies, Stevie's blindness and near-fatal auto accident, Curtis's paralysis. Drawing strength from the spirit and from their ever-shifting communities, they transformed tragedy into some of the most deeply democratic art the tormented republic has ever known. Each had turned to music in times of trouble, and holding to the gospel vision, each transformed personal misfortune into redemptive art. Resonating with the hope and hardships of the community that had supported them in times of need, their music powered the civil rights movement as it demanded the end of Jim Crow; it meditated on the meaning of Black Power, and it lamented the dimming of the dream. At every turn it kept faith with the gospel vision, and reminded us that it was a healing way of life, not a rigid set of rules.

As the war drums began to pound, it was a desperately needed call, and it sounded throughout the *Tribute to Heroes*. Although only Stevie Wonder was there in person, the spirits of Aretha and Curtis were equally present. Aretha's fear of flying, no doubt intensified by what had happened, kept her from participating in the *Tribute to Heroes* concert herself, but her vision echoed through musical granddaughter Alicia Keyes's soulful version of Donny Hathaway's "Someday We'll All Be Free" and Paul Simon's meditative "Bridge Over Troubled Water." Curtis Mayfield's voice and vision whispered through the chords and chorus of Bruce Springsteen's "My City of Ruins" with its call to "rise up" in renewed faith and dedication. A year later Springsteen used the song to conclude his blue-eyed gospel masterpiece, *The Rising*. When Springsteen toured in support of the album, the highlights included his Sam Cooke tribute "Meet Me at Mary's Place" and "Lonesome Day," which built up to a chorus of "It's all right"s. When he ended the concert with a verse from "People Get Ready," he was simply acknowledging the debt to the gospel vision that his music had been paying all along.

Stevie Wonder followed Springsteen at the *Heroes* concert with a version of "Love's in Need of Love Today" that summed up the meaning of the gospel vision in the post-9/11 world. Heard against the president's insistence that the attack on the World Trade Center was an attack on "freedom," his performance with the gospel group Take 6 conjured memories of the centuries-long struggle to make freedom real. Aware that the battle had not been won, Wonder cried out that the hate had already gone too far, that there had to be a better way. Even as the fires burned at Ground Zero and in our souls, he challenged all of us to look a brutal history in the eye and to keep on pushing until we reach the higher ground. If we hold to the gospel vision, we might yet, against all odds, begin to live the life we sang about in our song.

A NOTE ON SOURCES

Aretha Franklin

The primary sources of biographical information concerning Aretha are her auto-biography, *Aretha: From These Roots* (New York: Villard, 1999), written in collaboration with the premier autobiographer David Ritz; and two celebrity biographies: Mark Bego, *Aretha Franklin: Queen of Soul*, rev. ed. (New York: Da Capo, 2001); and Leslie Gourse, *Aretha Franklin: Lady Soul* (New York: Franklin Watts, 1995). The video *The Queen of Soul*, beautifully scripted by Nelson George, captures the core of Aretha's career better than any other source. Several overviews of soul music history include substantive interviews with Aretha, among them David Nathan, *The Soulful Divas* (New York: Billboard Books, 1999); Phyl Garland, *The Sound of Soul* (Chicago: Henry Regnery, 1969); and Gerri Hirshey, *Nowhere to Run: The Sound of Soul Music* (New York: Penguin, 1984). Both Bego and Gourse make extensive use of two well-known inter-views with Aretha: James T. Jones IV, "Soul of the Queen," *Vanity Fair* (Mar. 1994); and Clarence Walden, "Aretha Franklin Talks About: Being a Diva, Battle with Weight," *Jet* (May 1998).

Stevie Wonder

The best sources of information on Stevie are the celebrity biographies by Constanze Elsner, *Stevie Wonder* (New York: Popular Library, 1977), and John Swenson, *Stevie Wonder* (New York: Harper and Row, 1986). I have also made use of James Haskins, *The Stevie Wonder Story* (New York: Dell, 1979); and Martin E. Horn, *Innervisions: The Music of Stevie Wonder* (Bloomington, Ind.: 1st Books, 2000). Two books by people close to Stevie provide glimpses of his personal life, especially during his early years: Dennis Love and Stacy Brown, *Blind Faith: The Miraculous Journey of Lula Hardaway, Stevie Wonder's Mother* (New York: Simon and Schuster, 2002); and Ted Hull with Paul Stahel, *The Wonder Years: My Life and Times with Stevie Wonder* (Booklocker.com, 2002), which was published too late for me to make use of in this book. Several books on Motown give extensive attention to Stevie, among them Nelson George, *Where Did Our Love Go? The Rise and Fall of the Motown Sound* (New York: St. Martin's, 1985); Bill Dahl, *Motown: The Golden Years* (Iola, Wis.: Krause, 2001); and Peter Benjaminson, *The Story of Motown* (New York: Grove Press, 1979). Both Elsner and Swenson rely largely on published interviews with Stevie, the most important of which is, without question, Ben Fong-

Torres, "The Formerly Little Stevie Wonder" *Rolling Stone* (Apr. 26, 1973), reprinted in *Not Fade Away* (San Francisco: Miller Freeman Books, 1999). Other useful or frequently cited interviews include O'Connell Driscoll, "Stevie Wonder in New York," in Jann Wenner, ed., *20 Years of Rolling Stone: What a Long Strange Trip It's Been* (New York: Straight Arrow, 1987); Sue Clark, "Stevie Wonder Gets Good and Pissed," *Rolling Stone* (Sept. 30, 1971); O'Connell Driscoll, "Growing Up Stevie Wonder," *Rolling Stone* (June 19, 1975); Ellen Willis, "The Importance of Being Stevie Wonder," *New Yorker* (Dec. 30, 1974); Giles Smith, "Realms of Wonder," *New Yorker* (Mar. 13, 1995); Michael Goldberg, "The Timeless World of Wonder," *Rolling Stone* (Apr. 10, 1986); Ed Ward, "Jamaican 'Dream' Show: Will Wonder Never Cease," *Rolling Stone* (Nov. 20, 1975); "Stevie Wonder Discusses Car Crash," *Rolling Stone* (Sept. 27, 1973); and Stuart Werbin, "Stevie Wonder's Auto Accident: He's Recovering," *Rolling Stone* (Sept. 13, 1973).

Curtis Mayfield

All historians of Chicago soul music are profoundly indebted to Robert Pruter's *Chicago Soul* (Urbana: University of Illinois Press, 1991) and *Doowop: The Chicago Scene* (Urbana: University of Illinois Press, 1996). There has been no in-depth biographical study focused on Mayfield or the Impressions, but the liner notes to Rhino Records' box set *People Get Ready! The Curtis Mayfield Story* include a helpful compilation of quotations by and about Mayfield. Useful interviews include my own "Curtis Mayfield," *Goldmine* (July 4, 1997), reprinted in *Classic Rock Digest* (Iola, Wis.: Krause, 1998); Robert Gordon, "The Original Superfly Guy," *Q* (July 1993); Alan Light, "A Lasting Impression: The *Rolling Stone* Interview with Curtis Mayfield," *Rolling Stone* (Oct. 28, 1993); and Chris Salewicz, "Keep On Pushing: Curtis Mayfield," Rock's Backpages.com.

Reference Works

The indispensable sources of data concerning the record charts are the books compiled by Joel Whitburn: *Top Pop Singles 1955–1993* (Menominee Falls, Wis.: Record Research, 1994); *Top Pop Albums 1955–1996* (Menominee Falls, Wis.: Record Research, 1997); *Top R&B Singles 1942–1999* (Menominee Falls, Wis.: Record Research, 2000); and *Top R&B Albums 1965–1998* (Menominee Falls, Wis.: Record Research, 1999). The most reliable source of biographical details on popular musicians is Dafydd Rees and Luke Crampton, *VH1 Music First Encyclopedia: Rock Stars* (New York: DK Publishing, 1999).

Historical Contexts

The portrait of Chicago and Detroit in this book is deeply indebted to two brilliant works of urban history: Thomas J. Sugrue, *The Origins of the Urban Crisis: Race and Inequality in Postwar Detroit* (Princeton, N.J.: Princeton University Press, 1996); and Arnold R. Hirsch,

Making the Second Ghetto: Race and Housing in Chicago 1940–1960 (Chicago: University of Chicago Press, 1998). Adam Cohen and Elizabeth Taylor, *American Pharaoh: Mayor Richard J. Daley, His Battle for Chicago and the Nation* (Boston: Little, Brown, 2000), complements Hirsch's incisive analysis of race in Chicago by means of a compelling narrative biography of the elder Richard Daley. I have also benefited from Wilbur C. Rich's *Coleman Young and Detroit Politics* (Detroit: Wayne State University Press, 1989). My understanding of the civil rights movement in the North was aided greatly by Patrick Jones's dissertation, *The Selma of the North: Race and Politics in Milwaukee,* forthcoming from Harvard University Press.

Interviews

Joanne Bland, Oct. 2002, Madison, Wis.

Jerry Butler, Mar. 2001, Chicago, Ill.

Dave Marsh, May 2002, New York City

Curtis Mayfield, Apr. 1997, Atlanta, Ga.

Johnny Meadows, Feb. 2002, Chicago, Ill.

Gordon Sellers, Oct. 2002, Madison, Wis.

Mavis Staples, June 1997, Chicago, Ill.

Eddie Thomas, Feb. 2002, Chicago, Ill.

Ernest Withers, Apr. 2002, Madison, Wis.

Bobby Womack, Aug. 1999, Los Angeles, Calif.

NOTES

In the cases of Aretha Franklin and Stevie Wonder, much of the material included in reference works and celebrity biographies has been drawn from official Motown press releases and widely quoted interviews. When I have quoted interview material from a biography listed in "A Note on Sources," the citation refers to that relatively easily available source. When a quotation from an individual listed in the "Interviews" section has no citation here, it comes from a personal conversation with me.

Introduction
"Moving On Up"

2 **"You heard her three or four times . . . ,"** quoted in Ann Powers, "Aretha Franklin," in *The Rolling Stone Book of Women in Rock,* ed. Barbara O'Dair (New York: Random House, 1997), p. 93.

7 **"an impulse to keep . . . ,"** Ralph Ellison, *Shadow and Act* (New York: Random House, 1964), pp. 78–79.

7 **"the most fundamental of existential . . . ,"** Albert Murray, *The Hero and the Blues* (Columbia: University of Missouri Press, 1973), p. 38.

8 **"It's just like being in church . . . ,"** *Queen of Soul* video.

9 **"Gospel and the blues . . . ,"** quoted in liner notes to *Ray Charles: The Birth of Soul* (Atlantic Records).

10 **"For, while the tale of how . . . ,"** James Baldwin, "Sonny's Blues," in *James Baldwin: Early Novels and Stories* (New York: Library of America, 1998), p. 892.

Chapter One
"There Is a Fountain Filled with Blood"

16 **"taught me things . . . ,"** Gerri Hirshey, *Nowhere to Run: The Sound of Soul Music* (New York: Penguin, 1989), p. 231.

16 **"somebody would start . . . ,"** Mark Bego, *Aretha Franklin: Queen of Soul,* rev. ed. (New York: Da Capo, 2001), p. 15.

18 **"A voice spoke . . . ,"** Bill McGraw, "Style to Spare," *Michigan History* (Nov.–Dec. 2000), p. 73.

18 **"I was young . . . ,"** David Nathan, *The Soulful Divas* (New York: Billboard Books, 1999), p. 73.

19 **"Aretha's mother . . . ,"** Bego, *Queen of Soul,* p. 12.

19 **"People loved her . . . ,"** C.L. Franklin, *Give Me This Mountain: Life History and Selected Sermons,* ed. Jeff Todd Titon (Urbana: University of Illinois Press, 1989), p. 23.

19 **"for a black boy . . . ,"** Ernest Withers, personal interview, Feb. 2002.

20 **"A young black man . . . ,"** Timothy Tyson, *Radio Free Dixie* (Chapel Hill: University of North Carolina Press, 2000), pp. 41–42.

21 **"On weekends the traffic . . . ,"** Lars Bjorn with Jim Gallert, *Before Motown: A History of Jazz in Detroit, 1920–1960* (Ann Arbor: University of Michigan Press, 2001), p. 72.

22 **"No longer is the Valley . . . ,"** ibid., *Before Motown,* p. 66.

22 **"The people you saw . . . ,"** Bego, *Queen of Soul,* p. 16.

22 **"raising money in church . . . ,"** Daniel Wolff, *You Send Me: The Life and Times of Sam Cooke* (New York: William Morrow, 1995), p. 54.

22 **"the pull of those days . . . ,"** Aretha Franklin and David Ritz, *Aretha: From These Roots* (New York: Villard, 1999), p. 60.

22 **a nickname that suggested . . . ,"** Franklin, *Give Me This Mountain,* p. 16.

23 **"rocking back and forth . . . ,"** Mary Wilson and Patricia Romanowski, *Dreamgirl: My Life as a Supreme* (New York: St. Martin's, 1986), p. 22.

23 **"my main minister . . . ,"** B.B. King and David Ritz, *Blues All Around Me: The Autobiography of B.B. King* (New York: Avon, 1996), p. 96.

23 **"In no way, shape . . . ,"** Franklin and Ritz, *Aretha,* pp. 5–6.

24 **"had a brush and a case . . . ,"** Leslie Gourse, *Aretha Franklin: Lady of Soul* (New York: Franklin Watts, 1995), p. 22.

24 **"just bangin', not playin' . . . ,"** Phyl Garland, *The Sound of Soul* (Chicago: Henry Regnery, 1969), p. 197.

24 **"We poke our heads . . . ,"** Smokey Robinson and David Ritz, *Smokey: Inside My Life* (New York: McGraw-Hill, 1989), p. 29.

24 **"I keep cooking . . . ,"** Franklin, *Give Me This Mountain,* p. 38.

25 **"I'm good and mean . . . ,"** Franklin and Ritz, *Aretha,* p. 26.

25 **"a time of high optimism . . . ,"** ibid., p. 19.

25 **"My childhood was . . . ,"** Nathan, *Soulful Divas,* p. 74.

25 **"Daddy's personal affairs . . . ,"** Franklin and Ritz, *Aretha,* p. 27.

26 **"Most of what I learned . . . ,"** Garland, *Sound of Soul,* p. 199.

26 **"When he would get into . . . ,"** Franklin and Ritz, *Aretha,* p. 14.

27 **"God stirs the nest . . . ,"** King and Ritz, *Blues All Around Me,* p. 197.

27 The text of "The Eagle Stirreth Her Nest" can be found in *American Sermons: The Pilgrims to Martin Luther King, Jr.,* ed. Michael Warner (New York: Library of America, 1999), pp. 826–34.

28 **"Daddy preached self-pride . . . ,"** Franklin and Ritz, *Aretha,* pp. 19–20.

30 **"They had gone spiritually . . . ,"** Jerry Butler, *Only the Strong Survive: Memoirs of a Soul Survivor* (Bloomington: Indiana University Press, 2000), p. 17.

31 **"chronic urban guerrilla warfare . . . ,"** Arnold R. Hirsch, *The Making of the Second Ghetto: Race and Housing in Chicago, 1940–1960* (Chicago: University of Chicago Press, 1998), pp. 58–59.

33 **"In the early days . . . ,"** David Whitaker, *Cabrini-Green* (Chicago: W3 Publishing, 2000), p. 25.

33 **"When the red high-rises . . . ,"** ibid., p. 34.

33 **"I thought I was livin' . . . ,"** ibid., p. 36.

34 **"Everybody took care . . . ,"** ibid., p. 38.

35 **"was very much into poetry . . . ,"** liner notes to *People Get Ready! The Curtis Mayfield Story* (Rhino Records), p. 14.

35 **"I never really had to acquire . . . ,"** *People Get Ready*, p. 12.

35 **"I shrink away . . . ,"** Whitaker, *Cabrini-Green*, p. 43.

35 **"There was always talk . . . ,"** ibid., pp. 20–21.

36 **"He would get up there . . . ,"** William Barlow, *Voice Over: The Making of Black Radio* (Philadelphia: Temple University Press, 1999), p. 104.

38 **"The guitar used to . . . ,"** *People Get Ready*, p. 42.

38 **"he was an exceptional talent . . . ,"** Butler, *Only the Strong*, p. 32.

39 **"We had a lot of . . . ,"** Whitaker, *Cabrini-Green*, p. 21.

39 **"As far as dealing with Curtis . . . ,"** ibid., p. 21.

40 **"When I was telling Lula . . . ,"** Constanze Elsner, *Stevie Wonder* (New York: Popular Library, 1977), p. 14.

41 **"He stayed away . . . ,"** John Swenson, *Stevie Wonder* (New York: Harper & Row, 1986), p. 15.

41 **"Some jobs white folks . . . ,"** Thomas J. Sugrue, *The Origins of the Urban Crisis: Race and Inequality in Postwar Detroit* (Princeton, N.J.: Princeton University Press, 1996), p. 99.

42 **"the people in Conant Gardens . . . ,"** Elaine Latzman Moon, *Untold Tales, Unsung Heroes: An Oral History of Detroit's African American Community 1918–1967* (Detroit: Wayne State University Press, 1994), p. 114.

42 **"project boys . . . ,"** ibid., p. 115.

43 **"upper lower circumstances . . . ,"** Swenson, *Stevie*, p. 15.

43 **"My mother wasn't very happy . . . ,"** Elsner, *Stevie*, p. 30.

43 **"I never really wondered . . . ,"** Swenson, *Stevie*, p. 13.

43 **"We were poor . . . ,"** James Haskins, *The Stevie Wonder Story* (New York: Dell, 1979), p. 11.

44 **"I'm glad that I'm blind . . . ,"** Ben Fong-Torres, "The Formerly Little Stevie Wonder," *Not Fade Away* (San Francisco: Miller Freeman Books, 1999), p. 145.

44 **"When I was just a little baby ...,"** ibid., p. 146.

44 **"It was the playhouse trip ...,"** Haskins, *Stevie*, p. 21.

44 **"You know those small sheds ...,"** Swenson, *Stevie*, p. 12.

45 **"Great googa mooga ...,"** David Carson, *Rockin' Down the Dial: The Detroit Sound of Radio* (Troy, Mich.: Momentum, 2000), p. 55.

45 **"If it hadn't been for black radio ...,"** Barlow, *Voice Over*, p. 210.

46 **"They made me feel ...,"** Haskins, *Stevie*, pp. 15–16.

47 **"The first time I really felt ...,"** Swenson, *Stevie*, p. 15.

47 **"I was always beating things ...,"** Haskins, *Stevie*, p. 14.

47 **"I started playing the blues ...,"** Swenson, *Stevie*, p. 15.

48 **"I used to love ...,"** "Stevie Wonder: Lifesongs," Rock Around the World.com, issue 16.

48 **"We used to get ...,"** Swenson, *Stevie*, p. 22.

48 **"Detroiters were serious skaters ...,"** Franklin and Ritz, *Aretha*, p. 46.

49 **"I remember skating ...,"** Wilson and Romanowski, *Dreamgirl*, p. 26.

49 **"I fell in love ...,"** Robinson and Ritz, *Smokey*, p. 37.

49 **"Next thing I know ...,"** Hirshey, *Nowhere to Run*, p. 231.

49 **"Aretha had a way ...,"** Bego, *Aretha*, p. 25.

50 **"I got friendly ...,"** Hirshey, *Nowhere to Run*, p. 228.

50 **"All you needed to do ...,"** quoted in liner notes to *Ray Charles: The Birth of Soul* (Atlantic Records).

51 **"A's, B's, some C's ...,"** Bego, *Aretha*, p. 18.

51 **"In Detroit, the Franklin girls ...,"** Wilson and Romanowski, *Dreamgirls*, pp. 23–24.

51 **"I could have killed Aretha ...,"** Nathan, *Soulful Divas*, p. 74.

51 **"She always wanted to sing ...,"** David Nathan, "A Tribute to Erma Franklin," Rock's Backpages.com.

52 **"So we decided ...,"** Hirshey, *Nowhere to Run*, pp. 231–32.

52 **"we were too busy ...,"** Garland, *Sound of Soul*, p. 198.

52 **"When I was pregnant ...,"** Franklin and Ritz, *Aretha*, p. 71.

52 **"Many of the neighborhood girls ...,"** Bego, *Aretha*, p. 31.

53 **"a national leader ...,"** Jerry Wexler and David Ritz, *The Rhythm and the Blues: A Life in American Music* (New York: Knopf, 1993), p. 206.

53 **"He liked music ...,"** Gourse, *Aretha*, p. 59.

53 **"Women absolutely loved him ...,"** Bego, *Aretha*, p. 25.

53 **"Reverend was gone ...,"** Gourse, *Aretha*, p. 20.

53 **"Carolyn snapped into action ...,"** Franklin and Ritz, *Aretha*, p. 27.

54 **"That charisma he had ...,"** Bego, *Aretha*, p. 25.

54 **"He would spend Saturday night...,"** Al Young, "Brilliant Careers: Aretha Franklin," *Salon* (Aug. 3, 1999).

54 **"nothing inconsistent between...,"** Franklin and Ritz, *Aretha,* p. 16.

54 **"so amazed by Aretha's singing...,"** Willa Ward-Royster as told to Toni Rose, *How I Got Over: Clara Ward and the World-Famous Ward Singers* (Philadelphia: Temple University Press, 1997), p. 18.

54 **"You can't explain...,"** Hirshey, *Nowhere to Run,* p. 231.

55 **"The Reverend and Clara...,"** Ward-Royster, *How I Got Over,* p. 100.

55 **"Although Mom was jealous...,"** ibid., p. 117.

55 **"Daddy and Clara...,"** Franklin and Ritz, *Aretha,* p. 17.

56 **"I just cancelled...,"** Garland, *Sound of Soul,* p. 199.

56 **"helped shape my basic...,"** Franklin and Ritz, *Aretha,* p. 41.

56 **"He showed me some...,"** Garland, *Sound of Soul,* p. 198.

56 **"monuments of pure gospel power,"** Franklin and Ritz, *Aretha,* p. 51.

57 **"I'd have died to go...,"** Hirshey, *Nowhere to Run,* p. 232.

58 **"When the whites...,"** Craig Werner, *A Change Is Gonna Come: Music, Race and the Soul of America* (New York: Plume, 1998), p. 37.

58 **"As much as anybody...,"** Hirshey, *Nowhere to Run,* p. 233.

58 **"He did so many things...,"** Bego, *Aretha,* p. 27.

58 **"All the acts...,"** Peter Guralnick, *Sweet Soul Music: Rhythm and Blues and the Southern Dream of Freedom* (New York: Little, Brown, 1999), p. 334.

59 **"We'd drive thousands...,"** Bego, *Aretha,* p. 21.

59 **"driving 8 or 10 hours...,"** Nathan, *Soulful Divas,* pp. 74–75.

59 **"When you were singing...,"** Bego, *Aretha,* p. 20.

59 **"was just too shy...,"** Franklin and Ritz, *Aretha,* pp. 63–64.

59 **"I meet all kinds of people...,"** Robinson and Ritz, *Smokey,* p. 48.

59 **"Blacks had to stay with blacks...,"** Bego, *Aretha,* p. 20.

60 **"rainy night on a dark...,"** Mavis Staples, personal interview, May 1997.

60 The text of "Without a Song" can be found in Franklin, *Give Me This Mountain,* pp. 89–97.

Chapter Two

"Keep On Pushing"

64 The material concerning the use of the Impressions' songs in the Chicago movement is drawn in part from Guy and Candie Carawan, *Sing for Freedom: The Story of the Civil Rights Movement Through Its Songs* (Bethlehem, Penn.: Sing Out! Books, 1990).

64 **"Chicago is not that different...,"** Adam Cohen and Elizabeth Taylor, *American*

Pharaoh: Mayor Richard J. Daley, His Battle for Chicago and the Nation (Boston: Little, Brown, 2000), p. 331.

66 **"It was warrior music...,"** Gordon Sellers, personal interview, October 2002.

66 **"I started out...,"** Joanne Bland, personal interview, October 2002.

66 **"Curtis always seemed...,"** Brian Ward, *Just My Soul Responding: Rhythm and Blues, Black Consciousness, and Race Relations* (Berkeley: University of California Press, 1998), p. 76.

67 **"WVON played a big part...,"** Barlow, *Voice Over,* p. 211.

68 **"As a jock during that time...,"** ibid., p. 204

68 **"Curtis Mayfield was living around there...,"** Robert Pruter, *Doowop: The Chicago Scene* (Urbana: University of Illinois Press, 1996), p. 6

68 **"We were all into trying...,"** ibid., p. 174

69 **"At that time everybody...,"** ibid.

69 **"Joe [Breckenridge] and the guys...,"** ibid., p. 175.

69 **"Curtis was not easily convinced...,"** Butler, *Only the Strong,* p. 38.

69 **"We had a long debate...,"** Whitaker, *Cabrini-Green,* p. 43.

70 **"He convinced me...,"** Butler, *Only the Strong,* p. 38.

71 **"Dawson didn't want...,"** Cohen and Taylor, *American Pharaoh,* p. 172.

73 **"The snow was about five feet...,"** *People Get Ready,* p. 41.

73 **"They sang about five or six...,"** Robert Pruter, *Chicago Soul* (Urbana: University of Illinois Press, 1991), p. 31.

74 **"That's it! That's it!...,"** Butler, *Only the Strong,* pp. 42–43.

75 **"Why did that happen?...,"** Pruter, *Chicago Soul,* p. 26.

75 **"he had a great ear...,"** ibid., p. 25.

75 **"They pressed up the records...,"** Butler, *Only the Strong,* p. 50.

76 **"When the record came out...,"** Pruter, *Chicago Soul,* p. 32.

76 **"The place went up in screams...,"** Butler, *Only the Strong,* p. 54.

77 **"when she got to Curtis...,"** ibid., p. 66.

77 **"I used to get down...,"** ibid., p. 81.

78 **"We ain't going on...,"** ibid., pp. 70–71.

78 **"Back during those times...,"** Pruter, *Chicago Soul,* p. 32.

79 **"We scuffled some...,"** ibid., pp. 137–38.

80 **"not rigid. Very liquidy...,"** ibid., p. 75.

81 **"sense of humor...,"** Butler, *Only the Strong,* p. 92.

81 **"When Jerry called...,"** Pruter, *Chicago Soul,* p. 138.

81 **"a compelling account...,"** Ward, *Just My Soul,* p. 205.

82 **"It was something I'd lived...,"** Hirshey, *Nowhere to Run,* p. 258.

82 **"I had saved a thousand...,"** Pruter, *Chicago Soul,* p. 138.

86 **"When the fellows would go out . . . ,"** *People Get Ready,* p. 42.

86 **"Curtis and I, we knew . . . ,"** Pruter, *Chicago Soul,* p. 73.

86 **"The Chicago sound . . . ,"** ibid.

87 **"I must have had ten cups . . . ,"** ibid., pp. 81–82.

87 **"Gene seemed to sing . . . ,"** ibid., p. 64.

88 **"You would have to be careful . . . ,"** ibid., p. 73.

88 **"Motown used to put . . . ,"** ibid., p. 77.

89 **"Daddy and I had our sights . . . ,"** Franklin and Ritz, *Aretha,* p. 80.

89 **"untutored genius,"** Bego, *Aretha,* p. 42.

90 **"At first there was a quiet . . . ,"** Garland, *Sound of Soul,* pp. 199–200.

90 **"I'd never *really* leave . . . ,"** Hirshey, *Nowhere to Run,* p. 232.

90 **"Reverend, your daughter doesn't need . . . ,"** Franklin and Ritz, *Aretha,* p. 81.

91 **"she did everything wrong . . . ,"** Bego, *Aretha,* p. 38.

91 **"When you walk . . . ,"** Franklin and Ritz, *Aretha,* p. 85.

91 **"For the first three months . . . ,"** Guralnick, *Sweet Soul Music,* p. 335.

91 **"I was distracted . . . ,"** John Hammond, *John Hammond on Record: An Autobiography* (New York: Ridge, 1977), p. 346.

91 **"I went to the studio . . . ,"** ibid., p. 348.

91 **"to wed Barbra Streisand . . . ,"** Anthony Heilbut, *The Gospel Sound: Good News and Bad Times,* rev. ed. (New York: Limelight, 1985), p. 277.

92 **"I suppose you could say . . . ,"** Franklin and Ritz, *Aretha,* p. 86.

92 **"One night John called . . . ,"** Bego, *Aretha,* p. 43.

94 **"I came in and kind of upset . . . ,"** ibid., p. 54.

94 **"I think I made some very good . . . ,"** ibid., p. 53.

94 **"Aretha was so multi-talented . . . ,"** ibid., p. 69.

95 **"she could really sing . . . ,"** James Brown and Bruce Tucker, *James Brown: Godfather of Soul* (New York: Thunder's Mouth, 1990), p. 128.

95 **"Jazz was going through . . . ,"** Franklin and Ritz, *Aretha,* p. 91.

95 **"I sang to the floor . . . ,"** Bego, *Aretha,* p. 49.

95 **"After checking in . . . ,"** Ward-Royster, *How I Got Over,* pp. 225–26.

96 **"They don't respect each other . . . ,"** Gourse, *Aretha,* p. 47.

96 **"Ted beat her down . . . ,"** Bego, *Aretha,* p. 79.

96 **"It was a catch-22 . . . ,"** ibid., pp. 70–71.

97 **"It seems like they won't . . . ,"** Robinson and Ritz, *Smokey,* p. 123.

97 **"very little money . . . ,"** Bego, *Aretha,* p. 67.

97 **"a voice from up in the booth . . . ,"** ibid., p. 60.

98 **"Aretha went berserk . . . ,"** Gourse, *Aretha,* p. 47.

98 **"It was like I had no idea . . . ,"** Bego, *Aretha,* p. 62.

98 "There was another young artist...," Hirshey, *Nowhere to Run*, p. 239.

99 "upward mobility...," Guralnick, *Sweet Soul Music*, p. 338.

99 "A lot of people missed...," Bego, *Aretha*, p. 59.

99 "On Columbia I cut...," ibid., p. 77.

99 "road maps for gospel-based...," Nathan, *Soulful Divas*, p. 75.

99 "I cherish the records...," Wexler and Ritz, *The Rhythm*, p. 206.

100 "He was like our little...," Bill Dahl, *Motown: The Golden Years* (Iola, Wis.: Krause, 2001), p. 195.

100 "Everyone loved him...," Wilson and Romanowski, *Dreamgirl*, p. 113.

100 "When Stevie Wonder came there...," Dahl, *Motown*, p. 195.

100 "got around better than I did...," ibid.

101 "I was just a victim...," Elsner, *Stevie*, p. 41.

101 "I think his mother...," Hirshey, *Nowhere to Run*, p. 219.

101 "People were just walking...," Swenson, *Stevie*, p. 25.

101 "First of all let me tell you...," Elsner, *Stevie*, p. 43.

101 "You got to come hear this little kid...," Berry Gordy, *To Be Loved* (New York: Warner, 1994), p. 148.

102 "hyper, bright, and brimming...," Robinson and Ritz, *Smokey*, p. 112.

103 "His mother brought him...," Elsner, *Stevie*, p. 48.

103 "I was very fortunate...," Michael Goldberg, "The Timeless World of Wonder," *Rolling Stone* (Apr. 10, 1986), p. 153.

103 "I was *not* Little Stevie Wonder's baby-sitter...," Hirshey, *Nowhere to Run*, p. 220.

103 "He knew and loved my family...," Susan Whitall, *Women of Motown: An Oral History* (New York: Avon, 1998), p. 76.

103 "Me and my friend...," Swenson, *Stevie*, p. 25.

104 "He'd call my secretary...," Gordy, *To Be Loved*, p. 331.

104 "I'd call up and say...," Swenson, *Stevie*, p. 36.

104 "I like that suit...," Gordy, *To Be Loved*, p. 241.

105 "I remember a teacher...," Elsner, *Stevie*, p. 26.

105 "I cried and cried...," Haskins, *Stevie*, p. 33.

105 "The company, working through...," Swenson, *Stevie*, pp. 39–40.

106 "kind, studious young man...," Wilson and Romanowski, *Dreamgirl*, p. 133.

106 "I think the nicest compliment...," Swenson, *Stevie*, p. 44.

106 "Stevie made friends...," Elsner, *Stevie*, p. 52.

107 "one of the major forces...," Fong-Torres, "Formerly Little," p. 142.

107 "It was just amazing...," Elsner, *Stevie*, p. 47.

107 "It didn't take long...," Robinson and Ritz, *Smokey*, p. 112.

108 **"I think a harmonica...,"** Sue Clark, "Stevie Wonder Gets Good and Pissed," *Rolling Stone* (Sept. 30, 1971), p. 12.

108 **"This is the very best...,"** Haskins, *Stevie,* p. 42.

108 **"The first time I began to feel...,"** Swenson, *Stevie,* p. 31.

108 **"Motown's buses...,"** Otis Williams and Patricia Romanowski, *Temptations* (New York: Fireside, 1988), p. 78.

109 The description of the confrontation between West and Nash is drawn from the *Eyes on the Prize* video and from Taylor Branch, *Parting the Waters: America in the King Years, 1954–63* (New York: Touchstone, 1989), p. 295.

111 **"down in Alabama...,"** Swenson, *Stevie,* p. 42.

111 **"Holy smoke, that was really...,"** ibid.

111 **"He and Little Stevie Wonder remained...,"** Martha Reeves and Mark Bego, *Dancing in the Street: Confessions of a Motown Diva* (New York: Hyperion, 1994), p. 77.

111 **"So many of us have to demand...,"** Elsner, *Stevie,* p. 35.

112 **"It really was not like that...,"** David Freeland, *Ladies of Soul* (Jackson: University Press of Mississippi, 2001), p. 89.

112 **"I was on a lot of the Motown tours...,"** Nelson George, *Where Did Our Love Go? The Rise and Fall of the Motown Sound* (New York: St. Martin's, 1985), p. 74.

113 **"When Stevie got to...,"** Elsner, *Stevie,* p. 57.

113 **"It was never planned...,"** George, *Where Did,* p. 73.

113 **"It was neither easy...,"** Elsner, *Stevie,* p. 94.

114 **"We pulled up at 103rd Street...,"** ibid., p. 86.

114 **"You would not believe...,"** ibid., p. 90.

115 **"We hadn't taken advantage...,"** Gordy, *To Be Loved,* p. 226.

115 **"that young, undeveloped...,"** ibid., p. 226.

116 **"they would go through the list...,"** Adam White and Fred Bronson, *The Billboard Book of Number One Rhythm and Blues Hits* (New York: Billboard Books, 1993), p. 14.

116 **"We kind of clicked...,"** Dahl, *Motown,* p. 200.

116 **"What would happen...,"** Swenson, *Stevie,* p. 53.

116 **"That music wanted out...,"** White and Bronson, *Billboard Book,* p. 14.

119 **"provided a core of legitimate...,"** Ward, *Just My Soul,* p. 204.

120 **"I would sit there...,"** Pruter, *Chicago Soul,* p. 74.

120 **"There was nothing original...,"** ibid., p. 140.

121 **"We were in Nashville...,"** *People Get Ready,* p. 43.

123 **"You don't know what Chicago is like...,"** Cohen and Taylor, *American Pharaoh,* p. 348.

123 **"They wouldn't even give us...,"** ibid., p. 432.

124 **"the opposition it would face . . . ,"** ibid., p. 358.

124 **"The streets of Alabama . . . ,"** ibid., p. 415.

C h a p t e r   T h r e e

"Spirit in the Dark"

126 The description of Aretha at the Fillmore West draws on Michael Lydon, "A Spirit in the Dark: Aretha Franklin at Fillmore West, 1971," Rock's Backpages.com.

128 **"Aretha was continuing . . . ,"** Wexler and Ritz, *The Rhythm*, p. 206.

128 **"considered the musical tastes . . . ,"** ibid., pp. 245–46.

129 **"magic chord,"** Guralnick, *Sweet Soul Music*, p. 340.

129 **"I took her to church . . . ,"** ibid., p. 341.

129 **"To say we took her back . . . ,"** Bego, *Aretha*, p. 93.

129 **"to base the music around me . . . ,"** Franklin and Ritz, *Aretha*, p. 108.

129 **"no lawyers, managers, or agents . . . ,"** Bego, *Aretha*, p. 83.

130 **"I was not unhappy to see her . . . ,"** Hammond, *John Hammond*, p. 349.

130 **"At the end of the day . . . ,"** Bego, *Aretha*, p. 72.

130 **"below-the-Bible-Belt sound . . . ,"** Hirshey, *Nowhere to Run*, p. 294.

130 **"Stax was steaming . . . ,"** Wexler and Ritz, *The Rhythm*, p. 204.

130 **"Twenty-five thousand dollars . . . ,"** Rob Bowman, *Soulsville U.S.A.: The Story of Stax Records* (New York: Music Sales, 1997), p. 165.

131 **"Nobody knew those were white guys . . . ,"** Butler, *Only the Strong*, p. 193.

131 **"I knew about Aretha . . . ,"** Guralnick, *Sweet Soul Music*, pp. 339–40.

132 **"She hit that magic chord . . . ,"** ibid., p. 340.

132 **"It was a killer . . . ,"** Wexler and Ritz, *The Rhythm*, p. 210.

132 **"I couldn't believe it . . . ,"** Bego, *Aretha*, p. 86.

132 **"Walpurgisnacht, a Wagnerian . . . ,"** Wexler and Ritz, *The Rhythm*, p. 211.

132 **"the most fucked-up horn section . . . ,"** Guralnick, *Sweet Soul Music*, p. 340.

132 **"presenting Aretha and Ted . . . ,"** Bego, *Aretha*, p. 84.

133 **"A redneck patronizing . . . ,"** Wexler and Ritz, *The Rhythm*, p. 211.

133 **"a lot drunker than I thought . . . ,"** Guralnick, *Sweet Soul Music*, p. 342.

134 **"new national anthem . . . ,"** Ward, *Just My Soul*, p. 362.

135 **"I don't make it a practice . . . ,"** Franklin and Ritz, *Aretha*, p. 155.

135 **"the need of a nation . . . ,"** ibid., p. 112.

135 **"I just lost my song . . . ,"** Guralnick, *Sweet Soul Music*, p. 332.

136 **"like Minerva, full-formed . . . ,"** Wexler and Ritz, *The Rhythm*, p. 247.

136 **"When it comes to the ABCs . . . ,"** Hirshey, *Nowhere to Run*, pp. 243–44.

137 **"We had been fucked over . . . ,"** ibid., p. 242.

138 **"frenzied hand-clapping . . . ,"** Garland, *Sound of Soul*, pp. 194–95.

138 **"This was a 'love wave'...,"** Bego, *Aretha,* p. 108.

139 **"My first inclination...,"** Wallace Terry, *Bloods: An Oral History of the Vietnam War by Black Veterans* (New York: Random House, 1984), p. 167.

140 **"When you're talking...,"** Pruter, *Chicago Soul,* p. 142.

140 **"social conscience...,"** *People Get Ready,* p. 44.

141 **"Our purpose is to educate...,"** Ward, *Just My Soul,* p. 339.

142 **"beautiful beautiful...,"** Nikki Giovanni, *Love Poems* (New York: William Morrow, 1997), p. 34.

143 **"I wasn't a quitter...,"** Pruter, *Chicago Soul,* p. 304.

146 **"after the riots...,"** Whitaker, *Cabrini-Green,* p. 45.

146 **"It made you want to cry...,"** ibid., p. 26.

147 **"People ask me what soul is...,"** Swenson, *Stevie,* p. 57.

147 **"Categorization can be the death...,"** ibid., p. 81.

147 **"Some of that psychedelic music...,"** ibid., p. 57.

148 **"Stevie wanted to play...,"** *Hendrix: Setting the Record Straight,* ed. John McDermott (New York: Warner, 1992), p. 237.

148 **"When I think of the sixties...,"** Michael Goldberg, "The Timeless World of Wonder," *Rolling Stone* (Apr. 10, 1986), p. 153.

148 **"I just dug the effects...,"** Swenson, *Stevie,* p. 57.

149 **"Stevie wanted people in the studio...,"** White and Bronson, *Billboard Book,* p. 33.

151 **"Those whites takin' over...,"** Haskins, *Stevie,* p. 59.

151 **"Have you heard the Temptations'...,"** Swenson, *Stevie,* p. 67.

152 **"Writing is my thing...,"** Clark, "Stevie Wonder Gets Good and Pissed," p. 15.

152 **"I had the desire to move out...,"** White and Bronson, *Billboard Book,* p. 74.

152 **"This is the kind of freedom...,"** Fong-Torres, "Formerly Little," p. 147.

152 **"By the time he's 21...,"** Haskins, *Stevie,* p. 59.

153 **"I had to find out...,"** Goldberg, "Timeless World," p. 154.

155 **"I told Curtis...,"** *The Curtom Story,* liner notes, p. 8.

159 **"You can hear a lot of Curtis...,"** *People Get Ready,* p. 4.

159 **"I like the Impressions...,"** *Jimi Hendrix in His Own Words,* ed. Tony Brown (London: Omnibus, 1994), p. 91.

160 **"You learn the market...,"** Pruter, *Chicago Soul,* p. 308.

161 **"Of course I could relate...,"** ibid., p. 308.

163 **"My contract was made...,"** "Can a Black Man Sing the Whites?" *Rolling Stone* (July 6, 1972), p. 8.

164 **"It was a very important contract...,"** Fong-Torres, "Formerly Little," p. 49.

164 **"He was about 19 then...,"** Swenson, *Stevie,* p. 75.

164 **"I had some misgivings...,"** Gordy, *To Be Loved,* p. 305.

165 **"I knew I couldn't forever…,"** Swenson, *Stevie*, p. 78.

165 **"they began to understand…,"** Martin E. Horn, *Innervisions: The Music of Stevie Wonder* (Bloomington, Ind.: 1st Books, 2000), p. 105.

165 **"a woman's supposed to…,"** Swenson, *Stevie*, p. 82.

166 **"He'd be in the studio…,"** Elsner, *Stevie*, p. 166.

166 **"I recorded 40 tunes…,"** Swenson, *Stevie*, p. 76.

166 **"It really isn't so much to imitate…,"** ibid., p. 77.

167 **"Stevie showed up with…,"** George, *Where Did*, p. 180.

168 **"I thought at the very beginning…,"** Swenson, *Stevie*, p. 85.

169 **"My drummer had…,"** ibid., p. 83.

169 **"It was spontaneous…,"** ibid., p. 86.

169 **"He establishes rapport…,"** Fong-Torres, "Formerly Little," p. 141.

170 **"If you think of blacks…,"** Swenson, *Stevie*, p. 89.

171 **"Motown got caught…,"** Hirshey, *Nowhere to Run*, p. 191.

172 **"conjured up images…,"** Ward, *Just My Soul*, p. 367.

172 **"The most interesting thing…,"** Haskins, *Stevie*, p. 68.

173 **"it's a funky, dirty…,"** Horn, *Innervisions*, p. 121.

173 **"I was sitting…,"** Annette Carson, *Jeff Beck: Crazyfingers* (San Francisco: Backbeat, 2001), p. 112.

173 **"I told Motown…,"** Swenson, *Stevie*, pp. 87–88.

174 **"The black revolution…,"** Bego, *Aretha*, p. 145.

174 **"Soul music is music…,"** Gourse, *Aretha*, p. 90.

174 **"Sometimes she'd call me…,"** Wexler and Ritz, *The Rhythm*, p. 212.

175 Summaries and quotations from the June 18, 1968, *Time* cover story can be found in Heilbut, *Gospel Sound*, p. 277; Gourse, *Aretha*, p. 75; Garland, *Sound of Soul*, p. 202; and Bego, *Aretha*, pp. 103–104.

175 **"The story said her husband…,"** Nathan, *Soulful Divas*, p. 80.

176 **"String the titles together…,"** Gourse, *Aretha*, p. 76.

176 **"I think she may have cried…,"** Bego, *Aretha*, p. 126.

176 **"The songs she chose…,"** Wexler and Ritz, *The Rhythm*, p. 215.

176 **"I sing to the realist…,"** Gourse, *Aretha*, p. 81.

177 **"It should have been called…,"** Bego, *Aretha*, pp. 121–22.

177 **"Her taste could sometimes…,"** ibid., p. 122.

177 **"shocked and saddened…,"** Franklin and Ritz, *Aretha*, p. 132.

177 **"just a curtain, chair, and mirror…,"** ibid., p. 123.

178 **"gathering the bullets…,"** Franklin, *Give Me This Mountain*, p. 31.

179 **"The same people who left…,"** Ze'ev Chafets, *Devil's Night and Other True Tales of Detroit* (New York: Random House, 1990), p. 167.

179 **"I loved that phrase..."** Franklin and Ritz, *Aretha,* p. 136.

182 **"When Aretha records a tune...,"** Charlie Gillett, *Making Tracks: Atlantic Records and the Growth of a Multi-Billion-Dollar Industry* (New York: Allen, 1992), p. 211.

183 **"introverted musical genius...,"** Franklin and Ritz, *Aretha,* p. 140.

184 **"The thousands of black people...,"** Ted Fox, *Showtime at the Apollo* (New York: Henry Holt, 1985), p. 268.

184 **"the way black folk sing...,"** Michael Lydon, *Ray Charles: Man and Music* (New York: Riverhead, 1999), p. 270.

185 **"King Curtis could make me...,"** Hirshey, *Nowhere to Run,* p. 234.

185 **"return" to gospel...,** Gourse, *Aretha,* p. 98.

Chapter Four

Songs in the Key of Life

192 **"It's the last days of life...,"** Swenson, *Stevie,* p. 93.

192 **"Stevie is someone who goes...,"** Elsner, *Stevie,* pp. 208–209.

193 **"No, we do have a lot...,"** ibid., p. 210.

193 **"I think the deepest...,"** Swenson, *Stevie,* p. 93.

194 **"Since the jobs that are available...,"** William Julius Wilson, *The Truly Disadvantaged: The Inner City, the Underclass, and Public Policy* (Chicago: University of Chicago Press, 1990), p. 261.

195 **" 'Higher Ground' was a very special...,"** Swenson, *Stevie,* p. 94.

195 **"The people couldn't feel me...,"** Haskins, *Stevie,* p. 96.

196 **"It's a madhouse...,"** Gordy, *To Be Loved,* p. 330.

196 **"I knew that Stevie...,"** Swenson, *Stevie,* p. 95.

196 **"The only thing I know...,"** The best description of Wonder's recovery, based primarily on *Rolling Stone* reports, can be found in Swenson, *Stevie,* pp. 94–95.

197 **"I can usually tell a woman...,"** Haskins, *Stevie,* pp. 111–12.

197 **"We didn't have to do...,"** Swenson, *Stevie,* p. 97.

198 **"the only act who could have topped...,"** Haskins, *Stevie,* p. 119.

198 **"Sometimes he'll call me...,"** Swenson, *Stevie,* p. 91.

198 **"Steve has seeing-eye...,"** Elsner, *Stevie,* p. 97.

199 **"That'll tell you where I'm going...,"** Swenson, *Stevie,* p. 105.

199 **"If you were to turn on...,"** Robert Christgau, "Stevie Wonder Is All Things to All People," in *Grown Up All Wrong* (Cambridge, Mass.: Harvard University Press, 1998), p. 135.

200 **"The best way to get...,"** White and Bronson, *Billboard Book,* p. 144.

200 **"I would have been the only black...,"** Elsner, *Stevie,* p. 256.

201 **"I definitely feel that Marvin...,"** ibid., p. 234.

201 "Anyone who can stand up...," Haskins, *Stevie*, p. 130.

202 "I remember in Boston...," Elsner, *Stevie*, p. 224.

202 "His songs do more...," Swenson, *Stevie*, p. 112.

203 "America doesn't make people...," Elsner, *Stevie*, p. 252.

204 "There are faults at Motown...," Swenson, *Stevie*, pp. 111–12.

205 "That was probably no good...," Pruter, *Chicago Soul*, pp. 310–11.

206 "As far as my doing songs...," Chris Salewicz, "Keep On Pushing: Curtis Mayfield," Rock's Backpages.com.

207 "The album allowed me...," *People Get Ready*, p. 32.

208 "We were now setting up...," ibid., p. 46.

209 "We got great recognition...," Pruter, *Chicago Soul*, p. 309.

211 "The next thing I knew...," Bego, *Aretha*, p. 169.

211 "It proved the permanent power...," Franklin and Ritz, *Aretha*, p. 112.

211 "It took us about five days...," Nathan, *Soulful Divas*, p. 87.

212 "When she told me that Quincy...," Wexler and Ritz, *The Rhythm*, p. 277.

212 "I don't want to talk...," Bego, *Aretha*, pp. 159–60.

213 "Even though the lyrics...," Patricia Hill Collins, *Black Feminist Thought* (Boston: Unwin Hyman, 1990), p. 108.

214 "Aretha was right on time...," ibid., p. 108.

214 "you can see a lot...," *Rolling Stone Raves: What Your Rock and Roll Favorites Favor*, ed. Shawn Dall (New York: William Morrow, 1999), p. 142.

214 "The end of the seventies...," Franklin and Ritz, *Aretha*, p. 181.

214 "The song had wings...," ibid., p. 157.

215 "At one point, Natalie called...," ibid., p. 160.

215 "Someone told her I went around...," Bego, *Aretha*, p. 167.

217 "In disco the musical pulse...," Iain Chambers, *Urban Rhythms, Pop Music, and Popular Culture* (New York: St. Martin's, 1986), p. 147.

218 "It was definitely R&B dance music...," Anthony Haden-Guest, *The Last Party: Studio 54, Disco, and the Culture of the Night* (New York: Morrow, 1997), p. xxi.

218 "I didn't think it would be as big...," Nathan, *Soulful Divas*, p. 87.

219 "A song, like a person...," Franklin and Ritz, *Aretha*, pp. 160–61.

220 "the joy of love...," Both Mayfield's and Wonder's comments can be found in the liner notes to *The Philly Sound* (Epic Legacy Records).

221 "I was going on the road...," Pruter, *Chicago Soul*, p. 310.

222 "It was weird...," ibid., p. 320.

224 "True jazz is an art...," Ellison, *Shadow and Act*, p. 234.

225 "When I got the gig...," Swenson, *Stevie*, pp. 98–99.

225 "there were times when he'd stay...," Haskins, *Stevie*, p. 140.

225 "I'd made Stevie a huge blackberry cobbler...," Elsner, *Stevie*, p. 213.

227 "I had such a good time...," Horn, *Innervisions*, p. 176.

228 "flawed masterpiece," Christgau, "Stevie," p. 139.

229 "one of my favorite Stevie Wonder...," Dall, *Rolling Stone Raves*, p. 19.

230 "was forever telling us...," Gordy, *To Be Loved*, pp. 359–60.

230 "The more I heard people ask...," Swenson, *Stevie*, p. 120.

231 "It would have been nice...," ibid.

233 "I like what I wear...," Nathan, *Soulful Divas*, p. 71.

233 "Los Angeles was not the easiest...," Franklin and Ritz, *Aretha*, p. 172.

233 "I told him that I was interested...," Hirshey, *Nowhere to Run*, p. 237.

233 "I want everyone to know...," Bego, *Aretha*, p. 172.

234 "I couldn't bear to deny...," ibid., p. 192.

234 "A man of enormous energy...," Franklin and Ritz, *Aretha*, pp. 184–85.

Chapter Five

"Who's Zoomin' Who?"

236 "I know you've been standing...," Swenson, *Stevie*, pp. 126–27.

237 "Every time we did that song...," ibid., p. 135.

241 "I'm concerned because I can see...," ibid., p. 138.

241 "Mr. Reagan keeps asking...," Marshall Frady, *Jesse Jackson: A Biography* (New York: Random House, 1996), p. 305.

242 "Every minute you allow yourself...," Swenson, *Stevie*, p. 135.

242 "Lots of times when things are said...," ibid., p. 128.

243 "I just basically was saying...," ibid., p. 140.

243 "Stevie is a communicator...," Barlow, *Voice Over*, p. 269.

244 "the news and public-affairs...," ibid., p. 278.

245 "I felt something was happening...," Swenson, *Stevie*, p. 136.

245 "Prince has really been unique...," Dall, *Rolling Stone Raves*, pp. 191–92.

245 "Three days later he'd written...," Swenson, *Stevie*, p. 137.

247 "many characters, no one particular...," Horn, *Innervisions*, pp. 260–61.

248 "If being banned means...," ibid., p. 238.

248 "I'm very happy now...," Swenson, *Stevie*, p. 141.

248 "You can assassinate the man...," ibid., p. 136.

248 "As many whites as blacks...," Horn, *Innervisions*, p. 212.

249 "We have a monopoly on rats...," Frady, *Jesse Jackson*, p. 199.

249 "Now, Joe Louis milk...," ibid., p. 202.

250 "A kinder, gentler nation...," ibid., p. 64.

251 "Our time has come...," ibid., p. 385.

252 "**I'm certain she noted...**," Bego, *Aretha*, p. 182.

254 "**similarity in stylings...**," ibid., p. 206.

254 "**My brother would get...**," ibid., p. 204.

254 "**dealt with her as one singer...**," ibid., p. 207.

255 "**had so much fun...**," ibid., p. 208.

255 "**My good friend Miss Ree...**," Hirshey, *Nowhere to Run*, p. 34.

255 "**All of a sudden Luther...**," Franklin and Ritz, *Aretha*, p. 195.

256 "**Well, Mr. Vandross wanted to know...**," Hirshey, *Nowhere to Run*, p. 29.

256 "**the biggest lie ever told...**," Franklin and Ritz, *Aretha*, p. 233.

256 "*big mistake*," ibid., pp. 200–201.

257 "**At that point...**," ibid., p. 203.

257 "**I should have married Aretha...**," Bego, *Aretha*, p. 320.

258 "**He was born in poverty...**," Franklin and Ritz, *Aretha*, pp. 206–207.

258 "**You can't say the word 'death'...**," Bego, *Aretha*, p. 221.

258 "**She was delighted with what she heard...**," Nathan, *Soulful Divas*, p. 91.

259 "**In the voice you feel...**," Bego, *Aretha*, p. 226.

261 "**It was my first musical declaration...**," Franklin and Ritz, *Aretha*, p. 210.

261 "**I suppose the song's feminist...**," Bryony Sutherland and Lucy Ellis, *Annie Lennox: The Biography* (New York: Music Sales, 2001), p. 261.

262 "**I think we had a role-reversal...**," Bego, *Aretha*, p. 230.

262 "**I got along alright with her...**," Sutherland and Ellis, *Annie Lennox*, p. 261.

262 "**Annie had just had a photo session...**," ibid., pp. 262–63.

263 "**A lot of people forget...**," *Queen of Soul* video.

263 "**was looking to establish...**," ibid.

263 "**the best, quite simply...**," ibid.

264 "**I sounded like one...**," Franklin and Ritz, *Aretha*, p. 239.

264 "**She said she wanted to re-create...**," Bego, *Aretha*, p. 270.

265 "**when the choir walks down...**," Franklin and Ritz, *Aretha*, p. 217.

265 "**I am a traditionalist...**," ibid., p. 220.

265 "**For singers today...**," Bego, *Aretha*, pp. 269–70.

266 "**I sang between his words...**," Franklin and Ritz, *Aretha*, p. 217.

266 "**I need that old-fashioned...**," ibid., p. 222.

266 "**describes what my family...**," ibid., p. 224.

268 "**At that time, I wasn't...**," *People Get Ready*, p. 37.

270 "**Sampling allowed him...**," Steve Morse, "Setting the New Market in Sampling," *Boston Globe* (March 3, 2002).

273 "**The president let everyone know...**," Franklin and Ritz, *Aretha*, pp. 240–41.

274 "**There were eight minutes...**," Bego, *Aretha*, p. 328.

274 **"I did it . . . ,"** Franklin and Ritz, *Aretha*, p. 249.

274 **"No matter how far I may venture . . . ,"** ibid., p. 250.

279 **"It's not even the financial thing . . . ,"** Morse, "Setting the New Market."

281 **"Look at someone like Aretha . . . ,"** Chris Nickerson, *Lauryn Hill: She's Got That Thing* (New York: St. Martin's, 1999), p. 133.

282 **"Our podium, what we have to speak from . . . ,"** ibid., p. 17.

282 **"The rhythm, the syncopation . . . ,"** ibid., p. 129.

282 **"a young woman who knows . . . ,"** Franklin and Ritz, *Aretha*, p. 246.

283 **"old-fashioned down-home . . . ,"** ibid., p. 248.

284 **"A really heavy union . . . ,"** Horn, *Innervisions*, p. 296.

288 **"I sort of went out there . . . ,"** "Wonder, Hill, Clapton Praise Mayfield," *Rolling Stone* (Feb. 23, 2000).

DISCOGRAPHY

This discography is intended to provide a sense of the connections among the recording careers of Stevie, Aretha, and Curtis. The songs and albums listed in boldface reached either the Top Twenty on the singles charts (pop or R&B) or the Top Fifty on the album charts, while the remaining songs or albums failed to chart at that level. Starred and boldface songs or albums reached number one on at least one singles chart or the Top Ten on the album chart.

1956

Aretha, *Songs of Faith* (Chess)

1958

Impressions featuring Jerry Butler, "For Your Precious Love"
Impressions, "Come Back My Love"

1959

Impressions, *The Gift of Love*

1960

Aretha, "Today I Sing the Blues"

1961

Aretha, "Won't Be Long"
Aretha, "Rock-a-bye Your Baby with a Dixie Melody" / "Operation Heartbreak"
Aretha, *Aretha* (Columbia)
Impressions, "Gypsy Woman"

1962

Aretha, *The Electrifying Aretha Franklin* (Columbia)
Aretha, "I Surrender Dear"
Stevie, "I Call It Pretty Music (But the Old People Call It the Blues)"
Impressions, "Grow Closer Together"
Aretha, "Don't Cry Baby"
Stevie, *A Tribute to Uncle Ray* (Tamla)

Stevie, *The Jazz Soul of Little Stevie Wonder* (Tamla)
Impressions, "Never Let Me Go" / "Little Young Lover"
Aretha, "Try a Little Tenderness"
Stevie, "Little Water Boy"
Aretha, *The Tender, the Moving, the Swinging Aretha Franklin* (Columbia)
Aretha, "Trouble in Mind"
Impressions, "Minstrel and Queen"

1 9 6 3

Impressions, "I'm the One Who Loves You"
Stevie, "Contract on Love"
Impressions, "Sad, Sad Girl and Boy"
Aretha, *Laughing on the Outside* (Columbia)
★ **Stevie, "Fingertips—Part 2"** (R&B, pop)
★ **Stevie, *Little Stevie Wonder/ The 12 Year Old Genius/ Recorded Live*** (Tamla)
Impressions, *The Impressions* (ABC-Paramount)
★ **Impressions, "It's All Right"** (R&B)
Stevie, "Workout Stevie, Workout"

1 9 6 4

Impressions, "Talking About My Baby"
Stevie, "Castles in the Sand"
Impressions, *The Never-Ending Impressions* (ABC-Paramount)
Stevie, "Hey Harmonica Man"
Impressions, "I'm So Proud"
Aretha, *Unforgettable—A Tribute to Dinah Washington* (Columbia)
Stevie, *With a Song in My Heart* (Tamla)
Aretha, "Precious Lord" (Chess single released from 1956 session)
Impressions, "Keep On Pushing" / "I Made a Mistake"
★ **Impressions, *Keep On Pushing*** (ABC-Paramount)
Stevie, *Stevie at the Beach* (Tamla)
Stevie, "Sad Boy"
Impressions, "You Must Believe Me" / "See the Real Me"
Aretha, "Runnin' Out of Fools"
Aretha, *Runnin' Out of Fools* (Columbia)

1 9 6 5

Impressions, "Amen"
Aretha, "Can't You Just See Me"
Impressions, "People Get Ready" / "I've Been Trying"

Impressions, *People Get Ready* (ABC-Paramount)
Impressions, *The Impressions' Greatest Hits* (ABC-Paramount)
Stevie, "Kiss Me Baby"
Impressions, "Woman's Got Soul"
Aretha, "One Step Ahead"
Impressions, "Meeting Over Yonder"
Aretha, *Yeah!!* (Columbia)
Impressions, "Get Up and Move"
Stevie, "High Heel Sneakers"
Impressions, "I Need You" / "Never Could Be You"
Impressions, "Just One Kiss from You"
Impressions, "You've Been Cheating"
Impressions, *One by One* (ABC-Paramount)
Aretha, "A Mother's Love" / "Mockingbird"

1966

★ **Stevie, "Uptight (Everything's Alright)"** (R&B)
Impressions, *Ridin' High* (ABC-Paramount)
Stevie, *Up-Tight Everything's Alright* (Tamla)
Stevie, "Nothing's Too Good for My Baby"
Aretha, "Follow Your Heart"
Impressions, "Since I Lost the One I Love"
★ **Stevie, "Blowin' in the Wind"** (R&B)
Impressions, "Too Slow"
Stevie, "A Place in the Sun"
Aretha, "Cry Like a Baby"
Impressions, "Can't Satisfy"
Aretha, *Soul Sister* (Columbia)
Stevie, "Some Day at Christmas"

1967

Note: Beginning in 1967 with *Take It Like You Give It; Take a Look;* and two volumes of *Greatest Hits,* Columbia would flood the market with previously recorded material in an attempt to capitalize on Aretha's success with Atlantic. The best of these compilations, which occasionally included rarities and remastered cuts, are listed in the "Recommended Compilations" section.

Stevie, *Down to Earth* (Tamla)
★ **Aretha, "I Never Loved a Man (The Way I Love You)"** / **"Do Right Woman—**
Do Right Man" (R&B)
Impressions, "You Always Hurt Me"

★ Aretha, *I Never Loved a Man the Way I Love You* (Atlantic)

Stevie, "Travelin' Man" / "Hey Love"

★ Aretha, "Respect" / "Dr. Feelgood" (R&B, pop)

★ Stevie, "I Was Made to Love Her" (R&B)

Impressions, "It's Hard to Believe" / "You Got Me Running"

Aretha, "Lee Cross" (Columbia)

Impressions, *The Fabulous Impressions* (ABC)

★ Aretha, "Baby, I Love You" (R&B)

Aretha, "Take a Look" (Columbia)

★ Aretha, *Aretha Arrives* (Atlantic)

Stevie, *I Was Made to Love Her* (Tamla)

Impressions, "I Can't Stay Away from You"

Aretha, "(You Make Me Feel Like) A Natural Woman"

Stevie, "I'm Wondering"

★ Aretha, "Chain of Fools" (R&B)

Stevie, *Some Day at Christmas* (Tamla)

1 9 6 8

★ **Impressions, "We're a Winner"** (R&B)

Stevie, *Greatest Hits, Vol. 1* (Tamla)

Stevie (as Eivets Rednow), "Alfie"

Stevie (as Eivets Rednow), *Eivets Rednow* (Tamla)

★ Aretha, *Lady Soul* (Atlantic)

★ **Aretha, "Since You've Been Gone (Sweet Sweet Baby)" / "Ain't No Way"** (R&B)

Impressions, *We're a Winner* (ABC)

★ **Stevie, "Shoo-Be-Doo-Be-Doo-Da-Day"** (R&B)

Impressions, "We're Rolling On"

★ **Aretha, *Aretha Now*** (Atlantic)

Impressions, "I Loved and I Lost"

Stevie, "You Met Your Match"

★ **Aretha, "Think" / "You Send Me"** (R&B)

Aretha, "The House That Jack Built" / "I Say a Little Prayer"

Impressions, "Fool for You"

Impressions, *The Best of the Impressions* (ABC)

Stevie, "For Once in My Life"

Aretha, *Aretha in Paris* (Atlantic)

Aretha, "See Saw" / "My Song"

Impressions, "This Is My Country"

Impressions, *This Is My Country* (Curtom)

1 9 6 9

Stevie, *For Once in My Life* (Tamla)

Aretha, *Soul '69* (Atlantic)

Impressions, "My Deceiving Heart" / "Seven Years"

Aretha, "The Weight" / "The Tracks of My Tears"

Aretha, "I Can't See Myself Leaving You" / "Gentle on My Mind"

Impressions, *The Young Mod's Forgotten Story* (Curtom)

Stevie, "My Cherie Amour"

★ Impressions, "Choice of Colors" (R&B)

Aretha, *Aretha's Gold* (Atlantic)

★ Aretha, "Share Your Love with Me" (R&B)

Stevie, *My Cherie Amour* (Tamla)

Impressions, "Say You Love Me"

Stevie, "Yester-Me, Yester-You, Yesterday"

Aretha, "Eleanor Rigby"

1 9 7 0

★ Aretha, "Call Me" / "Son of a Preacher Man" (R&B)

Stevie, "Never Had a Dream Come True"

Aretha, *This Girl's in Love with You* (Atlantic)

Stevie, *Stevie Wonder Live* (Tamla)

Aretha, "Spirit in the Dark" / "The Thrill Is Gone"

★ Stevie, "Signed, Sealed, Delivered, I'm Yours" (R&B)

Stevie, *Signed, Sealed and Delivered* (Tamla)

Impressions, "Check Out Your Mind"

Impressions, *Check Out Your Mind*

Impressions, "(Baby), Turn to Me"

★ Aretha, "Don't Play That Song" (R&B)

Aretha, *Spirit in the Dark* (Atlantic)

Curtis, *Curtis* (Curtom)

Stevie, "Heaven Help Us All"

Aretha, "Border Song (Holy Moses)" / "You and Me"

Curtis, "(Don't Worry) If There's a Hell Below We're All Going to Go" / "The Makings of You"

1 9 7 1

Aretha, "You're All I Need to Get By"

Curtis, "Mighty Mighty (Spade and Whitey)"

Stevie, "We Can Work It Out" / "Never Dreamed You'd Leave in Summer"

★ Aretha, **"Bridge Over Troubled Water" / "Brand New Me"** (R&B)
Stevie, *Where I'm Coming From* (Tamla)
Curtis, *Curtis/Live!* (Curtom)
★ Aretha, *Aretha Live at Fillmore West* (Atlantic)
★ Aretha, **"Spanish Harlem"** (R&B)
Stevie, "If You Really Love Me"
Aretha, *Aretha's Greatest Hits* (Atlantic)
Aretha, **"Rock Steady" / "Oh Me Oh My (I'm a Fool for You Baby)"**
Curtis, "Get Down"
Curtis, *Roots* (Curtom)
Stevie, *Greatest Hits, Vol. 2* (Tamla)
Stevie, "What Christmas Means to Me"

1 9 7 2

Aretha, *Young, Gifted and Black* (Atlantic)
Curtis, "We Got to Have Peace"
★ Aretha, **"Day Dreaming"** (R&B)
Stevie, *Music of My Mind* (Tamla)
Stevie, "Superwoman (Where Were You When I Needed You)"
Curtis, "Beautiful Brother of Mine"
★ Aretha, *Amazing Grace* (Atlantic)
Aretha, "All the King's Horses"
Curtis, "Freddie's Dead"
★ **Curtis,** *Super Fly* (Curtom)
Aretha, "Wholly Holy"
Stevie, "Keep On Running" / "Evil"
★ **Stevie,** *Talking Book* (Tamla)
Curtis, "Super Fly"
★ **Stevie, "Superstition"** (R&B, pop)

1 9 7 3

Aretha, "Master of Eyes (The Deepness of Your Eyes)"
★ **Stevie, "You Are the Sunshine of My Life"** (pop)
Curtis, *Back to the World* (Curtom)
★ Aretha, **"Angel"** (R&B)
Curtis, "Future Shock"
Aretha, *Hey Now Hey (The Other Side of the Sky)* (Atlantic)
★ **Stevie,** *Innervisions* (Tamla)

★ Stevie, "Higher Ground" (R&B)

Curtis, "If I Were Only a Child Again"

★ Stevie, "Living for the City" (R&B)

Curtis, *Curtis in Chicago* (Curtom)

★ Aretha, "Until You Come Back to Me (That's What I'm Gonna Do)" (R&B)

Curtis, "Can't Say Nothin' "

1974

Aretha, *Let Me in Your Life* (Atlantic)

Stevie, "Don't You Worry 'Bout a Thing"

★ Aretha, "I'm in Love" (R&B)

Curtis, *Sweet Exorcist* (Curtom)

Curtis, "Kung Fu"

★ Stevie, "You Haven't Done Nothing" (R&B, pop)

★ Stevie, *Fulfillingness' First Finale* (Tamla)

Aretha, "Ain't Nothin' Like the Real Thing"

Curtis, "Sweet Exorcist"

Aretha, "Without Love"

Curtis, *Got to Find a Way* (Curtom)

★ Stevie, "Boogie On Reggae Woman" (R&B)

Aretha, *With Everything I Feel in Me* (Atlantic)

1975

Curtis, "Mother's Son"

Aretha, "With Everything I Feel in Me"

Curtis, *There's No Place Like America Today* (Curtom)

Curtis, "So in Love"

Aretha, "Mr. D.J. (5 for the D.J.)"

Aretha, *You* (Atlantic)

1976

Aretha, "You"

★ Aretha, "Giving Him Something He Can Feel" (R&B)

Aretha, *Sparkle* (Atlantic), produced by Curtis Mayfield

Curtis, *Give, Get, Take and Have* (Curtom)

Curtis, "Only You Babe"

Aretha, "Jump"

★ Stevie, *Songs in the Key of Life* (Tamla)

Curtis, "Party Night"
★ **Stevie, "I Wish"** (R&B, pop)

1 9 7 7

Aretha, "Look into Your Heart"
Curtis, *Never Say You Can't Survive*
★ **Stevie, "Sir Duke"** (R&B, pop)
Aretha, "Break It to Me Gently"
Curtis, "Show Me Love"
Stevie, "Another Star"
Aretha, *Sweet Passion* (Atlantic)
Curtis, "Do Do Wap Is Strong in Here"
Stevie, "As"
Curtis, *Short Eyes*
Stevie, *Looking Back*

1 9 7 8

Curtis, "You Are You Are"
Aretha, *Almighty Fire* (Atlantic), produced by Curtis Mayfield
Aretha, "More than Just a Joy"
Curtis, "Do It All Night"
Curtis, *Do It All Night* (Curtom)

1 9 7 9

Stevie with Marvin Gaye, Diana Ross, Smokey Robinson, "Pops, We Love You"
Curtis, "This Year"
Curtis, *Heartbeat* (Curtom)
Curtis with Linda Clifford, "Between You Baby and Me" / "You're So Good to Me"
Aretha, "Ladies Only"
Aretha, *La Diva* (Atlantic)
Stevie, "Send One Your Love"
★ **Stevie, *Journey Through the Secret Life of Plants* (Tamla)**
Aretha, "Half a Love"

1 9 8 0

Stevie, "Outside My Window"
Curtis with Linda Clifford, "Love's Sweet Sensation"
Curtis, "Love Me Love Me Now"

Curtis with Linda Clifford, *The Right Combination* (Curtom)
Curtis, *Something to Believe In* (Curtom)
Curtis, "Tripping Out"
★ **Stevie, "Master Blaster (Jammin')"** (R&B)
Aretha, *Aretha* (Arista)
★ **Stevie,** *Hotter than July*
Aretha, **"United Together"**
Stevie, "I Ain't Gonna Stand for It" / "Knocks Me Off My Feet"
Aretha, "Think," on *The Blues Brothers* soundtrack (Atlantic)

1981

Aretha, **"What a Fool Believes"**
Stevie, "Lately" / "If It's Magic"
Aretha, "Come to Me"
Aretha, **"Love All the Hurt Away"**
Stevie, "Did I Hear You Say You Love Me?"
Aretha, *Love All the Hurt Away* (Arista)
Curtis, "She Don't Let Nobody But Me"
Curtis, *Love Is the Place* (Boardwalk)
Aretha, "It's My Turn"
Curtis, "Toot an' Toot an' Toot"

1982

★ **Stevie, "That Girl"** (R&B)
★ **Stevie with Paul McCartney, "Ebony and Ivory"** (pop)
★ **Stevie,** *Stevie Wonder's Original Musiquarium* (Tamla)
Stevie, "Do I Do" / "Rocket Love"
★ **Aretha, "Jump to It"** (R&B)
Aretha, *Jump to It* (Arista)
Stevie, "Ribbon in the Sky" / "Black Orchid"
Curtis, "Hey Baby (Give It All to Me)"
Curtis, *Honesty* (Boardwalk)
Stevie with Charlene, "Used to Be" / "I Want to Come Back as a Song"
Aretha, "Love Me Right"

1983

Aretha, "This Is for Real"
★ **Aretha, "Get It Right"** (R&B)

Aretha, *Get It Right* (Arista)
Aretha, "Every Girl (Wants My Guy)"

1 9 8 4

★ Stevie, "I Just Called to Say I Love You" (R&B, pop)
★ Stevie, *The Woman in Red* (Motown)
Stevie, "Love Light in Flight"

1 9 8 5

★ **Aretha, "Freeway of Love" (R&B)**
★ **Aretha, *Who's Zoomin' Who?* (Arista)**
★ **Stevie, "Part-Time Lover" (R&B, pop)**
Aretha, "Who's Zoomin' Who?"
Curtis, "Baby, It's You"
★ **Stevie, *In Square Circle* (Tamla)**
★ **Stevie with Dionne Warwick and Friends, "That's What Friends Are For" (R&B, pop)**
Curtis, *We Come in Peace with a Message of Love* (CRC/Ichiban)
Aretha with the Eurythmics, "Sisters Are Doing It for Themselves"
Stevie, "Go Home"

1 9 8 6

Aretha, "Another Night"
Stevie, "Overjoyed"
Aretha, "Ain't Nobody Loved You"
Stevie, "Land of La La"
Aretha, "Jumpin' Jack Flash"
Aretha, *Aretha* (1986)
Aretha, "Jimmy Lee"

1 9 8 7

★ **Aretha with George Michael, "I Knew You Were Waiting (For Me)" (pop)**
Aretha, "Rock-A-Lott"
★ **Stevie, "Skeletons" (R&B)**
Aretha, "If You Need My Love Tonight"
Curtis with the Blow Monkeys, "Celebrate (The Day After You)"
Stevie, *Characters* (Motown)
Aretha, *One Lord, One Faith, One Baptism* (Arista)
Aretha with Mavis Staples, "Oh Happy Day"

1 9 8 8

★ **Stevie, "You Will Know"** (R&B)
Curtis, *Live in Europe* (CRC/Ichiban)
Stevie with Michael Jackson, "Get It"
Stevie with Julio Iglesias, "My Love"
Stevie, "My Eyes Don't Cry"
Aretha with the Four Tops, "If Ever a Love There Was"

1 9 8 9

Stevie, "With Each Beat of My Heart"
Aretha with Elton John, "Through the Storm"
Aretha, *Through the Storm* (Arista)
Aretha with Whitney Houston, "It Isn't, It Wasn't, It Ain't Never Gonna Be"
Aretha with James Brown, "Gimme Your Love"

1 9 9 0

Curtis, "Homeless"
Curtis, *Take It to the Streets* (CRC/Ichiban)
Stevie, "Keep Our Love Alive"
Curtis, "Do Be Down"
Curtis with Ice-T, "Superfly 1990," on *The Return of Superfly* (Capitol)

1 9 9 1

Stevie, "Gotta Have You"
Stevie, *Music from the Movie Jungle Fever* (Motown)
Aretha, "Everyday People"
Aretha, *What You See Is What You Sweat* (Arista)
Stevie, "Fun Day"
Aretha, "Someone Else's Eyes"
Stevie, "These Three Words"

1 9 9 2

Aretha, "If I Lose," from the *White Men Can't Jump* soundtrack

1 9 9 4

Aretha with Michael McDonald, "Ever Changing Times"
Aretha, "A Deeper Love," from the *Sister Act* soundtrack
Aretha, *Aretha Franklin's Greatest Hits, 1980–1994* (Arista)

Aretha, "Willing to Forgive"
Stevie with Whitney Houston, "We Didn't Know"
Aretha, "Honey"

1 9 9 5

Stevie, "For Your Love"
Stevie, *Conversation Peace* (Motown)
Stevie, "Tomorrow Robins Will Sing"
Aretha, "It Hurts Like Hell," from the *Waiting to Exhale* soundtrack (Arista)
Stevie, *Natural Wonder*
Stevie, "Treat Myself"

1 9 9 6

Curtis, *New World Order* (Warner Bros.)
Curtis, "New World Order"
Stevie, *Song Review: A Greatest Hits Collection*
Stevie, "Kiss Away Your Tears"

1 9 9 7

Curtis, "No One Knows About a Good Thing"
Stevie with Herbie Hancock, "St. Louis Blues"
Stevie with Babyface, "How Come, How Long"
Curtis, "Back to Living Again"

1 9 9 8

Aretha, "A Rose Is Still a Rose"
Aretha, *A Rose Is Still a Rose* (Arista)
Aretha, "Here We Go Again"
Aretha, "Chain of Fools," "Natural Woman," and "Testimony" on *VH1 Divas Live* (Epic)

2 0 0 0

Stevie, "Misrepresented People" and "Some Years Ago" on the soundtrack to *Bamboozled*

RECOMMENDED COMPILATIONS

The Discography includes greatest hits compilations only when they included a substantial amount of new material or when they played a significant part in the artist's career. Especially since the advent of the CD, there have been dozens of compilations focusing on different aspects of Aretha's, Stevie's, and Curtis's careers. The following compilations do a good job of introducing particular aspects of their music or providing overviews of their careers.

Aretha Franklin

Queen of Soul. A brilliantly executed four-CD compilation covering her great years at Atlantic. The Grammy award–winning liner notes are essential reading.

The Queen in Waiting or *Jazz to Soul.* Either of these two-CD sets provides a good overview of Aretha's Columbia years.

Delta Meets Detroit. A well-executed thematic compilation highlighting Aretha as a blues singer.

Aretha Franklin's Greatest Hits, 1980–1994. The definitive collection of her work with Arista. A nice complement to the *Queen of Soul* box set.

Stevie Wonder

At the Close of a Century. A four-CD set emphasizing Stevie's best-known and most successful music.

Song Review. A two-CD greatest-hits-style set that includes a number of songs from the eighties and nineties ("Redemption Song," "Ebony and Ivory") that had not appeared on Stevie's albums or other compilations.

Stevie Wonder: Early Classics. A fascinating compilation of hits and album cuts from Stevie's early days at Motown. Available only on import.

Curtis Mayfield and the Impressions

People Get Ready! The Curtis Mayfield Story. A three-CD overview of Curtis's work from the early days with the Impressions till the time of his accident. The third disk particularly is a gold mine of hard-to-find songs from his later Curtom albums.

Curtis Mayfield and the Impressions. A two-CD set from MCA that covers much of the same ground as the first two disks of *People Get Ready!* However, this set does a better job with the Impressions material, including several excellent songs that are otherwise available only on British or Japanese import CDs.

Curtis Mayfield Gospel. A compilation that emphasizes Curtis's explicitly gospel material. Includes several cuts that are not available on any other CD.

INDEX

ABC-Paramount label, 83, 121, 122, 143
Abner, Edward, 243–244
Abner, Ewart, 73, 74, 75, 76, 164
Ali, Muhammad, 111
Allman, Duane, 180
Althuser, Bob, 130
Arie, India, 281
Arista Records, 252
Atkins, Cholly, 90, 97
Atlantic Records, 99, 129–130, 177
Avent, Clarence, 83

Bacharach, Burt, 147, 264
Baker, Ella, 109, 144
Baldwin, James, 4, 10–11
Baraka, Amiri, 119
Barlow, William, 244
Beatles, the, 148
Beck, Jeff, 152, 171, 173
Beckett, Barry, 181
Belafonte, Harry, 26
Bell, Thom, 220
Benjamin, Benny, 106–107, 108, 118
Benson, Al, 36
Benson, George, 253
Bevel, James, 64
Billingslea, Joe, 171
Bishop, Louise, 129
Black Power movement, 5, 64–66, 118, 119,
        127, 134, 138, 140, 141–144,
        153–155, 179, 189
Blakely, Gerald, 42
Bland, Joanne, 66
Blues music, 7–8, 15, 16
Boardwalk label, 268
Bogart, Neil, 268
Booker, Kenneth G., 42
Bowles, Thomas "Beans," 21, 108
Boyce, Al, 39, 69
Bracken, Vivian Carter, 74, 75
Bradford, Janie, 100
Braun, Michael, 230
Bridges, Ben, 224
Brooks, Arthur, 69, 78, 119
Brooks, Richard, 69, 78, 119

Brown, James, 95, 264
Browne, Don, 139
Bryant, Ray, 92–93
Burrell, Kenny, 177
Butler, Billy, 68, 80
Butler, Herb, 69
Butler, Jerry, 30, 33, 35, 37, 38–39, 68, 69,
        70, 73, 74–79, 80, 81, 82, 131, 206
Bynum, Robert, 42

Cabrini-Green housing project, 29, 30–31,
        32–34, 145
Call and response, 8, 79
Carr, James, 180, 181
Carter, Calvin, 73–74, 75, 78, 79–80
Carter, Clarence, 180–181
Carter, Leora, 90
Carter, Ron, 177
Cash, Fred, 69, 119, 121
Cecil, Malcolm, 148, 167, 192, 193, 202
Chambers, Iain, 217
Chandler, Gene, 87–88, 222
Charles, Ray, 9, 50, 72–73, 107–108,
        127–128, 184–185
Chicago, 30–35, 63–65, 71, 123–125,
        145–146, 206
Christgau, Robert, 198, 199–200, 228
Civil rights movement, 2–3, 4, 5, 15,
        28–29, 45–46, 63–68, 70–72,
        109–110, 118–119, 123–125,
        134, 138–139, 140–141, 235,
        248–251
Clemons, Clarence, 260
Cleveland, James, 14, 16, 37, 56, 185, 186,
        232, 253
Clifford, Linda, 208, 221, 222, 232
Clinton, Bill, 272–273
Clinton, George, 7, 45, 159, 174
Cogbill, Tommy, 131, 134
Cohen, Adam, 124
Cole, Natalie, 215
Collins, Charlie, 198
Collins, Patricia Hill, 213–214
Columbia Records, 90, 91, 94, 96–97, 99
Combs, Sean "Puff Daddy," 283

Cooke, Sam, 9, 14, 16, 56–58, 72, 73, 89–90, 97–98
Cosby, Henry, 116, 149
Covay, Don, 137
Crockett, George, 178
Cropper, Steve, 130
Cunningham, Ken, 179–180, 214, 232, 233
Curtis, King, 126–127, 135, 137, 182, 184, 185
Curtom Records, 85, 143, 155, 156–158, 160, 205, 208, 221–222, 232, 268

Daley, Richard J., 32, 64, 71, 123–124
Davis, Carl, 86, 87, 88, 120
Davis, Clive, 252, 254, 256, 258, 263
Daylie, Holmes "Daddy-O," 36
Detroit, 19–22, 41–43, 178–179
Disco music, 190, 205–206, 216–221, 239
Dixon, Dallas, 39, 69
Dixon, Larry, 76–77
Dixon, Willie, 7
Doo-wop music, 68–69
Dozier, Lamont, 219
Driscoll, O'Connell, 201
Dupree, Cornell, 184, 186, 212, 252
DuPri, Jermaine, 283
Durham, Frantic Ernie, 45
Dylan, Bob, 98–99, 149, 243

Edmonds, Kenny "Babyface," 276
Edwards, Bernard, 219
Edwards, Dennis, 257
Edwards, Esther, 102, 103
Ellis, Ray, 82–83
Ellison, Ralph, 7, 224
Elsner, Constanze, 198, 225
Ertegun, Ahmet, 210

Fame Studios, 129, 130–131
Fenty, Philip, 161
Five Stairsteps, 207
Folk music, 149–150
Fong-Torres, Ben, 44, 169–170
Frady, Marshall, 250
Franklin, Aretha, 3–5, 6, 10
    awards and honors, 93, 136, 138–139, 213, 238, 266
    Broadway musical offers, 257
    call-and-response technique, 8
    childhood years, 15–17, 18–19, 22, 23–26, 58
    civil rights movement and, 2–3, 67
    crossover strategy, 92, 94, 97
    disco music and, 218–219

diva status, 282–283
    in eighties, 238, 243, 251–266
    C.L. Franklin's influence, 25–26, 54
    gospel highway, 58–60
    gospel vision and, 15–16, 128
    icon status, 273
    live performances, 13–15, 49, 67, 95–96, 126–128, 138, 184–187, 215–216, 273–274, 282–283
    Mayfield, work with, 210–212, 219, 286
    Muscle Shoals sessions, 129–133, 137
    musical education, 55–58
    in nineties, 272–276, 282–283
    as orchestrator of her own sound, 136
    as "Queen of Soul," 135
    racial consciousness, 28
    as role model for young singers, 279–280, 282
    romantic life, 52–53, 94, 96, 175–176, 179–180, 214, 233, 234, 257
    in seventies, 126–128, 179–187, 210–216, 218–219, 232–234
    show business initiation, 58
    singing career, decision on, 54
    in sixties, 89–99, 129–139, 174–177
    songwriting, 182
    teenage years, 13–15, 48–62
    tributes to, 288
    troubles of, 174–176, 214, 233–234, 256–257, 266
    women singers, conflicts with, 215, 275
    women's movement and, 134–135, 213–214, 261–262
Franklin, Aretha, music of
    "Ain't Nobody (Gonna Turn Me Around)," 137
    "Ain't Nothin' Like the Real Thing," 213
    "Ain't No Way," 137
    "All of These Things," 213
    "All the King's Horses," 182
    Almighty Fire, 219
    "Almighty Fire (Woman of the Future)," 219
    "Amazing Grace," 186
    Amazing Grace, 180, 184, 185–187
    "Angel," 17, 212, 214–215, 274
    "Another Night," 260–261
    "April Fools," 182
    Aretha (1961), 99
    Aretha (1980), 252–253
    Aretha (1986), 263–264
    Aretha Arrives, 136–137, 181–182
    Aretha in Paris, 138

Aretha Live at Fillmore West, 127–128, 180, 184–185
Aretha Now, 176–177
"Baby, Baby, Baby," 135
"Baby, I Love You," 137
"Bill Bailey Won't You Please Come Home," 91
"Border Song (Holy Moses)," 182, 212, 276
"A Brand New Me," 182
"Break It to Me Gently," 214, 219
"Bridge Over Troubled Water," 127, 183
"Bring It on Home to Me," 177
"Call Me," 176, 180, 182
"Can't Turn You Loose," 253
"Chain of Fools," 17, 137–138
"A Change Is Gonna Come," 135
the Cleopatrettes, 51–52
"Come Back Baby," 137
"Come to Me," 252
compilation albums, 276
"Cry Like a Baby," 97
"The Dark End of the Street," 180–181
"Day Dreaming," 182
"The Day Is Past and Gone," 185
"A Deeper Love," 276
"Dr. Feelgood," 127, 135
"Doctor's Orders," 264
"Don't Let Me Lose This Dream," 135
"Don't Play That Song," 127
"Do Right Woman–Do Right Man," 17, 132, 133–134
"Drinking Again," 98
"Drown in My Own Tears," 135
"Eleanor Rigby," 127, 180, 182–183
The Electrifying Aretha Franklin, 93–94
"Elusive Butterfly," 177
"Ever Changing Times," 264
"Everyday People," 264
"Every Lil' Bit Hurts," 283
"First Snow in Kokomo," 182
"Freeway of Love," 251, 258, 260, 274
"Gentle on My Mind," 177
Get It Right, 255–256
"Gimme Your Love," 264
"Give Yourself to Jesus," 186
"Giving Him Something He Can Feel," 211
"God Bless the Child," 95
"Going Down Slow," 137
The Great Aretha Franklin, 93
"Groovin'," 137
"Here We Go Again," 283

Hey Now Hey (The Other Side of the Sky), 210, 212
"Higher Ground," 265–266
"Hold On I'm Coming," 253
"How Deep Is the Ocean?," 92
"How I Got Over," 186
"I Can't See Myself Leaving You," 176
"If Ever I Should Leave You," 95
"If You Gotta Make a Fool of Somebody," 176
"I Knew You Were Waiting (For Me)," 263–264
"I'll Never Be Free," 177
"I Love Every Little Thing About You," 213
"I'm in Love," 212
"I Never Loved a Man (The Way I Love You)," 4, 91, 129, 132, 133, 134, 135
I Never Loved a Man the Way I Love You, 135, 181–182
"Integrity," 261, 262
"In the Morning," 283
"I Say a Little Prayer," 176
"It Hurts Like Hell," 274, 276
"It's Your Thing," 255
"I've Been in the Storm Too Long," 265
"I've Been Loving You Too Long," 182
"I Wanna Make It Up to You," 255
"I Wish It Would Rain," 256
"Jesus Hears Every Prayer," 265
"Jimmy Lee," 263
"Jump," 211
"Jumpin' Jack Flash," 263
Jump to It, 254–255
"Just My Daydream," 255
"Kind of Man," 253
La Diva, 219
Lady Soul, 136–137, 181–182
Laughing on the Outside, 94, 95
"Let It Be," 183
Let Me in Your Life, 212
"Look in Your Heart," 211
"Look to the Rainbow," 238, 251
Love All the Hurt Away, 252, 253
"Love Me Right," 255
"Love the One You're With," 127
"Make It with You," 127
"Mary Don't You Weep," 186
"Master of Eyes (The Deepness of Your Eyes)," 213
"Mr. D.J. (5 for the D.J.)," 213
"Money Won't Change You," 137
"Moody's Mood," 212
"Never Grow Old," 62, 185, 186

Franklin, Aretha, music of *(continued)*
 "Never Leave You Again," 283
 "Night Life," 137
 "Niki Hoeky," 137
 "96 Tears," 137
 "Nobody Knows the Way I Feel This
  Morning," 98
 "Oh Happy Day," 265
 "Oh Me Oh My (I'm a Fool for You
  Baby)," 182
 "Old Landmark," 185
 "Ol' Man River," 97
 One Lord, One Faith, One Baptism, 264–266
 "Operation Heartbreak," 94
 "Over the Rainbow," 91
 "People Get Ready," 137
 "Power of Love/Love Power," 254
 "Precious Lord (Take My Hand),"
  13–15, 61, 62, 185
 "Pullin'," 182
 "Push," 258, 261
 Queen of Soul, 219
 "Respect," 4, 17, 127, 129, 134–135,
  213–214
 "Rock-a-bye Your Baby with a Dixie
  Melody," 92, 93–94
 "Rock Steady," 5, 93, 182, 183
 "A Rose Is Still a Rose," 282
 A Rose Is Still a Rose, 283–284
 Runnin' Out of Fools, 97, 99
 "Run to Me," 211
 "Satisfaction," 127, 137
 "Save Me," 135
 "Say It Isn't So," 95
 "See Saw," 176
 "Since You've Been Gone (Sweet Sweet
  Baby)," 137
 "Sing It Again, Say It Again," 213
 "Sisters Are Doing It for Themselves,"
  261–262
 "Solitude," 95
 "So Long," 177
 Songs of Faith, 61–62
 "Son of a Preacher Man," 180, 182
 "Soul Serenade," 135
 Soul Sister, 97
 Soul '69, 176, 177
 Sparkle, 210–212
 "Spirit in the Dark," 5, 92, 127, 182, 184,
  276
 Spirit in the Dark, 180, 181–182
 "Surely God Is Able," 265
 "Swanee," 97
 "Sweet Bitter Love," 97

Sweet Passion, 219
 "Take a Look," 97
 *The Tender, The Moving, The Swinging
  Aretha Franklin,* 94–95
 "That's Life," 137
 "There Is a Fountain Filled with Blood,"
  62
 "Think," 5, 93, 139, 176, 274, 283
 "This Bitter Earth," 98
 This Girl's in Love with You, 180–182
 "This Is for Real," 255
 "The Thrill Is Gone (From Yesterday's
  Kiss)," 183–184
 Through the Storm, 263, 264, 266
 "Today I Sing the Blues," 91, 93, 176,
  177
 "The Tracks of My Tears," 176, 177
 "Trouble in Mind," 95
 "Try a Little Tenderness," 94–95
 *Unforgettable–A Tribute to Dinah
  Washington,* 94, 98
 "Until You Come Back to Me (That's
  What I'm Gonna Do)," 213, 214
 "Watch My Back," 283
 "The Weight," 212
 "What a Fool Believes," 253
 "What a Friend We Have in Jesus," 186
 What You See Is What You Sweat, 263, 264
 "When I Think About You," 219
 "When the Battle Is Over," 182
 "Whole Lot of Me," 253
 "Wholly Holy," 185
 "Who's Zoomin' Who?," 258, 262–263
 Who's Zoomin' Who?, 6, 239, 258–263
 "Why Do Fools Fall in Love?," 274
 "Why I Sing the Blues," 182
 "Willing to Forgive," 276
 "With Everything I Feel in Me," 213
 With Everything I Feel in Me, 212
 "Without Love," 213
 "The Woman," 283
 "Won't Be Long," 93
 Yeah!!, 97, 99
 You, 210, 212
 "You and Me," 182
 "You Can't Always Get What You Want,"
  253
 "You'll Never Walk Alone," 186
 "(You Make Me Feel Like) A Natural
  Woman," 137
 Young, Gifted and Black, 180, 181–182,
  183
 "You've Got a Friend," 186
Franklin, Barbara, 18–19, 23–24, 53

Franklin, Carolyn, 17, 51, 53, 133, 135, 137, 212, 213, 234, 258, 264, 266
Franklin, Cecil, 8, 17, 22, 49, 59, 234, 265, 266
Franklin, C.L., 4, 13, 14–15, 16, 17–19, 22–23, 24–28, 51, 52, 53–55, 56, 57, 58, 60–61, 90, 94, 96, 175, 177–178, 185, 233, 234, 257–258
Franklin, Clarence, 52, 90, 233
Franklin, Eddie, 53
Franklin, Erma, 17, 51–52, 53, 59–60, 133, 135, 256, 266
Franklin, Henry, 17
Franklin, Kirk, 280
Franklin, Rachel, 25, 266
Franklin, Vaughn, 17, 23
Fraser, C. Gerald, 184
Freedom Rides, 110
Funk Brothers, 99–100, 106

Gamble, Kenny, 220–221
Garland, Phyl, 90, 134, 138
Garrett, Lee, 40, 113–115, 198
Gaye, Marvin, 8, 162, 163, 245
George, Nelson, 239
Giltrap, Jim, 166
Giovanni, Nikki, 3, 142
Glover, John, 47–48
Gooden, Sam, 69, 78, 119
Gordy, Berry, 72, 101–102, 104, 105, 107, 114, 115, 116, 163–164, 196, 203–204, 229–230, 232–233, 245, 246
Gospel vision, 2–3, 7–9, 10, 15–16, 36–38, 49–50, 118, 125, 128, 191, 195, 199, 204, 217, 224, 235, 237–238, 239, 278, 280, 287, 290
Gregory, Dick, 2–3, 65
Group format, 79
Guralnick, Peter, 131

Hale, Faye, 230
Hall, Rick, 130, 131, 132, 133
Hammond, John, 19, 89–90, 91, 92–93, 94, 99, 129–130
Hampton, Riley, 120
Hardaway, Lula, 40–41, 43, 44–45, 102, 103, 105, 225–226
Harris, Norman, 220
Harris, Teddy, 96, 97, 98
Hathaway, Donny, 157–158, 183, 212
Hawkins, Roger, 131, 132, 134
Hawkins, Sam, Tommy, and Charles, 38
Heilbut, Anthony, 91

Heiman, Marv, 270
Hendrix, Jimi, 148, 159, 165
Hill, Lauryn, 281–282
Hinton, Eddie, 180
Hip-hop music, 6, 237–238, 239–240, 253–254, 278–279
Hirshey, Gerri, 255
Holland, Brian, 101, 103, 106, 107, 113
Holmes, Viola, 33
Houston, Cissy, 135, 255
Huff, Leon, 220–221
Hull, Ted, 105–106, 111, 112, 114

Impressions, the, 156. *See also under* Mayfield, Curtis, music of

Jackson, Chuck, 215, 252
Jackson, Janet, 229
Jackson, Jesse, 26, 143, 216, 236–237, 238, 241–242, 249–251, 257–258, 265, 272
Jackson, Mahalia, 14, 15–16, 24, 25, 36, 37, 59, 175, 185
Jackson, Michael, 242, 243, 247
Jamerson, James, 106, 108, 118, 149, 252
Jazz music, 95, 224
Jemmott, Jerry, 184
John, Elton, 197–198, 276
John, Mable, 100
Johnson, Colonel Stone, 110
Johnson, Jimmy, 131, 132, 134, 176, 181
Johnson, Roscoe and Ethel, 31
Jones, Gypsie, 225–226
Jones, Quincy, 212, 242
Judkins, Calvin, 40, 41

Kees, Gene, 152
Kelly, R., 280–281
Kent, Herb, 67
King, B.B., 23, 27, 46, 173–174, 247
King, Jo, 91
King, Martin Luther, Jr., 2, 4, 7, 15, 29, 63–64, 110, 123–124, 138–139, 140, 150, 183, 235
    holiday in honor of, 236–237, 248

Lance, Major, 87, 206
Latimer, Larry "Nastyee," 192
La Vette, Betty, 112
Lee, Bill, 93
Lee, Spike, 276, 277, 288
Leiber, Jerry, 99
Lennon, John, 201
Lennox, Annie, 238, 261–262

Lewis, Curtis, 91
Lewis, Ramsey, 33, 35
Ligon, Joe, 265
Lupper, Ken, 186
Lydon, Michael, 127

Mandela, Nelson, 238, 248
Mardin, Arif, 186, 252
Margouleff, Robert, 148, 167, 192, 193
Marley, Bob, 204–205
Marsh, Dave, 193
Mayfield, Anna Belle, 30, 37
Mayfield, Curtis, 1–2, 3–4, 5–6, 10, 11
  awards and honors, 271
  Black Power movement and, 119,
    142–144, 153–155
  childhood years, 29–30, 34–40
  civil rights movement and, 66–68,
    118–119, 125, 140–141
  control of his career, 84–85, 88–89, 143,
    155, 270–271
  crossover strategy, 160
  death of, 287
  disco music and, 218, 219–221
  in eighties, 239, 267–269
  Franklin, work with, 210–212, 219, 286
  funky explorations, 159–160
  gospel vision and, 2
  guitar playing, 38–39, 68, 80, 159, 269
  in nineties, 266–267, 269–272, 285–287
  romantic life, 121
  in seventies, 145–147, 153–163, 190,
    205–212, 218, 219–223, 232
  singing voice, 38
  in sixties, 82–89, 118–125, 139–145
  solo career, decision on, 155–156
  songwriting, 35, 80–82, 86–88, 206–207
  soundtrack work, 208–210, 221
  spinal injury, 266–267, 269–270
  tributes to, 271, 287–288
Mayfield, Curtis, music of
  "Ain't Got Time," 207
  "Ain't It a Shame," 87
  the Alphatones, 39, 69
  "Amen," 120, 122, 206
  "Baby, It's You," 269
  "(Baby) Turn On to Me," 145
  "Back Against the Wall," 208, 209
  "Back to Living Again," 286
  Back to the World, 162–163
  "Beautiful Brother of Mine," 154
  "Between You Baby and Me," 208, 221
  "Can't You See," 145
  "Celebrate (The Day After You)," 269

Check Out Your Mind, 145
"Choice of Colors," 139, 144–145
The Class of Mayfield High, 87
"Come Back My Love," 79
"Come Free Your People," 268
compilation albums, 277
Curtis, 154–155, 156, 159
Curtis in Chicago, 206
Curtis/Live!, 153, 155, 158–159
Curtis Mayfield's Chicago Soul, 87
"Delilah," 87
"Dirty Laundry," 268, 272
"Do Be Down," 269
"Do Do Wap Is Strong in Here," 208,
  209
"Do It All Night," 220
Do It All Night, 219, 221
"Don't Change Your Love," 157
"Don't Waste Your Time," 157
"(Don't Worry) If There's a Hell Below
  We're All Going to Go," 5, 139,
  146–147, 158
The Fabulous Impressions, 122
"Find Yourself Another Girl," 81
"For Your Precious Love," 73, 74–76, 77
"Freddie's Dead," 161, 162
"Future Shock," 163
"Future Song (Love a Good Woman,
  Love a Good Man)," 163
"Get Up and Move," 123
Give, Get, Take and Have, 219
"Giving Him Something He Can Feel,"
  211, 221
"The Got Dang Song," 286
"Got to Find a Way," 208
"Grow Closer Together," 81, 84, 119
"Gypsy Woman," 82, 83, 84, 158
Heartbeat, 219, 220, 221
"He Don't Love You Like I Love You,"
  81
"He Will Break Your Heart," 81–82
"Hey Little Girl," 87
"Hey Senorita," 79
hip-hop music and, 278–279
"Homeless," 269
Honesty, 268
"I Made a Mistake," 123
"I'm A-Telling You," 81
Impressed!, 87
the Impressions, 66, 69–70, 72–80,
  82–84, 85–86, 88, 119–123, 142,
  143–145, 206
"I'm So Proud," 66, 119, 121
"I'm the One Who Loves You," 81, 119

"I Plan to Stay a Believer," 154
"It Ain't No Use," 87
"It's All Right," 119, 120, 121, 223
"It's Been a Long, Long Winter," 66
"I've Been Trying," 66, 119, 122
"Jump," 211
"Just Be True," 87, 156
"Keep On Pushing," 5, 66, 73, 118–119, 122
Keep On Pushing, 122–123
"Keep On Trippin'," 163
"Kung Fu," 207
"Lemon Tree," 121
"Let's Do It Again," 206, 221
Let's Do It Again, 208, 209–210
"Little Young Lover," 84
"Look in Your Heart," 211
Love Is the Place, 268
"Love Me, Love Me Now," 223
"Love's Happening," 207
"Mama Didn't Know," 87
"Man's Temptation," 87
"Meeting Over Yonder," 64, 66, 119
"Mighty Mighty Children," 206
"Mighty Mighty (Spade and Whitey)," 144, 153, 154
"Minstrel and Queen," 84, 119
"Mr. Welfare Man," 208
"The Monkey Time," 87
"Mother's Son," 208
"Move On Up," 154, 220
"Ms. Martha," 286
The Never-Ending Impressions, 121
"Never Let Me Go," 81, 84, 119
Never Say You Can't Survive, 207, 208, 219
"Never Stop Loving Me," 223
"Never Too Much Love," 66, 119
New World Order, 6, 267, 270, 284, 285–287
"No Goodbyes," 220
Northern Jubilee Gospel Singers, 38, 39
One by One, 122
"Only You," 145
"Only You Babe," 208
"The Other Side of Town," 154–155
"People Get Ready," 5, 66, 73, 119, 122, 125, 137, 158
People Get Ready, 122–123
"People Never Give Up," 223
"A Piece of the Action," 206
A Piece of the Action, 208, 209
"Pusherman," 161
"Rainbow," 87
The Return of Superfly, 269

The Right Combination, 222
"Right On for the Darkness," 163
Roots, 154, 155
"Run to Me," 211
"Sad, Sad Girl and Boy," 119
"Satin Doll," 121
"September Song," 121
"She Don't Let Nobody But Me," 268
Short Eyes, 207, 208–209
"Show Me Love," 208
"So in Love," 208
"Something to Believe In," 223
Something to Believe In, 207, 208, 222–223
"Sometimes I Wonder," 87, 122
"Soul Is Love," 206
Sparkle, 210–212
"Stay Away from Me," 206
"Stay Close to Me," 157
"Stone Junkie," 154
"Stop the War," 145
"Suffer," 206, 208
Superfly, 156, 160–162
Sweet Exorcist, 207
"Sweet Sensation," 208
"Swing Low Sweet Chariot," 206
Take It to the Street, 268–269
"Talking About My Baby," 121, 123
"They Don't Know," 144
"Think Nothing About It," 87
"This Is My Country," 5, 66, 139, 144
This Is My Country, 143–144
Times Have Changed, 145
"To Be Invisible," 207, 208
"Twilight Time," 122
"Um, Um, Um, Um, Um, Um, Um," 87
"Underground," 220
"Up Up and Away," 122
We Come in Peace with a Message of Love, 268–269
"We Got to Have Peace," 154
"We're a Winner," 1, 2, 139, 140–141
We're a Winner, 122
"We're in Love," 123
"We're Rolling On," 139, 141
"We the People Who Are Darker than Blue," 154, 155, 158, 286
"What Now?," 87, 156
"Woman's Got Soul," 66, 122
"You Must Believe Me," 119, 123
The Young Mod's Forgotten Story, 143, 144–145
Mayfield, Curtis Lee, 29–30, 35
Mayfield, Helen Williams, 82
McCartney, Paul, 201, 238, 242, 243

McCoy, Sid, 36
McCullen, Tyrone, 158
McKee, Lonette, 211
McMullen, Craig, 158
McNeal, Velvelette Bertha Barbee, 100
Meadows, Johnny, 82–83, 84, 86–87,
    119–120, 156, 206, 268
Mersey, Robert, 94
Michael, George, 263–264
Mickelson, Jerry, 160
Midler, Bette, 98
Miller, Marcus, 253
Moman, Chips, 131, 132
Moore, Lola, 25
Moore, Phil, 90–91
Morales, Pancho, 186
Moses, Larry, 113
Motown Records, 67, 88, 89–90, 99–102,
    115, 116, 152, 163–165, 173,
    203–204, 246
Moy, Sylvia, 116, 117, 149
Murray, Albert, 7, 79

Nash, Diane, 109, 110
Nathan, David, 99, 212, 218, 233, 269
Neo-soul music, 281
New Bethel Baptist Church, 19, 22–23

Olazabal, Gary, 224, 227, 230
Oldham, Spooner, 129, 131, 132, 134
Otis, Clyde, 96–97, 98

Pate, Johnny, 120, 125, 141, 144
Paul, Clarence, 48, 102, 103, 107, 114,
    116–117, 150, 193, 245
Pavarotti, Luciano, 273–274
Penn, Dan, 131, 132
Phillinganes, Greg, 224
Philly International label, 220–221
Porcaro, Jeff, 253
Pounds, Raymond, 224
Preston, Billy, 126, 127
Prince, 245
Purdie, Bernard, 184, 186, 212, 252

Radio, 35–36, 45–46, 83, 243–244, 268
Rainey, Chuck, 186
R&B music, 9, 45, 50, 72–73, 129, 239–240,
    253–254
Redding, Otis, 128, 135
Reed, Jimmy, 80
Reeves, Martha, 102, 103, 110, 111
Reggae music, 204–205
Richards, Keith, 168, 263

Ritz, David, 275
Ritzema, Peter, 148
Robinson, Mickey, 116
Robinson, Smokey, 24, 49, 59, 97, 102, 107,
    156, 232
Rock 'n' roll music, 72
Rockwell, John, 228
Rodgers, Nile, 218, 219
Rolling Stones, 168–169
Roseman, Jan, 262
Rustin, Bayard, 123

Sager, Carole Bayer, 264
Sampling, 270
Satchell, Rochelle, 33–34, 146 .
Scott, Joseph "Lucky," 158
Scruggs, Chuck, 67–68
Sears, Zenas, 58
Sellers, Gordon, 66
Sembello, Mike, 224, 225
Shelby, Gene, 111
Shelley, Barbara, 255
Shore, Sig, 161
Sigler, Bunny, 220
Simmons, Daryl, 286
Simmons, Yolanda, 197
Simms, Gerald, 80
Simon, Paul, 183, 191
Sims, Altheida, 121
Sims, Gerald, 86
Smith, Reggie, 68
Soul music, 2–3, 4, 66, 67, 75, 81, 281
Springsteen, Bruce, 238, 243, 260
Staples, Mavis, 24, 84, 209, 210, 265, 269,
    286–287
Staples, Yvonne, 265
Starr, Ringo, 201
Stax Studio, 130
Steinberg, Martha Jean, 45–46
Stevenson, Mickey, 101, 106
Stewart, Jim, 130
Stuart, Marv, 155, 160, 205, 221
Swan, Dorothy, 24–25
Swenson, John, 115
Swope, Lillian Davis, 39

Tatum, Art, 55, 56
Taylor, Elizabeth, 124
Tee, Richard, 184, 212, 252
Terrorist attacks of 2001, 289–290
Thomas, Eddie, 66–67, 70, 73, 74, 75, 76,
    78, 80, 81, 82, 83, 84–86, 87, 88, 120,
    143, 155–156, 158, 160, 206, 221
Thomas, Emmanuel, 69

Thompson, Ray, 186
Tillman, Dorothy, 124
Todd, Willie, 53
Troutman, Roger, 269–270, 285, 286
Tucker, Ira, 196
Tucker family, 46
Turman, Glynn, 233
Tyson, Ronald, 220
Tyson, Timothy, 20

Vandross, Luther, 244, 254–256, 264
Van Dyke, Earl, 106, 108
Vee-Jay Records, 73–75, 78, 79–80
Vietnam War, 137–138, 162–163
Vigoda, Johanan, 164
Von Battle, Joe, 13, 14–15, 26–27

Walden, Donald, 174, 176
Walden, Narada Michael, 251, 258–259,
    263, 264, 286
Walker, David "T," 192
Walker, Junior, 112
Ward, Brian, 66, 67, 81
Ward, Clara, 14, 16, 49, 54–55, 96, 185, 186
Ward-Royster, Willa, 54, 55
Warwick, Dionne, 245–246, 252
Washington, Dinah, 14, 55–56, 97, 98
Washington, Marion, 30, 35
Washington, Zora, 39–40, 146
Watts, Nathan, 224, 225
Weems, James, 39, 69
Wexler, Jerry, 9, 53, 95, 99, 128, 129–130,
    132, 133, 134, 135, 136, 174, 176,
    177, 186, 210, 212
White, Gerald and Ronnie, 101
White, Ted, 94, 95, 96–97, 98, 132–133,
    138, 175–176
Whitfield, Thomas, 265
Wilder, Gene, 245–246
Wilkerson, Willie, 257
Williams, Andy, 203
Williams, Deniece, 171, 192–193
Williams, Jaspar, 258, 265–266
Williams, Marion, 14, 16
Williams, Otis, 49, 50, 108–109
Williams, Sherley Anne, 214
Wilson, John, 95–96
Wilson, Margaret, 33
Wilson, Mary, 23, 49–50, 51, 52–53, 54,
    100, 101, 106
Wilson, William Julius, 194–195
Wise, Stanley, 66
Withers, Ernest, 19
Wolf, Peter, 261

Wolff, Daniel, 22
Women's movement, 134–135, 141–142,
    213–214, 261–262
Wonder, Stevie, 3–4, 6, 10, 220, 252
    African interests, 203
    audition for Motown, 100–102
    awards and honors, 201, 238, 248
    blindness of, 40, 43–44, 100, 104–105,
        230
    childhood years, 40, 41, 43–48
    civil rights movement and, 67
    creative independence, 152–153,
        163–165
    education of, 105–106
    in eighties, 236–238, 240–249
    gospel vision and, 195, 199, 224
    harmonica playing, 47, 108
    head injury, 196–197
    humor of, 104–105
    icon status, 273
    influences on, 147, 148
    "Little Stevie Wonder" nickname, 102
    live performances, 112–113, 115–116,
        152, 168–170, 195–196, 197–198,
        200–201, 236–237
    Mayfield tribute, 287–288
    Motown contract of 1976, 203–204
    Motown Revue tours, 108–109, 110–113
    in nineties, 273, 274–276, 284–285
    political activism, 46, 170–171, 200–201,
        202, 238, 241–242, 243–244, 248
    racial consciousness, 170
    radio station ownership, 243–244
    romantic life, 44, 104–105, 112, 165–166,
        197
    in seventies, 163–174, 190–205, 223–232
    in sixties, 99–118, 147–153
    songwriting, 47, 116–117, 152
    soundtrack work, 230–231
    synthesized sound, 166–167
    work habits, 192–193
Wonder, Stevie, music of
    "Ai No, Sono," 231
    "All I Do," 241
    "All in Love Is Fair," 195, 197
    "Another Star," 229
    "As," 223–224
    "Baby Don't Do It," 151
    "Bang Bang," 151
    "Be Calm (And Keep Yourself
        Together)," 151
    "Beyond the Sea," 115
    "Big Brother," 171, 172
    "Black Man," 227, 228

Wonder, Stevie, music of *(continued)*
  "Black Orchid," 231
  "Blame It on the Sun," 171
  "Blowin' in the Wind," 149, 150
  "Boogie On Reggae Woman," 199, 200, 205
  "Can I Get a Witness?," 151
  "Cash in Your Face," 241
  "Castles in the Sand," 115
  "Cause We've Ended as Lovers," 173
  Characters, 244, 247
  "Cold Chill," 285
  compilation albums, 276–277
  "Contract on Love," 108
  "Contusion," 198, 227
  "Conversation Peace," 285
  Conversation Peace, 284–285
  "Dancing to the Rhythm," 277
  "Dark 'n Lovely," 229, 247
  "Did I Hear You Say You Love Me?," 241
  "Do I Do," 244
  "Don't You Worry 'Bout a Thing," 195
  Down to Earth, 151
  "Drown in My Own Tears," 108
  "Earth's Creation," 231
  "Easy Goin' Evening (My Mama's Call)," 226
  "Ebb Tide," 115
  "Ebony and Ivory," 242
  "Ebony Eyes," 229
  "Edge of Eternity," 284
  Eivets Rednow, 150–151
  "Fingertips, Part 2," 6, 99, 112–113
  "A Fool for You," 151
  For Once in My Life, 149, 150, 151
  "For Your Love," 284
  "Free," 247
  "Front Line," 244
  Fulfillingness' First Finale, 6, 167, 191, 198–200, 201, 228
  "Get It," 247
  "Go Home," 244, 246
  "Golden Lady," 195, 229
  "Hallelujah I Love Her So," 108
  "Happier than the Morning Sun," 168
  "Happy Birthday," 237, 242
  "Have a Talk with God," 226
  "Heaven Help Us All," 149, 152
  "Heaven Is Ten Zillion Light Years Away," 199
  "Hey Harmonica Man," 115
  "Higher Ground," 191, 195, 196, 197

  "High Heel Sneakers," 115
  hip-hop music and, 278
  Hotter Than July, 241
  "How Can You Believe," 150
  "I Ain't Gonna Stand for It," 241
  "I Believe (When I Fall in Love It Will Be Forever)," 171
  "I Call It Pretty Music (But the Old People Call It the Blues)," 108
  "If You Really Love Me," 153
  "I Just Called to Say I Love You," 244, 246, 248
  Innervisions, 6, 191, 192–195, 228
  In Square Circle, 229, 244, 245, 246–247
  "I Pity the Fool," 151
  "Isn't She Lovely," 226, 228, 229
  "It's Wrong (Apartheid)," 246
  "I Wanna Talk to You," 153
  "I Was Made to Love Her," 6, 116, 149
  I Was Made to Love Her, 151
  "I Wish," 226, 227
  The Jazz Soul of Little Stevie Wonder, 107–108
  Journey Through the Secret Life of Plants, 6, 228, 229–232
  "Joy Inside My Tears," 226
  Jungle Fever, 276
  "Keep On Pushing," 195
  "Keep On Running," 168, 198
  "Kesse Ye Lolo De Ye," 231
  "Land of La La," 246
  "Lighting Up the Candles," 245, 276
  Little Stevie Wonder/The 12 Year Old Genius, 113
  "Living for the City," 193–195, 198
  "Looking for Another Pure Love," 171
  "Love Having You Around," 167
  "Love Light in Flight," 246
  "Love's in Need of Love Today," 226, 290
  "The Masquerade," 108
  "Master Blaster (Jammin')," 241
  "Maybe Your Baby," 171
  "Misrepresented People," 289
  "Mr. Tambourine Man," 151
  "More than a Dream," 150
  "Move On Up a Little Higher," 195
  Music of My Mind, 6, 167–168, 173
  "My Cherie Amour," 149, 172
  My Cherie Amour, 150, 151
  "My Eyes Don't Cry," 247
  "My Girl," 151
  "My Love Is with You," 284

Natural Wonder, 277
"Never Dreamed You'd Leave in Summer," 153
"Never Had a Dream Come True," 152
"Ngiculela/Es una Historia/I Am Singing," 227
"Ordinary Pain," 226
"Overjoyed," 244, 246
"Part-Time Lover," 244, 247
"Pastime Paradise," 227–228
"A Place in the Sun," 149, 150
"Please Please Please," 151
"Put On a Happy Face," 115
"Rain Your Love Down," 284
"Redemption Song," 195
"Red Sails in the Sunset," 115
"Respect," 151
"Ribbon in the Sky," 244
"Saturn," 227
"A Seed's a Star," 231
"Send Me Some Lovin'," 151
"Send One Your Love," 231
"Sensuous Whisper," 284
"Shoo-Be-Doo-Be-Do-Da-Day," 151, 152
Signed, Sealed, and Delivered, 152
"Signed, Sealed, Delivered, I'm Yours," 149
"Sir Duke," 108, 227
"Skeletons," 244, 247
"Smile Please," 199
"Some Years Ago," 288–289
Songs in the Key of Life, 6, 191, 203, 223–224, 225–229
"Sorry," 285
"Spiritual Walkers," 246
Stevie at the Beach, 115
Stevie Wonder Live, 152–153
Stevie Wonder's Original Musiquarium, 244
"The Sunny Side of the Street," 115
"Sunshine in Their Eyes," 153
"Superstition," 171, 172–173
"Superwoman," 166, 168, 198
"Take the Time Out," 284
Talking Book, 6, 171–173, 228

"That Girl," 244
"That Lonesome Road," 151
"Thelonious," 173
"They Won't Go When I Go," 199
"Think of Me as Your Soldier," 153
"To Know You Is to Love You," 173–174
"Tomorrow Robins Will Sing," 284
"Too High," 195
"Travelin' Man," 150
"Treat Myself," 284
Tribute to Uncle Ray, 107–108
"Tuesday Heartbreak," 171
Tug of War, 242
"Uptight (Everything's Alright)," 116, 117–118
"Village Ghetto Land," 226
"Visions," 195
"Waterboy," 108
"We Are the World," 238, 242–243
"We Can Work It Out," 152
"What's That You're Doing," 242
"When You Wish Upon a Star," 115
Where I'm Coming From, 153
"Which Way the Wind," 150
With a Song in My Heart, 115
"With Each Beat of My Heart," 247
The Woman in Red, 244, 245–246
Wonderlove band, 168, 224–225
"Workout, Stevie, Workout," 113
"Yester-Me, Yester-You, Yesterday," 149
"You Are the Sunshine of My Life," 171–172
"You Haven't Done Nothing," 199, 200
"You Met Your Match," 151
"You've Got It Bad Girl," 171
"You Will Know," 244, 247
Woods, Ron, 263
Wright, Herman, 53
Wright, Syreeta, 165–166, 174

Yancy, Marvin, 215
Young, Mary, 54

Zawinul, Joe, 177